Working in Hollywood
How the Studio System Turned Creativity into Labor

Ronny Regev

University of North Carolina Press CHAPEL HILL

The University of North Carolina Press has been a member of the Green Press Initiative since 2003.

Library of Congress Cataloging-in-Publication Data

Names: Regev, Ronny, author.

Title: Working in Hollywood : how the studio system turned creativity into labor / Ronny Regev.

Description: Chapel Hill : University of North Carolina Press, [2018] | Includes bibliographical references and index.

Identifiers: LCCN 2017050787 | ISBN 9781469638294 (cloth : alk. paper) | ISBN 9781469636504 (pbk : alk. paper) | ISBN 9781469637068 (ebook)

Subjects: LCSH: Motion picture industry—California—Los Angeles— History—20th century. | Motion picture industry—California— Los Angeles—Employees.

Classification: LCC PN1993.5.U65 R44 2018 | DDC 384/.80979494—dc23

LC record available at https://lccn.loc.gov/2017050787

Cover illustration: Photograph of Katharine Hepburn checking her makeup in a park with several members of a film crew, during the making of *Morning Glory*, 1933. Used by permission of Photofest, Inc.

This work has drawn upon material originally published in "Hollywood Works: How Creativity Became Labor in the Studio System," *Enterprise & Society* 17:3 (2016): 591–617, published by Cambridge University Press, reproduced here with permission.

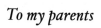

Contents

Acknowledgments

> I think if a man is an egotist and doesn't want his work touched ...
> I think that motion picture work is the wrong work for him to be
> engaged in; because motion pictures are necessarily collaborations.
> —DAVID O. SELZNICK

I have one thing in common with the Hollywood stars I write about; just like them I have acquired a large debt of gratitude to an extensive, unfailing support system. Indeed, so many wonderful people helped me throughout the past ten years that this book often felt like a collaborative effort.

Top billing goes to my academic mentors and advisers. I had the great privilege and fortune to study under the dedicated guidance of Daniel T. Rodgers. Dan's advice, encouragement, and intellectual stimulation were instrumental in shaping this book and in shaping me as a scholar. With his incredible mind and gracious manner, he strengthened my knowledge and understating of history, showed me new ways to think of culture, and taught me, among many other important lessons, to look for the discourse behind every "ism." Anson Rabinbach taught me that the cultural and even the pop cultural could also be intellectual. His endless knowledge and insightful comments about anything between Karl Marx and Groucho Marx were always thought-provoking, and I am deeply grateful to him for sharing them with me. Emily Thompson shared my Hollywood curiosity and helped expand my knowledge about it, while consistently providing a fresh take. Paul DiMaggio introduced me to the sociology of culture and inspired me to think about cultural production beyond the historical moment. Finally, T. J. Jackson Lears enriched my understanding of modernity and America. His ability to express complex historical phenomena in succinct and poetic language is a constant source of inspiration.

The opening credits to any history book must include archivists. This project took form in the special collections of the Margaret Herrick Library in Beverly Hills, and I am grateful to Barbara Hall, Louise Hilton, Jenny Romero, and the entire staff, who were always eager to help me find everything I needed. The dedicated personnel at the Oral History Division of

Columbia University, the Louis B. Mayer Library at the American Film Institute in Los Angeles, the Museum of Modern Art Library in New York, the Special Collections at the Dorothy and Lewis B. Cullman Center of the New York Public Library for the Performing Arts, the Wisconsin Historical Society, and the Warner Bros. Archive at the University of Southern California were all equally helpful. I am also thankful to the archivists of the National Archives at College Park, who searched until they found the NLRB records I was so desperately looking for. I wish they had signed their e-mails so I could thank them individually.

I owe an immense amount of gratitude to the Princeton History Department. Throughout my years in Dickinson Hall, I have benefited from the tremendous generosity and wisdom of Margot Canaday, Dirk Hartog, Tera Hunter, Kevin Kruse, Yair Mintzker, Martha Sandweiss, Sean Wilentz, and Julian Zelizer, all of whom taught me a great deal. The Princeton University Graduate School provided the intellectual and material support for many years of uninterrupted research and learning. Stanley Katz, Paul DiMaggio, and Mindy Weinberg at the Center for Arts and Cultural Policy granted additional research funds as well as a stimulating forum in which to discuss culture and organizations. The American Studies Program at Princeton offered similar financial support and an engaging environment, and I would like to thank Dirk Hartog, William Gleason, Judith Ferszt, and Candice Kessel for including me in it. The professional support of William Jordan and Judith Hanson during some of the crucial writing stages was vitally important, and I cannot thank them enough. Elizabeth Bennett, Reagan Campbell, Minerva Fanfair, Lauren Kane, Doris Kratzer, Etta Recke, Barbara Leavey, Pamela Long, Debora Macy, Kristy Novak, Max Siles, Jaclyn Wasneski, and Carla Zimowsk were always very attentive and made the work experience efficient and pleasant in an unmatchable way.

The history department at Princeton is home to an extraordinary intellectual community, one that I am very honored to have been a part of. Many of the people I met in the graduate lounge in Dickinson Hall, the reading rooms in Firestone Library, and the seminar meetings of the Modern America Workshop have left their mark on my work. Specifically, I would like to thank Alex Bevilacqua, Sarah Coleman, Henry Cowles, Rohit De, Will Deringer, Yulia Frumer, Matt Growhoski, Justene Hill, Jennifer Jones, Zack Kagan-Guthrie, Kyrill Kunakhovich, Radha Kumar, Valeria Lopez Fadul, Kathryn McGarr, Elidor Mëhilli, Paul Miles, Maribel Morey, Karam Nachar, Andrei Pesic, Helen Pfeifer, Suzanne Podhurst, Ben Schmidt, Margaret Schotte, and Sarah Seo for their thoughts and comments, and for making my time on campus friendly, exciting, and fun. More than anyone, Sarah Milov, always brilliant and razor-sharp, pushed me onward and upward. I cannot imagine a better companion to study American history with.

My fascination with history began thirty minutes north of Princeton, off a different New Jersey Turnpike exit. Remembering the wonderful years I spent at Rutgers University, I owe quite a bit to my professors at the history department in New Brunswick. Paul Clemens, David Foglesong, Ziva Galili, Bonnie Smith, and Virginia Yans all had a meaningful impact on my education as they taught me the basic skills a historian must have. Hilary A. Hallett deserves special recognition as she inspired me to think critically about Hollywood and introduced me to some of the sources any industry scholar should know.

Several exceptionally smart people graciously dedicated some of their precious time to read and comment on this manuscript or parts of it. Thank you so much, Ofer Ashkenazi, Eric Avila, Alec Dun, Chris Florio, Joe Fronczak, Dov Grohsgal, Doron Halutz, Caley Horan, Matt Karp, Beth Lew-Williams, Rosina Lozano, Charles McGovern, Andrei Pesic, Steven Ross, Moshe Sluhovsky, and Danny Walkowitz for every single useful comment. I would also like to thank Donna Haverty-Stacke and the Hunter College Labor and Working Class History Workshop Seminar, Yael Sternhell and the American Studies Seminar at Tel Aviv University, Sarah Milov and the Movement and Directions in Capitalism Seminar at the University of Virginia, Louis Warren, Emily Remus, Sarah Miller-Davenport, the Western Historical Association, the History of Capitalism Initiative at Cornell University, the Organization of American Historians, the Film and History Conference, and the Popular Culture Association / American Culture Association for providing engaging and productive forums in which to discuss my work.

I feel very lucky to publish this book with the University of North Carolina Press, where Chuck Grench provided his steady and expert editorial guidance while Jad Adkins, Kristen Bettcher, Mary Carley Caviness, Cynthia Crippen, Susan Garrett, Barbara Goodhouse, and Margaretta Yarborough added crucial final touches that turned my text into a book. I would also like to thank Lawrence Glickman and one anonymous reader for their productive and much-needed feedback.

One of the most important findings to come out of this project is that I have wonderful friends. Tidhar Wald, Shani Rozanes, Iddo Shai, Tal Pritzker, Nohar Barnea, Zuzana Boehmová, Maureen Chun, Nikolce Gjorevski, Jessica Levin, Ilana Nesher, Marko Radenović, Kelly Swartz, and Choresh

Wald were my New York family. Dana Arie, Zohar Avgar, Etty Avraham, Yael Bouton, Nohar Bresler, Jasmine Inbar, Julien Dubuis, Idit Duvdevany, Noa Epstein, Tamar Fein, Ofira Fuchs, Pazit Gez, Itaï Kovács, Leeat Perelmutter, Noam Reshef, Gil Rubin, Reut Tal, Hagit Tauber, Roie Telyas, Matt Trujillo, and Mimi Wiener provided additional and much-needed good company. A few incredible individuals held my hand so often it is hard to separate their invaluable professional help from their irreplaceable role in the other parts of my life. I could not have completed this book without the friendship of Nimisha Barton, whose wisdom, honesty, and sense of humor were a constant source of inspiration from the very beginning, as well as the friendship of Catherine Abou Nemeh, Hadas Aron, Yael Berda, Angèle Christin, Yiftah Elazar, Franziska Exeler, Rotem Geva, Udi Halperin, Yoav Halperin, Doron Halutz, Reut Harari, Daniel Hershenzon, Caley Horan, Rania Salem, and Michal Shapira.

Last but certainly not least is my family. I have a very supportive family filled with aunts, uncles, and cousins; I cannot name them all, but each one of them is important. In the closest circle, my grandparents Betty and Jacob Davidov, who always think I could do anything, and my sister Noa, with her liveliness and unbelievable strength, were always cheering me on. My most amazing uncle and aunt Doron and Hadas Davidov gave me a home away from home. Their dedication, support, and friendship throughout the years were greater and mean more to me than words can ever express. Finally, my parents, Motti and Irit Regev, have always been the most reliable and important source of support, comfort, and happiness. They taught me everything, I owe them everything, and I dedicate this book to them.

Working in Hollywood

Introduction

There is something magical about movies—something spellbinding about the fine-tuned images and coherent narratives they present, especially when compared to the nonglamorous and unintegrated experiences of our daily lives. As we are taken into their captivating alternative realities, they make us long for the illusions created on the screen. Moviemakers have forever capitalized on this allure. Ever since the first cameras started rolling, the people who work for the movies have wished to keep us enchanted.

Perhaps for this reason, stretching back to the industry's heyday, motion picture producers always preferred to keep the mechanisms behind the production process shrouded in mystery. Like trained illusionists, in public they constantly spoke about their trade in terms of randomness and wonder rather than foresight and expertise. Darryl Zanuck, the head of Twentieth Century–Fox, once claimed, "It [could] be said without fear of challenge that nowhere else in the world are so many millions risked under such hazardous circumstances and conditions." According to him, making movies was not "exactly like betting a million on the whirl of the ball at a roulette table but it's still always a gamble and the odds are even longer."[1] For Zanuck, it was a speculative and unpredictable game, filled with lucky high rollers such as himself.

Indeed, his fellow producers seemed to have been sitting right beside him at the table. "It isn't possible to make a successful picture [only] by selecting any good director and by engaging any good actors or actresses who happen to fit the parts for which they are selected—except, perhaps, by luck," affirmed Irving Thalberg, the legendary executive in charge of production at MGM.[2] His colleague at Warner Bros., Hal Wallis, added, "If there is an unpredicted business, it's motion pictures. Make one bad bet . . . and you'll find yourself in the unenviable position of having a picture on your hands in which people are no longer interested."[3]

Adopting the outlook presented by Hollywood executives, filmmaking appears to be nothing but a trade involving hunches and gut feelings. "It's a creative business. It's something new," said Adolph Zukor, the founder of Paramount Pictures and one of the men credited with inventing the studio system. "It's not like making shoes or automobiles when you have a model and you follow through for the year. Every picture is an individual enterprise by itself. There are certain ingredients you have to study," but there are also many times when you simply have to speculate: "I don't think I'll take that story, I don't think I'll make it, I don't think it's what the public will take." Even so, despite relying so much on tentative thinking, Zukor admitted, it was "a very pleasant occupation."[4]

THERE IS SOMETHING inherently disenchanting about writing history and, even more so, about writing the history of the movies. This book takes away some of the big screen's magic by revealing Hollywood's mundane apparatus. Uncovering the everyday commercial and labor practices that were responsible for the golden age of the Hollywood studio system, it brings into focus the stories of the men and women who produced the narratives, images, characters, and style of the American motion picture industry. Yet, the chronicles told here are neither these workers' sparkling, stardust-filled biographies nor their memoirs from Tinseltown nightlife. They also do not follow the granted ingenious travails of the filmmakers' creative process. Rather, the following pages bring to life the story of their employment and the routines and interactions they endured while navigating their careers within the big motion picture production companies. In that sense, this is a labor history of Hollywood, a study of the creative occupations that comprised it, which exposes the skill behind the showmen's veneer of luck.

Indeed, some of Hollywood's most famous employees defined their work in very different terms from those used by producers and managers. Joan Crawford, for example, thought, "It is very important to put in the story that we have jobs the same as any girl in a ten cent store, and we do what we're told."[5] Her fellow actor James Cagney felt that his job was "just like a shipping clerk. I was just a salaried employee." He added, "This was part of the times, for everyone. This didn't apply only to me; it applied to everybody under contract."[6] Of course, stars such as Crawford and Cagney are anything but obscure. Their personas were documented in countless biographies, newspaper articles, gossip columns, and the movies they appeared in. Yet, despite this onslaught of publicity, it is seldom mentioned that MGM had the option to lay off Crawford every six months. It is rarely pointed out that Cagney would, as he recalled, "get on the set at eight o'clock in the morning, and . . . [work] right on through till daybreak the next day."[7] It is often forgotten that Clark Gable only took on *Gone with the Wind* because if he refused the part, as he originally intended to do, his contract would have rendered him suspended without pay. Or in other words, despite their fame, the history of these Hollywood luminaries suffers from myopia, focusing narrowly on the glitz and glamor and overlooking the labor structure surrounding it.

Historians have paid much attention to the ways in which culture has become an industry and very little attention to how producers of culture have become modern workers.[8] As the above suggests, an important part of these people's stories, namely, their identity as workers, is repeatedly disregarded, hidden behind a discourse about entertainment and popularity that diverts the spotlight from the sphere of production.[9] This book seeks to redraw this glamorous image and present a historical study of Hollywood as a modern system of labor. It argues that the film industry's golden age, 1920–50, was not only defined by film content and celebrities but also by the people employed in the studio system, their work practices, and interactions on the job. These gave Hollywood its daily shape and are key to understanding it.

More importantly, this book shows how the Hollywood system institutionalized creative labor in the West[10] and how American motion picture companies essentially turned creativity into a modern form of work. By the late 1920s, filmmaking had matured into one of the most profitable industries in the United States; fifty million people went to the movies every week.[11] Consequently, the film studio evolved from an informal workplace where, as one employee put it, "anybody on the set did anything he or she was called upon to do," to a well-thought-out operation with function-specific divisions and tasks. By the 1930s, these were consolidated into specialized jobs: a cinematography department included first, second, still, and assistant cameramen; the actors' ranks featured stars, bit players, and extras. Thus, by systematizing and standardizing the work of actors, directors, writers, cinematographers, and many others, the motion picture companies delivered the first attempt to regulate creative work on a grand scale.[12] The success of their endeavor provided the blueprint for the streamlining of creative production in other forms of media and entertainment, as new business ventures extrapolated on Hollywood's way to embed artistic sensibilities into the efficiency-minded rationale of industrial capitalism.

A BEHIND-THE-SCENES glimpse into Hollywood quickly reveals what media scholar Thomas Schatz labeled "the genius of the system." It allows us to examine the delicate yet stable balance that was struck between "various social, industrial, technological, economic, and aesthetic forces" and yielded "a consistent system of production and consumption, a set of formalized creative practices," as well as "a body of work with a uniform style." Peeking into the studio systems' mundane apparatuses, this book follows in the footsteps of scholars such as Schatz, Janet Staiger, and Douglas Gomery, embracing their mission to uncover the mechanisms behind the production process and shed light on the complex cooperative effort that stood behind every studio and every film. Essentially, I build on their work and expose another side of the system's genius—its distinctive labor force.[13] However, instead of looking at how daily interactions shaped the quality and artistry of Hollywood films, this study focuses on work relations, or what Staiger calls the sociology of production.[14] The goal is to understand what it was like to work for a big Hollywood studio and to examine what kind of employee one had to be, or become, in order to make movies in an era and an industry that pioneered the standardization of cultural production. Or, to put it more simply, this book seeks to answer the question, How did Hollywood work?

The answer, as it turns out, lies mostly in carbon paper sheets. The American motion picture industry, as Schatz demonstrated, "left its legacy not only on celluloid but also on paper"—much paper. Bringing together the interests of moguls, managers, and creative workers, every film project was an arena of confrontation and negotiation. Numerous interoffice communications and memos were printed on small, colorful notepaper to "okay the script, to confirm casting, to approve sets, to suggest tests, to ratify make-ups, to assign crews, to instruct cutters, to recommend musical scores, to hold down performances and [even] to warn hat designers." Hal Wallis's secretary at Warner Bros. recalled "with awe a day in April 1937 when he launched 624 pink slips between dawn and dusk."[15] Such days were by no means unusual, and the countless slips produced contained more than dry instructions; they held the professional claims of the people who wrote them and the language they used to legitimize personal concerns within the overall good of the system. Therefore, while the popular films that came out of the system reflect the final product or the after-the-fact compromise, it is such colorful slips that capture Hollywood's most meaningful "contemporaneous struggles."[16]

These multicolored slips suggest that the everyday conflicts of this creative industry extended far beyond content and style. They represented broader struggles about hierarchy and control. Any slip, whether written by a producer, a director, a writer, or a costume designer, could serve as a claim for authority, an attempt to negotiate the balance of power on the studio lot. This ability or possibility to question authority stemmed in part from the newcomer status of the studio system. During the first half of the twentieth century, the major production companies in the United States were building a cultural industry. In that sense, what became an unprecedentedly successful entertainment business was also a work in progress, in which positions of power were not yet set in stone. In addition, as a creative industry, Hollywood was also an experiment, an attempt to reconcile a rationalized profit-seeking operation with a dependence on artistic taste. Motion picture companies subscribed to the industrial rationale emergent in America at the time, searching for ways to streamline production. Simultaneously, they had to rely on the unrulier talents of creative professionals. As a result, production facilities were sites of "constant and pervasive tension between innovation and control," arenas filled with creative visions, material interests, and a strong impetus to square them off.[17]

These many tensions left their mark. The constant maneuvering between creativity and efficiency was embedded in the sensibility of all those involved, forging complex and unique worker identities. As it was institutionalized to fit the demands of the modern film business, every toil became an amalgam of creativity and productivity. Each cinematic profession coalesced into its own particular mixture of an autonomous artist and industrial worker. Screenwriters, for example, were torn between their desire for the creative control traditionally enjoyed by authors and the available economic security offered by working for the movies. Thus, while contending with an ignoble division of labor that all but shattered the once-respected authorial voice, writers also bestowed on the industry some of the legitimacy of more established literary fields. Similarly, actors were subjected to two seemingly contradictory types of management. On the one hand, they were treated as regimented employees, bound by draconian contracts that essentially alienated them from their labor. On the other hand, the studios safeguarded and pampered them with exorbitant salaries and a network of professionals who worked day and night to make the stars look and sound good.

Directors, the celebrated auteurs of cinema, were indeed accorded a level of autonomy and responsibility that was unique in industry terms. This autonomy, however, was limited to the shooting portion of the production process. In most cases, directors had no say over scriptwriting or the editing of the picture. Furthermore, to maintain a studio career, directors had to demonstrate their conformity and commitment to the studio's material concerns. Conversely, for those working in the myriad other filmmaking crafts that composed the motion picture company, the struggle was less about control and more about recognition. Directors of photography, for example, sought to claim some of the respect and artistic stature accorded to directors and screenwriters. They struggled to form a tighter bond between the creative status of the film industry and the more traditional craft or technical work they introduced into it.

Finally, the most important but also the most ambiguous role in the system was that of the producer. Those employed in this role were the Henry Fords of the industry, responsible for turning Hollywood into an effective modern entertainment machine. They were the ones who shaped and personified the new Hollywood lots, turning them into intermediary spaces that accommodated the demands of profit-seeking corporate executives as well as artists. They served as brokers, embodying the contradictions of the system while closely supervising the production process of every picture and the studio as a whole. The conflicts of each group were not exclusive to it. Rather, some labor conditions epitomized the struggles within a specific line of work, while remaining merely occupational hazards for others. For example, division of labor was a hallmark of all but a few studio jobs, but it manifested most blatantly in screenwriting; every director or cinematographer who demonstrated unique talent was asked to sign an agreement that included some of the contractual demands placed on all actors; any creative employee sought more control over his or her work; everyone had to fight for their right to be considered employees under U.S. labor law.

Together, the people employed by the studios emerged as a new class: they were wage laborers with exorbitant salaries, artists subjected to budgets and supervision, stars bound by contracts. As such, these workers—people like Gable and Katharine Hepburn, director William Wyler, cinematographer James Wong Howe, and screenwriter Anita Loos—were the outliers of the American proletariat. Standing on the outskirts of the category, their position within the American class structure was soft. While experiencing some familiar elements of modern industrial production—such as alienation and commodification, Taylor's scientific management theory, and paradigms of Fordism—just as other factory workers did, for Hollywood creative employees "ownership relations were more complex." For one thing, they had a stronger identification with the product of their labor.[18] In addition, individual artistic skills or star persona made many film workers irreplaceable, or at least hard to replace. These unusual features, combined with the industry's high salaries, resulted in mixed loyalties that marked the emergence of a new class: an ambivalent working class.

Tracing the formation of this new class, which later spread into other creative industries, this book offers a new template for the study of popular culture that illuminates the role of companies such as MGM, Warner Bros., and Paramount in cultivating one of the leading modern forms of labor. It brings the story of these creative laborers to life by weaving together three narratives: first, the story of the American motion picture business and its expansion throughout the first half of the twentieth century into a vertically integrated oligopoly; second, the evolution of creative professions such as producing, acting, and directing and how they became central to the craft of filmmaking; and finally, and most importantly, it tells the story of the people themselves, of those working for the big studios in the new professions. It re-creates the everyday experience of Hepburn, Wyler, and many others, and presents a history of their employee sensibility and professional "way of being."

WHAT FOLLOWS, THEN, is a story about the experience of workers in a specific industry. This labor history of Hollywood examines the film industry's labor structure, how it came to be, and how those working in it "became vital subjects of and agents in histories of their own making."[19] Continuing the tradition of scholars such as David Montgomery and Herbert Gutman, this study is concerned with workers transitioning into a new section of industrial society, one which standardized and institutionalized creativity to an unprecedented scope and scale. It examines, as Gutman put it, "how that transition affected such persons and the society into which they entered."[20] Describing the practice of filmmaking in the studio system, this book shows how studio employees shaped this institution and its operation. Since the primary goal is to uncover the mechanisms that produced efficiency and functionality, in many ways this is a story about the formation of a capitalist hegemony. But, as the study of labor in capitalism often reveals, hegemony requires constant maintenance. Therefore, the following pages seek to capture both the consent and the constraint, both the alliances and the antagonisms, that formed the common daily experience within the dominant structure.

Unsurprisingly, the Hollywood structure was dominated by men. Women played a big part in Hollywood, both the place and the industry.[21] Nevertheless, film work, like any other kind of work, was shaped by assumptions about gender that were incorporated into the studio system and its practices, affecting both men and women. Most noticeably, the gendering of work roles in the film industry impacted the participation of women in specific creative fields, or, in some cases, resulted in their absence.[22] Indeed, professions such as cinematography that emerged in the early days of the industry and required technological expertise were almost exclusively masculine. They also remained that way until the 1970s. The acting and screenwriting ranks, those tasked with supplying the virtuous images and narratives of the screen, were brimming with women, who helped foster an image of respectability and wholesomeness. Furthermore, employees in these two categories, whether men or women, were treated by their superiors in a way that most resembles the attitude traditionally accorded to women in the labor market: either as menial and replaceable workers, in the case of screenwriters, or as commodified goods, in the case of actors. Most notably, the managerial positions, those of producer and director, were occupied by men. Women such as Lois Weber and Alice Guy Blaché, who flourished in those roles during the 1910s, virtually disappeared from the scene by the mid-1920s. The "masculinization" of several work roles is very noticeable in this study, as are the participation of women in and the "feminization" of other parts of the industry. However, neither of these discrete processes takes center stage here.

The dominant Hollywood structure was also white. Motion pictures were born in the 1890s, following the end of Reconstruction and the rise of Jim Crow. Hollywood flourished in tandem with a new and invigorated form of racism, one that was "more self-conscious, more systematic, more determined to assert scientific legitimacy."[23] It is therefore not surprising (though by no means was it inevitable) that the film that symbolized the potential of the new medium—D. W. Griffith's *The Birth of a Nation* (1915)—was also an affirmation of this new form of white supremacy. In such a pervasively racist atmosphere, African Americans and other ethnic minorities found few opportunities to work in the film industry, aside from the token screen appearances that confirmed and amplified cultural stereotypes. The story of black, Latino, and Asian labor in the studio system is similar to its counterparts in many other industries, revealing a pattern of exclusion, discrimination, and far too few exceptions that prove the rule.[24] Therefore, the absence of a meaningful discussion of racial inequality in this book echoes its upsetting absence in the industry itself.

PARALLELING THE DIVISION OF labor in the studios, *Working in Hollywood* is organized by profession. Each of the chapters follows one group of employees who carried primary responsibility for the creative content of the movies, namely, producers, writers, directors, actors, and cinematographers. The time frame underlying all chapters surrounds the formation of the classical Hollywood studio era. By this term I mean to identify not a style but a business model; to borrow the words of historian Steven Ross, I view Hollywood as "less a place than a new way of doing business."[25] The beginnings of this specific model can be traced back to the 1910s, and its decline to the late 1940s and early 1950s. Throughout those years, the American motion picture industry was, as most scholars tend to agree, a "mature oligopoly," that is to say, a market structure that "institutes a mixture of rivalry and tacit cooperation with regards to pricing policies."[26] Filmmaking in America was always a business, and, true to form, it was always accompanied by fair and unfair trade practices in search of monopoly. Thomas Edison was responsible not only for the first motion picture projector but also for the industry's first trust.[27] However, this routine mode took an enhanced form when a series of mergers and consolidations that had begun in the mid-1910s culminated, by 1930, in a vertically integrated industry controlled by five major companies—the majors—each of which owned theater chains, nationwide distribution systems, and studio production facilities. These five companies controlled key resources in the three branches of film supply. It was this march toward oligopoly that also created a uniform mode of production, including the standardization of labor practices across the industry.

The temporal focus of this project, therefore, starts with the first budding of the oligopoly, the formation of the five majors, in the 1910s. The first was Paramount, formed in 1916 by a merger between Adolph Zukor's production company, Famous Players, the Jesse L. Lasky Feature Play Company, and a newly formed network of regional distribution firms called the Paramount Picture Corporation. Soon enough, Zukor took over the entire operation and commenced buying his own theaters, a move that reached its pinnacle with the 1926 purchase of Balaban & Katz, the largest theater chain in Chicago.[28] Thus, Zukor created the first vertically integrated company that could make, rent out, and exhibit its own pictures.

Other moguls followed suit. Marcus Loew, the biggest theater holder in New York, bought the Metro distribution system, the Goldwyn Picture Corporation production facilities, and the Louis B. Mayer production unit, merging them in 1924 to form MGM, the production-distribution division of Loew's.[29] William Fox, of the Fox Film Corporation, also decided to build his own theaters, catching up with his two competitors.[30] Next came Warner Bros., incorporated in 1923 by the four Warner brothers, Harry, Abe, Sam, and Jack. This family venture ensured its place in the proverbial "big league" through serious investment in sound technology and the acquisition, in 1929, of the First National theater chain.[31] The final integration was that of RKO. David Sarnoff, the president of RCA, assembled this last major so that the sound equipment developed by its parent company could turn a profit. In 1928, Sarnoff partnered with Joseph P. Kennedy, who owned the little FBO studio, and the Keith-Albee-Orpheum vaudeville circuit, now turned theater chain, forming together the fifth vertically integrated company.[32]

By 1930, the merger movement had come to an end. The so-called big five were set with impressive production facilities, worldwide distribution networks, and strategically located theaters. These grand-scale operations were connected in a "symbiotic relationship" with two additional production-distribution companies, Universal and Columbia, and the distribution-only firm United Artists, all of which owned no theaters and are commonly referred to as the "little three."[33] Among all of them, they produced 60 percent of the American industry's output and collected 95 percent of the national film rentals.[34] They also found ways to work in unison.

The owners of the big companies sought to stabilize their status. They did so by pooling their interests and initiating trade practices that benefited them over smaller independent producers, distributors, and exhibitors. Outside the realm of production these practices included the acrimonious customs known as "blind selling," that is, the leasing of pictures that were not yet complete, and "block booking"—that is, the leasing of several films in fixed packages upon the condition that all would be exhibited without allowing the theater owner to pick and choose among them.[35] The majors also engaged in an effort to institutionalize these practices. In 1922, Zukor and Loew formed the Motion Picture Producers and Distributors Association (MPPDA), appointing as its head former postmaster general William H. Hays. As one scholar explained, this trade organization ensured that the motion picture business "worked on commonalities, whereby the insiders who joined together solved common problems while competing only among themselves in the marketplace."[36] Five years later, following an initiative of Louis B. Mayer, the partners also formed a joint company union, the Academy of Motion Picture Arts and Sciences.

Despite some fluctuation in revenue stream, this cooperative system maintained its stability through the Depression years, the New Deal, and World War II. Yet, toward the late 1940s, three disturbances pushed film production away from the studio system and toward a system based more and more on "spot production" or separate deals. One of these disturbances was the arrival of television, which introduced a new technological competitor to the market.[37] By the mid-1950s, television had taken over the average American household, while box office revenues were losing ground.[38] A second disturbance was policy-driven. A change in the tax code during World War II increased the tax rate on personal income, thus creating a strong incentive for the highly paid producers, actors, directors, or writers to form independent production companies and thereby reduce their effective marginal tax rate from 90 to 60 percent.[39] Finally, the largest disruption was a legal one. In 1948, the Supreme Court delivered its final ruling in a nearly decade-old federal antitrust case against the majors. In what is known as the *Paramount* decision, the Court found the big companies, including Universal, Columbia, and United Artists, in violation of the Sherman Antitrust Act and effectively ended their vertical integration by ordering them to divest. Studios were stripped of their theater ownership, and vice versa.[40]

These developments had many effects on the industry as a whole. One of the most meaningful was the change in employment patterns within the production branch. Throughout the "classical era" or the "studio era," the integrated nature of the industry ensured a steady cash flow from the box office back to the filmmaking facilities. As a result, in terms of labor, the studio operations of the majors could maintain their own stock companies. At any given moment, a studio like MGM had under its employment an army of producers, actors, writers, directors, editors, cinematographers, and many other kinds of personnel. Their various departments were always fully staffed, and their members signed contracts ranging from a few months to seven years. This ability to keep so many people on the payroll proved extremely important when it came to creative talent, particularly for the big stars, whose unique skills could be deployed upon request. After the *Paramount* decision, the stock-company model eroded. The reason was that film production did not generate any revenue on its own; distribution and exhibition did that. Without the theaters and the oligopolistic trade practices, the generous and steady studio budget that was necessary to maintain talent stables was no longer available. This erosion serves as an end point and helps frame the years of the integrated studio system and its distinctive mode of employment as a clear case study, one through which it is possible to isolate a particular type of organization and experience of creative labor in a modern cultural industry.[41]

LEGENDARY TITANS SUCH AS Zanuck, Thalberg, Wallis, and Zukor were lucky men, but they were also skillful workers and savvy managers. Though by stressing chance and fortune they might have been trying to protect the wonders of the screen, their unique methods and inventive work habits were in some ways no less magical. Another producer by the name of Pandro Berman once said that it was nothing short of a "miracle" when "you can get ten guys together to make a movie and all of them be right all the way through, so that you end up with a masterpiece." By no means an easy task, "it has to do with the inception of the story, with the treatment, with the director, with the producer, with everybody having to be right all the time to make a good picture, and who's right all the time?"[42] To understand how all these elements came together, we must shift our gaze from the mise-en-scène of the pictures to the mise-en-scène of the labor system behind them. The best place to begin such an expedition is with this small group of men, who spoke about luck but acted under the firm conviction that they knew exactly what was right.

CHAPTER ONE

Producing

Soon after Darryl Zanuck, head of production at Twentieth Century–Fox, bought the rights to John Steinbeck's *The Grapes of Wrath* in 1939, "rumor flooded Hollywood. It was said that Zanuck had paid $75,000 to keep it off the screen. Another report was that he had purchased it only in order to make a whitewashed version of it. A third report was that if the novel was made into a picture, the financial backers of the studio would withdraw their money."[1] Zanuck apparently loved it: "Show me a man who can prove that I spent $70,000 for a book in order to shelve it . . . and I'll make a picture about him!" As one of his employees pointed out, "Nothing improves Zanuck's disposition like a good stiff rumor that he'll never do it. His spirits rise, soft drinks flow like water in his office, and it is a first-rate time to hit him for a raise."

The rumors did hit some nerves, though, particularly those of Steinbeck. In April 1939, during his first meeting with Nunnally Johnson, the screenwriter assigned to adapt the novel, the author demanded to know "what the hell was this rumor that the company had got the story for the sole purpose of ditching it." Johnson tried to assure him that was not the case, but Steinbeck "remained skeptical—polite, to be sure, but clearly skeptical. Nor, incidentally, has his skepticism ever abated . . . he'll still be dubious until he has seen the picture on the screen."[2]

Though the rumors were false, Steinbeck had good reason to be skeptical about the prospect of a Hollywood adaptation for *The Grapes of Wrath*. After all, at the beginning even Zanuck was doubtful. Despite his personal belief in the project, the head producer feared that Winthrop Aldrich, chairman of the board at Chase National Bank, which essentially controlled Fox studios, "would probably raise hell with me because I was attempting a controversial subject that did not hold capital in too high a light." But when he ultimately met Aldrich, expecting "the ax to fall," the latter congratulated him on the project. "To hear one of the tycoons of the banking world express confidence in *The Grapes of Wrath* astonished me," claimed Zanuck, "because none of the Hollywood wiseacres shared this opinion."[3] Steinbeck was happy too. In a letter to his agent he wrote, "Zanuck has more than kept his word. He has a hard, straight picture . . . looks and feels like a documentary film and certainly it has a hard, truthful ring. No punches were pulled."[4] For Zanuck this was what he called "the pay-off": he made a successful picture that earned Steinbeck's approval as well as the big banker's blessing.[5]

This was Zanuck's professional position, standing between Steinbeck and Chase National. As an executive in charge of production, his job was first and foremost to make sure that the studio was profitable. Yet, to do so he had to negotiate and orchestrate the talents and aspirations of a diverse creative force. Men like Zanuck, assuming titles such as executive producer, head producer, or executive in charge of production, coordinated the entire operation of their respective studios. However, working in a taste-guided industry, theirs was not a conventional assembly line spitting out identical products. It was a different kind of production process, one in which they had to translate a budget handed down by the company's financial executives into a changing program of specific pictures, each of which featured an original plot, drama, and characters. This task required a unique capability. Indeed, as screenwriter turned industry anthropologist Leo C. Rosten pointed out, such producers developed a skill that included "a knowledge of audience tastes, a story sense, a businessman's approach to the costs and mechanics of picture making," and, on top of everything else, the ability to "manage, placate, and drive a variety of gifted, impulsive, and egocentric people."[6]

It was a complex skill, and throughout the 1920s and 1930s a number of successful executive producers used it not only to make movies but also to shape Hollywood's mode of production. They did so by organizing filmmaking around their negotiation abilities, turning the Hollywood studio into an intermediary space that accommodated the demands of profit-seeking corporate executives as well as the artistic ambitions of writers, directors, cinematographers, and actors. Making their job the key position in the industry, head producers enthroned a form of moviemaking that was itself intermediary, combining cost-effectiveness with extravagant sets, elaborate narratives, and high-priced talent. In a sense, the evolution of this work role and the stories of the people who filled it is the story of the industry incarnate. It charts the coming together of efficiency and art, bureaucrats and artists, big budgets and creative visions. It is a story of a few go-betweens who turned their liminal position into the throbbing center of the studio system.

Brokering an Unknown

To understand why studios developed the function of executive producer, one has to consider the economic structure they were operating in. Filmmaking is done in a market that sociologists generally refer to as "turbulent," or one that is "changing in ways that are incapable of analysis and prediction."[7] Most if not all culture-producing industries fit within this category, as their profits depend on inconsistent and intangible factors such as taste and fashion, which are essentially "unanalyzable."[8] Consumption of entertainment, as opposed to, say, liquor or vehicles, is not based on a fixed need, and its patterns are for the most part unpredictable. The capricious nature of the demand makes it difficult, in turn, to fix and standardize the supply chain. Or, in other words, "uncertainty is intimately related to the exigencies of product generation," since the ever-changing target offers very "few [certain] standards of creative competence or expertise." To make matters worse, supplying goods to a taste-guided market forces the management of cultural industries to "negotiate and renegotiate the norms and rules governing the creation of new products with writers, artists, and other creative personnel" who are often guided by sets of considerations that are foreign to the economic realm.[9]

Managers, therefore, are engaged in an everlasting effort to contain uncertainty. One way to do so is by trying to decipher the complex mechanisms of taste and preference.[10] Another is to find organizational structures that maximize creative output. Within this second framework, creative industries almost always embrace an organizational model in which they rely on brokers to "negotiate between the aspirations of artists for creative expression and the desire of management to predict and control."[11] These brokers function as mediators; they translate the objectives of management to popular culture creators, and vice versa. Such a system varies from the more common "managerial capitalism" prevalent in the "multiunit industrial enterprise" that became the standard for most industries in the United States in the first two decades of the twentieth century.[12] For, while conventional bureaucratic administration "is based on close supervision, repetition of routine, and compliance with orders," brokerage administration   "is characterized by ambiguity, informality, and negotiation."[13] Brokers offer an unconventional and dynamic type of leadership that is more entrepreneurial and hybrid, working outside normal channels, and forming novel combinations out of the available means of production.[14]

The Hollywood model of brokerage administration developed in tandem with the industry. Though motion pictures had already attracted audiences at the beginning of the twentieth century, it was only during the 1930s that the American film industry completed its transformation into a modern business enterprise. A series of mergers and consolidations leading up to that decade culminated in a vertically integrated industry. One outcome of this process was that big studios, such as MGM, Warner Bros., and Fox, were simply too big and could "no longer [be] run by their founders as family business[es]." Accountable for delivering a product to large theater chains and worldwide distribution networks, these studios were now under the orderly command of "hierarchies of salaried executives who rationalized operation to insure long term stability and profits."[15] In this sense, American motion picture companies were not different from other integrated and multifunctional corporations engaged in the manufacturing and processing of goods; companies such as Standard Oil or United Fruit went through similar processes roughly between the 1880s and World War I.[16]

This newfound bureaucratic structure was a direct result of the increased involvement of banks and financial corporations in Hollywood. Mergers required capital, as did the development of sound technology, an enterprise that consumed many industry resources throughout the 1920s. In addition, though the repercussions of the Great Depression were late to hit Hollywood, by 1931 most companies stopped registering profits. One by one, the majors filed for bankruptcy, while even those that managed to stay afloat, namely, Warner Bros. and Loew's, were losing millions. Wall Street bankers and other investment firms seized this opportunity to penetrate the film market. They subsidized business expansion, financed technological experimentation, and resurrected studios from receivership. Thus, Paramount, for example, found its board filled with stakeholders from Lehman Brothers and the Royal Insurance Company of Great Britain, while Fox was reorganized as Twentieth Century–Fox under the supervision of Chase.[17]

In other words, expansion introduced a new top layer of bankers and bureaucrats into the industry, one that was far removed from the filmmaking ranks. East Coast executives and board members were often foreign to the rhythms and discourse of the creative process; film production was simply not at the center of their attention. At the time, the economic soundness of the industry depended mainly on the dominance of the "big five" majors as distributors-exhibitors, not on the production centers on the West Coast. In that sense, the studios were subordinate to the two other branches of the business, and at the "center of gravity" stood the "stable profitability of the theaters." Indeed, inventive distribution practices such as block booking and blind selling were instated to guarantee rental revenues for the majors. Yet, even with these oligopolistic methods for collateral, the industry still rested on that "base of intangibles"—the movies, which had to be made in order to draw the crowds to the box office. Bankers and efficiency experts still ultimately needed to contend with creative personnel.[18]

Enter the producer, or, more accurately, the producers, the people whose unique job it was to serve as the ligaments between the business strata and the creative labor force in the studios. Connecting two such seemingly foreign elements was a complicated task. As Jesse L. Lasky, a producer and the executive vice president of the original Paramount–Famous Players–Lasky Corporation once said, the producer "must be a prophet and a general, a diplomat and a peacemaker, a miser and a spendthrift." He must have "the patience of a saint and the iron of a Cromwell." He essentially had to embody the internal contradictions of the system. Producers were the brokers of the Hollywood film industry. On the one hand, they were responsible for "the control of the artistic temperament, the shaping of creative forces and the knowledge of the public needs for entertainment."[19] On the other hand, as Lasky told a group of Harvard students in 1927, they were tasked with "justifying [the] negative costs" to the management and with "determining the profits that may be made."[20] They had to translate market rationale into creative work and explain artistic choices in terms of future earnings.

Of course, this was not a task for one person alone. When asked about the role of the producer in the studio, screenwriter Philip Dunne replied, "You say producer, and do you mean . . . Zanuck, who ran the whole studio, all the pictures, or do you mean Cliff Reed, who was subordinate to [John] Ford, or do you mean a staff producer who is grinding out 10 pictures, or is it the fellow sitting in an office in New York who is trying to raise the money?"[21] There were many kinds of producers. An industry churning out between 500 and 800 pictures every year naturally generates a high frequency of negotiations.[22] Every film had to be brokered individually while keeping track of the output as a whole. Due to this fact, every studio had a network of producers streamlining the creative work—a blood-circulating system channeling information to and from the company's headquarters.

If we think of producers as blood vessels, then the most important of them, the main artery, must have been the studio's head producer. As Lasky stated, "He is the producer of producers . . . he works as the co-ordinating force of functioning producers under him." This "major executive" chose his workers, inspired them, and directed them, and hence "the product of those workers inevitably [bore] the stamp of his personality and his mind." Lasky added that a wise producer "understands the artistic temperament enough to permit it to have its way within reason, so that the product bears not only the trademark of the mind of the general producer" but also the imprint of "the other creative forces that work under him."[23] A master of art and reason, the head producer was the central broker, the dynamo galvanizing the industry. Therefore, the rise of the film industry is also the story of how producers got to be at that center.

A Steady March to Efficiency

In the beginning, there was disorder. The technology to record and project motion pictures developed in the late 1890s, but it was only a decade later that one could speak of a real industry. Before that, "making movies was not yet an extensive business," claimed screenwriter and documentarian

Lewis Jacobs. All one needed to make motion pictures was "a business office, a camera, and enough money to pay for the film and to cover the cameraman's modest salary." After they were made, "films were sold outright to the exhibitors, largely by mail order."[24] Such a loose structure did not require a well-defined division of labor. Indeed, it seems this burgeoning business operation lacked any such division. A word search through the digitally available trade papers from the time reveals that, before 1907, the terms "producer" and "director" were virtually not in use in the motion picture world, at least not to describe any particular profession.[25]

These slapdash days were short-lived. The year 1907 was one of economic recession in America. Paradoxically, it was also the year during which "the little store shows known as Nickelodeons were doing a gold-rush business." Audiences flocked to the theaters in ever-increasing numbers, a surge that put a strain on the disordered production end of the industry. Simply put, the irregular shooting patterns left companies short on supply. That boom year, only about 1,200 one-reel films were released in the United States, and as few as 400 of them were made domestically. This was far from enough to satisfy the appetite of the thousands of "hungry Nickelodeons," most of which were changing their programs twice a week or even daily.[26] The market was ready for expansion, and expansion, said Jacobs, "necessitated more people and a division of duties to speed the output." Accordingly, by

1908 some roles, including "directing, acting, photographing, writing, and laboratory work," were already split into separate crafts.[27]

Under this primary division, the producer seems to have been the person commissioning and financing the filmmaking ordeal, the one standing at the head of the production company. "It is likely that before next Fall ground will be broken for one of the largest motion picture studios in the world somewhere near Denver," declared the *Moving Picture World* in June 1908. The paper reported that "Colonel W. N. Selig, the noted Chicago inventor and motion picture producer, will be in the city within a few weeks to decide on the plans which are necessitated by the constantly growing demand for films and the further necessity of making them where sunshine instead of electric lights can be utilized."[28] This was one of the very few times the paper mentioned the term "motion picture producer" that year, and it is clearly in reference to the financial endeavors of this minstrel company owner turned film business entrepreneur. That said, the term was still far from fixed. In fact, though there was definitely an increase in its use, through the early 1910s, "producer" was frequently taken to be synonymous with "director." "A producer for one of the large moving picture manufacturers, accompanied by a party of fourteen people, has been taking pictures from a special train on the Yosemite Valley Railroad," reported the *Nickelodeon* in July 1909.[29] "The eye of the spectacular producer dominates the entire production and eclipses the acting and the photography," commented the *Moving Picture World* in 1912 while evaluating the directorial feats of a picture titled *St. George and the Dragon*.[30]

Even so, the search for order was well under way. Already in the early 1910s, several companies were experimenting with labor division and efficiency. In June 1913, *Motion Picture News* reported, "Lubin is falling into line with Edison and Vitagraph," incorporating their policy "to put a working script up to a director with strict order to produce it."[31] This new "efficiency system of management" was orchestrated by Wilbert Melville, whose title was "producer-manager of the Western branch" of the company. Melville does not seem to have been supervising individual productions, but he did plan the structure of work in the Lubin studio. His planning, in addition to establishing an independent script-editing department, also had a spatial component, by which "the relative locations of the buildings were determined with a view to the part they play in the general scheme," making sure that "those which are most used in connection with the work on the stage," such as the property room, "are grouped around the stage."

According to the *Moving Picture World*, this new policy adopted by Melville "makes possible the production of pictures of high quality while effecting substantial economies of money—and of time."[32] It is probable that other studios adopted similar templates, and taken together, these well-crafted structures gave birth to a new organizational function.

By the mid-1910s, it was already possible to detect a separate craft: the creatively involved production manager. Around 1914, the industry adopted a new structure that "centralized the control of production under the management of a producer, a work position distinct from staff directors."[33] This change was in some sense part of a nationwide industrial effort to increase efficiency, which included a deskilling of labor as professed by theorists such as Fredrick Winslow Taylor, and an embrace of managerial hierarchy, in which a new stratum of middle management found new ways to expand markets and speed up production and distribution.[34] In the film business, the lengthening of motion pictures to seventy-five minutes on average and a shift toward a uniform style of production, incorporating such elements as "continuity, verisimilitude, narrative dominance, and clarity," spelled a need for production planning to ensure both "profit maximization" and "quality control." As a result, production firms began designating a specific person, the producer, who oversaw all filmmaking and was responsible for the entire firm's output. His job included developing a detailed shooting script, using that script "to plan and budget the entire film shot-by-shot before any major set construction, crew selection, or shooting started," and monitoring all post-shooting work.[35]

Consider the following transition reported by *Photoplay* in 1915. David W. Griffith, who, the magazine declared, had earned "the right to be known as the world's foremost director of motion picture plays," had recently been appointed "the chief producer of all Reliance, Majestic, and Griffith photo dramas." The writer of this piece was not simply conflating the two roles; he was emphasizing a change. As he explained, between them, the three film brands mentioned released "an average of five new photoplays every week," and naturally "it is impossible for Griffith personally to produce this number of plays each week." Hence, under his new role, "to each of them he devotes part of his time." Griffith was now a producer. He has "many directors work[ing] under him," and he frequently "casts their pictures, and, in all cases, he selects their stories."[36] Only with a few pictures, those released under the Griffith brand, did the master retain his original directing duties. Without much fanfare, *Photoplay* essentially announced the separation of "producer" from "director" and the emergence of the producer-as-supervisor work role.

Griffith was not the only director to be entrusted with managerial duties. Until that point, the mode of production relied on the organizational abilities of the director, but when the system expanded, the initiative these filmmakers demonstrated while coordinating their own productions seemed to suggest that they would be those most suitable to take charge of larger operations. Directors were the natural choice for the job. Specifically, the man who commanded such a complicated endeavor as *The Birth of a Nation* certainly proved to be a skillful and efficient producer. However, his interests lay elsewhere. As one historian explained, while the industry developed a system of specialization and divided labor in the studios, Griffith, "preferring his intuitive working method and full creative control," chose to focus on directing and ultimately "became more or less an outsider."[37]

One other director who did display a taste for organization was Thomas H. Ince. The son of two actors from Rhode Island, Ince, born in 1880, entered show business at a young age. He began acting when he was only six, joining various theater-touring companies. His career in motion pictures started in 1910. He returned to New York following an engagement in Cincinnati, and, he explained, "as it sometimes happens with actors and others, I found myself out of a job." One day, after "completing the rounds of the booking offices without success," he encountered an actor friend by the name of Joseph Smiley, who, to Ince's surprise, was now "an assistant director at the Imp studio on 56th street." Smiley took Ince with him to the studio, where the latter was immediately offered an acting job. The young actor took it, even though he claimed that the place reminded him of "some of my unpleasant one-night stands." In a similar and typically haphazard manner, "several months later, one of the Imp directors resigned before his picture was complete and [Ince] was given a directorship." Assuming the role, he made a name for himself by completing several very successful two-reel westerns.

Then came a very meaningful stage in his career. A year after he joined IMP, Ince heard that Adam Kessel Jr. and Charles O. Baumann, the owners of the New York Motion Picture Corporation, wished to expand their nascent operation in Edendale, California, and were looking for an able director to take a company out west. "I decided to apply for it . . . feeling that I would have greater possibilities in this new field than in New York. A little strategy was necessary, I felt, to impress my prospective employers with my importance, so I allowed a moustache to grow, and on the day of my interview with Baumann I borrowed a large and sparkling diamond ring. This I figured would make the impression that I was a man of means who did not have to work for the paltry $60 a week, which was my munificent salary at the Imp studio."[38] He got the job, a salary of $150 a week, and stock in Keystone, Mack Sennett's production unit in the Los Angeles region, which was financed by the New York Motion Picture Corporation.[39]

It was in Los Angeles that Ince created the studio that would serve as a dress rehearsal, so to speak, for the well-oiled production facilities of the golden age. After completing a couple of films in Edendale, the director realized that "the facilities had to be improved, if the infant art [of cinema] was to live."[40] In October, he convinced Kessel and Baumann to let him lease a farm of 18,000 acres on the shore north of Santa Monica. In what would soon be known as Inceville, the director constructed "a main stage 175 × 220 feet; a new glass stage 360 × 160 and two auxiliary stages 50 × 80 feet, an administration building, a restaurant, a commissary, a wardrobe building, a property building, a scene building, 200 dressing rooms, an arsenal . . . a power house . . . a reservoir . . . six stable[s]," and some additional structures. Even though it was near a variety of natural landscapes, the operation also included settings for "a Spanish Mission, a Dutch Village with a genuine canal, old windmills, etc.; a Japanese village with jinrikishas; an Irish village; a Canadian village; an East Indian street and a Sioux camp."[41] This was only the beginning.

Ince was interested in progress, or, as he termed it, in "the rapid and sustained growth of the picture industry, and the steady march to efficiency."[42] His Taylorist persuasion manifested itself even when it came to subtitles, which he considered "a very important phase of the industry." He decided on a form of lettering only "after experimenting with many types of letters." With regard to "the question of how long to run a title," that too, he explained "had been worked out scientifically."[43] Considering this frame of mind, one could imagine that Ince was uncomfortable with the prevalent production practice, in which "a director would get the germ idea of a plot, assemble a cast, go out on location and start to shoot, having only a hazy idea of what he was going to do." Especially as head of operations in Los Angeles, Ince could not contend with the "inevitable" and recurring situation in which a director "would have to hold up the picture and keep the cast standing around while he racked his brain for an idea."[44]

As explained, at the time the industry was about to turn the corner. With longer narrative films gaining popularity and with the demand for films only increasing, production had to become more organized. As Ince explained, "A director could no longer be the jack-of-all-trades, for the industry was out of its swaddling clothes." No, now "it behooved the director to concentrate solely upon directing, and to employ men and women who were especially qualified along certain lines to take charge of its various departments."[45] And so it was in Inceville. By 1913, Ince had stopped directing and began supervising the "520 . . . names on the weekly payroll."[46] He had a staff of six directors working under him, to whom he handed a detailed shot-by-shot continuity script, including setting and props.[47] He had specialized departments for every other part of production, such as wardrobe and acting, and he also introduced tight budget control.[48] Rather than directing films, he was directing a whole studio.

The executive producer was born. Ince was not alone, of course, but his innovations, together with those introduced by Griffith, Melville, and others, helped align Hollywood with what has been termed "monopoly capital's quest for organizing and supervising the potential for labor time and power." At the same time, the industry was also nurturing an ongoing creative quest for bigger and more ambitious movies. As it turned out, these pursuits went hand in hand. Two years after its establishment, Inceville was no longer big enough. Its success, manifested in the success of the pictures it produced, led to a distribution partnership with the newly established Triangle Film Corporation, as well as the construction of an additional gargantuan operation in Culver City, with even more workers, stages, and departments. This was the new normal. By 1915, a "pyramid of labor" was the dominant studio structure around Los Angeles, featuring a top manager, middle management, department heads, and workers. The Ince-type producer was at the head of the pyramid, and from that position he could avert some of the inherent problems of creative production, including "irregularity . . . slowness of manufacture, lack of uniformity, and uncertainty of quality."[49]

This was the first step. At that point, the new Hollywood studios, though constantly growing and certainly much larger than their East Coast predecessors, were still rather small in comparison to the vast and sprawling business operations that would emerge in the 1920s. They were also different in terms of hierarchy. Though Ince was contractually bound to powerful companies such as the New York Motion Picture Corporation and, later, Triangle, these were not parent companies in the traditional sense. They did not interfere in the production process. Furthermore, Ince owned his product. In 1915, for example, he held 65,000 shares in Triangle and received dividends from Keystone, Broncho, Kay Bee, Empire, and the Domino production brands.[50] He was not in the middle but at the top of his self-made pyramid. As the industry kept expanding, his craft relocated to the middle, and it is to this repositioning that we shall turn next.

The Evolution of a Motion Picture Producer

History is rarely about one man, but when it comes to the transformation of Hollywood producers from their role in the 1920s to the central position they occupied during the golden age of the studio system, one name seems to stand out, that of Irving Thalberg. One of the founding members of MGM, Thalberg updated and improved the system of supervision developed during the 1910s to fit the studio of the vertically integrated industry, the studio that was now only part of a production-distribution-exhibition mammoth. Simultaneously, he also adapted the role of the producer. During the 1920s, a creative and efficient manager such as Thalberg could no longer stand at the top of the pyramid. By mid-decade, those who filled the uppermost ranks were more often than not men like Thalberg's boss, Nicholas Schenck, an entertainment industry entrepreneur and a savvy businessman who served as the president of Loew's. Nor was Thalberg "the most artistic individual at the studio." Nevertheless, he found a focal position between those poles, "between New York and L.A., between capitalization and production, between conception and execution."[51] His power stemmed from his ability to bring them together.

Thalberg was not one of the pioneers. Born in 1899 and suffering from a congenital heart defect, he spent most of his childhood and adolescence in bed in Brooklyn while motion pictures transformed from a novice technology into a profitable industry based in Los Angeles. In fact, Thalberg reached California for the first time only in 1920, long after Thomas Ince and Carl Laemmle, his first employer, established themselves as leading picture showmen. Unlike for these men, for Thalberg cinema was not a new industry up for grabs; it was a passion. Or at least so claims Samuel Marx, who was head of the scenario department at MGM. Marx met Thalberg while both were junior employees at the New York offices of Laemmle's Universal Film Manufacturing Company. Thalberg was working as Laemmle's personal secretary. The two coworkers bonded while working overtime and dining at Thompson's Cafeteria at the bottom of the Mecca Building on Broadway. As Marx suggested, it was there that Thalberg already expressed his integral managerial vision. "The people have to take what we give them," he professed to Marx, "[and] it seems to me they deserve better." He wanted to be in charge, to "make them do it my way so they never know if their way was better." Thalberg was concerned with quality, in particular the poor quality of production at Universal, but he also believed in the power of management—his own management.[52]

As is often the case with Hollywood legends, there is no way of knowing if Marx's recollections are accurate. In any case, whether he was as explicit about them or not, soon enough the young secretary got a chance to demonstrate this dual set of concerns. In March 1920, Carl Laemmle took Thalberg on a trip to Universal City, his five-year-old studio in the San Fernando valley.[53] Impressed by the young secretary's ideas about production, he left him there, and, by the end of the month, also appointed him general manager in charge of production.[54] Thalberg went right to work, putting things in order à la Ince. He introduced mandatory shot-by-shot scripts, schedules, and budgets, all to make sure that "one big picture after another went to the screen on schedule." He worked "quietly, earnestly, [and] efficiently" in order to "keep the big plant running."[55] By the fall of 1921, he was able to proudly announce, "seven companies are now at work, and . . . within a fortnight some twelve or fourteen will be busy."[56] As the *Los Angeles Times* declared, Thalberg was "a driver" of the kind that "asks for twice as much as he can possibly expect from every man, and, in consequence gets every man's full effort."[57]

To achieve this kind of authority could not have been easy, especially not for someone who lacked any real background in filmmaking. While knowledgeable about the methods employed by the producers who preceded him, which were regularly reported on in the trade papers, Thalberg did not have any practical experience. Unlike Griffith or Ince, he never directed a motion picture. Despite that fact, he felt competent to purchase stories, supervise script writing and casting, and oversee the cutting and editing of every film. In 1920, it is important to remember, efficiency-guided management systems were common in Hollywood but not preeminent. At the beginning of the decade "creative power was [still] concentrated in the hands of a relatively small group of filmmakers capable of conceiving, orchestrating, and executing specific projects."[58] One of these directors was Erich von Stroheim, an industry pioneer who, like many of his peers, was ill disposed toward the idea of scientific management.

The standoff between Thalberg and Stroheim is yet another famous tale. However, underneath the embellished, exaggerated, irresistible details stands a deciding moment in which a young executive producer asserted his authority over an artistically talented star/director. Stroheim was not only successful on his own; he was responsible for making Universal successful. His first feature for the company, *Blind Husbands*, which he wrote, directed, and starred in, grossed almost half a million dollars and marked the first time "the little studio had a film that was both profitable and prestigious."[59] The movie was also quite expensive to make, as Stroheim ignored the allocated budget of $25,000 to spend $250,000. When Thalberg became head of production, the celebrated director was busy running behind schedule and above budget on his next feature, *Foolish Wives*. Thalberg attempted to curb Stroheim by appealing to his reason, cutting off money, and even removing him from the production altogether. But to no avail—as Stroheim was both the director and the lead actor, it was impossible to get rid of him without letting the extensive footage he had already shot go to waste. As Stroheim saw it, he was an artist, and Thalberg a clerk, and "since when does a child supervise a genius?"[60] That was round one.

Round two ended quite differently. In 1922, Stroheim and Thalberg put their differences aside and started work on another project, titled *Merry-Go-Round*. And once again, problems abounded. This time Thalberg had the upper hand. Before the film went into production it was agreed that Stroheim would stay behind the camera, and other actors were cast for the leading roles. Therefore, on October 6, after costs, rather as expected, went over budget, Thalberg could write to Stroheim, "You have time and again demonstrated your disloyalty to our company . . . and have attempted to create an organization loyal to yourself, rather than to the company you were employed to serve. . . . You are discharged from our employ."[61] As Thalberg saw it, art could not trump the organization. Creativity was important and often merited increased spending, but it had to be checked. It was such thinking that won him the trust of businessmen like Laemmle. Still, despite this display of organizational conformism, it soon turned out that Thalberg also had a little bit of Stroheim in him.

Swearing by efficiency and order, when it came to film content, Thalberg proved to be a perfectionist with a flair for extravagance. Soon after he got rid of Stroheim, he turned to producing his first grand picture, *The Hunchback of Notre Dame*. The production was lavish, including the construction of a full-size façade of the Parisian cathedral in addition to nineteen acres of sets and a cast numbering 2,000 people. Laemmle originally authorized the project, but, while supervising the editing, Thalberg was not pleased, and he ordered, without the big boss's approval, a restaging of the crowd scenes. This pushed the budget and the film into the realm of a "prestige epic."[62] Lacking an in-house theater chain, Universal was not in the habit of producing such pictures, which committed the company to a robust promotional budget. Laemmle preferred to leave such expensive productions to Paramount or Fox and concentrate on low-budget films. He let Thalberg off the hook this time, but despite *Hunchback*'s great success as Universal's top-grossing movie of 1923, it was unclear whether Laemmle would authorize such a project again. This conflict only added to what was already a fraught relationship between the young producer and his boss. Thalberg decided to move on and find a company that would share his vision of organization as well as ambitious movies—one in which he could negotiate with the management.

He found it in the newly merged Metro Goldwyn Mayer. The triangular trademark MGM is somewhat of a misnomer, since the balance of power it implies had little to do with the company that was signed into existence in 1924. For starters, Samuel Goldwyn never took part in it. But, even more importantly, the name does not account for Nick Schenck, the head of the Loew's theater chain, who orchestrated the merger of the new company in order to better compete with industry giants such as Paramount. In 1920, Loew's Inc. was the dominant theater chain in New York City, but its production branch, including only the small Metro Pictures Corporation, was unable to deliver a sufficient number of quality pictures. Schenck decided to overcome this problem by acquiring Goldwyn Pictures, a company with considerable production facilities that lacked competent management. For that latter component, he turned to the Louis B. Mayer Company, which was short on facilities but included the expert team of Mayer himself and his newly appointed head of production, Thalberg. Despite their skimpy studio, which was located on the same lot as Colonel William Selig's zoo, Mayer and Thalberg managed to create solid A features, which was exactly what Schenck needed.

Loew's and later MGM were in a way the exact opposite of Laemmle's Universal. Even after acquiring the Goldwyn Company, Loew's theater chain was comparatively meager. Schenck's strategy imitated the model of the Keith-Albee-Orpheum vaudeville circuit, which meant controlling the New York market and owning a few first-run houses in the biggest cities around the country.[63] First-run theaters demanded high-end product to justify the expensive admission prices.[64] Therefore, unlike Paramount, which owned around 1,200 movie houses of all kinds, or Universal, which relied on the distribution of lower-budget films, Loew's, which owned only about 130 theaters, needed a steady supply of quality features.[65] This is where Schenck's business model aligned with Thalberg's vision of cinematic production; both men believed in prestigious pictures. It was Thalberg who proved he knew how to make them.

From his new position as vice president in charge of production, earning $650 a week, Thalberg developed a system of tripartite consensus: pleasing audiences, hence pleasing Schenck, but also satisfying the aspirations of his creative staff.[66] To achieve this consensus, one had to negotiate. That probably came naturally to Thalberg, who from the outset saw motion pictures as an intermediary product. As he once stated, "Nobody had been able to say definitely whether picture making is really a business or an art." In his view, it was both. Filmmaking was a business "in the sense that it must bring in money at the box office," but it was also art "in that it involves, on [the part of] its devotees, the inexorable demands of creative expression." In short, Thalberg wrote, "it is a creative business," and it should be managed as such, "with budgets and cost sheets" but without "blue prints and graphs."[67] Movies were in-between products, therefore their production had to take place in a middle ground between the possibilities of unbound creativity and the constraints of profit-driven management. Such an organization demanded compromise on both ends.

First, creative personnel had to submit to regulation. Holding the reins at MGM, Thalberg expanded on the centralized system he instigated at Universal, introducing even more rigorous specialization and division of labor. With the help of Mayer's managerial skills, the two men were able to develop the most impressive production facilities in Hollywood. In 1927, their stock company included twenty-five directors, forty-five actors, and forty-one writers. In addition, they oversaw an expansive art department headed by Cedric Gibbons and a vast studio with multiple sets and an army of technical staff supervised by Eddie Mannix. This vast operation "required meticulous scheduling and script development, close collaboration with the various department heads ... and careful supervision of each picture." To ensure a steady flow of information, Thalberg introduced middle management in the form of five supervisors: Harry Rapf, Bernie Hyman, Hunt Stromberg, Al Lewin, and Paul Bern. Each of these "Thalberg men" was responsible for several pictures and reported directly to the head office. Centralization gave way to steady output. A report from 1925, for example, indicates that "MGM had seventy-seven projects in some stage of development. . . . Ten pictures were in production, seven were completed . . . two were reissues," and "the remaining fifty-eight were in some stage of preproduction."[68]

Thalberg was very proud of this operation. In fact, he claimed that due to it "the director ... has a greater opportunity to express his individuality." Echoing Ince's statement that directors should concentrate on directing, Thalberg proclaimed, "Thanks to efficient organization, [the director's] mind is relieved of all the multifarious, important but time-consuming details of production." As a result, "he has just one thing to do, instead of many—to infuse all his artistry and ability into making a good picture." As Thalberg saw it, efficient management actually liberated the artist. It was "distributing the burden on many shoulders, employing many minds," thus affording "the director the greatest opportunity for self-expression that he has ever had."[69] Indeed, it was a remarkable creative opportunity, albeit one that was now limited to shooting the picture, as opposed to orchestrating the entire production process.

All the same, armed with its regulation mechanisms, the Mayer-Thalberg system was making a name for itself across town. Pandro S. Berman, who was working as a producer at RKO at the time, remembered the two MGM managers as the fathers of the "producer system": "With Thalberg, [Mayer] was able to set up a method of making pictures. . . . He [could] hold the directors more or less in check financially by giving the producers authority. He made [the latter] responsible for finding the properties, and watching over the development of the screenplay with the writer." Due to their jack-of-all-trades status in the early days, directors were the loose cannons of the modern studio. As indicated by Stroheim's behavior, they were the most likely to oppose forced measures of control. Not so at MGM. There, as Berman explained, the "stable of directors which was rather extensive would be called in to make a picture two weeks before the production started"[70]— that is, after most of the script was written and the lead roles were cast. As Ed Woehler, a unit production manager at MGM, recalled, "When you had a script from Thalberg, it was ready to shoot, and when you took it on the stage, you shot it. And that's where this man was clever." Clever because "this way it stopped all of the set changes that the director would find late in the picture and had to change the script."[71] Creative caprices, which often led to more spending, were virtually gone, as a network of supervisors curtailed individual directors and subjected them to strict monitoring by Thalberg.

But directors were not the only ones who had to compromise. Corporate executives were also paying a price, literally. Thalberg believed that "a bad picture, or even a fairly good picture which is not so good as it should be, may do the company which puts it out many times as much harm as the cost of the picture itself. . . . In other words, the cheap pictures are the expensive pictures." Therefore, "the intelligent producer will go on experimenting—which, in pictures, means going on spending—until he believes in his own mind that he had made the best possible product." Thalberg's philosophy was not necessarily frugal. On the contrary, despite his efforts to curb directors, he was sensitive to the needs of the creative process. He understood that "pictures not only cost a great deal of money"; they also "require comparatively leisurely production in the factors of time and energy—particularly time—which must be consumed in searching for the human ideas on which the success of every picture depends." In fact, he expressed these ideas in an op-ed he wrote for the *Saturday Evening Post* in 1933, denouncing any intention to cut back on production costs, which he considered a "blow at the very life center of the business." This op-ed was tacitly aimed at his employers, suggesting that if Loew's was to be profitable, it had to start spending, since only "assured quality will mean assured attendance," which in turn will entail assured revenues.[72]

And spend MGM did. Surveying the studio's ledgers reveals that in the silent era the average cost of an MGM film was between $125,000 and $400,000, depending on the year, with several prestige productions ranging from $400,000 to $800,000. For example, *The Big Parade* from 1925 had a budget of $382,000, while *The Temptress*, from the same season, was made for $669,000. Between 1927 and 1928, *White Shadows in the South Seas* was produced for $365,000 along with *The Student Prince*, which had a budget of $1,205,000. To compare, in this same season the average production cost at MGM was $277,000, while Warner Bros. spent only $104,000. To be sure, in industry-wide terms MGM was not overspending, as the cost of an average Hollywood feature film in 1924 ranged between $150,000 and $500,000. Still, the annual presence of several prestige pictures with excessive budgets, combined with a relatively small number of low-budget productions, confirms that Thalberg was pushing for the higher end of the normal.[73]

Raw numbers, however, account for only part of the picture. The Thalberg philosophy demanded more money but, as he stated himself, also more time. Despite the fact that, on the whole, MGM churned out a sufficient number of pictures every season, the time spent on each specific feature was far from standardized. As testified by writer Anita Loos, "Sometimes, certainly with Thalberg, one was on any picture at least five years. I don't think Thalberg ever produced a picture that five years work hadn't gone into."[74] The time was spent on "conferences, rewrites, conferences again."

Loos recounted that "at least twelve scripts were written on every story that was ever done. . . . Retakes were done for the slightest reason—they'd do a whole sequence over, to improve something you hardly could find was wrong."[75] This relaxed procedure could, on occasion, appear superfluous or even wasteful: "I remember that one time I was working on a story with Irving, and we used to wait for story conferences, and sometimes we would wait for six weeks, three months, six months. While I was waiting, I was knitting a scarf, and by the time the scarf was finished, I figured that scarf cost MGM about $70,000. And it wasn't a very big scarf at that."[76] Yet, whether one chooses to view such time consumption as extravagance or as one of the necessities of creative expression, it is definitely not just business-oriented. In fact, the time factor is a great indication of Thalberg's inter-mediary status and brokerage abilities—he was both efficient and lavish. He allowed for creativity to reign on a film-specific level but made sure well-organized productivity was maintained overall, that is, that there was always a steady stream of completed pictures headed to the theaters.

Another indication of Thalberg's capabilities as a broker was his high approval rating across jurisdictions. In his biography about the producer, Samuel Marx declared that he had "never found anyone who hated Thal-berg."[77] This is probably an exaggeration, but superlatives are indeed not hard to come by, especially in the creative ranks.[78] Despite the discipline Thalberg enforced, many directors seemed to have appreciated their MGM boss. George Cukor, who worked under Thalberg in the 1930s, observed that he "was very creative" and "had a good sense of what was melodrama and what was tough." Artists like Cukor, who belonged to the New York literati circles, recognized that Thalberg was not exactly one of their own and still held him in high regard: "He wasn't well educated but he was by no means ignorant. He would talk about Shakespeare and analyze it the way no professor ever did, from the showman's point of view."[79] King Vidor, one of the few directors at MGM who maintained artistic control over his pictures, was far from dismissive of his supervisor's contribution, claiming, "Thalberg's consciousness of the responsibilities of his position was far above the average."[80] In his autobiography, Vidor describes a very fruitful and supportive relationship with Thalberg, who, he says "knew instinctively when someone presented a good idea or at least one which that person con-sidered really important, and didn't try to talk him out of it."[81] It seems most directors found that Thalberg was no hindrance to creativity.

Even more than directors, it was writers who were in awe of the head producer's capabilities. MGM was notorious for its attitude toward its writing staff. It employed more writers than any other studio, which allowed management to assign several of them to work on every script and to withhold any artistic control, while assigning screen credits as the producers saw fit.[82] Most writers were not appreciative of this system. "MGM's scheme of making movies was found to be the most Humpty-Dumpty notion that ever hit the entertainment world," claimed famed screenwriter Ben Hecht. "Movies were made by people who not only didn't know how to make movies, didn't know how to look at them, but who were for the main part illiterate."[83] Despite his successful and lengthy career in the industry, Hecht was often dismissive of Hollywood, to the extent that one might write off his remarks as a provocation. Nevertheless, even he was sympathetic when it came to Thalberg: "[He] was a genius. I worked with Irving, and he was different. Irving was a naturally born storyteller. . . . He had a flair for telling stories like comedians have for telling jokes. He could make them up. It was a fantasy-ridden head he had, and it was good. Then, he had a flair for telling movie stories, he knew about the medium, much more than most writers knew. He lived two-thirds of his time in the projection room. . . . He hadn't the faintest idea what human beings did, but he knew what their shadow should do."[84] Hecht was not the only one who reserved his praise for Thalberg. Loos was similar in her observations. "I went back to work for Irving, who was another great genius, and [an] extraordinary man," she said. However, "when Irving died, I saw the writing on the wall, and I knew that the fun was over and the magic was gone. There were no geniuses around anymore."[85]

With such appreciation and cooperation from his creative staff, Thalberg could win the approval of the most important group in show business, the audience. He did not get it directly. Since Thalberg refused to take screen credit, he was probably anonymous to most people outside the world of moviemaking. The pictures he made, on the other hand, were well known. Like a true showman, Thalberg believed his business depended "as almost no other . . . on the emotional reaction of its customers," and he sought to avoid "public apathy."[86] The central producer system he developed proved capable of doing just that. The tremendous success of MGM under the Mayer-Thalberg administration is evident in the statistics of their first four seasons at the helm: seasonal earnings and profits doubled, a fact that "marked MGM's arrival as one of Hollywood's leading studios."[87] Surprisingly, one of the early triumphs of the system was a cooperation between Thalberg and none other than Erich von Stroheim. *The Merry Widow*, which was completed only after the director was fired by Mayer and then rehired upon Thalberg's insistence, was the top-grossing movie of 1925, earning $1,933,000 domestically.[88] Staying true to his conviction that only quality assured attendance, Thalberg was willing and able to negotiate even with Stroheim to fill the theaters.

All this was, needless to say, extremely pleasing to Schenck. Thalberg's positioning helped make Loew's/MGM one of the most profitable picture companies, second only to Paramount, and not for long. The chief executive acknowledged Thalberg's importance to the company by boosting his salary from $650 to $2,000 a week in October 1926, only to adjust it again a year later to $4,000 weekly, with a guarantee for a minimum income of $400,000 annually.[89] The head producer won corporate approval, and not only from his own corporation. In his unfinished novel *The Last Tycoon*, F. Scott Fitzgerald wrote about the main protagonist, who was modeled on Thalberg: "He was a marker in industry like Edison and Lumière and Griffith and Chaplin. He led pictures way up past the range and power of the theatre, reaching a sort of golden age." Fitzgerald was no stranger to movie-town as, on top of selling the rights to several of his stories, he also dabbled in screenwriting for several of the studios. The fact that he chose Thalberg as the inspiration and vehicle through which to exhibit and illuminate the film industry is telling and indicative of the stature held by the producer throughout the 1930s. As Fitzgerald observed in the novel, "Proof of his leadership was the spying that went on around him—not just for inside information or patented process secrets—but spying on his scent for a trend in taste, his guess as to how things were going to be."[90] Soon, spying was not enough, and other studios were searching for a Thalberg of their own.

The Boy Wonders

Thalberg's MGM lot quickly became a coveted paradigm. Indeed, by 1927, his "central producer system was being heralded as a model of filmmaking efficiency, productivity, and quality control" to the extent that "other studios developed similar management setups."[91] Of course, setups on their own were incomplete, as was simply placing an individual at the head of West Coast studio operations. For the paradigm to work, a company had to find a capable broker who could understand both ends of the industry while having some effective philosophy on motion picture aesthetics. What Thalberg essentially did that was so worth replicating was to synthesize the interests of both the managerial strata and the creative ranks. He did so by personifying this synthesis, by inspiring creativity and at the same time being mindful of those factors of uncertainty so threatening to a modern business. Essentially furthering the modernization brought about by Ince and others, Thalberg helped carry the studio into the vertically integrated age by reformulating it as a creative space within a big business. Consequently, by the early 1930s, all major movie companies were on the lookout for their own "boy wonder" to turn their studios into such a workplace.[92]

The search was one of trial and error. Between the mid-1920s and the early 1930s, a cross-industry reorganization wave bred a cohort of producers who copied, experimented with, and expanded the original MGM setup. Whether they replicated Thalberg to a T or followed his example more loosely, all the producers who came up through the studio ranks embodied the broker sensibility. They showcased an aptitude to speak the language of both art and commerce as well as an ability to translate from one to the other. Together, as a group, they solidified and entrenched their work function within the film industry.

One successful follower was the man who would become perhaps the most recognized producer in the business, David O. Selznick. In fact, he claims to have "originated the title of Executive Producer, which had not previously been used."[93] Selznick, the producer of *Gone with the Wind* and the man who brought Hitchcock to Hollywood, started his career in Tinseltown working for Thalberg. It was not his first encounter with the movie business, but it was a fresh start. Like Thalberg, Selznick, born in 1902, was not one of the pioneers. His father was. Back in New York, Lewis J. Selznick was an important entrepreneur whose company, Selznick Pictures, was big enough to unsettle the monopolistic intentions of Adolph Zukor, president of Paramount Pictures, to the extent that the latter made it his mission to bring Selznick down. David and his brother Myron both worked in the family business: "I worked for my father's companies when I was in my teens. I was trained by my father in distribution and finance and advertising, his idea being that Myron would take care of the producing end and I would take care of the other things. . . . It is unfortunately true that there are very few producers in the picture business who know what they ought to know about domestic and foreign distribution, merchandising and advertising, and finance. I don't think there is any branch or any phase of the picture business in which I have not worked, except as a cutter."[94] When Selznick Pictures collapsed in 1923, David wanted to stay in the business, and three years later he made his way from the center of motion picture finance to the new capital of filmmaking.[95]

Whether it was due to his experience or simply to high self-esteem, David Selznick was not satisfied with the lower ranks of studio hierarchy. He had bigger plans for himself and for pictures, and he began spreading those around without delay. On October 5, 1926, only his second day working as a reader at MGM, he sent a memo, an action he was going to become very famous for, to his boss, Harry Rapf, saying, "It is immediately apparent to the newcomer that the organization is so vast, and its departments so varied and unrelated in duties, that contact is practically impossible." Later that same day, he also felt the urge to point out that "beyond doubt . . . astonishing almost unbelievable grosses can be rolled up in the foreign countries on pictures that are both big and local."[96] His potential and zeal for organization were noticeable, but MGM already had its architect. Indeed, a little over a year later, Selznick was fired after he indignantly questioned Thalberg's authority, demonstrating that a successful broker also knew how to get rid of any real or possible challenges to his throne. During the short span of time he was employed at MGM, Selznick still managed to serve as head of the writers' department and as a story editor, and even to produce with great efficiency two low-budget Tim McCoy westerns.

His reputation was established to such an extent that his next job was for Paramount, the company owned by the man who was Selznick the elder's most bitter competitor. It was not Zukor himself who hired David, but Paramount's general manager of West Coast operations, B. P. Schulberg. In Selznick's own words, "Schulberg was the most efficient general manager of a studio I have ever known . . . a really great mill foreman"—not a broker. This different set of skills was adequate, Selznick claimed, as this "was in the days when . . . pictures were sold en masse, and when a difference in quality made extremely little difference in the gross on the picture."[97] Up to the early 1930s, Paramount was the most profitable motion picture company. That did not necessarily mean it had the most profitable studio. What it did have was a very well-orchestrated chain of theaters, and in particular a network of subsequent-run theaters. That is to say, "unlike MGM with its emphasis on the first-run market, Paramount was a volume outfit."[98] While the former released between forty and fifty films per year, the latter had a program of around seventy.[99] For this reason, a competent general manager like Schulberg, who held a position similar to that of L. B. Mayer, was all the company needed to turn a profit. Schulberg, however, was rumored to envy MGM's success in producing A features, and so he hired Selznick in 1928 and soon made him his executive assistant.

Unlike a mill foreman, Selznick was a visionary. His philosophy regarding film production, which he developed throughout his extensive memos, manifested a strong desire to imprint his own brand of brokerage administration. "I have many misgivings concerning our own individual policies as a studio," he wrote in June 1931 in a memo to Schulberg that he never sent. "Production is being influenced to what I consider as being an extremely unfortunate degree by men who are, to my mind . . . completely unqualified," yet they "have more influence on executive decisions than the directors and writers of respective pictures." Though he did not name names, Selznick was dissatisfied with the balance of power in his workplace. "We have the players, the directors, the writers—a staff comprised of people of enormous talent and great ambition," he exclaimed. Unfortunately, he added, "the system that turns these people into automatons is obviously what is wrong." He acknowledged that "there must . . . be an executive head to a studio"; however, such a position did not necessarily entail that one person will "[carry,] in his mind, the plans of seventy pictures yearly, plus the enormous amount of material from which these seventy are selected, plus the executive work involved in the management of a large studio."

Unlike his old boss at MGM, Selznick believed that there was a limit to what one man could do. He thought movies could improve and the process be made more cost-effective by "breaking up production . . . into smaller units," each run by an executive such as himself and responsible for one or two features per year. This, he claimed, was "the best way out of the pit of bad and costly pictures in which we are now sunk."[100] Close attention was the key for getting more value out of the studio's money, and the way to achieve this goal was by focusing the master producer's concentration. With what he called "production units," Selznick in fact foresaw the future of the industry, a future he would help realize. Back in 1931, though, Hollywood was still thinking in Thalberg's terms.

In fact, Selznick's next job was as the Thalberg of a brand-new vertically integrated company. RKO was established in October 1928 by RCA.[101] Two not very successful years later, David Sarnoff, general manager of RCA, hired Selznick as vice president in charge of production. In a letter he wrote to his new father-in-law, Louis B. Mayer, Selznick mentioned a key element behind his motivation for taking the job: "I want to continue to develop my own people and my own stars and my own facilities from the scratch line where I started a year ago. Then truly, if I put it over, I will have done something—and that is the best reward!" Selznick seems to have written this letter in response to some sort of a job offer from Mayer, therefore he added that while he had "the most enormous respect for Irving Thalberg" and regarded "him as the greatest producer the industry has yet developed," he could not work under him. He was now a member of the head producers' rank, an equal and a competitor, therefore his goal was not only to match Thalberg's achievements but also "one day to surpass them."[102]

He did his best. During his first and only year at RKO, Selznick "produced forty-seven features, and a like number of shorts at a cost of $10 million, $5 million less than during the previous year." In addition, he "brought in new directing and writing talent, including George Cukor, William Wellman, Ben Hecht, [and] Dudley Nichols . . . [and] signing unknowns Katharine Hepburn and Fred Astaire."[103] His reforms produced such films as *A Bill of Divorcement*, *Bird of Paradise*, and *What Price Hollywood?* Unfortunately, RKO began as and continued to be a struggling studio, and despite his efforts to establish what he termed "a rigid economy policy in making capital expenditures," Selznick found it very hard to negotiate with the corporate wing of the company. "It is hampering and discouraging to me to be constantly criticized on costs," he wrote in 1932, especially since "no studio in the business has ever had such great reduction in costs, considering quality."[104] This letter was never sent; another one from January 27, 1933, was, and it essentially ended Selznick's association with RKO.

The reasons for Selznick's resignation were many. As his biographer points out, Selznick "was at times foolish and idealistic; at others, he was an arrogant manipulator."[105] Either way, upon his departure he stated at least one complaint that illustrated the sort of workplace he hoped for. Simply put, he objected to the demand of Merlin Aylesworth, the president of the corporation, to approve all matters concerning production. On January 27, 1933, he wrote to Benjamin B. Kahane, the vice president of RKO, "While recognizing you as the head of the company in matters of finance and policy, I could not consider accepting the possibility of any veto power on the part of anybody on stories which I might select." Selznick understood his own position as "being in charge not merely of costs but also of everything that went into the making of a picture." While he was willing to accept advice on the former from Aylesworth, and about the latter from his creative staff, the reverse order was unacceptable. He insisted on standing "on [his] record on both costs and quality," something he could do only if he continued "to have final authority—and by final, I mean final." He proceeded with a comparative argument, claiming, "Irving Thalberg has never been subjected to the word or approval of Nicholas Schenck."[106] He was wrong, but, that being said, he had a point. If the heads of the RKO Corporation were capable of making both financial and creative decisions, what was the benefit of having a broker like Selznick?

Selznick understood his own value. Corporate executives made several attempts to assume complete responsibility of studio operations, without much success. As one film scholar explained, time after time, "bankers and financiers proved singularly inept in managing motion-picture businesses," since "they did not have the know-how or the temperament to make pictures audiences liked."[107] Take for example the case of Paramount. Following, *but not due to*, Selznick's departure the company went into receivership, during which time, reported *Fortune* magazine, "fifty-three different law firms, banks, protective committees, and experts yammered and bled for two and one-half years over the sick giant."[108] The result, as one studio employee pointed out, was that "for the first time within my recollection, Paramount had no picture among the first ten for the year 1934." The reason, as far as he was concerned, was simple: the executive in charge "had no experience in the production of feature pictures prior to his advent at the studio."[109]

The situation continued to deteriorate. The new board of directors, established in 1935 and controlled by Lehman Brothers, Electrical Research Products Inc., and the Royal Insurance Company of Britain, appointed as the new president John Otterson, a "solid businessman . . . [who] bombarded the studio with cost-accounting procedures, efficiency schemes, and personnel forms."[110] Once again, the result was abysmal. A report on the studio claimed, "The negative costs were exceeding their budgets . . . shooting schedules were being disregarded [and] the planning of the 1936–37 program was hopelessly inchoate." The composer of this report, former film executive Joseph P. Kennedy, advised the board "to get rid of their quality businessmen or prepare for another receivership."[111] Only after Barney Balaban was appointed president, in July 1936, was the studio reorganized. Balaban, one of the pioneers of the exhibition business in Chicago, appointed executives such as Y. Frank Freeman and producer William LeBaron in addition to arranging, as per Selznick's vision, production units centered on individual producers or producer-directors.[112] All this is to say that while Selznick's abilities as an efficient broker might have suffered from his hotheadedness, he did seem to understand the organizational demands of a creative industry.

This structural understanding manifested itself in creative interactions as well. By the late 1930s, Selznick began realizing his "production units" vision by starting his own company, Selznick Int., in which he supervised a limited number of films each year. At the beginning of 1938, amid pre-production for *Gone with the Wind*, he shot one of his famous memos to George Cukor, who at that point was still the assigned director for the film. The executive was busy crafting the script with screenwriter Sidney Howard, and he was "worried that all this painstaking work is going to be largely in vain" if they did not have "a pledge" from Cukor, promising that he "won't use the book during the course of production to add three lines here and four lines there." The reason for this worry was economic. As Selznick explained, "Even the addition of five or six words per scene is going to count up to a thousand feet or more that we have taken out with terrific agony." Additional feet of film translated of course into an increased budget, and a possible "tremendous loss to the company." Selznick was not trying to eliminate the director's creative control. "Certainly," he said, "I am not going to have any objection to your raising any points about lines or cuts on anything else in advance of our starting in production ... which we can then thrash out in a few final conferences." But he wanted all such creative additions to be discussed in cooperation, before filming, and not have Cukor "trying to sneak [them] into the picture on the set." Appealing to his director, reasoning with him while implicitly restricting him, Selznick was carving out the intermediary work space in which the film would be made.[113]

Between them, Thalberg and Selznick disseminated brokerage administration into the operations of four of Hollywood's major studios: Universal, Loew's/MGM, Paramount, and RKO. The early 1930s saw the rise of two additional production-distribution-exhibition firms, namely, Warner Bros. and Twentieth Century–Fox. Both companies understood the importance of a capable central producer, and both recognized this capability in Darryl Zanuck.

In December 1935, *Fortune* labeled Zanuck "the new crowned boy genius of the films."[114] This followed his appointment, earlier that year, as vice president in charge of production of the newly merged Twentieth Century–Fox. On its own, Fox had been around since the 1910s, but a series of debacles in the late 1920s left the company in financial disarray and lacking proper management. In a move similar to the one made by Nick Schenck in 1924, the corporation's vice president, Sidney Kent, who understood the necessity of management, orchestrated the purchase of Twentieth Century, a year-old production company headed by Zanuck and Joseph Schenck, Nick's brother.[115] At that time, Zanuck was already a hot commodity around Hollywood, as he had spent the past decade establishing his reputation with a different group of Hollywood siblings.

Warner Bros. was a family-owned business, and it remained that way throughout the studio era. The main reason behind the company's ability to survive without falling into the hands of big banks was the fiscal conservatism of Harry Warner, the president of the corporation and the brother in charge.[116] As a financial operator, his vision was simple: he sought an inexpensive movie factory, which could produce a sufficient number of pictures for the company's theaters each year. Like Paramount, the production branch of the company "operated on a volume basis, trying to make a small profit on every film."[117] However, the Warners had far fewer theaters than Paramount, even after their consolidation with the First National theater cooperative in 1929. What the company did have was sound. Warner Bros. was the first studio to experiment with and seriously pursue talkies. On April 1926, Harry signed an exclusive deal with Western Electric to use its Vitaphone technology, a deal that enabled the company to release *Don Juan*, *The Jazz Singer*, and *The Singing Fool*, three productions that signaled both the end of the silent era and the company's admission into the vertically integrated major league.[118] The transition to sound required good stories and good dialogue; therefore, it is not surprising that to back their expanding operations, the Warner brothers chose a writer.

Born in 1902, Darryl Zanuck was not a pioneer, and neither was his father. He simply wanted to work in the movies and was indefatigable by nature. To illustrate, in 1917, despite being underweight and underage, he joined the Omaha National Guard and was stationed in France during World War I, all before his seventeenth birthday. By 1924, as his biographer wrote, "Charlie Chaplin was the biggest star in the world, Irving Thalberg was running production at the expanding Metro-Goldwyn-Mayer . . . and Darryl Zanuck was writing dog pictures."[119] The dog in question was Rin Tin Tin, the star of a series of movies produced by Warner Bros., which for Zanuck presented an opportunity to start writing for the pictures instead of for pulp newspapers. He quickly rose up the ladder until, in 1927, he was made "an associate executive to [Jack] L. Warner." His responsibilities included "writing original stories, adapting manuscripts, books or plays already written, collaborating with authors, directors and scenario writers, editing and titling films in the making, to be made, or the finished product." In addition, his contract stipulated that he was to serve as a "general overseer of production, acting in an executive capacity with J. L. Warner in and about the business of making motion pictures."[120] Following the merger with First National, he also received the title chief executive in charge of all production.

Working under Harry's regime was very different than the conditions at MGM. One main difference was that the executive producer could not rely on increased spending. As the company's president once said, "A picture, all it is, is an expensive dream. Well, it's just as easy to dream for $700,000 as for $1.5 million."[121] Zanuck managed to do just that. This was particularly apparent in his revival of gangster films such as *Little Caesar* and *The Public Enemy*, the latter made for only $230,000 and grossing $557,000. The profits generated gave Zanuck a chance to further experiment with content rather than cost. He produced such pictures as *42nd Street*, a low-budget musical that generated earnings of $2,281,000, and *I Am a Fugitive from a Chain Gang*, a controversial story that proceeded to earn $1,599,000 as well as critical acclaim, including praise from the National Board of Review.[122] He learned how to inspire creativity under a tight budget, a quality that was immensely important as the Depression set in. Evidence of his success included the multiple job offers he got after submitting his resignation from Warner Bros. in 1933, whether from Joe Schenck, who immediately took him under his wing, or Kent, who recognized in him the potential to revitalize the Fox lot.

A typical Zanuck day at Fox's Movietone City in Beverly Hills illustrates the creative involvement of this executive producer. Not the first one on the lot, he usually started his day at ten thirty, when he "roll[ed] in through the gates." First, "there are treatments and synopses to be read," of which "he reads the best dozen or so himself." Then, "at eleven thirty there is a story conference" with the scenario writer and the associate producer of specific productions. These meetings followed a somewhat standard procedure: "[Zanuck] mentions what pleased him about the script or treatment. Then he dismembers it" for about twenty minutes, "then there is some discussion and there are some suggestions from the writer and the producer." At three in the afternoon, he enters the projection room, where he will stay until late at night, talking to the editor, "re-editing scenes as they [are] run." Throughout the day "he talks incessantly of whatever comes into his head," recording everything on one of his many Dictaphones.[123]

Zanuck stuck to his schedule, and he expected his employees to do the same. He saved both "time and money by laying down a rigid schedule for his productions," and to "guard against delay he [would] make any sacrifice—even replacing the star." With writers, for example, "he [tried] to keep their time on scripts down to ten weeks," when "in most studios twenty [was] the average." To be on the safe side, he also exacted "weekly reports to check on their progress." However, if Zanuck's writers proved reliable, they were "given more responsibility than is customary in Hollywood."[124] The same went for the cinematographers and directors; as long as they stayed on script, Zanuck "never went on set."[125] As Ben Hecht remembered it, "You could make a good movie with Darryl, because he adored efficient work, and if you made your work efficient, he would go along."[126] He rewarded competence with creative freedom in the hope of building an organization that enjoyed both.

A case in point was the production of *Jesse James*. In late September 1938, Zanuck sent a telegram to director Henry King, who was filming out in Missouri, stating, "After reviewing everything that has been shot to date, I am definitely convinced that the entire location trip was, to a great extent a financial mistake. . . . At the rate we are going the picture will never break even, no matter how successful it is." Shooting on location, rather than on a studio stage, was costly, and companies tried to limit it to only when absolutely necessary. Having watched the dailies sent from King's unit, Zanuck realized that "there is nothing in the way of scenery or background that we could not have photographed near here at far less expense and trouble." Due to the lack of efficiency, Zanuck decided to enforce his authority and interfere in the director's work. But he was not angry, writing, "I blame no one but myself for not acting on my original hunch, and realize that in the history of our industry there has never been a successful location trip that lasted longer than two weeks." Furthermore, he wrote to King, "I appreciate your desire for authentic location, which prompted you to suggest the trip. And I also realize that you have no confidence in process shots."[127] Despite having doubts about such expenditure, Zanuck approved it; he was attentive to his director, allowing him to experiment and stepping in only when he felt the budget was overly compromised without superior results. It was a negotiation between a purely profit-based rationale that would deny such shots altogether and a wholly artistic one that would let the director experiment endlessly.

Compromise and negotiation were expected from the managerial ranks as well. While pictures could not be entirely subjected to artistic integrity, Zanuck was similarly unwilling to expose his productions to the complete control of the corporations. Screenwriter Philip Dunne remembered "sitting in the projection room one night" when Zanuck said, "Lock the door." Again, to be on the safe side, he called the projectionist and told him to lock the door too, saying, "Spyros is on the lot." He was referring to Spyros Skouras, who became the president of the Twentieth Century–Fox Corporation in 1942, and was apparently on a visit to the West Coast. The writer recounted that "later [they] heard this knocking on the door and this voice [calling] let me in." But Skouras remained outside; Zanuck was unwilling to let the president monitor the creative production process. According to Dunne, "He was absolutely right that he just would not permit any interference with the studio operation."[128] It is hard to imagine that Zanuck would treat his superior like that. Indeed, it may very well be that Dunne was overstating this standoff, or that Zanuck was merely trying to impress his employees. Even so, this recollection by a writer signals that Zanuck wanted to maintain a perceived buffer, a comfort zone for the creative personnel to work in.

Such votes of confidence in his creative staff made Zanuck someone worth working for. As Nunnally Johnson stated in 1959, "I miss Zanuck—I miss him terribly at Fox. No picture-maker, no focal point, no feeling of strength at the top." He missed having "a boss up there who was watching, and whose opinion you respected," someone who would say, "This is going good," or "That's not going good," or "Nunnally, I think you ought to do this over."[129] Director Anatole Litvak noted, "He helped me enormously, and I have the greatest respect for Darryl, for having the courage of allowing me to do [*The Snake Pit*]."[130] Even Fritz Lang, whose relationship with Zanuck was troubled, to say the least, admitted that this boss was "very responsible," "not a fool," and "a very good producer."[131] However, Zanuck's ability was probably best described by Cukor, who stated that he was simply a "very imaginative showman."[132]

ON SEPTEMBER 14, 1936, Irving Thalberg died. He was only thirty-seven when his weak heart succumbed to severe pneumonia. "The wheels at Metro-Goldwyn-Mayer studio ... were stopped at midnight last night in his memory," reported the *Los Angeles Times*, "and not a camera will turn for twenty-four hours."[133] The grief spread beyond the gates of the Culver City studio. The whole industry was in mourning. United Artists conducted memorial services, the Samuel Goldwyn, Walter Wanger, and Pickford-Lasky companies gathered for a eulogy, and all "the famous and the great of Hollywood, about 1500, stopped their work to assemble in Temple B'Nai B'Rith, Wilshire Boulevard, to join in the last tribute to the 'boy wonder' of the screen."[134] In a way, it was an end of an era—the Thalberg era. As the newspaper reported, "No successor is to be appointed to fill his shoes" because "there is no one who could." Or in the words of one executive, "He made his own job. It ends with him."[135]

But in many ways "it" had only just begun. Thalberg molded a culture of production that spread to the industry as a whole. The balance he struck in studio operations was emulated and elaborated on by Selznick, Zanuck, and other influential producers such as Hal Wallis, Pandro Berman, and Dore Schary. By 1936, some form of the Thalberg balance was deep-seated in the main office of every studio in Hollywood. It is true that aside from Zanuck, and perhaps Wallis, who replaced the latter as head producer at Warner Bros., none of these men were responsible for or directly involved with such an extensive setup as MGM. But all practiced what Thalberg preached. All embodied the "in-between" position of their work role, and all continued to preserve their studios, and by implication filmmaking, as an intermediate workplace.

CHAPTER TWO

Writing

Veteran screenwriter Charles Brackett used to reserve the following warnings for "potential dramatists" who "have an eye on picture studios": First, "if you are only happy in an ivory tower, don't go into motion picture writing." Furthermore, "if every word you set down was dictated to you from on high and mustn't be questioned, don't go into motion picture writing." Working in Hollywood, proclaimed Brackett, was a team effort, so, "if you can't subordinate your ego enough . . . forget the studios. Write magazine stories, write novels, write plays." Fame seekers in particular were advised to take heed: "If you do go into the studios and are successful . . . you'll run into another irritation," Brackett cautioned. "Your work will never be recognized as satisfactory . . . you'll never be as familiar to the general public. Nobody will fight for your autograph. When you drive to a premiere, the crowd in the bleachers will peer into your car and say, 'oh, that's nobody.'" For those who insisted on pursuing a career in screenwriting, the best advice he could offer was to "reconcile yourself to that anonymity."[1]

Indeed, writing for a Hollywood studio was often frustrating. "I know of two men whose names are widely known to all of us, who wrote competitively the same story for a well known company," exclaimed the screenwriter John Howard Lawson. He added that after pitting them against each other, "the executive in charge of the production never read either of the scenarios." The creative verdict "was left entirely in the hands of a reader who was getting $25 a week." Lawson, a former president of the Screen Writers Guild (SWG), was complaining about the condition of the Hollywood writer in a hearing held before the House Patent Committee on March 1936. "We have in the motion picture industry a situation where we find that the writer has none of the protection, none of the dignity he has attained in other fields," he claimed. In the studios "creative energy is not allowed free play," therefore writers who had already demonstrated their technical abilities elsewhere and were summoned to the filmmaking capital to "give certain definite creative value are deprived of the rights to those values." What the industry needed, per Lawson, was "legislation strengthening authors' rights to dictate how their writing should be handled in Hollywood."[2]

These dispirited views were by no means unanimous. Fellow screenwriter Joe Mankiewicz was more sanguine, claiming, "As far as so-called control over material is concerned," it "should be said and remembered" that "the Hollywood writer is paid anywhere from $300 to $3000 a week to write screenplays." Remarkably, "if a screenplay is not good, he does not give the money back." That is, "you get paid whether or not the buyer wants what you write," which is "a security that [no] artist in history ever had." When an author works on a novel or a play, Mankiewicz claimed, he or she can say, "I have put in a year or two years of my life on this. I want to control it." Equally, he charged, "I think it's idiotic—I know it's idiotic—for a writer to draw two or three thousand dollars a week, 52 weeks a year, sometimes not writing at all, playing golf or tennis, and writing with no guarantees that the writing is good or that the buyer will like it, and under no compunction to give back the money if it's not good." With this kind of security, you cannot ask for control, he said. "I don't think you can have both."[3]

To be sure, Mankiewicz was exaggerating somewhat. Very few writers earned $3,000 every week. In reality, as late as 1938, payrolls at major studios suggested that 40 percent of employed writers earned a weekly salary of less than $250, with only around 12 percent exceeding $1,000.[4] Many of these writers were not employed for fifty-two full weeks out of the year. Yet, Mankiewicz's point—namely, that Hollywood screenwriters, unlike their fellow wordsmiths in other creative industries, were employees— remains salient. They were paid to write, on a weekly basis—not as an advance—and without precise commitments with regard to the quantity or quality of their output. The reconciliation of such an obviously creative process as writing with conventional labor practices was not an intuitive process. Indeed, the introduction of the screenwriting profession to the studio system proved challenging, as both writers and studio heads were recalcitrant, each for their own reasons, and concerned about the implications of submitting lyrical composition to a punch clock. Moguls and producers had to come to terms with the economic and legal implications of maintaining a creative workforce. As for writers, Mankiewicz was not off the mark suggesting that they wished and endeavored to maintain some combination of both security and control.

During the early 1930s, after movies became talkies, many men and women of words were caught between two worlds, that of traditional authorship and that of screenwriting. Changes in leisure and consumer culture in the previous half century had loosened the margins of the more traditional world of the literati to include playwrights as well as fiction writers for magazines, and even some news reporters or columnists. Screenwriting, however, was still on the outskirts. Nevertheless, the increasing need for stories and the sudden need for dialogue, combined with the heavy wallets of motion picture producers, contributed to an influx of talent from that old guard of novelists, short-story writers, and playwrights into Hollywood. The rationalized operation that developed in the studios throughout the 1910s and 1920s was very different from the atmosphere of the literary circles in New York or the Ivy League universities. As one writer put it, "In the beginning of the world there was the word. But in the beginning of Hollywood . . . only the picture."[5] Words were new to the movie capital, and it, in turn, was new to the people who wrote them. As Mankiewicz implied, Tinseltown offered the prospect of financial security, but in return it demanded control over the writers, their time, and their output.

Reactions varied. Some, like Lawson, were frustrated. Others, like Mankiewicz and Brackett, were more receptive to the new opportunities. There were also the veterans, people like Frances Marion, Anita Loos, or Casey Robison, who had been in the business since its silent days or even its East Coast days, and took tremendous pride in it. Together they formed a very diverse and articulate crowd, whose coming together as a group into a union was in some ways the familiar "making of the writing class" story. Yet in other ways, their history presents a more complex and dynamic tale about the transformation of an industry by its practitioners and the repositioning of this industry within the larger framework of American art and entertainment. For, whatever they thought about their nontraditional workplace, studio writers formed and maintained another link between East and West, this time the East of bohemians and intellectuals rather than bankers and stockholders. Lawson and Mankiewicz may have been at odds when appraising their condition, but both presented it in comparative terms, relative to "other fields" where authors worked on novels and plays. They knew how writers in other industries lived and worked; they understood the pros and cons. Many screenwriters kept one foot firmly planted on the other coast, and from that split position they could at least hope to combine the best of both worlds.

Worlds of Possibilities

Images were certainly at the origin of motion pictures, but words were quick to follow. Soon after their appearance in the late 1800s, moving images grew out of their novelty phase and, increasingly, had to rely on narrative to attract audiences. Narratives not only brought people to the box office but also proved to be a useful and efficient organizing mechanism, with a potential to limit the costs of production. Then again, narratives added some costs too. They required a labor force to write them, as did the intertitles filmmakers relied on prior to and in lieu of sound. When talking pictures became a technological possibility, dialogue further elevated prose from its off-screen, descriptive, and plenary role to an essential on-screen feature. This evolution translated into an increased demand for writing skill. Indeed, particularly from the late 1920s, but stretching back to the early 1910s, Hollywood was constantly on the lookout for people who could not only write but write for the screen, a distinction that, while subtle, as it soon turned out, was very meaningful.

To better understand the position of screenwriters within the burgeoning movie industry, it is necessary to take a step back and look at the art world as a whole. Sociologists often portray structures such as the Hollywood studio system as a subfield or world of interaction that is embedded within a larger, overarching field/world of American art and entertainment. This larger field consists of the sum of "people and organizations who produce those events and objects that world defines as art."[6] Every subfield functions independently and contains its own agents, rules, norms of conduct, and resources. Subfields also interact and compete with one another, often over resources and prestige, as well as over the right to be included in the realm of the art world. In fact, when motion pictures first appeared, they were quickly snubbed by more established subfields, particularly theater, and as a result were deprived of some highbrow employees and audiences who did not wish to be associated with them.

The people operating in the art world typically follow a specialized professional trajectory. Therefore, most habitually remain within one subfield; playwrights work for the theater, opera singers in the opera, sound engineers in the recording studio, and so on. However, some agents may operate in more than one subfield either serially or simultaneously. In such transitions, they use resources and skills that are "transposable" and "polysemic" and "can be applied to a wide and not fully predictable range of cases outside the context in which they are initially learned." Or in other words, expertise is both unique and adaptable. Subfields or industrial structures are not "impervious" to such transference, and rather than constrain it they enable it, thus allowing various fields/worlds to "intersect and overlap."[7] With the advent of sound, this overlap between Hollywood and other parts of the art world became very pronounced. The need for words invited a new cohort of writers into the industry who carried with them the skills and resources they acquired in other subfields.

Screenwriters were not the first to "cross worlds" in such a way. Many of the moguls and actors turned to cinema from vaudeville and Broadway, as did practitioners such as costume and set designers. Screenwriters were also not a wholly new phenomenon, as mentioned above; a considerable number of them had been operating in the movie business since the early 1900s. Nevertheless, writers were a new force to be reckoned with, for several reasons: First, because there were many of them. Sound created a new sort of rush in California, one for dialogue. New writers therefore came en masse and were soon taking up space on the lots and in the budget sheets. Second, due to timing: they were newcomers. In the late 1920s and early 1930s, when studios hired new writers by the dozens, one could speak of an integrated movie industry with its own creative system already in place. Writers were the new kids on the block, and they had to be absorbed or assimilated into the existing mode of production. Finally, particularly due to their in-between status, they were outsiders. Writing, like acting, is not unique to the movies, and in fact, most of the practitioners who poured into Hollywood gained their experience in other creative fields such as playwriting, the magazine world, and literature. They were not novices but transfers, not native-born but immigrants. Indeed, acting like a migrant community as they moved out west, while coming to terms with the habits and practices of the movie world, writers also strengthened the ties between that world and the other creative fields back in New York from which they came.[8] They helped solidify the union of image and text.

Words for a Silent World

In the beginning of Hollywood there were unspoken words. Scenarios were a by-product of the shift away from documentary and toward narrative pictures starting around 1907. This shift was the result of an increased demand for motion pictures generated by the booming vaudeville and nickelodeon markets. Staged films were more predictable and manageable in terms of manufacture, because they were shot in a studio under a schedule, a method that proved more suitable for mass production than outdoor filming of topical subjects. In addition, longer narrative films were relatively cheaper than short ones, since a larger amount of footage was produced with the same sets and the same workers.[9]

The demand for stories was reinforced on other fronts as well. In 1911, the Supreme Court ruled that motion pictures were in fact dramatic productions, thus subjecting them to copyright laws and sending companies on a hunt for original material.[10] The star system that developed throughout the teens pushed for character-driven stories that could serve as vehicles for screen actors such as Mary Pickford or Douglas Fairbanks. These circumstances, combined, brought about what film historians call a "scenario fever," which subsequently gave rise to a group of "pioneer scenarists." Like those who would follow them in the 1930s, many of these first writers for the screen emerged from diverse backgrounds within popular culture, bringing to the screen their know-how in journalism, theater, and literature.[11] Their incorporation into the industry at such an early stage was rather smooth. In this prestandardized phase of filmmaking, the division of labor was not yet rigid, and there was more room for experimentation. In fact, appearing on the scene before standardization, these pioneers helped solidify the initial mode of production.

Writers were not hired merely to write scripts; they helped invent them. In the early days of cinema there were no scripts. "They used suggestions—they were called suggestions—and they might be very brief, just ideas, or they might be cribbed from some book or play. Nobody considered anything as copyrighted in those days," remembered one of the pioneers, Frank E. Woods. There was no standard method of submitting "suggestions" either; he recalled submitting them "as I happen to write them; sometimes orally; sometimes the director would be told the story. Sometimes they would start out and say, well, what will we shoot today? . . . I expect the director usually had some thought about how he was going to shoot it, but very frequently I was without any preparation."[12] Woods is credited with submitting the first "continuity," which means the splitting of the story into scenes. Of course, as he stated, "we never knew the word until about 1912 or 13. It was all, previous to that, merely cutting a picture into scenes, consecutive scenes."[13] A native of Pennsylvania, Woods, who started his literary career as a reporter for the *New York Dramatic Mirror*, was also among the first to write critical reviews of motion pictures. It all started due to a feud in the theater world that cost the *Mirror* some of its advertising accounts and forced it to look for new patrons in the "previously disregarded [and] vulgar realms of the motion picture industry."[14] In return for the studios' business, the paper began publishing film reviews written by Woods under the byline "The Spectator."

From critic, he turned insider. Woods started selling story suggestions to the Biograph film company, and in 1908, one of them, a version of Tennyson's poem *Enoch Arden*, was the first to be submitted in the form of a continuity.[15] Or so he was told. "I couldn't swear it was the first one written. Some other studio may have had a similar one, but I never knew of it, and I was always credited with having written the first continuity."[16] First or not, it marked a watershed, Woods was certain about that. After 1909, he claimed, "the importance of a well prepared script increased continuously from the very start until the present day." Companies started employing "what they called a scenario editor, and as it grew, pictures grew in length and quality, they employed writers to put the script into continuity form, and at the time I was with Griffith, about ten or fifteen writers were on salary, and then I was with [Jesse L.] Lasky [and] we ran up to about fifty on salary."[17]

The scenario fever had begun. Producers were partial to the idea of having a script before shooting started. Such rigorous attention to narrative made organizational sense, as "it was cheaper to pay a few workers to prepare a script and solve continuity problems at that stage than it was to let a whole crew of laborers work it out on the set or by retakes."[18] As producer Edwin Thanhouser, the owner of a studio in New Rochelle, was reported to have said, "When I had my theatrical company . . . I never told the director, 'Go and put on a play,' and trusted to his inventive genius. I selected a manuscript I liked, and he followed it. And I don't see any reason why the same course shouldn't be a success in the motion pictures game."[19] Certainly, pretty soon the success of these instructional manuscripts was undisputable. By 1911, many "firms had a story reading/writing department with head, readers, and writers," and, by 1913, these departments underwent a "splitting of expertise," with "some workers excelling in creating stories, others in re-writing," and with their ranks further bolstered by title and subtitle draft-men and even "inter-title specialists."[20]

Specialization was undoubtedly well on its way, but on the studio grounds the division of labor was still not well defined. One of the earliest scenarists, Beulah Marie Dix, recounted that "in those early days of silent pictures . . . a writer often sold an original to the company and then worked on it, frequently in collaboration with the director." The Famous Players–Lasky Company hired Dix, a children's book author, in 1916. She was a writer, but as it seemed to her "it was very informal in those early days. Anybody on the set did anything he or she was called upon to do. I've walked on as an extra, I've tended lights—and anybody not doing anything else wrote down the director's notes on the scripts."[21] Fellow writer Clifford Howard had similar impressions. He claimed that "the scenario department, destined to become the most important and most expensive features of a studio," and comprising a "corps of readers, a staff of story adapters, a staff of continuity writers, a bunch of gag-men, and a coterie of title writers," was "a development that none could have foreseen even as late as 1913."[22] That was the time when he took a position as a scenario editor in the Balboa Amusement Company, one of the first such editors to set foot in Southern California.

It was only after World War I that one could truly speak of an integrated screenwriting profession. The push for specialization came, for the most part, with the decline of a freelance scenario market. An important part of the "scenario fever" was "public promotion of the craft" through contests and magazines, resulting in a flood of "public screenwriting," that is, scenarios submitted to the studios by practically anybody.[23] Public enthusiasm was manifested in letters such as the one sent to writer Lloyd Lonergan from a small town in Pennsylvania: "This play is written by my son, Thomas, who is 16 years old. He is too delicate to go to work and since he had a bad fall, two years ago, has been very backwards in school. The doctor thinks that in time he may outgrow his feeble mental condition, but in the meanwhile he has turned his attention to motion pictures writing, and perhaps there may be a place for him there, so I send this story which he wrote after supper last evening."[24] This system had its problems. For one, submissions were so vast in number that effective quality control became difficult. Furthermore, irritated authors whose work was plagiarized by members of the enthusiastic public began pressing charges.[25] Such troubles were extremely undesirable to an industry whose center of gravity had just moved from east to west and which was trying to establish itself as a respectable, reliable, and consolidated business.

Though in terms of organization the Hollywood studio system would not reach its zenith before the mid-1930s, the road to integration began in the early 1920s. It was during those years that Adolph Zukor of Paramount began purchasing theaters across the United States, that Nicholas Schenck consolidated Metro-Goldwyn-Mayer, and that the up-and-coming moguls, facing the threat of censorship and foreign trade limitation, created a cooperative trade organization, the Motion Pictures Producers and Distributors of America.[26] The search for order did not skip the writing departments, which by then were very much in existence. With the shrinkage of the freelance market, studios were focused on acquiring contract writers from among the professionals who had been with the industry for several years. Names like Woods, Dix, Anthony Paul Kelly, Charles Kenyon, Anita Loos, Bess Meredyth, Jeanie MacPherson, Hector and Margaret Turnbull, and June Mathis would repeatedly appear in the writing credits, which now became a standard practice.

Many of the leading scenarists were women, and most of them joined the business in the 1910s. This disproportionately large percentage of female writers, occasionally even in the executive positions of production companies, was partially due to the fact that movies were still not taken seriously as a business. In the early days of the industry, the chaotic nature of production rendered it "ungendered," or at least temporarily unbound by the conventional gender norms governing labor. In addition, the lowbrow status of motion pictures placed them "outside the boundary of legitimate business," and it was believed that the presence of women would accord respectability. This, combined with the labor shortage created by the "scenario fever," enabled, if not forced, companies to tap talent pools that were relatively uncharted by more traditional industries.[27]

As a result, the business was teeming with women, especially in the writing quarters. The informal setting of early studio work, where anybody did whatever he or she was called upon to do, "reduced the sex segregation of labor" and replaced it with a culture that "responded to performative rather than ascriptive modes[s] of authority." Lack of ascription accorded women the opportunity to participate and advance.[28] When, in 1924, Frances Marion, one of the leading screenwriters of the studio system, assumed a position in the writing department of the newly incorporated MGM, "over a quarter of the scenario writers were women and many of them were already friends." Marion herself had been writing screenplays for about a decade, having collaborated with such towering female filmmakers as Mary Pickford and director Lois Weber. She and many of her fellow women writers were among the pillars of the industry, and they were treated accordingly. Marion's contract with MGM stipulated a weekly paycheck of $3,000 and the option to assist in supervising and editing her productions.[29] This was not a common prerogative.

To the contrary, the specialization process introduced the infamous practice of "writing on committee." Early in the 1920s, it was already not uncommon "for scripts to travel through several writers or groups of writers," and "seldom did one person do all the work all the way through."[30] Writer Anita Loos recalled, "This is true—they had an enormous number of writers, and of all those writers, 10 percent of the writers did all the writing."

She explained that it was "[Irving] Thalberg's theory to have an enormous staff, so he would hire writers by the dozens," and continually kept them engaged in rewriting one another's assignments. "It's a very special technique," said Loos, "and if you're not the type who will rewrite a hundred times, you're no good for motion pictures." Part of the turn to committees was related to the intensifying division of labor, which, on top of stories, continuities, and titles, now also included the writing of "treatments." These new additions consisted of "a narrative story of the picture as it is proposed to produce it," explained Woods. "It is like a short story," he elaborated; "you might call it a short story, except it confined itself to the material to be used in preparing a continuity."[31]

Most pioneer writers took this ignoble splitting of their expertise in their stride. These men and women were used to the informal atmosphere described by Dix; they were accustomed to the cooperative aspect of filmmaking. Some, like Grover Jones, even started out working in other departments. Writing screenplays through the 1940s, Jones had been in Hollywood "since the latter part of 1913." Prior to that, he noted, "I was a sign painter. Prior to that I was a coal miner." He came to Hollywood to write, sort of: "In those days everything was labeled in the pictures. The man who was the janitor had a sign 'Janitor' across his cap. The fellow who took pills—it said 'Pills' on the box." He figured that "seeing so many pictures" that needed so many signs, he could make those and "get rich."[32] Indeed, Jones spent five years in technical positions at studios such as Universal and Vitagraph until one day he was "watching Gilbert Pratt direct these two comics, trying to get into a dancing school," and he made a suggestion: "I said, 'Wouldn't it be funny if one of the comics hid in that suit of armor in the hallway?' Gilbert Pratt looked at me and said, 'what for?' I said, 'And then when the professor walks in and he throws his cigarette away and he throws it in the suit of armor, look what will happen.' He thought that was funny, and they wrapped the story around it." Later that night one of the executives at the studio hired Jones as a gagman for fifty dollars a week. At the time, Jones "had never heard the word 'gag.' I didn't know what they meant, but I did know the difference between $35 and $50, and I said, 'Yes.'" That started him on a career of "what you call writing."[33]

Coming up with gags was not exactly a writing job. As Jones explained, "The gag man . . . is a fellow who sits on the set, disliked by everybody, who tells the Director that it would be very funny if Gary Cooper caught his coat tail in something as he went out of the door."[34] In other words, it was not part of the preshooting preparatory stage. However, many of these practitioners, who lingered on sets helping comedy directors add funny bits while shooting was taking place, were later incorporated into the writing departments, and some of them, like Jones, metamorphosed into full-fledged screenwriters. Such interindustry promotions strengthened the communal feeling and loyalty of many of these pioneers, who learned to write for the movies at the same time the industry, as a whole, learned how to make them.

In the late 1920s, Clifford Howard tried to sum up what he believed was the overall tenor uniting him and his fellow screenwriters. He claimed that "novels are written; pictures are fabricated." He observed that "literary creation is solo work; cinema producing is collaborative, composite, multifarious, and vastly intricate." For that reason, while "many writers are called to Hollywood . . . few are chosen. And the elect are content to become and remain . . . individual cogs in the giant machinery of picture making."[35] Early Hollywood writers were overflowing with team spirit and proud to be a part of this newly emerging art world. Howard's language is patriotic. He thought it was his professional duty to "keep in touch with the developing technicalities and intricacies of picture making and its constantly fluctuating conditions and requirements."[36] He linked his own success to that of the industry. Such views were by no means unusual. Many early screenwriters understood their newly formed profession to be rooted in the world of motion pictures. The next cohort of scribing cogs was not so readily content with the place accorded to them in the giant machinery.

Days of Dialogue

The arrival of talking pictures did not happen overnight, and neither did that of newcomer writers. Film scholars have established that the transition to sound was years in the making and that "motion pictures did not turn topsy-turvy because of the talkies." On the contrary, sound filtered in gradually, over a period of ten years, beginning in the early 1920s. All the while, "the studios tried to anticipate the outcome of the audible cinema trend by hedging," that is, by continuing to produce silent pictures while adapting to new sound technology, practices, and techniques. It was only in 1929 that the studios declared an "all-sound product for the next season," and only after 1931 that production and projection of sound pictures had been standardized.[37] By then it was also clear that dialogue writing was a necessary new talent. Perhaps not coincidentally, it was around that time that other art worlds experienced a decrease in demand for such talent.

Like any migration, the one experienced by writers who traveled from the literary circles of the East Coast to Hollywood had both a push and a pull factor. The pull was Hollywood and its money; the push was coming from the decline of other writing markets. Although some of the pioneer writers, such as Loos, Marion, and Jones, adapted well to the practice of writing for sound, their numbers were not sufficient to handle the increasing workload. With a planned all-talkie output, the studios needed a large quantity of fresh talent that, as one screenwriter put it, "could turn out polished, swift, and effective dialogue" that "was fit to be spoken."[38] Naturally, they looked to the New York network of publishing houses, literary agencies, theater companies, newspapers, and magazines. As it happened, explains historian Richard Fine, the desire for serious writers reached a peak a few years after the conversion to talkies, when the Depression hampered the publishing industry and commercial theater.[39] By 1933, "the bull market for the writers' work ended." In the publishing world, the number of new titles printed sank, and on the legitimate stage the number of openings shrank to 130, half of what it was in 1926.[40] Hollywood probably deserved some of the blame for this decline, as it offered cheaper and quicker entertainment that, at least initially, won out in the competition over audiences. Now, after claiming the patrons, the film industry was ready to lure the creative workforce as well.

It is hard to determine the exact quantity of writers who migrated west beginning in the late 1920s. Fine identifies 138 of them, while other scholars put the number at 157. Either way, the total is considerable, particularly when compared with the number of writers working in Hollywood during those years, which industry insider Leo C. Rosten estimated to be around 800.[41] Moreover, in his analysis of the industry, Rosten also lists seventeen writers who earned the highest salaries in 1938; ten of them started working for the pictures after 1929.[42] Even without accurate statistics, clearly the newcomers were significant both in percentage and impact.

The experience of these eastern transfers in the studio system was summed up nicely by one of them. Dudley Nichols, who would become one of the most influential and well-paid writers in the business, producing the screenplays for *Bringing Up Baby* (1938), *Stagecoach* (1939), and *For Whom the Bell Tolls* (1943), among many others, started his career as a newsman. Before coming to Hollywood in 1929, he worked as a correspondent for the *New York World* and the *Nation*, covering criminal trials, foreign affairs, and, occasionally, the theater.[43] In a 1936 article for the *Screen Guilds' Magazine*, he observed that once "those reprehensible inventors, who might have left well enough alone, developed the sound track," Hollywood lost its peace and quiet. "Authors dropped from the Chief in droves," he explained, and "they were paid wonderfully well." Conditions were good too. Writers "were supplied with typewriters, charming stenographers, luxurious homes and parked cars. For a time they were happy." But only for a time, since, "having emerged from dingy newspaper offices and garrets into the sunlight, they began to remember certain joys that even poverty had not denied them, but which Hollywood certainly did."[44] Briefly blinded by the light and stupefied by warm weather and comfort, writers soon regained their sharpness. Though initially taken in by what another one of them termed "the tremendous excitement of a vast growing industry," Nichols claimed that he and his friends soon began to notice the shortcomings of their new habitat.[45] As a result, before long they were searching for fixes that would reconcile the world they knew with the one they were now living in.

The old worlds of writing shaped how many screenwriters experienced and reacted to Hollywood. Nichols's interpretation of the movie city only makes sense considering the "beliefs, attitudes, and values attendant to the identity of the writer," which individuals such as himself acquired in the East Coast's literary marketplace. He and others arrived in Hollywood to work as writers, a career that had a certain fixed meaning in the theater and publishing industries. Quickly, they discovered that, in the studio system, their profession was defined in radically different terms than in the labor market from which they came. For many of them, this was more than just a practical variance; it was essential evidence indicating that in the studio system "the profession of authorship as they knew it" was "under attack."[46]

Indeed, Los Angeles was not New York. Eastern intellectuals, used to the leisurely and romantic routine of fiction writing and the social gatherings at the Algonquin Round Table, had a hard time adjusting to the environment and atmosphere of their new workplace. "What happened to us out here Charlie?" asked actress Constance Collier. "In the East we used to be people going about with people. Not out here. We've become people in aspic." The friend she was writing to, screenwriter Charles Brackett, was in complete agreement: "All the composure and perspective I acquired in the East collapsed like foam. May God give me strength never to accept a really silly project again."[47] Brackett was an exemplary product of eastern composure and perspective. The son of a prosperous lawyer and bank owner from Saratoga Springs, New York, and a graduate of Williams College and Harvard Law School, he was brought up to become what one biographer called "a cultured man of the world."[48] As such, he also dabbled in writing;

in the mid-1920s, after publishing two novellas in the *Saturday Evening Post*, he decided to move to the big city and become a full-time writer. He published three novels and served for a while as the drama critic of the *New Yorker*, when, in 1930, a job offer at RKO brought him to Los Angeles, a big city in the making.

In California, he quickly made a name for himself. Brackett spent his first six years out west under contract at Paramount until August 17, 1936, when he learned that he was to be teamed with another writer named Billy Wilder to compose a script for *Bluebeard's Eighth Wife*. Wilder, as Brackett remembered, was "a young Austrian" he had "seen about for a year or two and liked very much."[49] The duo formed a partnership that lasted until 1950 and produced such classics as *Ninotchka* (1939), *The Lost Weekend* (1945), and *Sunset Boulevard* (1950). Though until this matchmaking none of Brackett's films gained much success, he himself was thriving, earning a weekly salary of $1,000.[50] Perhaps because he was already accustomed to economic security, Brackett was not entirely happy. Something in the nature of the work frustrated him. "I found myself in agony of thinking I was neither funny nor competent," he wrote in 1935; "finally I reached the comforting conclusion that nothing but the absolutely commonplace pleases anyone at Paramount. Oh, well, maybe now and then something with a kind of high-school foolishness about it."[51]

Such dreary depictions of Hollywood were quite commonplace among newly arrived writers. Samson Raphaelson grew up in the immigrant Jewish community of New York's Lower East Side. He was perhaps the quintessential eastern writer, except that he started his career in Chicago, writing short stories and working for publishing and advertising agencies. In the early twenties, which overlapped with his early twenties, he returned to work and write in New York. One of his short stories, "The Day of Atonement," was published by *Everybody's Magazine* in 1922 and then rewritten to become Raphaelson's first stage play. In the process, it was also retitled *The Jazz Singer*. Starring George Jessel, the play became a huge Broadway hit, which made its author, who owned the rights to the original story, a wealthy man.[52] One of the royalty checks Raphaelson received was from Warner Bros., which bought the cinematic rights to the play. Starring Al Jolson, the film *The Jazz Singer* was one of the first to feature sound, and its success signaled the economic potential of talking films.[53] The movie also signaled the potential its young author might have in the picture business.

While his play made it to Hollywood in 1926, it took the playwright four years to follow. Raphaelson was not in the least tempted by Hollywood. "I felt you lowered yourself," he said. "I had no historic sense of the meaning and significance of movies." As for the hit movie he was credited with, he felt that he "had nothing to do with it. I would neither be proud nor [*sic*] ashamed of it. . . . It's something that the movie people did. They took a play of mine, they mangled the hell out of it." After that, "if a lot of people went to see it, for reasons that I can't fathom to this day, I take neither credit nor blame."[54] After the stock market crash, what he did take was a cross-country train. Having lost most of his savings in 1929, Raphaelson accepted a job with the newly formed RKO studio for $750 a week. Less than a year later, he moved to Paramount, where, much like Brackett, he was introduced to the man with whom he would collaborate for nearly twenty years, director Ernst Lubitsch. Though he would ultimately be responsible for such hits as *The Merry Widow* (1934) and *The Shop around the Corner* (1940), back in 1930 Raphaelson was still suspicious.

His view of the movies had somewhat improved, but his experience remained that of an outsider. "Not that pictures aren't interesting," he wrote to a friend, "they are. They are too engrossing. It is hard to live in this town without measuring . . . yourself by your salary." That was exactly the problem. "The assignments, the politics, the salaries of the various lots are of such intense immediate interest," he felt, "that you find after months have gone by you've talked and thought about nothing else."[55] A couple of months later he explained to a different friend, "The first thing needful is to accept that fact" that "here . . . not great stories, but practical ones written quickly, are the point. Let some more naïve soul than I strive mightily to write the great picture; I will content myself with the simpler imitation of a fine play or a fine novel."[56]

Behind the frustration expressed by Brackett, Nichols, and Raphaelson loomed the crisis of lost authorship. Studio work deprived screenwriters of control over their creations, a feature most eastern writers understood as an essential part of their profession. Indeed, the standardization brought to the system by managers such as Irving Thalberg stressed the product over the practitioners who made it. According to the film industry's version of modern managerial theory, a movie was a collaborative effort, and as such it belonged to the studio that orchestrated and determined the conditions of the collaboration. This theory was confirmed by the Copyright Act of 1909, which determined that the employer is the de jure "author of the work made for hire."[57] Thereby, actors, directors, cinematographers, and writers were more akin to resources, albeit indispensable and precious ones, than sui generis geniuses or artists. Leo Rosten, who worked as a screenwriter for most of the 1940s, pointed out that "the writers who find it easiest to adjust to Hollywood are [ones] who have served as writer-employees before coming to Hollywood," that is, "newspapermen, advertising writers, publicist[s]," since "these men do not invest too much self-esteem in their work."[58]

Consider the screenwriting process as described by the vice president of Columbia Pictures, Benjamin B. Kahane. The senior executive was testifying in a 1937 hearing before the National Labor Relations Board (NLRB) regarding conditions of employment in Hollywood.[59] One would assume that, under these circumstances, Kahane tried to paint a pretty picture of harmonious labor relations. Yet, his account seemed to validate a charge made by screenwriter Philip Dunne, who claimed that in Hollywood "the writer was slightly a second-class citizen, but the script was first class, because the script was his"—that is, it belonged to the producer.[60] Per Kahane, any movie indeed started with a producer, who chose a property, which could be "a stage play, [or] it may be a novel, a book, a poem, or an original written expressly for screen purposes." Then "a contract is made with a screen writer, or a screen writer under contract is assigned to write either a treatment or a first draft of a screen play script." All the while, "the writer operates under the general direction of the producer. The producer confers with him as to the subject matter and as to scenes and situations. The writer does the work." He or she will start by writing a treatment. "Assuming that the producer approves [it] and concludes to go ahead with the productions," Kahane explained, "the next step will ordinarily be the preparation of the first draft of a screen play." However, if the treatment is not approved, "either changes are required to be made or the treatment is abandoned and production is abandoned," or "another treatment is made by another writer."

Next comes the first draft, which is "a complete script indicating all of the actions, all of the dialogue, the themes and the continuity, indicating the sound, sound effects and everything that enables—well, everything pertaining to the shooting of the particular photoplay." The first draft is followed by "conferences between producer and executive and writers" or "sometimes the director." Conferences generate more and more drafts until the producer is satisfied. During this process of draft writing and rewriting, the screenwriters may be replaced; in fact "this is frequently done," and "in many instances more than one writer is involved at the same time in the preparation of a script." Kahane offered a simple logic that stood behind this practice: "One writer's particular ability may be along the line of construction. Another may be able to write good dialogues. Another may be a comedy or gag man." In any case, "the rule now is for more than one writer to be engaged in the preparation of a screen play."[61] Authors were like technicians, each utilized for his or her particular expertise. Creative control, which used to be the essence of their work, was now not even in question.

This work routine was the source of much discontent. For one, writers had to come to terms with the fact that the producer had the final word, even if his understanding of story or drama was inferior to theirs. As writer Sheridan Gibney testified at the same hearing, a script would be changed "if [the producer] doesn't like a scene as it is written, or if he doesn't like a situation as it is developed; if he doesn't like the character and wants the character changed." In case of a disagreement, "sometimes it is a discussion[,] sometimes it is a very heated argument," of which the writer wins "only minor ones." In general, said Gibney, producers will only "give up their point after they have had five or six different writers trying to write what they suggest, and then they decide it was wrong."[62] Or, as dramatist Ben Hecht saw it, "they never ask you to think of anything because . . . the producer is lurking in the woodwork with something he's thought up, and he being your boss . . . he's the man who tells you what to do."[63]

Another point of contention for writers pertaining to literary integrity was the practice of "writing on committee" or "mixing writers." Sidney Howard, one of the seventeen writers who worked on *Gone with the Wind*, and one of the four who actually received credit, thought this system was practically an absurdity: "This [collaboration] not only wastes untold quantities of money—such producers have more than once spent close to a half a million dollars in screen writers' salaries—but deprived the finished picture of any homogeneity of style."[64] Edwin Justus Mayer, one of the five writers credited in the 1939 film *Rio*, added that "every writer had had the experience of seeing his name on the screen and recognizing that he was not responsible for moods and lines in the picture."[65] The union of the author and his work was broken.[66]

There were practical problems too, on top of the attack on authorship. As demonstrated with the cases of Howard and Mayer, often a picture would carry multiple writing credits to accommodate the entire village that raised the child. Maurice Rapf, one of the six people to be accredited with composing Disney's *Song of the South* (1946), who at one point also served as the Screen Writers Guild chairman of credits, explained that "a writer's position in the motion picture industry is determined by his screen credits. The size of his check depends both on the quality and the number of pictures which bear his name, with emphasis on quality."[67] There were multiple kinds of credits; a script could be "written by," or "based on a story by," or "based on an idea by," and it could feature "added dialogue by." Sometimes the list would grow so long that the names of some writers were reluctantly left on the floor of the editing room, so as not to belabor the opening titles. Perhaps it did not matter, since when a story has so many names attached to it, who can really take credit? Then again, when one's career depended on the number of pictures that bore one's name, being literally and figuratively cut out had material consequences.

Unsurprisingly, editorial nonchalance about credits produced many grievances. Ferdinand Reyher arrived in Hollywood in the early 1930s after publishing a novel and having spent most of his twenties in Europe, where he formed a friendship with Bertolt Brecht and was later instrumental in bringing the German playwright to America.[68] In 1938, he wrote for Paramount the screenplay of a western titled *Ride a Crooked Mile*. At first, "the credit was assigned to me, accredited to me, and the original story had been assigned to another writer," but then "two days later the studio changed it." Reyher was not denied credit; "it was a question of the placing of the credits." He explained, "You see, the value of the credit is in the original thing. I would have had the original screen play based on a story," but after the change "I had credit of the story and screen play [together with] the other man," rather than being given exclusive credit for the screenplay alone.[69] Reyher did not want to receive credit for someone else's idea; likewise he refused to share credit for his own story. He complained to the studio to no avail. Now and again screenwriters refused undue credit. Brackett remembered that while working with Wilder on *Blossoms on Broadway* (1937), "Mr. [B. P.] Schulberg was kind enough to have our names on it, and we felt it was not fair and took them off." Their contention was that "the young man who rewrote it deserved the credit."[70] However, in a town where credit determined position, such chivalry was not always forthcoming.

The alienation of the writer was actually quite a formal matter. As of the early 1930s, in the studio system, the rights over creative material were officially waived the moment a writer signed a contract, a practice that, as mentioned, abided by U.S. copyright law. Most basic studio contracts, as if written for a case study in *Das Kapital*, contained some variation of the following paragraph: "The writer agrees that all material composed, submitted, added and/or interpreted by the writer hereunder shall automatically become the property of the Corporation which, for this purpose, shall be deemed the author thereof, the writer acting entirely as the [corporation's] employee."[71] That was not all. Many of the long-term contracts also included a layoff clause according to which the producer had an "arbitrary option" to dismiss the writer without pay for a specified duration, usually spanning several weeks. Since the layoff period was part of the contract, the latter remained in force throughout it; that is, even though the writer was technically laid off, anything he or she wrote during that time was, at least in theory, the legal property of the studio. It was a far-reaching contract that embodied a complete separation of writers not only from their work but also from their product.

Still, the objective, for most writers, was to land just such a contract. As Kahane explained, "There are different types of deals. There is the writer who is employed under contract for a particular period," and "there is the writer who is engaged for a particular assignment—that is, one assignment from week to week."[72] The latter, also known as freelance writers, in addition to having no stable source of income, were exposed to other forms of maltreatment, such as "writing on spec." Working on speculation implied that one would be "writing something in the hope that a producer will buy it." That something would not be an original story, play, or novel by the writer, but rather a treatment based on a specific idea handed down by a producer. Often, as one freelancer commented, "a producer would employ as many as eight on that basis," as it was clearly a cost-effective method for developing stories.[73] More often than not, their work was for nothing. Writer Martin Field sarcastically observed that when the freelancer submitted the on spec work, the producer, "who by this time had made four trips to Santa Anita, played six gin-rummy sessions, flown one quick round trip to New York, and in general undergone a mental change of regime, had no interest left in what had once been a hot story angle." Unsurprisingly, he lamented, "not a red cent crossed palms."[74]

Writing on spec might have resembled the labor conditions some writers experienced in New York, with one notable distinction—in Hollywood they did not own the material. Writers in other fields regularly composed sans contract. As Mankiewicz implied, they might spend anywhere from a few days to a few years on a short story, novel, or play with the hope of selling it when it was finished to a publisher, a magazine, or a theater company, and, if they were really lucky, also to a motion picture company.[75] In fact, the studio story departments all had extensions in New York whose role was to obtain information on available completed material and purchase rights to it directly from publishers or writers.[76] However, when a story was sold, whether to a publisher, a Broadway producer, or a studio, the writer still held some rights over the original copy. And it goes without saying that if a work failed to sell, the author remained with the property in hand. Not so in Hollywood. When one wrote on speculation, it was usually in order to develop an idea that was already bought and paid for—an idea that belonged to someone else. Therefore, if the producer chose to pass on the speculative treatment, the writer was left with nothing but lost time and energy.

Outside the spec business, red cents did cross palms in Hollywood, of course, a fact that, as mentioned, was one of the initial draws of Tinseltown. Perhaps the best illustration for the migratory status of writers in Hollywood was their attitudes about remuneration. On the one hand, regardless of their film industry status, screenwriters were making more money than in any other writing industry, and they knew it. Frances Goodrich and her husband, Albert Hackett, moved to Hollywood in 1931 after writing and acting together on the New York stage since the early 1920s. "In those days, writers made lots and lots of money," said Hackett. "I think the top men were making about $5000 a week. We went out there at a contract of $750 for the two of us, a team."[77] Edwin Justus Mayer may have complained about writing conditions, but he was honest enough to admit that "salaries are large and comparatively sure."[78] Some writers even used the money earned in Hollywood to compensate for the lack of it in other fields. Ben Hecht liked to brag that he "was working at Metro . . . very happily," but never for more than "eight or ten weeks" consecutively. He "got paid by the week" and received "bonuses for every movie that was finished," staying only "till I got enough money to quit for the year."[79]

On the other hand, by the mid-1930s, writers were also measuring their paychecks in intra-industry terms, comparing themselves to their current coworkers rather than to the meager paychecks they left back east. In 1935, Dudley Nichols granted that "Hollywood writers are hacks creating or trying to create entertainment for money," but the real question, he claimed, was "whether such writers are overpaid hacks." His answer was a categorical no. "The total salary paid to writers in Hollywood is well under five per cent of the total cost of pictures," he claimed. "That is not much, considering that pictures today could not begin to be produced without the writers' ideas and talents."[80] Nichols had a point. In his study, Rosten found that while "the top movie writers are very well paid," they were "by no means as well paid as Hollywood's directors, actors or producers." While, in 1938, the top seventeen writers mentioned by Rosten earned over $75,000, there were, for comparison, "80 actors, 54 producers and executives, [and] 45 directors" in the same pay bracket.[81]

The sidelining of writers relative to the other creative forces in the industry was often commented on. To some it was nothing short of a conspiracy generated by "the Star-Director-Producer triumvirate—the Trinity of Egoism, Power, and Dollars, which consciously and unconsciously conspire to keep the Writer outside the Gates of Paradise."[82] Separated from their work and their product, writers now saw themselves as splintering from their fellow filmmakers. In such a frame of mind, even a small affront could serve as a casus belli. As luck would have it, writers did not have to seek high and low for such a cause, which soon presented itself in the form of a full-blown attack on 50 percent of their paystub.

Talking Back

At the same time eastern writers were assimilating to the world of moviemaking, a series of external events shook the system and opened up new possibilities for change. The Great Depression hit the picture business late but did not pass it over completely. By March 1933, like many companies in other industries, the studios found it increasingly difficult to meet their payrolls. Taking advantage of the recently announced bank holiday on March 6, studio executives introduced an emergency measure of their own that they claimed was necessary to avoid a looming general shutdown. Coming together in a time of crisis, the big production companies made a joint decision to enact an industry-wide wage cut. Employees whose weekly wages amounted to $50 or more would receive a 50 percent cut, while those earning less than $50 would receive a 25 percent cut for the duration of eight weeks.[83] The response from the ranks was quick to follow, and it was organized.

In April, almost immediately following the pay cut announcement, the SWG was officially launched.[84] A month later, on June 30, the Screen Actors Guild was also formed. Initially, the studios refused to recognize these unions and further antagonized them with the approval, in November, of a Code of Fair Competition for the Motion Picture Industry, which was sponsored by the National Recovery Administration (NRA). The code was signed without adhering to or seriously consulting with the special committees representing the newly formed talent guilds. With the passing of the National Labor Relations Act and the formation of the Congress of

Industrial Organizations in 1935, Hollywood unions gained political leverage, and indeed, by May 1937, the actors had forced the studios to recognize their guild. The Screen Directors Guild, which sprang up early in 1936, reached an agreement with the studios by early 1939. The longest battle was waged by SWG, which after two sets of hearings in front of the NLRB finally won recognition only in May 1940. All this was happening while other forces in the industry, such as the electrical workers and projectionists, were waging battles of their own with and against the International Alliance of Theatrical Stage Employees.[85]

The New Deal, with the various programs it undertook to combat the Depression, served as a double-edged sword for the studio system, echoing the conditions in many other industries during the 1930s. The Emergency Banking Act and the NRA helped the big companies solidify their oligopoly by sanctioning pay cuts and other control mechanisms under the pretense of "codes of fair practice." By contrast, measures such as section 7(a) of the National Industrial Recovery Act, as well as the Wagner Act, and especially the formation of the NLRB, were instrumental in enabling the establishment of various Hollywood guilds and helped set in motion the industry's transformation into a union shop.

While the impetus behind the writers' crusade might have come from this broader sociopolitical framework, the meaning and methods of their struggle were transposed from the contiguous creative worlds of New York wordsmiths. Writers on the East Coast had a history of collective action, which predated the national political developments of the 1930s. Though hardly a union, the Authors' League, established between 1911 and 1912, standardized the use of contracts in the publishing business and created a forceful assembly of writers under which various groups could operate. One such group, which had a significant influence on screenwriters, was the Dramatists' Guild, which began as a committee within the league around 1919.[86]

Playwrights in New York were subject to various forms of manipulation by producers.[87] As one of them recounted, "It was not by any means usual to get an advance against royalties . . . a manager owned world rights. . . . We had no say about the deal," and "though theoretically an author could object to changes in the script, this was true only in proportion to the fighting strength of the author."[88] In 1926, the Dramatists' Guild, backed by the Authors' League, managed to achieve a minimum basic agreement with the important theatrical production companies.[89] The agreement, among other things, "wiped out practically all [pay] abuses" and "preserved integrity of scripts," so that there could be "no change without Author's consent." Most importantly, though, according to several playwrights, "the agreement cemented League Dramatists into a compact entity."[90] In the words of the Pulitzer Prize–winning playwright Owen Davis, it proved to him and his colleagues that "collective power through organization . . . enforces their rights," and that it "certainly made [the] road easier" for young writers upon which "the future of the theater depends [as well as] that of experienced writers."[91]

Many of the screenwriters forced to accept a studio pay cut experienced the Dramatists' Guild battle firsthand. Among the participants in the 1933 inaugural meeting of SWG sat at least three men who were intimately familiar with the playwrights' struggles in the 1920s: Raphaelson, Lawson, who was a veteran of New York's New Playwrights Theater, and Mayer, an established author. At the meeting, these men "pointed out that the task to be accomplished by writers in Hollywood was far less difficult."[92] They saw the parallels. As Raphaelson once wrote to a friend back east, "I suppose [Hollywood is] as mad an industry as you hear it is, but I don't think it's any more grotesque than the sort of thing you and I went through daily with the Phillipe Boys, or with the delightful but equally fantastic Mr. Douglas."[93] Hackett and Goodrich expressed similar sentiments. "We were accustomed to Actors' Equity and Dramatists Guild," they agreed. "We didn't feel dependent upon the industry, so we weren't intimidated by the nature of studio antagonism."[94] Broadway battles prepared eastern writers for their fight in Hollywood.

Screenwriters in the film industry wanted to import their eastern achievements to the West Coast. In other words, they wanted a guild shop. Throughout their negotiations and confrontations with the Hollywood moguls and producers, writers brought forward various demands pertaining to their conditions of employment. They wanted contracts to be "required in all cases" and the prohibition of writing on speculation; they sought for writers not to be "on call during lay-off" so that they "may do other work"; they demanded the prohibition of any blacklist; and they insisted that credit arbitration be "disinterested," so that the "writer [will] pick [the] organization to act for him."[95] Some of these claims, like the call for universal contracts, harked back to the wrangles of authors and dramatists. However, encompassing all these requirements was one goal—the right for collective bargaining in the form of the Dramatists' Guild's 1926 minimum basic agreement.

In 1935, Ernest Pascal, the president of SWG, proclaimed, "The guild is fighting for one thing—guild shop." He explained that such a condition "opens its door to every Writer regardless of qualification. The Writer merely agrees to abide by the rules of the Guild—and no writer, except a Guild Writer, may be employed in a Motion Picture Studio." Pascal stressed that they were not proposing a "closed shop," which might "result in a virtual monopoly of the labor market." As opposed to it, he explained, "The guild shop idea has been tried and proved conclusively."[96] The SWG president based his claims on New York experience, and he did so explicitly. He explained, "Through guild shop [the Dramatists' Guild] corrected all the evils that existed for the Dramatists in the theatre." Playwrights on the East Coast realized that "only through guild shop could they negotiate a deal with Producing Managers that could be binding and enforceable." He proceeded with a direct analogy: "Screen Writers are the dramatists of Motion Pictures," and therefore "the key that solved their problems . . . will solve our problem."[97]

For some writers, analogy was not enough; they wanted unity. In April 1936, as part of an attempt to force the studios' hand into recognizing it, the SWG board proposed an amalgamation of the guild with the Authors' League and the formation of "one organization for all American Writers." The rationale behind this proposition was that "basically the problem of all writers is the same, and always has been." Therefore, it is a collective interest to "consolidate all writers in all fields into one strong and unified organization, strong and able to protect writers against the invasion of his rights [*sic*] and to fight for and win what is rightly his."[98] Beyond the utopian language, the proposition had specific practical implications. Even if the guild won recognition, which at that point it had not, acting alone SWG was "unable to cut off the supply of man-power and material."[99] In case of a screenwriters' strike, producers could always reach out once more to the pool of talent on the other coast. A joint union with a minimum basic agreement, "so that all persons employed are members of the League and all sellers of material are members of the League," would prevent that from happening.[100] It would mean the best for both worlds.

The call for amalgamation was not unanimous. As one would expect from a group of erudite political activists, they did not speak in one voice. In addition to their experience as writers in other industries, many SWG members were armed with their various and often conflicting political persuasions. Much has been written about the association of Hollywood writers with the American Communist Party (CPUSA). Indeed, several guild members, such as Paul Jarrico, Ring Lardner, Donald Ogden Stewart, Dorothy Parker, and Lillian Hellman, were affiliated with the party in one way or another.[101] Among the members and fellow travelers, some, including John Howard Lawson, Albert Maltz, and Clifford Odets, became involved with the CPUSA back in New York.[102] Beginning in 1935, party headquarters placed great emphasis on recruitment of new members from the motion picture industry. It initiated "studio study clubs," which were "held twice a month, rotating from one member's [sic] home to the next." As screenwriter Lester Cole remembered, his branch was "made up mostly of film people," and they "took turns giving 'educationals,' which for us were mainly on literature and art."[103] However, as several historians pointed out, strong antifascist sentiments, as well as the existence of a loose popular front coalition affiliated with the Democratic Party, meant that "in Hollywood in the thirties, the Communist Party was barely distinguishable in policy and activities from the noncommunist Left."[104] As Raphaelson explained, "I felt that if the world was going to go communist or fascist, I'd rather see it go communist, though I never joined the Party."[105]

Despite the vocal presence of some Communists, SWG was by no means a Communist organization. A close look at the propositions made by the guild's board reveals a very careful choice of language, which indicates an attempt to avoid terms that gravitated too far to the left. The emphasis on "guild shop" as opposed to "closed shop" is one example. Another is the inclusion, in the amalgamation proposal, of a clause providing "against the contingency of two Guilds being able to call a third Guild out on strike."[106] Even the choice of the term "guild" rather than "union" suggests an ambivalent attitude toward organized labor.[107] Such caution was not coincidental. For one thing, members of the guild wanted to avoid accusations by studio bosses that they were used as a front for the CPUSA. More important, though, was the active membership in SWG of moderate and even conservative writers. Pascal might have been speaking for the guild's board, but sitting right beside him was Nunnally Johnson, who self-identified as a "Southern white Methodist" and, in later years, claimed that "if you had to put a name on it, it would be liberal Democrat," though "a radical wouldn't call me very liberal."[108] Also on the board was Brackett, who often testified that he "happen[ed] to be a born Republican, a tried-in-the-fire, voted for Landon Republican."[109] People like them, while consistently advocating for "a stronger, tougher guild," were also adamant about keeping labor politics and left-wing causes out of it and vigorously opposed any attempt to "grind someone's political axes."[110] Even when it was calling for the writers of America to unite, the SWG was far from a radical organization.

Still, for some, even these moderate demands were too much. Pioneer writers were particularly divided in their views about the new organization.

Some, like Frank Woods and Anita Loos, joined enthusiastically. Frances Marion even served on the board for two years. However, for the most part, the veterans of the silent period were antagonistic to the idea of a union, especially one that included professionals who did not write for the screen. Indeed, several of them, encouraged by studio heads, resigned from SWG, claiming that "they didn't want to be governed from New York."[111] But even the newcomers were not of one mind. The leader of the dissenters was James K. McGuinness, one of the first contributors to the *New Yorker*'s "Talk of the Town" segment. This writer arrived in Hollywood in 1927 and settled comfortably at MGM. Despite his East Coast beginnings, McGuinness did not share the inferiority complex of other screenwriters. He believed that different writing worlds were exactly that—different— and therefore should remain separate. "Their interests were New York interests and the legitimate theater interests," he said about the authors and dramatists. "It seems to me," he added, "that there was a danger . . . that the writers in moving pictures . . . could be used as a weapon in the fight between moving picture producing companies and the Dramatists Guild or the Authors Guild who were interested chiefly in novels and short stories."[112] For McGuinness, the natural alliance was horizontal, between picture people, and not a vertical coalition of writing people.

This cinematic loyalty naturally appealed to the sensibilities of studio management, and with their help, in May 1936, McGuinness formed an alternative writers' organization, the Screen Playwrights. Screen veterans Casey Robinson, Grover Jones, Howard Emmett Rogers, Bess Meredyth, Carey Wilson, Rupert Hughes, and Waldemar Young joined him. While the lines of this political conflict were not neatly drawn between east versus west or old versus young, acclimatization did play a role. One of the harshest critics of SWG was Patterson McNutt, who came out west from New York in the mid-1930s after publishing short stories in the *Saturday Evening Post* and the *American Magazine*, among other publications. The reason for his move was material. He was offered $350 a week to "clean up" a story called "Salable Ware."[113] His reasons for staying were ideological. "I consider myself to be one of the luckiest white men in the world," he testified.[114] Even though he was working in Hollywood for a couple of years, McNutt saw no need to combine the best of both worlds, because the world of the studio system was already the best. He was dismissive of the amalgamation plan and believed it ensued from an attitude that was "typical of Hollywood," but also "rather dangerous to Hollywood writers": "We come out here and we get on a gravy train, and after you have been on that gravy train for a certain length of time, I think you tend to get into the frame of mind where you think you belong on that gravy train; no matter what you do, that that is the normal state of life."[115] For people like McNutt, SWG and its demands represented this dangerous way of thinking. Whether they migrated to it or not, some writers saw Hollywood as a creative world one should be thankful for rather than tamper with.

Despite this, the claims of SWG and the language introduced by it had an influence across the board, even on the Screen Playwrights. To present a viable alternative to SWG and perhaps also to disprove their own reputation as studio puppets, in March 1937, the Screen Playwrights signed a contract with the producers. The agreement featured accomplishments such as "a minimum wage, standardized contracts," due notice upon request "on whether other writers were working on the same material, no speculative writing without payment, and participation in the credit allocation procedure."[116] Noticeably, the organization did not negotiate an exclusive guild shop, which might have been a bad call on their part, since, while fearful of aligning with the persecuted SWG, most writers chose not to join the ranks of the Screen Playwrights. As a result, the Screen Playwrights never turned into a serious tool for collective bargaining and representation. Eventually, with the help of the NLRB, the original writers' guild reclaimed its membership. In 1941, SWG, now formally recognized, signed an agreement with the studios that featured "85 per cent union shop for three years, when it would become 90 per cent," as well as "exclusive control over credits."[117] The proposed amalgamation with the Authors' League never fully materialized; still, screenwriters managed to create a protective union modeled after this organization, bringing motion pictures and the traditional writing worlds somewhat closer.

In this sense, the effect of migratory writers extended beyond improving their own status within the studio system. They transformed the status of the film industry as a whole. Although amalgamation was ultimately discarded, the fact that it was seriously considered suggested that, as Pascal said, "screen-Writing . . . became the same as any other kind of writing. It wiped out the distinction between the 'legitimate' writer and the 'Hollywood' writer." To be sure, this was an overstatement. Many wordsmiths would have challenged Pascal and his contention that the different writing professions had all "become one."[118] But his use of the word "legitimate" is meaningful. The willingness of authors and playwrights to come together with screenwriters validated Hollywood to some degree. It ascertained that the presence of migrant writers lent some respect and validity to what was formerly a questionable line of work. The transition of "legitimate" writers into the screenwriting ranks made screen work a bit more legitimate. Writing for the screen might still have been looked down upon, but it moved up a peg or two. With their history, their struggle against the studios, and also the quality of their work, by the late 1930s, screenwriters had turned their profession into one that was worthy and valuable enough to be included within an idyllic, hypothetical coalition of all writers.

In fact, the Authors' League's failed plan was by no means the last word. Ten years after the proposed amalgamation, author James M. Cain, whose novels were a hot commodity in Hollywood during the 1940s, was advocating for an "American Authors' Authority." This wished-for organization would administer copyright and protect writers' contracts no matter who they signed them with, "a magazine, a publisher, a radio station, or a picture company."[119] Gone were the attitudes of the 1910s, when "a self-respecting author" like Clifford Howard, who wished to "retain the confidence of his friends and admirers," would "speak softly" about working for the picture business "if he was caught at it." A screenwriter no longer had to treat "his undignified work as a trifling side issue, done just for the fun of it."[120] Writing for the movies and, by implication, the movies themselves were now part and parcel of the unofficial league of American authors.

Once the page had turned, there was no going back. The newfound closeness between screenwriting and "legitimate" writing enabled some penmen to continue living between worlds. This was most apparent when addressing the grail of authorial control. The question of ownership or, more accurately, lack of it, remained a sensitive topic among screenwriters, who never fully surrendered the dream of owning the rights for scripts. This privation was such a sensitive matter that Philip Dunne once referred to it as "dynamite." He admitted that "control of material" was "what the writers really want . . . of course it was. No writer in his senses could want anything else."[121] Indeed, in 1945, the author and screenwriter Raymond Chandler went as far as claiming that a writer without "power of decision over the uses of his own craft, without ownership of it," was in essence "almost without honor for it."[122] These were poignant words. Dunne reflected that "by controlling source material" the screenwriter "would undoubtedly have won by now a far greater degree of recognition and respect than he has." Alas, he concluded, in Hollywood it was impossible that the "craftsman, the salaried mechanic, should have a legal right to dictate [to] the manager, the entrepreneur who has a responsibility to his stockholders."[123]

In reality, by the mid-1940s, screenwriters had found roundabout ways to gain more control over their work. The most common method was to hyphenate their writer status with another role, such as director or producer, that carried greater prestige and authority. Brackett and Wilder turned from being a team of writers to being a writer-producer and a writer-director, respectively, as did Ben Hecht and his partner Charles McArthur. Dunne and Nunnally Johnson began producing, while Dudley Nichols metamorphosed into a writer-producer-director.[124] Another way to gain control was to participate in the financing of the movie, or, in industry parlance, "to work in profit-sharing independent ventures as partners and not as employees." That meant working without a studio contract, but under SWG protection independent deals were safer and offered their own perks. Advocating these ventures, Mary McCall Jr. described her deal with producer Sam Jaffe: "My contract called for the payment to me of fifteen thousand dollars for ten weeks work. If the screenplay, as finally shot, was less than seventy-five per cent my work, that fifteen thousand dollars would be the total payment to me. If seventy-five per cent or more of the screen play which was used was my work, I was to receive five per cent of the producers' share of the picture. The fifteen thousand dollars would then be considered an advance against my percentage." The result was satisfactory. McCall received $1,500 above the advance and was expecting additional income from world market profits. She described this writing assignment as "the most profitable experience of my working life," and added that she wished her "fellow writers no better fortune than a contract of this sort."[125]

However, despite these efforts, and despite what was, by the mid-1940s, a complete assimilation into the motion picture world, some writers remained dissatisfied with the status of authorship in that world. As Dunne once again conceded, while "the writer who becomes a writer-producer is . . . accepting both authority over and responsibility for his work, while assuming a far more realistic position vis-à-vis the director," he is still "not completely free." Underneath it all, no matter how "glorified," the writer was still an "employee, subject to the directions, and in some cases the apparent lunacies, of the studio executives. His chain may have become a mere web of gossamer, but he is still caught."[126] For some, the only way to gain real control was simply to leave.

In 1942, shortly after the SWG agreement went into effect, Casey Robinson, a former member of the Screen Playwrights who started his career as a titles writer in the mid-1920s, sent a letter to his boss, Jack L. Warner. Essentially, he wanted out of his Warner Bros. contract, saying, "After much deliberation I feel it is to our mutual advantage to call off our marriage." He confessed that it was not "physically possible for [him] to complete that much work and at the same time maintain the measure of quality [he] insists upon at all time." He felt he was "approaching stagnation" and working under "irksome and restricted conditions." He wanted to make it absolutely clear that "it was not money [he was] after"; rather, "It is my freedom I want." By freedom he meant "the opportunity of choosing my own subjects—the privilege of writing original screenplays—a partner's voice in casting and direction—and a full partner's reward in, primarily, satisfaction, and secondarily, financial rewards (great or small) which result from the free and unrestricted use of my full talents, whatever they may be." This veteran writer, who originally opposed amalgamation, perhaps because he had no experience working in other fields outside cinema, was now asking for more control—for traditional authorship rights. He was begging to be "fired immediately."[127]

Robinson understood that what he was asking for was "unheard of in those days," not to say "revolutionary."[128] He also knew that "Jack Warner despised writers," and therefore was not likely to grant his request. He tried to increase his odds by appealing to Hal Wallis, the studio's head producer, a "very strong man in his job," albeit one whose "door was sort of open."[129] He wrote to Wallis, saying, "I hope [Jack] sees the light," and that he "would appreciate boundlessly any support you feel like giving."[130] But despite the strides made by screenwriters since the silent days and through SWG wars, despite the change migrant writers brought to the screenwriting community and to the status of their profession, for studio bosses, a writer's quest for authorship still sounded like a foreign language. Dumbfounded by Robinson's request, Warner wrote to Wallis the next day, "I cannot understand the attached note from Casey Robinson. I gave him a good deal and straightened everything out to his satisfaction, and now he sends a letter like this. I think it is uncalled for and isn't cricket. Will you tell Casey for me, to live up to his agreement?"[131]

A FULL MERGER between the screenwriting field and other writing worlds was yet to come. In the meantime, the give-and-take of ideas, demands, techniques, and practices continued, and by the early 1940s, screenwriters had managed to transform the world of moviemaking enough to make most of them enthusiastic and utterly loyal to it. Conceivably, it was exactly this combination of newfound loyalty to motion pictures and a longstanding alliance with other literary fields that condemned writers in

Hollywood to a constant migratory position, to an ongoing, contested process of identity formation. Following the patterns set by other waves of labor migration, screenwriters established a line of exchange between their new place of work and the industries they left behind. This new channel of communication was not a one-way street; a study of Broadway or the publishing business, not to mention radio and television, during the same years would surely reveal similar borrowing and adaptation inspired by Hollywood. Furthermore, as is often the case with émigré communities, screenwriters never reached a consensus about the merits of their prevailing line of work. Some continued to see their role as nothing more than "first-rate cabinetmakers" who mold raw material made by other people and "work it into an acceptable form."[132] Others, like Charles Brackett, maintained that "writing for the screen is a living and important art" that carries a "burden unique among writers," namely, "sustaining the interest of an audience without interruption."[133] Either way, as a group they assimilated and as individuals they reconciled themselves to the anonymity writing for the screen entailed.

CHAPTER THREE

Directing

During the golden age of the Hollywood studios, what was the difference between the creative status of a screenwriter and that of a director?[1] Consider the production of *The Lives of a Bengal Lancer*, a Paramount picture based on a novel by Francis Yeats-Brown that followed the struggles of three British soldiers in India. Initial work on the screenplay was assigned to two writers, Malcolm Stewart Bailey and Harvey Gates, in early 1932. As writer Grover Jones testified, "In those days we used to write scripts alphabetically as the sequence came, A, B, C and so on. Well, they wrote and wrote and got a little discouraged, and finally got down to F and said, 'the hell with it,' and quit." Then the job was handed over to Jones and his partner William Slavens McNutt. They wrote a script, but the studio decided not to pursue it. Subsequently, "two or three years went by, maybe four. Writers came from all over the world to work on *Bengal Lancer*. They were from every place. And the cost accumulated—I have forgotten the exact figure now—almost up to $300,000, $400,000 or half a million."[2]

At that point, director Henry Hathaway came on board. "The reason they gave him *Bengal Lancer*," said Jones, "was because he got discouraged . . . drew out his savings of $2,000, and took a trip around the world . . . and, by chance, he went through a place called India. So when he got back he was the only guy on the lot who had been in India."[3] Hathaway was an in-house director at Paramount who worked mostly on low-budget westerns. As he remembered, *Bengal Lancer* was his "first really important movie." He decided to shoot the picture, as he did with all his westerns, in Lone Pine, California, explaining, "I had been up in India . . . and it wasn't unlike the country that we were in." He had one request, though. He asked the company to supply an elephant, for cinematic credibility. He wanted to film an elephant going over the hill, and make the audience think, "My God, this isn't a place I've been, here's an elephant."

"Then a funny thing happened." The night before shooting was about to begin, Hathaway was cruising the set in search of his elephant. When he could not find it, he approached one of the production assistants, who informed him that the studio decided not to send one: "They said that they think it's a whim of yours and they don't want to spend the money." The director was furious. He called the main office and said, "I understand you're not sending me the elephant . . . well, I'll tell you one thing. You start him out right now in a truck, start him or start another director." They said they would send another director. Then, about an hour later, "the assistant director came around and said the elephant's on the way." Hathaway admitted, "It was more a matter of principle. But there was [also] a great shot."[4]

The film, released in 1935, featured an elephant, as well as Gary Cooper, one of the first screen appearances by Akim Tamiroff, a directing credit for Hathaway, an adaptation credit for Jones and McNutt, a suggestion credit for Yeats-Brown, and additional writing credits for Waldemar Young, John L. Balderston, and Achmed Abdullah. Here lay the difference. While writers accumulated, assigned and reassigned for no particular reason, the director was irreplaceable, even at the cost of carrying an elephant up the Alabama Hills.

Hollywood directors were part of a production team together with producers, writers, cinematographers, art directors, editors, actors, and many others. Just like their teammates, they were studio employees who worked under the command of an executive producer or head of production. But, unlike their colleagues, directors enjoyed a certain degree of authoritative autonomy. On first glance, this autonomy appears to conflict with the systematic division of creative labor embraced by most studios beginning in the mid-1910s. In a process that took around ten years, filmmaking was slowly divided into small tasks, which were clumped in dedicated departments with supervisors and specialists. In one such department, writing a story became an umbrella term for the labor of scenarists, title writers, dialogue writers, continuity writers, and gagmen. Somehow, within this organizing frenzy, the directing profession remained relatively unbroken. Particularly during the filming stage of the production, when the cameras were rolling, studio involvement in the director's job was reduced to a minimum. Even such towering figures as Irving Thalberg or Darryl Zanuck generally "never went on set" and "left the director pretty much alone."[5]

This disengagement was not the result of respect for artistic freedom. On the contrary, the reality of production required an independent director above all for commercial expediency. When films became longer and more complex, featuring elaborate settings and the growing expenses tied to the star system, the actual production of footage on the set became very expensive. Efficiency was of the essence. However, since cinema was still a creative business, it had to be accompanied by a genuine talent for pictorial storytelling, good acting, and visual originality. Hence, successful studio directors, those who proved they had the skill to shoot a "good" film while remaining within budget, were given a limited autonomous sphere, between the preproduction preparatory stage and the postproduction tasks of cutting and editing.

Directing had a history of autonomy. Stage directors in theaters and particularly on Broadway were responsible for many of the creative aspects of a play. Similarly, in the early days of cinema, between 1900 and 1914, the director fulfilled nearly all functions in film production save for acting. The maintenance of this freedom, however, should not be taken for granted. After all, writing was perhaps the quintessential self-sufficient task, a tradition that Hollywood quickly transformed. Rather than an organic necessity, directorial authority was a reasonable recourse, one that helped to bridge the creative complexity of the task and the growing demand for efficiency and productivity.

The Function of Autonomy

As a business that relies on perpetual creative innovation, the motion picture industry cannot operate exactly like a conventional assembly line. The ignoble division of labor that was part and parcel of any modern industry did not spare filmmaking. Yet, at the core of the cinematic production process stood a mission that proved very difficult to shatter into minimal automatic tasks. That mission was unifying various elements, including script, scenery, and actors, into a unique and popular motion picture. Producers of mass culture always face commercial uncertainty, since they are unable to predict the exact ingredients that will constitute a successful product. Even proven crowd-pleasers such as the western genre or a certain star actor may one day, unexpectedly, fall out of fashion. Novelty is necessary. Novelty, though, comes with an organizational cost. It disrupts the "conventionalization" of production activities, defies routines, interrupts procedures by introducing individual choice, and is often unsatisfied by the available resources. As a result, cultural industries attempt to protect the convention of production by containing originality. One way to do so is to isolate the innovative functions and confine them to specific skill-based work roles that are relatively unstructured and unconstrained.[6]

Theoretical studies of labor and capital long ago called attention to the correlation between skill and autonomy. The industrial rationale emergent between the late nineteenth and early twentieth centuries generally sought to reduce any production process to "simple labor," thus divorcing it from "special knowledge." However, whether in the coal mine, the steel mill, or the automobile factory, there were some crafts that relied on training and were therefore harder to break up, supervise, and control. Frederick Winslow Taylor, the father of scientific management theory, referred to these crafts as possessing "rule-of-thumb" or "traditional knowledge."[7] More critical onlookers named this phenomenon "the manager's brain under the workman's cap." Either way, the juxtaposition of simple tasks with more elaborate ones split the workforce in two. On the one hand, there were "common laborers, who fetched and pushed at the command of their gang bosses," and on the other, "craftsmen, who learned their trades by doing and who clearly directed their own work and that of their immediate helpers."[8]

For the most part, industrial efficiency and rule-of-thumb decision making were at odds. Management sought to "destroy the craft as a process under the control of the worker" and reconstitute it as a series of clear and easy to supervise tasks. Workers often attempted to fight the division of labor and maintain their own control. They did so mostly by organizing, forming formal or informal groups, and establishing ethical codes that protected their interests and values. Indeed, the attainment of employee autonomy was more often than not the result of struggle.[9] But that was not always the case. Autonomy could on occasion be functional.[10] Since some skills proved to be indivisible, sometimes setting aside designated pockets of autonomy assisted and even enhanced the mode of production. For some industries, leaving a certain class of workers to their own devices was simply more practical.

American cinema was one such industry. As filmmaking evolved into a modern business, keeping the director somewhat autonomous proved to be beneficial. There is no question that the owners of motion picture companies sought to exercise as much control as possible over the production process. However, even at its most domineering, the studio system failed to break down the craft of directing and left it almost completely in the hands of its practitioners. This was despite the fact that there was never formal or any other kind of meaningful resistance from the ranks. Organization also came late; the Screen Directors Guild was established only in 1936, failed to gain recognition until 1939, and never went on strike. Nevertheless, between the late 1910s and the early 1930s, Hollywood developed a production routine that relied on the director's "rule of thumb" during the shooting part of the filmmaking process.

There were four main reasons for the maintenance of this autonomy. First was the force of habit. During the early days of cinema, before any kind of managerial system was put in place, directors did enjoy, or endured, sole responsibility for all aspects of filmmaking. When the financiers of the companies started to increase their involvement in the details of production, the pattern of an independent director was already in place. Second, the film directors' counterparts in theater and foreign film industries, who were also self-sufficient to some extent, influenced the Hollywood version of the profession. Third, the nature of directing, that is, the orchestration of the shooting of a motion picture, is a creative task that, like writing, acting, or designing, requires some level of freedom.

Finally, on top of all these lies the fact that the actual process of filming is a complicated and expensive endeavor whose successful and punctual completion demands the command of a skilled and experienced professional. Shooting a movie involves film, a costly product. Shooting a movie also takes time, and in motion pictures time equals loads of money. Shooting a movie that features clear footage with good lighting, a dramatic story, and credible acting calls for care, attention to detail, and some level of perfectionism—all qualities that often lead to waste of either film or time. Therefore, shooting a film with care and without wasting too much money demands skill, and, as indicated, a high level of complexity and skill usually entails autonomy. It is worthwhile taking a closer look at the evolution of directorial autonomy in Hollywood. In order to do so, though, one has to go back to the days when the director was not just autonomous: the director was everything.

Making Bricks without Straw

When production of motion pictures had just started, in the first fifteen years of the twentieth century, the director was "the mainspring of the new industry ... for he knew how to make bricks without straw." At least that was how one anonymous director writing for the *Saturday Evening Post* saw it. "It was all a wild hurly-burly to throw film onto the market," he claimed. "Exhibitors were clamoring for new pictures," since "the ten-cent customers stood in line with their dimes in their hand." The feeling was that "any old thing would draw a crowd, and the cameras could not grind fast enough to supply the demand." A director was anyone who could answer the call for "footage, and still more footage": "unlimited money was poured into his lap and he was told to make pictures and to keep on making pictures as fast as he knew how."[11]

What appeared to be an unlimited demand was the only guideline in the early days. Eager investors were constantly in the market for anyone who thought they were up to the task of churning out pictures quickly. As one film historian put it, "If you were twenty and thought you could direct, one company or another would probably give you the chance."[12] That was exactly the case with the *Saturday Evening Post* director: "The motion-picture game was new in those days, and I thought I saw a future in it for a young man." He started at "the grease-paint end" of some studio and was "permitted to remain on the lot long enough to study the making of pictures—long enough to qualify as a director in the days when almost anyone could qualify—and almost anyone did."[13] Indeed, as it was a new profession, film directors came from everywhere. Some, like D. W. Griffith, G. M. Anderson, and Al Christie, had theatrical experience. Others brought with them any other kind of experience: "Sam Wood had worked on pipelines for an oil company . . . James Cruze had worked in a medicine show . . . Clarence Brown had been an auto salesman. W. S. Van Dyke had been a lumberjack, gold miner, railroader, and mercenary."[14]

Take Allan Dwan's case. "It was a funny thing," he remembered. While working as an electrical engineer in Chicago in 1909, he "was sent out to the old Essanay studio . . . one day to install some Cooper-Hewitt lights. They were new then, and took an expert to handle them. While I was adjusting them, I watched things that were going on and became interested." He asked Essanay for a job: "The company was being reorganized in some ways—a lot of the old bunch had left to go west to form the American— and they made me scenario editor."[15] A couple of months later the company sent Dwan to California to write some stories for director Frank Beal. As mentioned, production was disorganized in those days, and it took Dwan a long while just to locate the film crew he was looking for. "I finally found [them] at San Juan Capistrano. . . . There were about eight actors, a lot of cowboys, some horses, and everyone was sitting there doing nothing." Beal apparently chose to vacation in Los Angeles, where alcohol was more readily available. Dwan wired Chicago, saying, "I suggest you disband the company. You have no director." The wire that came back read "You direct."[16] The rest he learned on the go.

The high demand also inspired women to see a future in the profession. Labor shortages, together with the decentralized nature of the new industry, left filmmaking a somewhat "ungendered" terrain. To boot, the presence of women both in the audience and as members of the industry helped legitimize the business at a time when exhibitors and producers sought for middle-class authority. Indeed, between 1910 and World War I, many women jumped on the bandwagon.[17] The names behind the titles included Margery Wilson, Ruth Ann Baldwin, Grace Cunard, Cleo Madison, Ruth Stonehouse, Ida May Park, Elsie Jane Wilson, and Lois Weber. The door was open, and behind it waited a perfect career for the "New Woman" of the era. As the very successful director Alice Guy Blaché commented in 1914, "It has long been a source of wonder to me that many women have not seized upon the wonderful opportunities offered to them by the motion picture art to make their way to fame and fortune."[18] She herself grasped this opportunity with both hands, serving as the head director of the Solax Company, which she owned with her husband, and was recognized as one of the most experienced and respected filmmakers in the world.[19]

It was the golden age of the "director system." The function of the director became prevalent in 1907, when a separate worker was hired by companies to take over production. During the next two years, one could speak of a system in which "one individual staged the action and another person photographed it." The first was probably called a director because a turn to fictional narrative made the role analogous to that of the stage director, "who controlled the choices of scenery, costumes, and acting, and used a script as an 'outline' of the narrative."[20] In those days, the producer and the director were the same person, and the terms were even used synonymously. After 1909, demand increased and companies needed more "footage, and still more footage." The problem was that one director could shoot only about one or two pictures per week. As Dwan recalled, "We would work say, Monday, Tuesday and Wednesday shooting and make two pictures. Then on Thursday and Friday I'd develop and cut them. . . . We wouldn't ship them until we had maybe six, and then they'd release them in their own order."[21] Companies responded to this production lag by hiring more directors, sending each of them out to work independently with their own crew.

Even though firms commissioned the work, the director was the one in charge; he or she was writing, staging actors and camera, editing footage, and sometimes even developing the film. Everything except distribution and exhibition was in their hands. The anonymous director in the *Saturday Evening Post* remembered one time he was hired, which was "typical of the period":

"Want to work for us["]? [a]sked Mr. Jones, who was and is a man of few words. I said that I might consider a proposition. "Consider the proposition made . . . How much?" I told him how much and he grunted: "All right! You're hired." "When do you want me to begin?" I asked. "To-morrow." "But my people—my company? I'll need a camera man and a property man and a—" "Get 'em," said Jones briefly. "Get all the people you need." I next wished to know whether he had any stories in sight—any scenarios in preparation. "Get your own stories," said he[.] "Same kind of stuff you've been doing. Get everything and start shooting as soon as you can."[22]

By this point—the mid-1910s—proven experience in turning out one-reel pictures or features was especially sought after.[23] Raoul Walsh was making films with Griffith when, in 1915, Winfield Sheehan of the newly formed Fox Company set out to hire him. "Nobody ever heard of the Fox Company," and Walsh, who wanted to remain with Griffith, figured that "the best way to get out of this [was] to blast him with a big salary." He told Sheehan he wanted $400 a week, an astronomical figure. He received a contract the next day.[24] Everyone wanted reliable directors, whatever the cost.

Demand for directors remained constant, but beginning in the mid-1910s the system around them started changing. "The outlines of the new industry," as most film scholars contend, began to take form around 1913, with the appearance of "new feature-production companies" that would end up taking control of distribution and exhibition.[25] The process, which culminated only a decade and a half later, was triggered mostly by competition over markets between companies seeking to control a bigger share of this still rather novel and certainly mushrooming business. But it was also goaded by the latest marked audience preference for longer feature films. The success of lengthy, ambitious, and expensive pictures such as Griffith's *Enoch Arden*, a two-reeler from 1911, and the nine-reel, two-and-a-half-hour-long Italian production of *Quo Vadis?* in 1913, signaled a new phase in motion pictures. By 1916, the crowds seemed to be turning away from shorts. As *Photoplay* reported with a somewhat frustrated tone, it was "impossible to make exhibitors understand that a short picture may have a bigger drawing power than a long one."[26] The "vogue of feature length films," as industry historian Lewis Jacobs referred to it, combined with the escalating reliance on a star system, "caused revolutionary changes in every department of the industry." Simply put, production became a good deal more expensive. Moviemaking now had to be a large-scale operation, and the companies' new goal was "the achievement of an organization and techniques to meet the new conditions."[27]

Luckily, some templates for efficient production organization were already in practice. It just so happened that one of them was developed by a director. Thomas H. Ince began his career as an actor. Around 1910 he started directing, working first for Carl Laemmle's Independent Moving Pictures Company (IMP). Soon after, he took a job with Kessel and Baumann's New York Motion Picture Company. They sent him out to make westerns at their new studio in Edendale, California.[28] It was there that Ince developed his innovative operation, dividing production into a "two-stage labor process—the work's preparation on paper by management followed by its execution by the workers." One could also refer to these stages, as they would later be known, as "preproduction" and "production." The preproduction phase, as devised by Ince, included the formation of a detailed script or "continuity" in which scenes were numbered consecutively and the location in which they were to be shot was noted. It also contained a detailed description of the mise-en-scène or action in each scene. The scripts were not prepared by the director, and were often accompanied by an injunction reading, "It is earnestly requested by Mr. Ince that no change of any nature be made in the scenario either by elimination of any scenes or the addition of any scenes or changing any of the action as described, or titles, without first consulting him."[29] Enthralled by the managerial aspect of moviemaking, Ince gradually stopped directing. In 1915, he collaborated with Griffith and Mack Sennett to form the Triangle Film Company, assuming a role that was essentially an early version of the latter-day executive producer and enabling him to continue his experimentations with organization.

It is hard to determine whether there was a creative motive behind Ince's shakeup of production routines, but there was certainly an economic motive. Ince was not alone in his quest for structure and convention. The material benefits were rather obvious: a preproduction phase helped control the outflow of cash by limiting impulsive, on-the-spot expenses—it introduced economic planning. Our *Saturday Evening Post* director once again painted a valuable picture. Speaking in praise of organization, he described the days before it was introduced: "When a director wanted anything he wanted it bad—had to have it that instant or the next.... It was so much simpler to send one of the hired men scooting in an automobile after the stuff . . . And our pay roll . . . I had twelve actors under salary all the time, and it was seldom that a scenario demanded the full strength of my stock company. . . . Our big stage as it used to be in the old days—crowded . . . a dozen or more directors excitedly bawling orders at their assistants; hundreds of employees."[30] Each director was acting alone, and resources were accumulated ad hoc, while sharing and cooperation were unheard of. The integration of new top-down operations with managers and specialized departments regularized shooting not only by introducing the script, which was the blueprint, but also by forming procedures that fostered coordination in the use of players, stages, props, and other equipment. In the words of the *Saturday Evening Post* director:

> Not only did I have an estimate sheet, setting forth in detail authorized expenditures for every part of my work, but I had sketches of all my sets, prepared by expert draftsmen, showing just exactly what I needed, and what I was told I would get. . . . Gradually it came to me that I was having less trouble in making pictures. It was easier to get the props I needed; if I turned in an order to the technical department for a special set I got that set when I needed it. Stage space and location became more available; a long quiescent scenario department began to turn in real stories. Unconsciously I was being speeded up at my work. . . . I found that I was getting more footage than ever before with less hurry and worry.[31]

This anonymous director was obviously advocating for the new system. Other directors seem to have held similar views. "Most directors are not business men," said Dwan back in 1920, "therefore the films have had to arrange for . . . men who, when the director had laid out the thing artistically . . . will find out how it can be done at the lowest cost."[32]

The question of artistic control may be somewhat irrelevant, since, in the early days, it is unclear whether anyone in particular, let alone the director, really had any authority over the way a picture was eventually exhibited. Writer Casey Robinson remarked that it was never "the day of the director," because once he had finished shooting, "the producer and the subtitle writers would come in and actually determine the nature of the movie."[33] Director Howard Hawks concurred. He had a brief career as a title writer, and claimed that those "could change a whole story, change a whole picture. I could change the leading lady to a heavy and the heavy to a leading lady—and I did a couple of times."[34] Dwan also recalled how "we'd be astonished when we went to a theatre," to see a picture he made; "the whole aspect of the movie was frequently changed."[35] Then again, how often did the director actually see the movie? Dwan was shooting in California, then sending his pictures to the main office in Chicago, which would later distribute them across the country as it saw fit. There was no way of knowing for sure when and where his pictures would feature, especially not at the rate he was going. "I once tried to draw up a list of pictures I'd done," said Dwan in 1964. "Someone sent me a list with eight hundred titles on it, and I tried to help him by adding on the rest. I got to fourteen hundred and I had to give up. Just couldn't remember the others."[36] Paid by the reel and producing at least one per week, most pioneer directors were too busy to worry about protecting their artistic integrity.

There were a few exceptions. A great deal has been written about the career of D. W. Griffith, the leading director of silent cinema. His extraordinary talent and contribution to the medium are undoubtedly worthy of attention. However, it is exactly due to his exceptionality that he will not be discussed at length here.[37] Having already achieved unprecedented success by 1910, Griffith was able to obtain unusual commercial benefits such as percentage deals or commissions for each film of his that was leased or sold.[38] As the director himself attested in an advertisement he published in the *New York Dramatic Mirror* in December 1913, "For two years from the Summer of 1908 [he] personally directed all Biograph motion pictures," and "thereafter . . . he superintended all Biograph productions and directed the more important features."[39] These were privileges enjoyed by a select few, including Ince, Sennett, and Blaché. Griffith would probably have disagreed with the anonymous *Saturday Evening Post* director about the merits of system and efficiency. Such a disparity, together with his idiosyncratic career, is in many ways the exception that proves the rule. With an unyielding creative integrity and an unwillingness to concede to supervision and organization, Griffith helped invent and sustain the idea of an artistically autonomous director. Though far from realized, this model of complete control and rule-defying creativity remained the coveted ideal.

Considering Griffith's ideology, it is somewhat ironic that Triangle, the hallmark of the silent auteur, was purchased in 1918 by producer-mogul Samuel Goldwyn. The latter incorporated its facilities with his own and went on to sell both to the Loew's Company in 1924. Under Loew's the lots became part of the Metro-Goldwyn-Mayer kingdom, which was commanded by the newly enthroned executive producer Irving Thalberg. Perhaps it is also not surprising that the careers of the company's original owners faded or, in Ince's case, abruptly ended as Hollywood entered the age of the producer.

Sadly, the new age also saw the fading of women from the directorial ranks. Shortly after World War I, female filmmakers all but disappeared. Only Lois Weber maintained a visible presence for a few more years. This was following what appeared to be an increase in women's cinematic power during the late 1910s, with stars such as Mary Pickford breaking free from their bosses and disseminating what one scholar termed a "her-own-company epidemic." As film companies began to identify progress with a "sound profit center," masculine codes of business and fraternal societies quickly redefined directing as work more suited for men.[40] Alas, the rise in efficient production also saw the decline of the capable woman director. For the remainder of the studio era, she was gone, and the director was practically always a he.

Alone on the Floor

It is hard to pinpoint the exact moment the director lost his absolute creative authority. As shown, one could suggest he never truly had it. Still, at least through the mid-1910s directors were responsible for most major decisions in the production process—they selected stories, locations, and players; hired staff members and equipment; and, most importantly, decided what and how to shoot. In this regard, the first significant signs of change occurred around 1914, when producers, efficiency experts, and standard production-line practices took charge of what up to that point had been the responsibility of the director and cameraman, leaving the latter only with orchestrating the "integration of production, and maintenance of production performance."[41] The age of the director was not entirely over. Between 1915 and the mid-1920s, most producers were "little more than glorified production managers," and, viewing the industry as a whole, "creative power was [still] concentrated in the hands of a relatively small group of filmmakers capable of conceiving, orchestrating, and executing specific projects."[42] This reign of creative aptitude persisted to some degree until the early 1930s, when the concept of authorial freedom had become a rarity around Hollywood.[43]

Nothing happened overnight. The penetration of organization, standardization, and division of labor into the American film industry is best thought of as a process. Attempts to insert systematization and efficiency began very early on in setups like Ince's. The struggles of Irving Thalberg and Erich von Stroheim on the Universal lot, and Thalberg's triumph during the production of *Merry-Go-Round* in 1922, served as one decisive moment in the assertion of the studio and head producer's authority over directors. Another such moment was the formation of MGM in 1924; the operation developed there by Thalberg and Mayer marked an important development toward greater concentration of power. Finally, a definitive and crucial change occurred following the introduction of sound and the onset of the Great Depression, when bankruptcies and receiverships brought big studios like Fox and Paramount under the control of Wall Street.[44] Heavily involved and invested in the film business, big banks and stockholders now had a considerable stake in transferring management from creative and often impulsive people to compliant and responsible executives. As one economist put it back in 1933, "The biggest production obstacle [is] the director.... Any man who is so unsure of what he is doing ... that he has to shoot 100,000 feet of film to be sure of 7,500 ... should be sent back to whatever he was doing before he began to infest the picture studios."[45]

So, after all that, what was the director left with? It depends on whom you asked, and on October 1, 1937, the National Labor Relations Board (NLRB) asked Henry King. This veteran director, who entered the film business in 1914 as an actor, testified in a hearing concerning the labor conditions of screenwriters. Cautioning that his testimony reflected only his own experience, King proceeded to describe the job of "a film director" in a Hollywood studio. "First," he explained, "our story, of course, is selected ... and it is submitted to him [the director] to read." Then, the director decides whether he feels "that he can make a picture that will justify the cost" for said story. If he deems it impossible, "why he immediately says so to the producer, and the producer then ... takes him off." Then "there is a conference called" with the writer, who gives his suggestions, and "if they [are] approved by the producer and the director ... the writer will add those to his story." Following the scriptwriting, "there is a breakdown made of the story by the different departments, the art department, the construction department, property department, paint department, location department," and so on, and "we have a budget meeting, at which the director sits at the corner of the table where he can see everyone, and there is generally sometimes 40 or 50 people that participate in those budgets meetings." The function of these meetings, according to King, was to enable the director to give "all of them the same viewpoint of what will be needed in the making of the picture."[46]

King offered an illustration that, possibly because he was testifying at a hearing, pertained to the production of a court scene. He claimed that each director would picture such a scene differently: "One man might visualize that he was going to do it with 100 people, another might visualize that he was going to do it with 10." In the breakdown conference, the director would say, for example, "We will use 20 people in the audience, four lawyers, and two for this and two for that, and we will have a clerk, a judge and so on. And he will enumerate those." As a result, the different departmental professionals will be able to estimate "what the cost will be fix[ed] against." The director will also declare "how important an actor you will have for each of those parts." The same goes for the way the courtroom is to look, that is, the furniture, props, and lighting. For those, "the art department submit their sketches, and [they] are approved by the director and the producer and the associate producer." Next is a conference on casting, "in which there will be the casting director, the producer, the associate producer, and the director, who will sit in, and each one will have made a list of suggestions." Here, King probably understood it was impossible to downplay the well-known dominance of the star system in determining casting; therefore he added, "So far . . . my experience has been that the people I have suggested I have always got—that is, if they are available."[47]

When preproduction is over, it is time to roll the camera. "On our starting day we start shooting," said the director of such pictures as *State Fair* (1933) and *The Song of Bernadette* (1943), not forgetting to add, "It is probably clear to everybody that each scene of the picture passes through the director's mind," and "naturally, everybody must see it in his way." King offered a convincing creative rationale for this authoritarianism: "Transferring [a story] from paper to the screen is just as individual in its undertaking as it is [to write a] story," and "you cannot have 16 different ideas in the scene." Filmmaking required one uniform creative vision. The director was the one who could supply this uniformity. Thus, the director's opinion trumps all. He can even change the script. Not big changes, but during the filming stage the director can alter "all things pertaining to dialogs or change of dialog, or minor things in writing that haven't any great structural change in them," since he "must be familiar enough with the story by that time." That said, admitted King, "If a new sequence were to be written, out of deference to the writer . . . they give it back to him to do that. Sometimes they call in another writer."[48]

On to postproduction. "When the picture is completed," explained King, "the director supervises with the cutter the putting of the picture together, getting it into the first cut." Actually, he begins this process while still "in production"—"each morning I run the rushes, and I cut the pick takes which, in my opinion, [are] the best." What makes them the best? "Various reasons—sometimes photography, sometimes for action, many little things we have to keep in mind." So, when shooting is over, "those pick takes are assembled, and when they are put together, then I run them with the cutter, and we eliminate, fit together tightly"—all so as to "develop and tell the story in its best, I mean to make it pictorial on the screen at its best." When the first cut is ready, the director "shows it to the producer" and "from then on the director and producer work together in whatever changes they make until the picture is in its final form."[49]

Judging by King's account, it appears that not much had been lost by way of directorial authority. His view, however, was nowhere near unanimous. Screenwriters, for example, painted a far less glorified picture. Philip Dunne remarked that this idea of the director "creating the film" was, simply put, "nonsense." As he remembered it, "in the assembly line days" at Fox, "the director was never assigned until [Darryl] Zanuck," the executive producer, "considered the script finished."[50] Fellow writer Nunnally Johnson exclaimed that directors "deserve little more credit, say, than the engineer who brings the Twentieth Century Limited [train] from Chicago to New York. There's very little he can do except stay on the track . . . He didn't create the track" and "had no choice about which way he was going."[51] Producers shared this misgiving about the exaggerated role of the director. Pandro Berman, who served as the executive producer of RKO and later worked at MGM, claimed that "under Mayer's system the stable of MGM directors which was rather extensive would be called in to make a picture two weeks before the production started," and "very often the director would be finished within six days or so after the picture finished."[52] That is, the director did not supervise editing.

Legendary executive producer David O. Selznick, who worked everywhere from Paramount to MGM and RKO, offered a similar account. "The director," he said in 1937, "operates differently in different studios." Speaking in front of a film-study group at Columbia University, he explained that at MGM, "for instance, the director, nine times out of ten, is strictly a director. . . . His job is solely to get out on the stage and direct the actors, put them through the paces that are called for in the script." At Warner Bros., the situation was even worse. There, said Selznick, "the director is purely a cog in the machine." He "is handed a script, usually just a few days before he goes into production." The filmmaker could not be more involved, since that would make it impossible for him to churn out the "five or six pictures a year" he was expected to complete. Seeking to differentiate his own budding independent company from such humdrum operations, whose methods, incidentally, were developed to a great extent by Selznick himself, the producer bragged that with him, the director "is on the script as far in advance as it is possible." He is there "in the story conference with me and the writers . . . and I always have my director in on the cutting." But, he added, "that is not obligatory . . . nor is it the custom in most of the larger studios."[53]

Perhaps it is only natural for writers and producers to play down the role of the director. Still, they were not alone. In 1939, Frank Capra, arguably the most successful director in the business, complained in an op-ed in the *New York Times* that in most cases, a practitioner like him is not guaranteed a right to "read the script he is going to do and to assemble the film in its first rough form for presentation to the head of the studio." There was no right to "final cut." Furthermore, he estimated that "80 per cent of the directors today shoot scenes exactly as they are told to shoot them without any changes whatsoever," and "90 per cent of them have no voice in the story or in the editing."[54]

Despite these complaints, it is hard to believe that King's outline was entirely false. After all, Capra had his own reasons to underplay the director's role. He was on a campaign to get the Screen Directors Guild recognized and probably used the op-ed as an opportunity to attract both attention and sympathy. It is also possible, as King suggested, that his own experience was exactly that—his own—and in that sense was unique and rather fortunate. For that matter, due to Capra's celebrity status at Columbia Pictures, his experience could not have been much different.[55] To be sure, King's account is exaggerated: the director did not command the entire production in such a way, he did not supervise budget or breakdown meetings, and neither the producer nor the head of the studio was a marginal character to be consulted with only on casting and after the final cut was complete. King's narrative presents, at most, a best-case scenario for a director, albeit one that was very atypical. A more mainstream experience was offered at the same NLRB hearing only twenty-four hours before King took the stand.

Benjamin B. Kahane was vice president of Columbia Pictures. A lawyer by training, Kahane was a member of the executive committee of the Keith-Albee-Orpheum Circuit, which, in 1928, became part of the RKO film company. After serving as the head of the company's studio for four years, he was invited by Harry Cohn to work under him at Columbia. As vice president, his responsibility was primarily to manage public relations, though due to his kindly nature Kahane also acted as father confessor to many employees following frequent disputes with the somewhat less avuncular president.[56] Summoned by the NLRB lawyers to explain "the problems that confront a producer in the making of a motion picture," this executive might have been in the best position to comment on day-to-day practices. Assuming a noncreative position, and testifying in a hearing about the role of writers, one could presume he did not have very much at stake while explaining the position of a studio director.

Beginning, again, at the preproduction stage, Kahane, when asked how the director is selected, responded that he "either happens to be under contract to the studio at the time or is engaged for the particular picture." As for his participation in the script writing, "Well, there is no rule about that," said the vice president; "sometimes the director is involved in the preparation of a screen play several weeks or several months before the final play is drafted. Sometimes he comes in when a first draft or even . . . final draft has been completed." If it is a "more important production," then "the director is concerned a little earlier and has considerable to do with the preparation of the screen play, collaborating with the writer." That said, Kahane emphasized, "The director always has a certain amount of preparation." How about casting? Did the director have complete charge of casting characters? "No," he responded. "I would say the selection of cast is the province of the producer. The director is consulted, but the producer has the decision." Kahane then went on to explain the details of the budget meeting; his description included the director only as an item on the expense list.

The vice president did not have much to say when it came to the shooting process itself. Kahane mentioned that the director must "work for carrying out the script, adding business." Asked to explain what "business" meant, he offered an illustration: "A director may have a scene with a man and a woman that are having a conversation. It is up to the director to determine where they will be placed, what they are to do, and [so] on. It may be that the man goes to take a drink, they may walk around . . . the things that each will occupy himself with while carrying on the dialog. That is the invention of the director." Kahane confirmed that if small dialogue changes are necessary, "most directors will take care of that." But here he added an important detail that King failed to mention. Although the director oversaw all the "business" while shooting, the producer did not simply wait on the sidelines. "Usually," he said, "each day after shooting has been completed the negative is developed . . . and a print is made." The following day "that print is projected . . . for the producer and executives in the company, so that they may view the work done the previous day." This viewing did not function merely as a rubber stamp; studio heads wanted "to see how your production is progressing, how the scenes are being played and what quality you are getting in photography and performance and scenes . . . that the script is being followed and that the script as written is right." If a problem was detected, such as "incorrect or improper" characterization, or if they thought the "lighting is bad," "the camera man is not getting the results expected," or "a performer is not giving the proper performance," then "the producer who had that opinion would discuss the matter with the director."[57]

Kahane's version brings the producer back in. While acknowledging the director's creative importance, the vice president reminded his listeners that in the picture business everyone had to answer to the head producer. Two other accounts from the late 1930s, this time by directors, both confirm this picture and add one more important element that seems to have been overlooked by King—cooperation. Describing his job to a lay audience, George Cukor wrote that, ideally, "the director makes his appearance very early on in the life story of a motion picture." That said, he added, in the "usual case he makes his entry when he is summoned by a producer." This director, who was responsible for such classics as *A Bill of Divorcement* (1932) and *The Philadelphia Story* (1940), chose to portray the production process as "a series of collaborations which go on . . . until the film is ready for showing." He described how, from the moment the producer hires him, the director spends his time in conferences with all the professionals the studio has to offer. In fact, "the essence of the directorial approach," according to Cukor, is "the art of knowing exactly how much to take from each of his collaborators." Throughout, the director "must constantly select and reject, extract, modify, repulse and refine a continuous output of suggestion[s]."[58]

John Cromwell, who directed *Of Human Bondage* (1934), among many other films, saw it much the same way. With regard to the script, he claimed back in 1938, "The director adds only enough interpolations of his own to give the story the fluidity a screen story must have." Otherwise, "it must be conceived and formulated by the writer and the director as a complete entity." When it comes to sets, lighting, and camera angles, he wrote, "the greatest danger to avoid is any set or predetermined ideas . . . which are not amenable to suggestions from the author, the art director or the cameraman." About casting: "His star or stars have already been chosen by the producer. He must accept or reject the casting director's final choice of players." Finally, on the topic of budget, he explained: "A director should be able to determine what it would cost to shoot successfully the story agreed upon," but "of course the production manager supervises the various details," including "the estimates of all departments involved."[59]

Consolidating all these versions, the director in the golden age of the Hollywood studios emerges as what might be termed a contingent auteur, one whose authority rests on "institutional constraint." Directors in the studio system enjoyed both creative freedom and artistic control, but those were sanctioned by the studio and conditioned on cooperation with and acceptance of its "fusion of resources, personnel, management style, and market strategy."[60] For the most part, the final word belonged to the head producer, who could defer to the director on matters of artistry. During the preparatory and editing stages, the frequency of such surrenders varied and depended on the status of the director, the temperament of the producer, and the nature of their relationship. In between pre- and postproduction, this balance of power was interrupted. As all accounts seem to imply, when it came time to start shooting, producers not only deferred; they capitulated.

The expensive nature of resources, particularly during shooting, called for the director to be alone "on the floor." Studios wanted their product to have quality while staying within budget, and to achieve these goals, following a rigorous preparation process, a skillful director had to be given some autonomy. At least, this is how most studio heads saw it. Executive producers such as Thalberg, Selznick, and Zanuck rarely went on set, and as the latter was reported to have said, "On the set the director has 90 percent control. You may be able to persuade him to do this or that, but only within 10 percent. The rest of it, he's going to do it." Even screenwriters admitted that "once the picture is on the set and the director's in charge . . . the producer has no control. . . . It's in the hands of the director."[61] Kahane's testimony supports this view, as he claimed that "the business" of "carrying out the script" is "the invention of the director on the set."[62] Considering the towering position of head producers, it is reasonable to assume that this autonomy was not preordained; it was expedient. To Selznick again, nothing was "obligatory" when it came to studio practice. However, it appears that leaving directors to their own devices made the most economic and creative sense.

The failure to divide the directorial labor was not for lack of trying. Irving Rapper, who came to Hollywood after a directing career on Broadway, mentioned that he "first arrived at the studio to become a dialog director."[63] Indeed, he received such credit in over twenty titles, including *The Life of Emile Zola* (1937) and *High Sierra* (1941). Cukor, who occupied this position as well, said that "there were no specified duties" for dialogue directors.[64] He claimed that "what happened [was] the talkies came in and the movie world split in two." Since many of the established directors did not know how to handle sound, "they invited . . . as many stage directors as they could get to come out here . . . and the movie directors would tend to the movie part and the dialogue director was supposed to coach or listen to the dialogue."[65] Overall, Cukor held several halfway positions until he finally simply "directed" *Tarnished Lady* in 1931. Prior to that he "co-directed, and that was also—that was even more tricky, because there were two men." Theoretically, the work was to be divided so that "one ostensibly took care of the visual part of it and the other the acting part." These jobs, or what Cukor termed the "peculiar positions they had in those days," testify that the autonomy accorded to the director on the set was not taken for granted.[66] In the same way that big companies divided the work of screenwriters into suggestions, continuities, dialogue, and gags, there were probably similar attempts to split up the directing profession. The fading of these by-roles suggests that something stood in the way of division and systematization.

Cooperation and supervision were the essence of efficient filmmaking, but they were hard to implement while the cameras were rolling. Cukor managed to capture the importance of preproduction quite clearly, claiming that "when the time comes for a scene to be shot," the director "ought to have a very clear idea of what [he wants] to achieve." To elaborate: "In the modern studio there is no room for inefficiency, for anything but clean-cut, fool-proof preparations. If your cameraman has not been given a chance to see the designs for the settings, you may find that a beautifully built scene simply cannot be lit to advantage, nor action in it photographed properly. If a discovery like that is not made until the picture is actually in-production, the waste of time and money is enormous."[67] These remarks, made in 1937, echo the anonymous *Saturday Evening Post* director who in 1916 claimed that organization "speeded up" his work. Yet, without making a value judgment praising the system, Cukor's description underlines a simple matter of fact: by the time the director was sitting in his black canvas chair with his name printed on it and yelling orders into a megaphone, there was no room for any more consultations, because any delay was very expensive.

If we compare filmmaking to war-making, picture shooting is like actual shooting. It is D-day. Almost everything that had to do with moviemaking was expensive: cameras, sets, lighting, salaries—in particular those of stars—and raw film. If you were a major studio producing anywhere between forty and seventy films per year, then your expenses were very high, and you did what you could to contain them. One way to cut spending was to limit the usage of valuables, that is, of actors, specifically loaned or freelance actors, and film. Preparing a detailed shooting script, scheduling multiple conferences about sets, and endless discussions about lighting and camera angles were conducive to creativity, of course, but these preparations also assured that when Clark Gable or Greta Garbo came on set, he or she was not being paid to idle around the set while the director and the producer argued about a line in the dialogue.[68] As one assistant director put it, "Artistry, in this day and age, is not by any means a cheap commodity: it demands time, time is money, and production costs mount with amazing rapidity."[69]

Another expensive commodity was film. Raw film, film stock, or the material from which one produces the negative of the picture, was a whole technological field with its own innovations and competition. To begin with, very few companies produced raw film, and the few that did, including Eastman Kodak in the United States, Pathé and Dupont in France, and Agfa in Germany, often had preferential trading agreements in their countries. In addition, printing, that is, the development of a negative into a positive or "processed shot"—the one that is eventually screened in theaters—was also a costly procedure.[70] Lack of planning or disagreement on the set could cause a waste of film, as takes and scenes had to be shot multiple times to cover all available options and opinions until a consensus was reached.

Whether it was due to wasted time or film, the cost of an inefficient set was definitely enormous. Take the case of *For Whom the Bell Tolls*, produced by Paramount between 1940 and 1942. The original budget had an estimated cost of $2,149,000. It included $150,000 for the rights to Ernest Hemingway's story, $78,375 for the three writers who worked on the script, $79,157 for director Sam Wood, and $283,437 for cast fees, including Gary Cooper and Ingrid Bergman in the lead roles. The cost was fixed to an estimate of 60 shooting days. In reality, however, production lasted 125 days, and reports from the sets that were erected in Blue Canyon, Relief Canyon, and the Sierra Nevada often listed delays due to "slow progress," "weather conditions," and "difficult locations." As a result, the eventual cost of the movie was $2,986,231, $837,231 above the original budget. It is interesting to note that the most expensive items in the "over budget" column included a cast fee that inflated costs by $195,226, location and living expenses that required an additional $90,000, raw film that cost $42,957 on top of the $89,853 specified in the original budget, and finally Wood's own paycheck, which was boosted by a sizable $32,793.[71]

To prevent such misuse of time, money, and film required skill. What made a skillful director? Assistant director Robert Edward Lee suggested the following considerations: "Can he shoot out of continuity . . . and still get a good picture? Can he jump all over the script, a portion of one sequence here followed by another there, and when the finished product is shown on the screen will it be good box office?"[72] The filming process was designed for efficiency, and as a result it was often chaotic. The schedule was set to assure cost-effectiveness, and scenes were grouped according to location or the actors who performed in them. Players often came on set just for a few days, and the studio did not wish to call them back for another paycheck.[73] The time a company had on a studio lot stage or off-studio location was also expensive, and therefore limited. A skillful director had to know how to work within these limitations. To do that, he had to know what he wanted and how to verbalize his wishes so that actors, cameramen, and other crew members would understand. He had to know how to shoot everything that was necessary without being superfluous. He had to do all that fast while keeping the final product coherent, appealing, and preferably also profitable. As one producer put it, a director had to "pull together the work of others" to make a film that is a "synthesis" but not "synthetic."[74]

This was not an easy task, and indeed there were not that many skillful directors. In the study he conducted of the industry, Leo C. Rosten found that in 1938 there were 244 active directors in Hollywood. That might sound like a considerable number, but it pales in comparison to the 800 writers he counted and the 1,753 class A actors who were members of the Screen Actors Guild at the same time.[75] Taking into account that 769 pictures were released throughout that year, it appears that when it came to running the set, studios no longer trusted simply anybody.[76] In order to be worthy of autonomy, a director had to prove that he had the necessary skill to either bring the movie in within budget or bring in profits that would make up for the cost overrun. He had to demonstrate a creative side as well as a conformist one, a balance that could be maintained only by understanding the circumstances of his industrial position. Acquiring such skill was not a straightforward mission; it was built up slowly, through creative experimentation and institutional negotiations. Maintaining the skill, as well as the autonomy it bestowed, required a continuous, career-long, daily practice.

Willy, I Would Be Grateful for Your Consideration . . .

The career of William Wyler is a fine example of such workplace acumen. He spent his first ten years in Hollywood learning the profession as an in-house director at Universal. In 1935, he started a long-term engagement with independent producer Samuel Goldwyn that lasted until 1946. During the more than a decade he spent with Goldwyn, Wyler experienced more freedom. His contract allowed him to take outside projects with other studios. The same contract also allowed his boss to loan him out, and, together, these two features enabled the director to experience production operations at three of the majors—Warner Bros., Twentieth Century–Fox, and MGM.[77] Following World War II, Wyler, along with directors Frank Capra and George Stevens and producer Samuel Briskin, formed an independent production company called Liberty Films. The company did not fare well on its own and, in 1948, was sold to Paramount.[78] Thus, Wyler's interaction with his various superiors presents an excellent case study through which to examine the workplace experience of a studio director.

Like many others in Hollywood, William Wyler got his break from Carl Laemmle. The head of Universal was a relative, his mother's cousin, to be exact, and when Wyler was eighteen, Laemmle offered him a job in his film company in New York. William, whose given name was actually Willi, was born in Alsace in 1902. He came to America in 1920, following his uncle Carl's proposition, which was presented shortly after the two had met for the first time in Zurich. "I owe everything to him," Wyler commented in a eulogy for Laemmle. "He brought me to this country . . . and started me at $20 a week" working in the mailroom, "from which he deducted $5 in repayment of my passage. . . . He was both generous and shrewd."[79] As Universal had operations on both coasts, Wyler made his way to California, where he worked as a production assistant until 1925. Then he was given a chance to direct when the director he was assisting, Arthur Rosson, got an offer from Paramount and walked out in the middle of production. The movie was a two-reeler titled *Underworld*, and Wyler asked permission from his uncle to take over the production. The answer was yes, which made the newest and youngest director on the Universal lot very excited. He wrote to thank Laemmle, saying, "I feel surer of myself this time than in anything

I have ever attempted . . . because I frankly believe that I have the material within me to develop some day into one of your best commercial directors."[80]

It was not unusual for a director to be foreign born. Rosten estimated that by the late 1930s, 28.7 percent of directors operating in Hollywood were born outside the United States. The main reason was that, particularly after World War I, directors, like many others in the film business, "found a readier market in Hollywood for their experience and skill."[81] Or, in other words, the American industry had more buying power. As Dwan recalled, "There wasn't too much we got from [foreign films]—except the people who made them: we got them, all of them. The minute a fellow would make a picture, somebody would send for him right away."[82] Always in search of reliable filmmakers, it is not surprising that the studios tapped all available resources for directors who had proved their creative, practical, and commercial ability—especially since, unlike acting or writing, directing did not require a high proficiency in the English language. And so they came: Mack Sennett hired Chaplin in the early 1910s, Ernst Lubitsch was brought over by Mary Pickford in 1922, and MGM summoned Fritz Lang. The rise of Nazism inspired another wave of German migration to Hollywood, including directors like Billy Wilder and Robert Siodmak, and right before the war Selznick sent for England's finest, Alfred Hitchcock.

Wyler was not hired due to his foreign success, but as a Jewish immigrant with a German accent he fitted right in. Exactly because he was not a well-known superstar when he came to Hollywood, his career is useful in demonstrating the development of a true studio-made auteur. Though it is hard to talk about a typical career trajectory when it comes to film directors, Wyler's progress, from two-reel westerns to prestige high-budget features, offers a glance into various modes of directorial practice, beginning with remuneration.

Studio directors made a lot of money. As Rosten's study uncovered, "The amount of money paid to movie directors is a potent testimonial to the importance which the motion picture industry attaches to their talents."[83] Like their fellows in other branches of filmmaking, most directors were under contract to a studio that engaged them for periods ranging between the time it took to produce one film and seven years. In most cases, contracts included an "option" clause, which enabled the studio, and only the studio, to cancel the contract at the end of every year. Wyler's first director's contract with Universal in 1927, for example, was for five years with a weekly salary of $250 and a studio "option" coming every six months.

However, each time Universal decided to pick up the option and keep him, Wyler's wage per week was to increase by $50.[84] This was a modest income in movie business terms, probably fitting for an unknown beginner. A confidential Universal memo from 1926 that lists the market value of "the most important directors" suggests that established professionals made between $1,000 and $2,500 weekly, with some, like Dwan and King, making $50,000 per film. The most expensive directors on the list were Stroheim, who earned $100,000 for his services, and Lubitsch, who received $175,000.[85]

Skill, that is, experience and success, increased one's value. In 1931, after Wyler had completed several nonwestern feature films, including *Hell's Heroes*, a very profitable talkie from 1929, his salary "leaped to seven hundred fifty dollars a week."[86] Three years later, following the release of *A House Divided* (1931) and *Counsellor-at-Law* (1933), the director reported to his brother that he had "finally signed a new contract with Universal," allowing for "$1125.00 per week with [a] forty-two week guarantee" and yearly options that "run as follows: $1375; $1550; $1750; $2250." If he was to be laid off for the remaining ten weeks, he had "the privilege of making one picture in Europe each year." Wyler was pleased, writing, "I can feel very content and satisfied with this agreement. Very few companies are handing out yearly contracts these days and free lancing, that is, going from studio to studio for one or two pictures is only good for a few big directors."[87] Though still not one of Hollywood's top earners, Wyler had moved up. The fact that he was guaranteed employment for only forty-two weeks was nothing out of the ordinary, as was the fact that during his layoff period he was still under Universal's control. Signing a studio contract implied many personal limitations, however, as Wyler indicated; at least until the late 1930s, very few directors, and for that matter few writers and actors, were successful enough to afford the uncertain path of freelancing, and given the option, most chose to avoid it. Even Capra, who was the most profitable director in the business, was committed to Columbia.[88]

How did one acquire the necessary skill to land a contract? Judging by Wyler's career, the answer seems to be a mixture of gift, audacity, and the ability to adapt these to studio needs. A director was guaranteed employment if he could produce consistent box office success. But of course, no one knew exactly how to do that. When a director had a track record one could assess his chances of producing cost-effective pictures. In the case of a new director, however, all a studio had to work with was potential. Wyler had potential. After completing one of his first feature-length pictures, *The Shakedown* (1929), a series of inside-studio reviewers sent their favorable impressions, including one who wrote, "Excellent picture. Fine ending. Good suspense. Great Fight. Action and drama all the way. Think Willie Wyler deserves a good break after this one. Certainly seems to show high percentage of intelligence in his direction."[89]

Laemmle thought so too, and he hoped he could mold this intelligence to Universal's benefit. In 1932, he wrote to Wyler, saying, "You have demonstrated that you know how to make excellent pictures but, unfortunately we have not made money on them." Uncle Carl was not giving up; he was simply trying to enhance his young relative's business consciousness: "You are smart and observing enough to see that there is always a good future for a fine commercial director, while the day of the other kind is gone forever." The head executive was responding to the director's request to be assigned a new project titled *Laughing Boy*. Perhaps due to their familial ties, Laemmle tried the following manipulation: "If you can make [the picture] in such a way as to let us get by with even a small profit, I will be the happiest man in the world because it will not only justify my faith in you as a director but as a commercial success as well."[90]

Cultivating a new director was not an easy matter, and it proved especially difficult with Wyler. At some point, producer Henry Henigson complained to Laemmle that "personally" he thought "the business of 'building directors' is an expensive method of procedure." If it were up to him, he wrote, "I would rather let the other fellow put them into school and then take them after they have had their schooling."[91] However, if the process was fruitful, the studio was likely to find itself with exclusive rights to a top-grossing director who usually had several years left in the draconian contract he signed when he was nobody, making him quite a valuable commodity. To achieve this result, the company had to teach the director how to work for it, a process that often required exactly what Laemmle employed in his letter—patience and negotiation.

As mentioned, once the director was released to the set, he was in control, therefore the main goal was to imprint the notion beforehand that it was worthwhile for a director to be cost-effective. He needed to understand that despite his creative autonomy while shooting, the studio still had the final word with regard to both the movie and the career of its maker. Movie companies wanted their directors to understand that their autonomy, while respected, had clear limits. They wanted them to know that, as George Cukor once put it, "there were certain things a fait accompli."[92]

The easiest place to assert studio authority was during the preproduction phase. While taking into consideration the director's will, studio heads carefully maintained their authority to decide which projects were to be made, by whom, and with how much. In April 1928, producer William Lord Wright informed Wyler: "I am handing you herewith the first four continuities [for] the Laemmle Novelties idea. Please read these carefully then come in and see me." These Novelties, conceived by the head of the company, were very particular in nature: "We will try to [do] a $750 estimate on a four-day shooting schedule [and] we have only 700 feet top of negative that we can get into this product for they are one-reelers." Wright wanted the director to cooperate with the writer of the scripts, but emphasized that "we must have any changes, which you and [the writer] may decide on . . . on paper and an estimate taken before we go in[to] production." To drive the point home, the executive added, "This is only business and in conformance with Mr. Laemmle['s] . . . ideas of combining art with commercialism."[93]

Wyler was not excited about this assignment. He wrote back, saying, "Although having much faith in the general idea of Laemmle Novelties . . . I wish to register my opinion that the subjects as written are without cleverness. . . . Being assigned to make these, I will naturally do my best, though regretting an honest lack of enthusiasm."[94] In studio terms, that sounded like a threat or at least a challenge. To reaffirm the hierarchy, Wright shot back that same day: "I do not think it is up to you or me to decide what product the organization should make, but it is up to us to be good soldiers and go ahead and try to make as good product as we can, and with the common sense idea of conserving Mr. Laemmle's money." He instructed Wyler to keep on working on the Novelties and to leave "the policy of the class of material we are to make [to] be set by those who carry this responsibility and authority."[95] The young director's autonomy was not extended to story material.

Even ten years later, when Wyler was already a well-known director, the chain of command was not much different. In 1938, he already had several commercial successes behind him, including *Dodsworth*, which he had made two years earlier. As a result, while no longer working for Laemmle, he had a more lenient contract, which, the director himself recalled, included a clause "whereby . . . after each film I did for Sam Goldwyn, I had the right to do one elsewhere."[96] Then he was "simply asked by Hal Wallis, who was in charge of [Warner Bros.] at the time," to direct Bette Davis in *Jezebel*. "The script was submitted to me, and it was already a finished script," said

Wyler. He added, "If I hadn't liked the story I wouldn't have done it."[97] That was only because he was working out of contract. When, in 1940, Wyler refused one of Goldwyn's suggestions, the latter "in accordance with contract . . . deemed [Wyler] suspended for a period of 16 weeks."[98] In almost all cases, the studio chose the story for the director. As a freelancer, the filmmaker had a right to say no. Under contract, even that liberty had a price.

Studio executives were not necessarily out to get their directors; they simply had broader concerns. While a director like Wyler was worried about his own career and the specific movie he was working on, people like Laemmle and Goldwyn were trying to coordinate a yearly program of features and a whole stock company of employees. When, in 1939, Jack Warner decided to "switch assignments" and have Anatole Litvak "do *Twenty Thousand Years in Sing Sing* . . . with Raoul Walsh doing *World Moves On*," it was because the former was "getting nowhere" with his original assignment, and not because of a grudge Warner held against the director.[99] Furthermore, unless something conflicted with studio interests, in most cases head producers attempted to satisfy their directors. When, in 1944, Michael Curtiz told Warner he "would be truly grateful if you could assign me to something else until such time when *God Is My Co-Pilot* is re-modeled into the script we all hope it eventually will be," his request was granted.[100] Similarly, even back in 1931, if Wyler felt strongly against something, such as directing a Tom Mix western, Universal tried to reach an agreement with him. In this case, it was decided he would "direct and have the choice of stories available for the first Tom Mix picture"; however, "at [Wyler's] opinion, [his] name will be left off the screen this particular picture." In addition, Wyler was guaranteed "that the company will not ask [him] to direct any other picture of this series," and that he would "definitely [be] assigned to direct the new Lew Ayres picture."[101] It was a give-and-take relationship with the power scale tipped in favor of the studio.

When preproduction ended, however, the balance was shifted. Head producers and executives were now at the mercy of the director. During production, there was very little a producer could do to manage the way a picture was shot. The director was in charge, and it was up to him to decide how much time to spend on rehearsals, what angles to shoot a scene from, and how many takes to shoot until he got the right one. To be sure, studio executives never left their filmmakers completely alone. They had spies in the form of production assistants, line producers, and script clerks. Over at Warner Bros., for example, Wallis was keeping in close touch with ongoing productions even when he was on vacation. In 1942, while abroad, he kept receiving daily reports such as this: "I have spoken to assistants and briefly to Hawks, Shumlin and Curtiz, and they all say everything is going along smoothly and well."[102] Sometimes the news was not so encouraging. In October 1941, an assistant to the production of *King's Row* sent the following memo:

> Yesterday, Monday, this company was called for 9:00 A.M. shooting on Stage 14, had their first shot at 9:10 and finished shooting at 6:00 P.M. last night.
>
> This company shot 5 script scenes.... This will be 23 days over the schedule and very considerably over the budget. Considering the broken manner in which this show has been shot as regarding sets, cast, etc., I only hope it fits together right. I have never seen a picture shot in such a hurried manner as this picture had been made. Most of these circumstances were beyond our control and the insistence of Mr. Wood that we have Robert Cummings play the lead in this picture.[103]

Such reports, which were all too common, spelled out very expensive delays, but even in these cases, executive producers could not do much except plead, or, sometimes, resort to begging.

Wyler was a master of delay, mostly because he was infamous for shooting every take multiple times, earning such nicknames as "Once More Wyler." He saw it a bit differently. "It's true that in some cases" he shot scenes "too many times over and over." But, he claimed, "I do [it] until I get it the way I want it . . . there's always a purpose behind it and a reason for doing it over."[104] The various studios he worked for quite obviously respected his creative sensibilities, as they kept hiring him. Yet, whether it was with Universal, Goldwyn, or Warner Bros., producers kept trying to rein him in. This audacious director revealed his penchant for extravagance very early on. As early as 1927, his uncle wrote to him, observing: "You have only shot 73 scenes so far on your picture, spending $46,000.00[.] Therefore you have only $45,000.00 more to spend and still have 256 scenes to shoot." There was still hope for the young director, and so Laemmle emphasized, "Willie, don't forget you are on trial now.... Please, for your own sake more than for the company's sake, do your darndest to bring this picture in on estimate and still give us a good production."[105] Thus began the miseducation of William Wyler.

A couple of months later, while shooting *The Shakedown*, production was behind schedule once again. "Willie, I must impress upon you the necessity of making these pictures . . . for sixty thousand dollars," his producer wrote. "If you cooperate with me on this picture," he pleaded, "I promise to do my utmost on the next picture you make, and obtain permission to give you a little more leeway."[106] Such promises were rather useless, as Wyler was fairly comfortable taking his own leeway. Sometimes he would change the script while shooting, triggering a request from Laemmle "to have such changes as you may desire to make, submitted to this office for my approval before shooting."[107] Other times, Wyler would be careless with film: "At the termination of each scene it is important that you arrange with your staff to call a signal, preferably the word 'cut' . . . thus saving the film which is being unnecessarily exposed."[108] Nevertheless, even the mild sarcasm did not help. Nearly a decade later, executives were still "astounded to note that you took one scene 14 times and of these takes 10 of them were complete ones, approximately 1'35" long. The cost of the film alone for these takes is a big sum." They were still trying to convince Wyler that he was "a very good director and no one can tell me you can't make a scene in at least 2 to 4 takes top and print the one you really know is right."[109] And they were still begging: "I must ask you again to co-operate with us as you know we cannot spend the time on this picture. . . . Willy, I would be grateful for your consideration."[110]

One reason for this repeated ceremony of entreaties was that, as wasteful as a director could be, it was more expensive to replace him. When a film changed directors, everything almost always had to be done over. Take the case of *The Wizard of Oz* (1939). "Dick Thorpe started it," remembered producer Mervyn LeRoy, but he "just didn't have the feeling of the [picture]." Then "George [Cukor] started it too, and George is a great director . . . but he wasn't happy in what he was doing, so we got Victor Fleming." It was not really anybody's fault; "they were all honest." Nevertheless, "everything that George shot or Dick shot was not in the picture at all."[111] Cukor himself experienced a similar problem in 1932, when he worked with Lubitsch on *One Hour with You*. He was asked to take over the direction duties until the latter finished another picture he was involved with. When the German master returned, he discarded most of the work already done. The problem, as Cukor saw it, was that though he "directed quite a lot . . . it didn't have the style of Lubitsch"; despite "the best intentions in the world, I was not Lubitsch, and I could not shoot a Lubitsch picture."[112] The making of a motion picture, it appears, required a coherent vision. In practical terms, that meant that once shooting started, it might be cheaper to contend with an inefficient director than to make a switch.

All of these troubles ended as soon as the shooting process was over. As Capra mentioned in his 1939 op-ed, Hollywood filmmakers did not have the right to compose the final cut of their picture. Though they were often involved in the editing process, the decision on what takes to use and in what order, or, in other words, on how the movie would appear to the paying audience, belonged ultimately to the studio and its head producer. During postproduction it was once again the director's turn to beg. "You have given instructions to have the 'E' sequence cut without consulting me or giving me the benefit to see the sequence assembled and instructing the cutter," Wyler wrote to his producer in 1933. This correspondence came following the filming of *Her First Mate*, and the director felt that the "result is very unfortunate and the first half of 'E' sequence . . . is very disappointing and . . . almost unrecognizable, for it has lost its effectiveness." He wanted to "recut scenes in the manner [he] visualized," an operation he considered "an important part of [his] work." That said, he acknowledged, "I fully realize, that you [the producer] are in full jurisdiction over the production of this picture and would like to know how you stand in the manner."[113]

In the same way executives attempted to appeal to their directors' commercial sense, the latter seem to have phrased their pleas in creative terms. Later in 1933, Wyler was producing *Counsellor-at-Law*. While viewing the edited version of his footage, he noticed the deletion of one line—"Tell him to go to hell"—from the last reel. He wrote to Laemmle Jr., Carl's son, who took over the studio in the late 1920s, "respectfully calling [his] attention to the fact that the deletion . . . is extremely damaging to the picture." This was "not because of the humor of the particular line, but because with the deletion the climax of the picture remains unrelieved and we eliminate the only bit of comedy relief in the ending of the picture." The director believed that the line "was absolutely necessary, in order to obtain the proper change of mood from any audience for the ending of the picture to [include this] piece of comedy relief."[114] Since the line does not appear in the film, one could assume that with most executives the use of creative jargon had about the same effect as using commercial language to speed up directors.

WYLER WAS NOT in full control over the films he directed, but neither were the moguls who hired him.[115] It was more complicated than that. Like his fellow directors, Wyler was a competent practitioner working in a system that rewarded his particular skills, since those were helpful in tackling the uncertainty embedded in the entertainment market. Making movies in this studio system, which attempted to limit his independence, the director constantly searched for ways to assert his control. He was working within the boundaries while constantly checking them. Ultimately, he internalized the rules of the game and demonstrated enough conformity to the system. Wyler once even chastised another director for being too slow. "It really is incredible to think of the time you have taken to make your picture," he wrote this starting filmmaker, who happened to be his brother; "no matter how good it may be, it is too much time to take nowadays."[116] A system-made artist who learned to operate in the space created between his vision, the vision of fellow practitioners, studio resources, and studio demands, Wyler embraced the everyday negotiations in his craft, as did most of his contemporaries. They learned how to direct motion pictures for a profit and to direct their own careers according to the intricacies of their workplace and industry. Successful directors understood the system; they knew how and when to behave like artists as well as how and when to behave like conscientious employees. Thus, they helped define their profession as a semiautonomous labor, serving art and company.

CHAPTER FOUR

Acting

Margaret Mitchell was a little troubled. It was October 1936, and she had recently published her first novel, *Gone with the Wind*. It was an instant sensation. Her debut was so successful that the book sold 176,000 copies, at three dollars a copy, in just one month. These figures spurred interest in Hollywood, and recently she had sold the picture rights to the book for an unprecedented sum of $50,000 to producer David O. Selznick.[1] Of course, it was not her career she was troubled about. It was Clark Gable. "Life has been awful since I sold the movie rights!" she wrote to one of Selznick's representatives. "I am deluged with letters demanding that I do not put Clark Gable in as Rhett. Strangers telephone me or grab me on the street, insisting that Katharine Hepburn will never do." As much as she tried to explain that "it is Mr. Selznick and not [her] who is producing this picture," Mitchell was still caught in the casting commotion, a fact that prompted her to plead, "I wish to goodness you all would announce the cast and relieve me of this burden!"[2]

Selznick knew casting would be an issue. In fact, he almost passed on *Gone with the Wind* because of it. "I do feel that [the book's] only important showmanship values would be in either such star casting or in a tremendous sale of the book," he wrote to his story editor in May 1936. His independent film company, Selznick International, was established only a year prior, and though he was a successful and respectable producer, his operation was much smaller in comparison to studios such as Warner Bros. and MGM. He thought that one of those "larger companies can afford [to] buy it now in the hope or expectation of such casting opportunities and such a sale, but I do not feel we can take such a gamble."[3] His reservations were not unfounded. The American people wanted to see Gable play Rhett Butler; there was no way around it. Gable was under contract to MGM; there was no way around that either. "L. B. [Mayer] called me today to suggest that they would be interested in buying 'Gone with the Wind' together with my services as a producer," Selznick wired his company's chairman. "I believe an announcement would be accepted that we had made [the] deal because of my feeling that the public demanded Gable and we could have him in the film in no other way."[4] Ultimately, the rights to the book did not change hands, but the price paid for the star was high. Selznick agreed to distribute the picture through MGM and cut it some of the profits. Since he already had a distribution deal with United Artists, it also meant he had to postpone production until that agreement expired.[5]

Clark Gable was also troubled. He did not want to play Rhett. He thought that the role did not fit him, and complained to Metro's story editor that "it's the first time that the girl isn't sure that she wants me from the minute she sets eyes on me." Nevertheless, Gable found himself "trapped" by what he considered a "series of circumstances over which I had no control." Even though he was a Hollywood star, one that this particular movie could not do without, his contract with MGM—as was the case with most other actors in the studio system—did not accord him the right to turn down roles. If he refused to play Rhett, he risked being suspended without pay for the entire duration of production. Whether it was due to the financial strains caused by his ongoing divorce, the rumored bonus of $50,000 promised to him by Mayer, or both, Gable conceded. "It was a funny feeling," he commented years later. "I think I know now how a fly must react after being caught in a spider's web."[6]

Of course, one does not need to feel very sorry for Gable; there are worse things that could happen to an actor than being forced to appear in *Gone with the Wind*. However, his situation does bring out the irony embedded in the practice of film acting. While certain stars became as or even more important than the picture product itself, in the daily reality of the industry, despite their value, those same stars possessed very little control over their careers. If a studio felt that the success of a picture required Gable, Gable was required to be in the picture.

In this sense, Hollywood movie stars occupied an interesting position within the system: they were both regimented employees and precious commodities. In reality, that meant that the studios had two seemingly conflicting goals: to enhance players' value and standardize their employment. They had to find a way to make a player like Gable a unique product, one that theaters would pay a high price to screen, while at the same time making sure his independent value did not exceed that of the company itself, so that he would not be able to work outside of it or against its needs. The method they employed included a combination of big salaries, highly strict and demanding contracts, and paternalist care for screen players' creative development. Hollywood studios signed actors to long, exclusive commitments in which they had little or no control over their craft. They could not choose the parts they played. In return, the studios compensated the players generously and developed a network of professionals whose role it was to create box office stars and maintain their success. Creating and maintaining stars was a serious effort that included selecting good stories and diverse roles; investing in wardrobes, makeup, and lighting; and supervising publicity. It was a creative endeavor.

Union of Role and Person

Commodification, in the Marxist sense, was not unique to the acting profession. As in most other modern industries, the labor of motion picture craftsmen such as directors or writers was valued according to its contribution to production and based on its usefulness to the system. In line with the traditional theoretical model, these crafts were subjected to an ignoble division of labor and alienation from the film product. As employees, that is, as screen performers, actors experienced the same treatment. First, the acting profession was divided into extras, bit players, supporting players, and leading players. Second, the lower ranks of this division, or almost anyone below the "supporting" level, fit the definition of what labor historians call "common laborers": they had "the most elementary form of wage dependence," whereby they exchanged what were regarded as simple services for a daily wage.[7] Finally, at all levels, performers did not own the films they participated in or have any meaningful control over the formation of the motion picture.

For those in the highest rank of players, however, there was an additional and different form of commodification at play. In the case of stars such as Gable or Hepburn, they themselves, not only their labor, became an object of commerce. They as people were the marketable product. This actor-as-commodity function was different from commodified labor, since while the value of acting—the labor—was limited to exchange within the production process, the value of the actor—the persona—did not matter much in terms of actual work, but it did impact the distribution and exhibition of motion pictures. The work of screenwriters, for example, had an exchange value only inside the Hollywood studios; the presence of Gable in a picture, however, carried an external value to owners of theaters and audiences. The American film industry had already begun exploiting the popularity of screen actors to sell tickets at the box office in the early 1910s. This dependency on the star system has only intensified since then and is still apparent today. Specifically, until the late 1940s, by casting popular players in pictures, the companies that held them under contract could increase the rental fees of their productions and their percentage from box office receipts. To be sure, such casting did not necessarily facilitate or improve the quality or efficiency of the production process itself. The fact that the actors were stars was utterly unimportant to the filming process. Rather, it helped create the market for the films. For, just like the motion picture itself, stars were on sale.

At first glance, the cult of personality surrounding film stars might even seem contrary to Marxist critique. After all, as opposed to the classical assumption that labor under capitalism is reduced to a state of "depersonalized objectivity," the film star, by contrast, "stands as the resplendent, full center of a personalized teleology, a place where the distinction between role and person is meaningless."[8] In addition, while due to their employment contracts, the actors' labor and image were supposedly under the "legal ownership" of the studios, because actors were physically and endemically linked to their persona, each one of them was by implication the "ultimate possessor" of his or her own image.[9] Furthermore, the role accorded to famous players in stabilizing the market and decreasing uncertainty would suggest that they held a unique position of power within the industrial structure. To the contrary, despite this unique union of role and person and their advantageous market position, at least during the years of the oligopolistic Hollywood studio system, between the early 1920s and the early 1950s, movie stars did not escape the standardization of their profession.

The reasons were twofold. First, the oligopoly of the big picture companies, which controlled the industry via vertical integration, stripped the market of any real alternative employment options. Or, in other words, if one wanted to become or remain a movie star, one had to work in Hollywood under the terms of the major companies. Second, as it embraced the star system, the American motion picture industry also developed a managerial method to handle the human product. It found a way to partially separate the person from the star by signing a contract with the person and harnessing the star persona to the studio operation. Understanding the challenge star power might present to their economic control, these same Hollywood producers and executives developed a system of dual treatment by which actors' encompassing employment conditions correlated to their place in a standardized workforce, while their salaries and day-to-day management correlated to their commodity status. Players' contracts, whether they were stars, potential stars, or supporting actors, restricted them as employees and put them under the complete control of the studios. At the same time, studios paid their stars exorbitant sums and created a network of support whose role it was to develop, maintain, and even increase the value of the commodity. If the star was the "ultimate possessor" of her own image, the studio operation created a situation whereby it was unclear how much of that image existed or should remain without the support of the company. Big studios such as MGM and Paramount were conglomerates of various creative professionals. The expertise they offered and the care they invested to look after their star product were very difficult to replace.

Unexpectedly, the management of players as both employees and commodities applied to women and men alike. Though the attention to the personality of screen players began with female actors, the commodification of male actors followed very shortly after, all in the same year. Through the 1920s, 1930s, and 1940s, both sexes were subjected to the same contracts, conditions, modification of appearance, and publicity. To be sure, appearance and publicity were designed to agree with popular and traditional gender perceptions, but this conformity affected actors as well as actresses. Even the attitude of executives, which was often condescending and paternalistic in nature, did not seem to discriminate between men and women. Sociologists who study the world of fashion modeling suggest that the careers of people who work in such industries all "resemble women's historically contingent relationship to the labor market, as goods themselves exchanged in marriage."[10] This lesson seems to apply in Hollywood as well. Unlike the work routine of producers and directors, which resembled that of the traditional masculine professional guilds, the work of film acting followed a more feminine pattern. In their transformation into a dual employee-commodity status, male actors were subjected to a kind of treatment labor markets usually reserved for women. But before any of that could happen, all players alike had to change, turning from the anonymous screen performers who appeared in the early silent pictures into the important and famous picture personalities of the golden age.

From Team Players to Stars

On March 12, 1910, a large ad by the IMP Film Company appeared in *Moving Picture World*. It read, in large, bold letters, "We Nail a Lie." An accompanying paragraph told the readers: "The blackest and at the same time the silliest lie yet circulated by enemies of the 'Imp' was the story foisted on the public of St. Louis last week to the effect that Miss Lawrence (the 'Imp[']) girl, formerly known as the 'Biograph' girl) had been killed by a street car. It was a black lie because so cowardly. It was a silly lie because so easily disproved. Miss Lawrence was not even in a street-car accident, is in the best of health, will continue to appear in 'Imp' films, and very shortly some of the best work in her career is to be released."[11] Legend has it that this was the moment the star system was born. Until the events surrounding this publication, it is commonly held that although audiences were already "favoring certain players and expressing their preferences," the "names of their screen idols were unknown." Most film historians maintain that the reason behind this anonymity was that "manufacturers diligently kept such information secret," believing that "any public recognition actors received would inspire demands for bigger salaries."[12] Instead, producers encouraged a credit system based on either company names or roles played. For example, actresses were known as the "Vitagraph girl," "Little Mary," or "Wife," and in the case of men as "Husband" or "Banker." When rumors about the death of the "Biograph girl" started circulating, her real name, Florence Lawrence, was revealed by the resulting press coverage, and "the anonymity of players was breached."[13]

It was indeed uncommon for a film performer to attract such great attention at the time. But other evidence suggests that the birth of the named movie star was not so sudden. The Essanay actor Ben Turpin, for example, had already appeared under his own name in the *Moving Picture World* pages on April 3, 1909.[14] In advertisements published by the Edison Company in September 1909 and February 1910, players were not only mentioned by name but were even presented with a short biography. Kalem, another pioneer film company, distributed lobby display cards of performers and their names to be placed at nickelodeons and other theaters as early as January 1910.[15] Viewed within this context, Lawrence's incident, all of which was probably a publicity stunt orchestrated by IMP, appears less like a watershed and more like a sign of the times.

Upon concluding its first decade, the cinema business in the United States was going through several transformations, one of which was the simultaneous emergence of the film acting profession and the star system. After all, before 1908 there could hardly be any stars, since there were only a few regularly employed actors.[16] Indeed, media scholar Richard deCordova claims that the star system was the result of two processes that took place around that time. The first was economic. The rapid expansion of the industry between 1907 and 1909 introduced a need "to rationalize production and produce a larger and more predictable supply of films."[17] The turn to narrative film, which helped regularize production schedules, was one of the responses to this need. Another was the adoption of the stock company model, prevalent in the theater business, which assured a steady supply of trained workers.[18] The resulting sizable output of films presented producers with the auxiliary need of differentiating their product from the hundreds of other motion pictures on the market.

The second process was discursive. DeCordova claims that, in 1907, audience "attention began to be focused away from the projectionist and the mechanical capabilities of the apparatus and towards the human labor involved in the production of film," specifically to those appearing in it. It was around this time that the theatrical verb "to act" gained prominence over others such as "to pose" or "to fake" in reference to screen performance. Together, these two processes accentuated the role of the performers and marked them as the primary instrument in product differentiation. Now, "films with actors could be differentiated from films without actors, and, as the presence of actors became accepted as the norm, particular actors (their identities) could be differentiated from other actors."[19] Further cinematic changes, such as the introduction of the close-up shot and the production of longer two- or three-reel pictures, also contributed to players' visibility. Precedent certainly played a role as well. The use of actors for market differentiation was a tried and true technique practiced in European and particularly British theater for over 200 years, and was a leading organizing mechanism in American theater since the mid-nineteenth century.[20]

Gradually, more and more actors began to be featured steadily in pictures and advertised by name. People were noticing them. In November 1910, a *Moving Picture World* editorial announced, "The public is getting to know these moving picture players," and therefore the paper suggested that from now on "each picture or reel be preceded by the full cast of the characters in the play, with the names of the actors and actresses playing the parts."[21] As the "picture personalities" system was being integrated into standard industry practice, producers also began coming up with new ways of exploiting it. Players' presence was further heightened through cooperation between newly founded studio publicity machines and fan magazines. Those turned star performers into "sights of knowledge" by constantly producing information about "the professional existence" of actors and, toward the 1920s, also about their private lives[22]—anything that might increase the performers' box office draw.

The formation of a well-oiled star system took time. In the meantime, throughout the early years, while the status of their profession was still unstable, screen players were just part of the team. "It was a whole life," remembered Gloria Swanson. "You had a routine . . . You get up very early . . . and off you go to the studio," then "by the time you've finished shooting, and then you look at the daily rushes, and you get home all you can do is take your make-up off, get some food, go to bed—and look at your lines for the next day."[23] Blanche Sweet painted a similar picture. "You see," she explained, "we couldn't do any of that frivolity during the week, because we were working. You had to be early, you had to get up early, work all day, by the time you were finished you didn't have time or want to go to parties or things."[24] Sidney Blackmer claimed that since "there was no union then that restricted the hours," one "could work till midnight and still be called at 5 in the morning." According to him, demands were so high that fellow actor Wallace Reid "became physically exhausted and began to resort to some little medical pick-up, and from this got into an addiction."[25] Other actors saw it a bit differently. Lillian Gish acknowledged, "There were no unions, no hours." But that was not necessarily a bad thing. "We worked twelve hours a day, seven days a week, and liked it," she said, "because no place was as interesting as the studio."[26]

Such convivial statements are not uncommon among the pioneers. Perhaps this was because, at least until 1913, the early film companies reproduced the theatrical practice of traveling stock companies. The "enforced mobility" accompanying this lifestyle contributed to a sense of "unity among film-makers, giving them a group consciousness that was important when there was as yet no film 'capital.' "[27] Actress Mae Marsh referred to it as a "very homey atmosphere."[28] Perhaps the lack of cultural capital and highbrow legitimacy is precisely what made all those who helped build the industry and its capital take such pride in it and remember it so fondly. It was a kind of lowbrow pariah solidarity. Either way, a sense of camaraderie was undoubtedly helpful in the experimental and not-yet-organized environment of most companies. Actors were expected to fulfill all sorts of roles during production. "When I first got my job with [J. P. McGowan], I had many duties," recounted A. Edward Sutherland. "I was an actor, and we were doing a railroad serial, so I had to learn how to run a train. Also I was a property man, or an assistant prop man. I was an assistant cameraman." In those days, he said, "everybody did anything on a picture. . . . If there was a camera to be carried, you carried it."[29]

Sutherland was not alone. Norma Talmadge used to "assist in the making or mending of costumes." Florence Turner, who was already one of Vitagraph's most important players, "helped with the wardrobe and even looked after the petty cash."[30] It was only natural in a way. Gish, for example, knew "all about lighting," because "the place where they developed and printed the film was right across from [her] dressing room." So when she had time, she recalled, "I'd be in there with Joe Aller, watching the developing of the negative and then the printing of it."[31] And Sweet made it clear that all this "wasn't a case of force. Nobody forced anybody. You volunteered. Or you naturally said 'okay.' There was no question of whether you would."[32] It was just the case that at the beginning, "there was a wonderful spirit," and "everybody was involved. If somebody had to brush off the stage, somebody picked up a brush and brushed it. It wasn't that it was beneath your dignity.... Whatever job there was to do, you pitched in and did it."[33]

The easy transition from actress to stage-sweeper makes sense considering the equal facility with which one could turn into a screen performer. Blackmer recalled that he "came to New York" during his university days to see if he "could break into the theatre." It was 1914, and he was "down in Union Square." He saw "a crowd gathering over on the sidewalk," and thought "it was a fight." He approached "to see what the trouble was." Someone signaled him to step forward and said, "I want you here at 8 o'clock tomorrow morning, in dinner clothes." Just like that, said Blackmer, "I had been cast in a motion picture!"[34] Stories like that have always been part of the industry and persist to this day. Legends of actresses being discovered next to soda fountains underpin the magic of movies and help blur the lines between players and their fans, between stars and the rest of us. However, studies of the star system have revealed that something closer to the truth usually involved a request to "get out there and round up all the good-looking females working in that department store and fix their teeth."[35] That said, at least through the early 1910s, tales such as Blackmer's were the rule rather than the exception.

Take the case of Marsh. As she told several interviewers, her first appearance on film occurred in early 1912. Her sister Marguerite was working for Biograph, and one day she took Mae with her to "work with Mack Sennett at Redondo Beach." While there, Mae served as an extra, "watching Mabel Normand dive into the ocean." To be clear, she emphasized, "I wasn't a bathing beauty. I was watching the bathing beauties."[36] Then she simply kept on working as an extra and part of the Biograph stock company. From there anything could happen. In a book she wrote about film acting in 1921, Marsh claimed, "After the beginner has done his extra work, or small bits, if he is of [the] right stuff, he will some day be given a part. He may be unaware of it, but that will be the biggest moment of his screen career."[37]

She had a reason to believe in such chances. Hers came the very same year she started, while D. W. Griffith was producing a picture titled *Man's Genesis*. As Mary Pickford, Sweet, and Marsh remember, in this seventeen-minute short, "the heroine must wear a grass skirt that shows her limbs practically from her waist down." Pickford, who was supposed to play the heroine, "refused to show her legs," pointed at Mae, and said to the director, "You give it to that little kid over there, she doesn't care if she shows her legs or not."[38] The extra turned into a leading lady.

This incident was not out of the ordinary. Gish and her sister Dorothy also got their start as extras at the Griffith company and climbed from there. Of course, all of these players showed an interest in the picture business. The point is that during these Devil-may-care days, the business showed an interest in most of them. Swanson may have said it best: "Maybe if I had been born ten years earlier or ten years later, I might not have had any of this." She understood well that "it was timing." She was simply "born at a time when they were so glad to have anybody stand in front of a camera." The actress, who started her career as a "guaranteed extra" for Essanay, captured the spirit of vanguard screen acting, stating, "I didn't stand in line, I didn't beg for parts, I didn't write letters to anybody or beg for anything. It all happened."[39]

Swanson was right to emphasize her birthdate. Though back then it was easier to get one's foot in the door of film studios, the camera, or, more accurately, the director, did not take just anybody. It is hard to pinpoint what constitutes a star, but looking back it is easy to see what most early screen actresses had in common. Age was definitely crucial, especially for women. Griffith, for example, knew what he was looking for. "When I consider a young woman as a stellar possibility," he stated in a *Photoplay* article in 1923, "I always ask myself: Does she come near suggesting the idealized heroine of life?" He claimed that "in order to have the real germ of stardom," a girl must suggest "the vaguely conscious ideals of every man" and "the attributes most women desire."[40] In more specific terms, looking at most of this director's heroines, as well as those of his colleagues, it appears that what men idolized and women desired to be was young—so young that perhaps they should not be thought of as women at all. Pickford and Marsh were seventeen in their first screen appearance; Dorothy Gish was fourteen, and Sweet only thirteen. Not that anyone asked. And if they did, the girls might even have shaved some years off. In those days it was the norm, and actresses always "registered as an adolescent 'girl' or a child-woman ambiguously poised between childhood and womanhood."[41] It was not the same for men, although they too had to endure the scrutiny of directors. Actor Arthur Johnson recounted that when he applied for a role at Biograph in 1908, Griffith told him that he was "too tall," but "if you cut down the heels off your boots you might do."[42] The age requirements for men, however, were not as stringent. Johnson got a job that year; he was thirty-two.

The demand for some specific physical attributes did not change the fact that, for those who held those attributes, breaking onto the screen in the early 1910s was rather uncomplicated. Whether for men or women, however, the days of the open-door policy were soon over. The more producers and exhibitors learned to rely on star power, the less they were inclined to feature unknowns in their pictures. New companies were established, such as Adolph Zukor's Famous Players, which, as its name suggests, relied on its roster of acting talent. When Zukor created his company in 1912, he assigned management positions to two well-known Broadway producers, the brothers Daniel and Charles Frohman, to assure the steady flow of bankable names from the stage.[43] Yet, with the growing popularity of films, theater cachet was not enough.

A screen star's identity was created by "intertextuality." As deCordova explains, "The spectator was encouraged to follow through all of the associations created through a specific actor's appearance from film to film." In that sense, an actor's fame was something the audience could feel it was contributing to or "actively participating in, by watching, familiarizing with, and embracing a pre-established canon."[44] A one-time film appearance by theater star Sarah Bernhardt could not inspire the same personal association and familiarity created through the dozens of pictures made by Florence Lawrence in one year. Moreover, due to the greater availability of cinema, the popularity of screen stars across the country exceeded that of stage luminaries. As Pickford's biographer stated, even when the actress returned to play in the theater, "fans at the stage door cried out more often for film's Little Mary than Belasco's Juliet."[45] To distribute its pictures, a company needed stars who were movie natives, a fact that Zukor understood rather quickly; soon enough he signed Pickford for $500 a week.

Contracts and high salaries were the next logical step. Five hundred dollars per week was a lot of money for an actress. When Pickford started, only three years earlier, Griffith hired her for five dollars a day with no guaranteed employment. By the end of 1910, at IMP, Carl Laemmle was paying her $175 a week, and at the time of Zukor's offer, Biograph and Griffith were still unwilling to go above $300. As players were, up to that point, part of the team, they did not earn such distinctive sums. But Pickford kept on making even more. In 1914, her wages were raised to $1,000 a week, and they reached the $4,000 mark in March 1915.[46] In turn, her meteoric fame and astronomical salary overhauled the entire industry's employment practices. Others were soon to follow. As the income of producers and exhibitors relied more and more on the names that appeared on the marquee, those names started understanding their value. Marsh claimed that Biograph was paying her "$85 a week" when, in 1916, "Sam Goldfish offered me $2,000 a week for 52 weeks for the first year."[47] When the matinee idol Douglas Fairbanks joined the industry that year, Harry Aitken of Triangle signed him for an initial weekly salary of the same amount.

With these figures the integration of the star system was complete. It is interesting to note that the work itself did not change. Movies were getting longer, but even so it would be hard to imagine anyone in pictures working harder than "twelve hours a day, seven days a week," as Gish claimed, or necessarily becoming a better actor. The change that occurred between 1909 and 1915 was not in labor practices but in market value. Those actors who became stars were receiving more money not for their work but for their name; they were commodified. To illustrate, in 1915 director Frank Powell and his boss William Fox wanted to save on costs and decided to cast an unknown in their upcoming feature, *A Fool There Was*. They hired Theodosia Goodman for a mere seventy-five dollars per week, and changed her name to Theda Bara. While star salaries climbed, the price for the actual work—for acting—was still very low. Of course, Fox had another plan here. He was operating under the assumption that he could "put the girl [they] choose under contract, as the part will make her." Instead of letting the market decide the matter for him, he would control the market. Indeed, the picture was a great success, and by the time Bara left the company, four years later, her value had climbed to $4,000 per week. Fox could manipulate her salary only for a little while.[48]

The Bara tale highlights another effect of the star system—the division of acting labor. As implied by the stories of Marsh and the Gish sisters, until the early 1910s there were extras and there were players, but the transition from the first group to the second was relatively effortless. Toward the late 1910s, as all the major studios began "experimenting with the 'all-star' policy," the acting category was split. Now there were extras, actors, and a first rank of stars, and "those below the first rank began to feel the squeeze of a saturated market."[49] Writing in 1931, Benjamin B. Hampton, who had worked in Hollywood in the previous decade, observed that in 1917–18 "the industry was so thoroughly obsessed by star frenzy that only a handful of people believed the public would ever accept anything different." Though he did not offer a source for this observation, he also claimed that "the extent of the star craze is demonstrated by the fact that of the six hundred or more features then produced in America each year, not more than five percent dared to seek a market unless bolstered by a real or alleged 'box-office name.'"[50] Whether that number is accurate or not, it is clear that the picture business had gone a long way from the days when Biograph refused to reveal players' names, when they were all equally anonymous.

Equality was certainly lacking. As is often the case in the American economy, black workers "felt the squeeze" ensuing from the new trade practices more violently than others. In general, African Americans found few opportunities in the motion picture industry. As journalist Geraldyn Dismond commented in 1929, blacks mostly entered the studios "through the back door" as servants of white stars.[51] Among the mainstream companies, there was no attempt to portray themes related to black life or to recruit African American creative talent.[52] Moreover, until the late 1920s, the limited number of black film parts were predominantly performed by white actors in blackface. When employed, black actors were relegated to minor, stereotypical, and one-dimensional roles such as waiters, maids, laborers, musicians, slaves, janitors, and servants. The star system made this discrimination more conspicuous. Without major roles, black performers could not develop the popularity and market presence necessary to become film stars. The only place for them was in the lower echelons of the acting category. In addition, most film producers were not immune to the prevalent racist attitudes of the time and, as a result, African American actors such as Ernest Morrison, Stepin Fetchit, Nina Mae McKinney, Paul Robeson, Rex Ingram, and Ethel Waters, who did manage to achieve relative, albeit limited, success in later decades, received less money than their white counterparts and were often denied credit.[53] Thus, while the star system was flourishing, black actors were shut out, facing a labor market that was not only divided but also racially segregated.

For the white acting elite, however, labor stratification was a welcome development. In fact, toward the late 1910s, it seemed as if star power were spiraling out of control. Some players, like Pickford, Fairbanks, and Charles Chaplin, gained such status that when they feared Zukor and other producers were plotting to curb their salaries, they created their own company. In January 1919, United Artists was signed into existence. This new setup was to unite those actors mentioned as well as William S. Hart and Griffith, and "release [their] combined productions through [their] own organization."

Essentially, it was a distribution arrangement, whose intention was to by-pass the growing power of new studios such as Zukor's Paramount. Big producers did their best to belittle the new company. Richard Rowland, the head of the Metro studio, famously remarked, "So the lunatics have taken charge of the asylum."[54] Whether the plot that spurred Pickford and company into action was anything more than a rumor is unclear. Nevertheless, reactions like Rowland's as well as actions like the Bara buildup by Fox did suggest that the up-and-coming Hollywood moguls were trying to find ways of containing their movie star galaxy. Though competition among producers played an important role in driving up actors' salaries, as Hollywood entered the age of standardization, companies were looking for ways to capitalize on the commodity while keeping the employee in check.

Containing the Galaxy

Standardization did not occur overnight. It was a long process that in some ways had accompanied the film business since its inception. By the late 1910s and throughout the 1920s, however, oligopolistic expansion expedited the regulation of production practices. In March 1915, Laemmle launched his company's impressive West Coast studio in Universal City. The following year Zukor's Famous Players consolidated with the Jesse Lasky Feature Play Company and the Paramount Picture Corporation to create an impressive production-distribution firm. Four years later, that firm also started buying theaters. William Fox did not stay behind, and soon he too acquired several movie houses. In response to the rising power of these producers, an organization of powerful distribution companies from across the United States joined to form First National in 1917. The Loew's-MGM merger, with its outstanding Culver City studio, arrived in 1924, quickly followed by the growth of Warner Bros. and its eventual union with First National. These big companies devised various ways of controlling the motion picture market both individually and in cooperation with one another. Their box office stars remained a central part of the system.

Despite owning their own theaters, movie companies still used the popularity of screen performers to determine the market value of their pictures. Since each company's theater chain was concentrated in a different region of the country, to reach a national audience the majors had no choice but to exhibit each other's pictures. For example, to get exposure in the New York metropolitan area, Paramount, whose theaters were concentrated around Chicago, had to reach an agreement with the Loew's theater chain, and vice versa. In addition, as the majors often leased their pictures a season before they were produced, they developed a "differential pricing policy" by which B pictures were rented for flat fees and A pictures on varying terms, based on percentage of the gross. Lacking a superior metric for success, percentage deals for A pictures were often calculated based on the past box office performance of the actors who were cast to appear in them. Of course, this marketing rationale filtered back into production practices, assuring that most pictures included stars in order to guarantee profitable rental deals. One could say that by the late 1920s, "the star system became the prime means of stabilizing the motion-picture business."[55]

Interestingly, while at first the marketing of performers was one of the basic strategies fueling competition and the expansion of picture companies, as the industry became vertically integrated under a few large corporations that controlled production, distribution, and exhibition, the competition somewhat subsided. Already in the early 1920s, one could see how the employment of stars was undergoing standardization. While it is true that, at least until the end of World War I, "accidents and bizarre coincidence seem to have been responsible for a disproportionate number of major careers" in Hollywood, at least in the acting profession, entry into the business was no longer that haphazard.[56] Despite their centrality to the marketing of motion pictures, the career development and labor routine of actors were becoming more and more regimented.

First, as we have seen, many companies had already begun using exclusive contracts to assure the employment of both established names such as Pickford and new talents such as Fairbanks and Bara. In addition, it seems that by the early 1920s most studios had developed similar mechanisms with which to identify and sign newcomers. When Janet Gaynor came to Hollywood in 1924, she "made the rounds of the studios . . . to try to sign up for work as an extra. That meant waiting in the casting office." It was not a complicated procedure; "you just had your photograph taken, and gave them in through a little window." One day she got a call back from the office at the Hal Roach Studio. "They made two-reel comedies at that time, and they had lots of little young girls. You never knew what you were doing. You were background. It was extra work. I would get a day, maybe, once in six weeks or something like that."[57]

Then she moved to the next stage. After serving as an extra for a while, though this "didn't go on too long," Gaynor was "put into what at that time they called 'stock' at Universal Studios." As part of a company's stock "you were paid by the week $50. . . . You did extra work, and then maybe one day you'd have a lead, again in a little two-reel comedy or short Western or something like that." After stock came the contract. "At that time," explained the actress, "five year contracts were the usual thing if a young player had any possibilities at all: they signed them up for five years, which meant they paid $75 a week the first six month[s] and then could let them go if they didn't do anything with them." With this system, she noted, the studios "didn't jeopardize a great deal of money or time, but at least they gave you an opportunity. You had a little bit of security for six months." Gaynor got such a contract from Fox in 1926, and she remembers that it felt "so encouraging, I can't tell you. Just to be put in stock made you feel you were well on your way."[58]

Once again, the experience of this actress, who later starred in such classics as the 1927 silent *Sunrise*, does not seem extraordinary. Joan Crawford remembered things in much the same way, only she worked for MGM. "This was 1925," and she was "one of several dozen girls, including Dorothy Sebastian, Anita Page, Gwen Lee and Sally O'Neil, given contracts that year." It was standard procedure. "Every year, a flock of girls and boys were signed by the big companies. If they made good, that was fine for the studios; if they did not, nothing much was lost and they could always be used as extras for the duration of their contracts." All of them had to do a screen test of sorts. It was not "the painstaking and expensive procedure" it later became; in those days, it was more like "a moving photograph." At the beginning, she "thought the signing of [the] contract made [her] automatically, a five year fixture on the MGM lot." However, as Crawford discovered the next day, it was not that simple. First, she was "faced with an unexpected ordeal, that of an 'acting' test," and then, "to add to [her] discomfort," she had been told about "options, those frightening little clauses in contracts which give studios the right to dispense with players at the end of three to six months period."[59]

Option clauses were not unique to players, and they became a fixture in the careers of most creative personnel, including writers and directors. But the appearance of typical contracts, clauses, casting offices, and screen tests suggests the formation of a standardized practice. Furthermore, on January 2, 1926, the Motion Picture Producers and Distributors Association (MPPDA) established the Central Casting Corporation with the purpose of ordering the employment of extras.[60] As the casting director Phil Friedman explained, "When the studio first needed extra talent, great throngs of people, lured by the promise of good wages[,] flocked to Hollywood. . . . There were always crowds in front of their offices." Therefore, it became necessary to have one reliable source of extra talent. From 1926 onward, "the studio casting directors" began sending "their orders for extra talent over three teletype machines to Central Casting." The order was "automatically typed out," and it listed "the date, the time the extras must report, the name of the director, the number of the production, the type of make-up necessary," and "the number of extras, their ages, costumes, salaries, and any extra specifications required." Since pictures utilized many extras, Friedman boasted that the Central Casting Corporation Agency "has become the largest employment agency in the world, giving three hundred and fifty thousand jobs each year."[61] Extras were outsourced; they no longer just happened to come to work with their sister. All other players, as the experience of Gaynor and Crawford illustrated, were put in stock.

By the 1930s, studios developed a rather uniform formula to manage their talent pool. Friedman, who served as head of the casting office at Universal, Fox, the Pickford-Lasky Studio, and RKO, elaborated on it: a "studio roster consists of stars, feature and bit players." The first kind, the "contract player or star," is "an actor or actress who has a term contract for six months. This contains options renewable up to seven years, a guaranteed salary for twenty out of twenty-six weeks, whether or not the player works, and a lay-off period of six weeks." Friedman added that such a contract "also provides for a rising salary scale" after every option. Of the supporting players, those "considered important in bolstering up a picture, but are not box-office attractions themselves"—the feature players—are "contracted for a week at the minimum, while bit players are engaged by the day." This studio executive made sure to emphasize the constructive aspects of being a stock player, such as the "guaranteed salary" and the "rising salary scale." But the agreements players signed with studios did more than give them a chance at fame. They in fact committed the aspiring performers to a very rigid labor routine, one that assured that behind every potential star was also a disciplined employee.

The devil, as always, was in the details. With the option contract, as one film scholar claimed, the studios in fact "devised an ingenious legal document to control their high priced talent."[62] While motion picture companies adapted and enriched it, the option arrangement was almost certainly inspired by Major League Baseball's reserve system, practiced by team managers since the 1870s.[63] According to this system, the right to renew an option belonged exclusively to the employer. The infamous Hollywood clause explicitly stated: "In consideration of his employment hereunder by the

Corporation, and in order to induce the Corporation to enter into this agreement, the Artist grants to the Corporation the following options to engage and employ the Artist to render his exclusive services, as an actor, performer or entertainer." The artist grants an option, but is not granted one in return. In addition, during the time of employment artists agreed to "act, pose, sing, speak or otherwise appear and perform as an actor in such roles and in such photoplays and other productions as Producer may designate." However, "there shall be no obligation on Producer to cause or allow Artist to perform any services hereunder."[64] Essentially, the company was not required to cast the player in any picture while under contract, but if it did, she or he had to appear in it.

Simply put, most actors had no control over the roles they played. "People have the gall to write in to picture people and criticize them for the choice of their pictures," Crawford once complained. "I think it is very important to put in the story that we have jobs the same as any girl in a ten cent store, and we do what we're told." If she ever got a role that she actually wanted, it has "only been out of the goodness of Mr. Mayer," since among the actors "who have long term contract[s], none of us have the rights to choose our parts." She could think of only two exceptions: Greta Garbo and Norma Shearer. The first was undoubtedly MGM's greatest possession, and the second the wife of the head producer.[65] James Cagney felt the same. "Just like a shipping clerk," he reflected, "I was just a salaried employee. But this was part of the times, for everyone. This didn't apply only to me; it applied to everybody under contract."[66] Bette Davis would have concurred. In her words, "Studios employ many talented people for the sole purpose of finding suitable material for their top players, and only in rare cases is the star permitted to make her own selection."[67]

In general, players participated very little in the crafting of the story or the picture. Gable once remarked, "It's true that actors, today, have only one job to do—and that's acting. It's true that we have nothing to say about direction, production, very little to say about a script, very little influence, if any, in helping new talent get a start."[68] Indeed, the names of stars hardly ever appear in the preproduction correspondence or script conferences. Leslie Howard, who played Scarlett's other love, Ashley, in *Gone with the Wind*, once complained that "the conglomerate work" that is the script "is handed to the actor anything from a few days to a few hours before he reports for work, and even if he is important enough to be allowed to criticize, he will hesitate to add another cook to the many who have concocted the broth." Considering the fact that players were also excluded from the editing stage, Howard added, "so much for the control of the artist over his medium!"[69]

To be sure, there were exceptions. As Paul Muni said, some actors, like himself, "are fortunate enough to be able to choose their own stories and work with the writer from the beginning, watching the story develop and helping to mold the characters they will play on the screen."[70] Some were even given a choice of directors. Before work started on *Alice Adams* in 1935, RKO's head producer, Pandro Berman, sent a memo to Katharine Hepburn, saying, "As a final check-over I have taken a list of all the directors in the industry and from that list selected those who could . . . successfully direct a class picture. . . . Strangely enough, the final result brings us right back to a choice between two men—[George] Stevens and [William] Wyler." Berman stated that he had to make a choice that same day and asked the actress to "give me a concrete expression of your opinion so that I will avoid doing something which will make you unhappy."[71] However, throughout the 1930s and most of the 1940s, such cases were few and far between.

As a rule, players had to do as they were told or suffer the consequences, which were also specified in the contract. It was agreed that "in the event of the failure, refusal or neglect of the Artist to perform his services in accordance with this agreement, then, at the Producer's option and without notice, the obligation of Producer to pay the Artist any compensation shall cease from the time of commencement of such default." Furthermore, "upon the happening of any such default, Producer shall have the further separate rights or options to terminate this agreement as a whole or as to the particular picture with respect to which such default shall have occurred."[72] Actor Ralph Bellamy explained this clause in his own words: "If there were no provision in your contract for story approval, which was extremely rare, you could be assigned to any picture." Such assignment, he claimed, "could be done punitively, even, and was. I've had it done to me." In this case, "your only recourse is to say, I won't do it, which means that you go on suspension. If they want to take it to court, they can."[73]

Suspension without pay became the preferred threat of studio executives. Although according to many contracts, the studio could dismiss a player altogether for "failure to perform his services," such action carried the risk that she or he would immediately sign a contract with a different company. Withholding funds was much more effective. After Dana Andrews's successful portrayal of a police detective in *Laura* in 1944, Twentieth Century–Fox wanted him to play a similar role in *Fallen Angel*. He read the script and "thought it was pretty bad." He refused to do it, and "it got to the point where they were going to put [him] on suspension." Then his agent reminded him, "You won't work for a year, probably, or six months." Andrews played the part.[74] Maybe because it was their only recourse and because many of them could afford it, some actors welcomed suspension. Myrna Loy, for example, claimed that she was suspended from MGM on more than one occasion. "Well, of course, that sounds dreadful," she said, "but it's part of your contract." Even though "sometimes this can get rather uncomfortable on both sides," at other times, Loy admitted, "you have to do it." In her case, she did it once because she felt overworked; "I thought that I had done too much in one year, and I was very, very tired and wanted to get away and rest." On another occasion, "I thought I was very wrong for the part and I just said no."[75]

Stock contracts included even more demands. Players' services had to be extended to any publicity interviews or photograph sittings the studio deemed necessary. In addition, following scandals such as Roscoe "Fatty" Arbuckle's alleged murder of Virginia Rappe in 1921, or Wallace Reid's death by drug overdose in 1923, both of which caused unwelcome public uproar, actors and actresses were also asked to sign a morality clause. These came in various forms but essentially demanded that the player "conduct himself with due regard to public convention and morals," and that he or she "will not do or commit any act or thing that will tend to degrade him in society or bring him into public hatred, contempt, scorn or ridicule, or that will tend to shock, insult, or offend the community, or ridicule public morals or decency or prejudice." Once again, if they did, the "Producer may, at its option . . . cancel this agreement for breach of the provision of this paragraph."[76]

One more interesting detail to note is that, at least until the establishment of the Screen Actors Guild in 1933, the work schedule remained similar to the one described by the pioneer performers. Cagney remembered that his "first experience" of Hollywood, around 1930, "was the hours we worked. We would get on the set at eight o'clock in the morning, and we worked—on a Saturday—right on through till daybreak the next day. How many hours? Eighteen, twenty, hours a day."[77] Or as Gaynor recounted, "We had no hours at all. Usually you would start to work at 9:00 o'clock and work till 9:00 that night. I have worked a whole day and a whole night through."[78]

Ironically, the justification for the standardization of actors' labor was the magnitude and value of their uniqueness. When dealing with players' contracts, as well as with those of directors, writers, some cameramen, and composers, companies took every measure to create regimented employees. They inserted various exacting clauses, such as those designating that the artist shall perform his duties "at all times as instructed by the Corporation, including Sundays and Holidays, and at such places as the Corporation may direct." Side by side with these, the big companies also integrated a clause that explained this strict and uniform discipline as an attempt to preserve distinctive and exceptional abilities. Most individual agreements included some version of the following statement: "It is distinctly understood and agreed by and between the parties hereto that the services to be rendered by the Artist under the terms hereof, and the rights and privileges granted to the Corporation by the Artist under the terms hereof, are of special, unique, unusual, extraordinary and intellectual character, which gives them a peculiar value, the loss of which cannot be reasonably or adequately compensated in damages in an action at law, and that a breach by the Artist of any of the provisions contained in this agreement will cause the Corporation irreparable injury and damage."[79] Within one document, one page forces the artist, be it an actor, a director, or a composer, to "renounce his artistic independence." Then, on the very next page, embodying the corporation's legal need "to protect itself against possible breach of the contract," it endows that same artist with "the traditional dignity of a work of art."[80] It was a masterpiece of contradiction.

To be sure, there was indeed something unique about actors' services. Players, and particularly box office stars, were unusually well compensated by the studios. The draconian nature of the contract prompted some observers to assert, "Behind the grandeur of being a movie star . . . lay all the gradations of servitude."[81] Well, perhaps all gradations except for the pay. Once actors or actresses were successful enough to become "contract players," they were usually accorded a relatively high salary. Professional independence was exchanged for cash. It is hard to define as serfdom a situation where a rising star like Melvyn Douglas earns $900 per week in 1931, an actress like Hepburn receives a weekly paycheck of $1,500 in 1932, and even a young supporting actor like Tim Holt is guaranteed $350 a week as a basis for his "rising salary scale" in 1938.[82] As a point of comparison, the average *yearly* income per person in the United States that same year was $1,230.[83] Players not only earned a great deal of money; they also cost the studios much. An almost guaranteed fixture in the production files of Hollywood pictures is that the cast accounted for the most expensive item on the budget sheet. In the 1943 production of *Double Indemnity*, for example, the salaries of Fred MacMurray, Barbara Stanwyck, and Edward G.

Robinson amounted to $319,870, about a third of the overall budget. A similar ratio occurred in *Hold Back the Dawn*, from 1941, where the wages paid to Charles Boyer, Olivia de Havilland, and Paulette Goddard throughout shooting came to $237,129.43, about a quarter of the $978,000 budget.[84]

These sums suggest that at least in terms of remuneration, actors were not part of the conventional workforce. Their labor was not commodified only according to its value to the production process. These sums imply that, unlike directors or writers, famous actors needed a special incentive to sign a contract, special because of the additional function they fulfilled in the industry—their status as a product. Therefore, while contracts normalized the relationship between the studio and the player-employee, the generous compensation specified in them links to another set of practices that standardized the actor-commodity relations—a set of interactions that made sure the MacMurrays and the de Havillands maintained an extraordinary value and, more significantly, that they absorbed the fact that the studio was essential for this maintenance.

Not Born but Made

If some actors compared their role in the studio to that of a "girl in a ten cent store" or a "shipping clerk," others came up with different analogies. "How it feels to be a star today?" Gable contemplated in late 1940. "It feels like being a safety deposit box in a bank! A box full of gilt-edged securities and high-interest bonds." He felt that way "because of the terrific sums of money invested in us," that is, "the stories bought for us, the production costs that 'mount' us, [and] the salaries paid our co-stars and supporting casts."[85]

Indeed, the economic dependence on star power that was built into the system placed many players in the position of a prized possession: a valuable commodity that had to be handled with care. This status becomes clearer when one considers the personal nature of their appeal. As screenwriter Leo C. Rosten wrote in 1941, every star "is a monopoly. A Charles Boyer or a Claudette Colbert has a monopoly on those graces of voice, eyes, manner, attitude which constitute the individual personality." After all, "there is only one Clark Gable, only one Bette Davis." Although companies often tried to build up a "Gable type" or a "Davis type," there was never any assurance the public would be "won over" by the "synthetic substitute."[86] For that reason, companies tried to make stars out of the players they had in stock and used the tried-and-true ones with the utmost efficiency.

Many scholars attempted to answer the question, How does a studio develop and maintain a star? Cathy Klaprat suggests that aside from stars, the industry relied on narratives. Thus, a better question is, "How were stars matched to narratives and thus to the scriptwriting, publicity, and advertising strategies of a studio?" Analyzing the career of Davis, Klaprat finds that, usually, the industry would cast a player in different roles and test how audiences responded to each one. The nature of audience reaction would be determined by "fan mail, sneak previews, and exhibitor preferences," as well as "box office grosses printed in trade papers." Studios used these to assist in the "fitting of player to character." Once the fit was made and "the correct role was determined"—that is, the role producers assumed audiences expected and wanted to see the actor play—"advertising and publicity took over" and presented a version of the star's personal life that matched the traits associated with the star's screen persona. Klaprat shows how, at Warner Bros., Davis, who started out playing the "comely coquette," was later fixed to the role of "the vamp" after her successful appearance in the 1934 picture *Of Human Bondage*, a fixture that created a new, specific market for her films.[87]

Part of this process included the often-discussed makeover and training. As film and theater costume designer W. Robert LaVine emphasized, "A star was not born, but made":

> Hair was bleached or dyed, and, if necessary, to "open" the eyes, eyebrows were removed and penciled in above the natural line. Studio-resident dentists, expert at creating million-dollar smiles, capped teeth or fitted them with braces. Cosmetic surgery was often advised to reshape the nose of a new recruit or tighten her sagging chin. A "starlet" was taught how to walk, smile, laugh, and weep. She was instructed in the special techniques of acting before a camera, perfecting pronunciation, and learning how to breathe for more effective voice control. Days were spent in wardrobe, situated in separate buildings within the studio communities.[88]

To this entire operation one might add that, with every new picture project, studios had to pick the right stories, as well as the right screenwriters, directors, costars, wardrobe, makeup, and publicity. A whole expensive machine of specialized knowledge was employed to decipher what was the bankable character and then sustain it without wearing it out. This costly procedure was not foolproof; there were many actors and actresses who never became Gable and Davis despite the sincere efforts of the studios. For this reason, when an actress did become a starlet, the studio wanted to make sure it would get a return on its investment.

It was a catch-22 of sorts. Companies had an incentive to make stars, but once they did, they were held hostage by the success of these stars. This conflicting dependency of the studios inspired a special treatment toward actors within the organization. In the daily reality of the studios, actors were, by virtue of their personal value, subjected to two forms of management. First, as mentioned, they were objectified, that is to say, producers, other executives, writers, and directors often treated actors as a product rather than as participating creative employees. Second, their dual commodity/employee status often exposed contract players to a sort of managerial paternalism: while studios carefully safeguarded them, that protection took the form of arrogance, whereby those in positions of authority assumed that they held exclusive knowledge with regard to the players' best interests. The latter of these attitudes was unique, the former unique in its intensity, and both, together with the network of expertise described above, attempted to break the monopoly held by the actor over the star persona. All were part of an endeavor to tie the valuable star product to the picture company.

Even a superficial search through interoffice communications in any studio illustrates the tendency to commodify actors. Consider how Friedman, the casting agent, described his directory. Players were catalogued according to different categories: "the main classification . . . are stars and feature players: male and female. . . . Other classifications include character men and women, comedians and comediennes, colored people, orientals, musical and specialty talent." An actress such as Gaynor, for example, would be listed "both as an ingénue and as a young leading woman," while other players could be listed "in four or five classifications such as a young leading man, a heavy, a character actor and a foreigner." During the casting process, explained Friedman, "from his directory, the [executive] makes his suggestions for the various players on an assignment sheet which he sends to the producer and the director with his reasons . . . then all three discuss them in a conference." If the producers or directors were unsure of the selections made by the casting director, they would arrange for a "production test" for the players in question.[89] At least per this casting agent's experience, it seems that the actors themselves were not involved in the casting process. They were utilized like resources.

Undeniably, players were not the only workers the industry treated this way. Conforming to principles of scientific management and other features of a modern business, including a rigorous division of labor, Hollywood studios subjected the labor of writers, directors, cinematographers, and all other personnel to similar terms of exchange. That said, with actors and actresses, this practice took an extreme form; it was much more common, front and center, and it took into account physical attributes and personality rather than mere professional capabilities. In other words, it was not their acting ability—their labor—that was the commodity. Rather, it was their bare presence, the people themselves. The reason, of course, was that while the producer wanted to hire the best cameraman for the picture, he was not selling the cameraman to the public. Actors, on the other hand, were treated like a commodity because in many ways they were one.

The casting of *Gone with the Wind* once again serves as a great exemplar. Selznick International, the producing firm, was not among the major companies. It was an independent, which essentially meant a production operation with no distribution and exhibition branches. As a result, the company did not have the resources to maintain a large stock company and relied, to a great extent, on players loaned from other studios. Exempt from the task of building up talent and matching contract actors with the right roles, the production team could discuss possible cast members only in terms of its own needs. "What are your feelings about Vincent Price?" Selznick asked George Cukor.[90] "I have no strong feelings," he answered. "I think maybe we can do better."[91] The producer and then director had many such discussions.[92] "It might interest you to know that Frances Dee reads absolutely thrillingly with great temperament and fire. She is a most accomplished and technically efficient actress," wrote Cukor. "I have only one reservation about her for Scarlett," he added; "has she the shallow external minx quality that Mrs. Chaplin realized so brilliantly in private life?"[93]

Throughout 1937 and 1938, such exchanges between Selznick and his team were frequent. "George darling have found perfect Tarleton [twins] in London famous English aristocratic family but can be whipped into Southerners at drop of hat," specified one telegram.[94] "I am forgetting about Estelle Winwood because . . . I understand that she is not looking very well, and if her looks have gone off any I'm afraid she's scarcely the very chic and attractive woman that we want for the part," declared another.[95] One undated copy of a casting options form simply stated, "1. Sussan Carnahan: Pretty—not very experienced—gay and appealing 2. Ann Gillis: experienced—pretty 3. June Lockhart: Wistful—rather appealing 4. Marilyn Knowlden: Very good for type—little hard 5. Betty Moran . . . experienced—not very appealing." And a note at the end added, "None of these ideal for Blossom . . . in every case their speech is unladylike and not correct for the part."[96]

Just to be clear, this treatment was not reserved only for women. The discourse in the studios was just the same for male actors. "As to [the part of] Frank Kennedy," wrote Selznick, "I feel very strongly that much the best type physically is Conrad Nagel. He is exactly thin-blooded enough looking for the part, and fits perfectly the description, 'an old maid in trousers.' Even his baldness is of value; he is obviously a gentleman; and just weak enough."[97] With regard to the role of Ashley, he thought, "[Melvyn] Douglas gives the first intelligent reading of [him] we've had, but I think he's entirely wrong in type, being much too beefy physically."[98] Granted, physical appearance and personality were relevant features in a screen performance, yet they often seemed to gain prominence over the professional qualifications of actors. Cukor was worried that Dee was not as convincing a minx as another actress was in her "private life." Dee's ability to act the minx was not under discussion. In contrast, while considering other craftsmen, the discourse hardly ever strayed away from their formal expertise. When considering a cinematographer for his big production, Selznick's comments were strictly professional: "The more I think about [cameraman] Lee Garmes, the more I feel that he might be the best man for us, especially in view of his skill with angles and his ability to get the sort of effects which are so essential to our picture."[99]

The objectification of players was also visible in the studios' habit of trading in them. Like the option contract, another famous component of Hollywood agreements was the loan-out clause. It stated that "the Artist hereby expressly gives and grants to the Corporation the right to lend any of the services of the Artist provided for herein to any person, firm or corporation for any motion picture or pictures in connection with which the Corporation may be entitled to the services of the Artist hereunder."[100] Such loan-out agreements were made among the companies, not directly with the actors, and "all checks in payment of the Artist's services" were exchanged exclusively between them. They were "made payable to [the lending company] and . . . delivered to [it] each week at [its] studios."[101] These compensations almost always exceeded the weekly salary of the player in order to, as Friedman explained, "reimburse his studio for carrying the actor during his idle period, because when he is loaned to another studio it may interfere with his home studio commitments."[102] In other words, there was a profit involved, and generally the studio pocketed most if not all of it.

Once again, this practice applied to other creative employees as well, although in the case of actors it seems to have been more frequent. Besides, a loan-out of a player was different, since it was more than an efficient use of the company's labor resources; it was an investment in the star product and had to be treated as such. A casting agent by the name of Bill Grady, who headed the casting department at RKO as well as that at MGM, claimed, "Another source of worry without praise is the loaning out of our contract players to other studios." It was a source of worry, since "whenever this happens, the script must first be read carefully, to see if the role is suitable for that person," as there is always the worry that "an uncongenial part might do him more harm than good."[103] Here we begin to see the paternalist aspect of the management at play. Studios generally treated loan-outs of personnel as best practice; the lending of players, however, was thought of in terms of value enhancement.

Producers kept a close watch on the films for which they loaned their players. In 1944, for example, negotiating with the production team of the movie *Love Letters*, Selznick "made as a condition of . . . going any further with the [Jennifer] Jones and [Joseph] Cotten lending agreements, that the part of Dilly be not cast with Ann Richards but cast with some younger character actress, in order not to rob or detract from the worth of the role of Singleton," which Jones was intended to play in the picture. In addition, Selznick wanted "to make known that the part of Roger must not be portrayed by too young and handsome a boy," as it might harm Cotten.[104] Producer Hal Wallis, who was the intended recipient of the previous letter, had much the same concern when he was about to loan Joan Bennett to Walter Wanger. "I finally got around to reading *The Blank Wall*," he wrote in 1948, "and I think it will make a very good starting vehicle for Joan. It will, of course, require some developing of the leading male characters as they are pretty sketchily portrayed."[105] Unlike the trade of any other employee, when a player was leased, his or her home studio became involved in the external production. The loaned players were more than just hired hands; they became part of the property—that is, the motion picture—and it in turn became a part of their star property.

With regard to both loan-outs and in-studio work, producers often felt they knew best when it came to choosing the right role for their contract players. People like Wallis, Irving Thalberg, or Darryl Zanuck assumed that their experience in the business, and their economic as well as creative investment in their stars, made them the absolute experts about the latters' career paths. Consider a long telegram sent by Berman to Hepburn in 1936. The actress was apparently uninterested in fulfilling her latest assignment, a picture somewhat fittingly titled *A Woman Rebels*. She thought neither the script nor her part was well developed. Her executive producer was quick to put her in her place. "Dear Kate . . . I think you are making a big mistake in this whole matter," Berman wrote. "If you will recall there has never been a picture you have made about which I have been honestly enthusiastic from my own opinion that has turned out badly." The producer then proceeded to enumerate his right decisions with regard to her career: "I have strongly advocated production of *Morning Glory*, *Little Minister*, *Alice Adams*, and *Mary of Scotland*. . . . Needless to say each of them has extraordinary merit." He reminded Hepburn how there were "arguments over *Little Minister* and *Morning Glory* both of which I persuaded you to do."

Then Berman pointed out the perils of disobeying him by bringing up Hepburn's flops: "I never had any enthusiasm for *Break of Hearts* as you well know." Concerning *Spitfire*, "which you were keenly desirous to do . . . I tried to unsell [*sic*] you from making it." The producer claimed that he was "not trying to avoid responsibility," but emphasized, "I have never been wrong when I have been personally convinced insofar as your productions are concerned either from box-office angle or from angle of pleasing the most people with you." Finally, turning to the picture at hand, he argued that it "falls into category of those pictures about which I have . . . my own enthusiasm . . . is box office sympathetic in character, [and is] different from anything you have done in that it gives you opportunity to display another side entirely." Berman ended by stating, "I earnestly recommend you put aside all these discussion[s] and come here immediately to make this picture and I close with the confidence you will thank me for this wire within six months."[106] He was confident that he had the better judgment.

Actor Joel McCrea received a similar scolding from Selznick. "I have your note about *Our Betters* and will be glad to consider your complaint against the part," he wrote when he was still serving as RKO's head producer, immediately adding, "although you must believe I would not cast you in it unless I had given very serious consideration to what it would do to your future." Selznick was apparently less disturbed by McCrea's objection to the part. For that he had a clear answer: "You are under contract, Joel, you are receiving a weekly salary and decisions as to what parts you will play will be made by us, and not by you." No, the producer was more offended, not to say "surprised and disappointed," by one specific sentence in the actor's letter that stated that McCrea had "no intention of ruining [his] future" by participating in *Our Betters*. Selznick charged at the actor: "Your advance since this administration has been many, many times greater than what you achieved in your previous years in pictures, and I cannot conceive how you can have other than complete respect for and faith in our judgment." If there was ever any doubt, the producer wanted to affirm, "if you are cast in *Our Betters*, it will be because we think it will further you and not hurt you, and at the same time serve the best interest of the picture and the company." He concluded by referring to McCrea's qualm as "a ridiculous Hollywood attitude."[107]

In his letter, Selznick too was expressing a common Hollywood attitude, one that often carried beyond casting and into the players' private lives. As part of the star-building apparatus, studio publicity departments were constantly busy "fusing character and actor," by manipulating the public image of the star as an individual.[108] Sometimes, to maintain such fantasies, the paternalist regard for an actor's professional course included recommendations about his or her personal business. "The build-up, in the studio, of people they were interested in was very calculated and very interesting," said Myrna Loy. "It was quite remarkable ... to become this kind of 'fabulous person' that they manage to create through this constant publicity." Though, she added, "you had to deliver ... It was very, very interesting— and also very destructive for the person herself, I think." In her case, it was the name. Originally, it was Myrna Williams, and she "liked it very much," but "at that time everyone felt there had been a Kathleen Williams. . . . They were looking around for a sort of different name, and someone came up with the name Loy."[109] Crawford remembered that her given name, Lucille LeSueur, "sounded affected, and was difficult to pronounce," so "the [MGM] publicity department then conceived the idea of arranging with one of the motion picture magazines to conduct a contest, a prize to be given the person finding an acceptable name for [her]." Finally, producer Harry Rapf sent for LeSueur and, as she remembered, "told me that my name was Joan Crawford."[110]

The best story probably belongs to Dana Andrews, who "had gone to Mr. Goldwyn's vice-president in charge of the studio and told him [he] wanted to get married." The man answered, "Look, you haven't worked in pictures yet and we need a little publicity. What about squiring some girls around town to the nightclubs, so we can get a little publicity for you, which will help you along? I would suggest you wait a while." Andrews did as he was told, and when he tried again a couple of months later, Mr. Goldwyn himself said, "I'll think about it and let you know."[111] The moral clauses discussed above were another measure taken to direct the course of famous players away from ugly scandals, which were harmful to their popularity.

One could always ask whether all this attention to players, both on and off the set, was truly in their best interest. Bette Davis once said that while she believed that "actors and actresses are notoriously bad judges of story material," it does not "follow that the studios are always right." She noted that, while under contract, players "must be paid whether they are working or not; and when they are not working they are a worrisome item of expense." Therefore, "if the studio has scheduled nothing suitable for the star at such a time, she may be requested to go into this production even though they know it is unjust."[112] Or in other words, with all the fanfare about "furthering" their stars' careers, head producers and executives did have other, more material concerns than an actor's artistic development. The paternalist language, though arguably sincere to some extent, could also serve to soothe egos and mask what was essentially fiscal efficiency. Lauren Bacall once referred to this as "Svengali-ing" the player.[113]

Then again, one must remember that in many ways the system worked. Many actors who made it into the contract player category had very long careers. Reginald Owen, a British stage player who began his film career in Hollywood in the late 1920s and was never a leading man, admitted, "From the actor's viewpoint . . . the years have never been like it. I was under contract for sixteen years with Metro, which is a long, long time for anybody to be under contract."[114] Looking back, Cukor, who was privy to backstage star handling, also observed that overall they were treated very well by the studios: "They were given pictures that were, in fact, vehicles to show them to their best advantage, or to try sometimes to show a different facet of their talent. As a result, these people had long, long careers."[115] Davis might have had a point about unjust casting, but the concerns of Wallis and his team at Warner Bros. were definitely broader than mere profitability. "I am returning to you the Ben Hecht story," wrote one of Wallis's advisers. "It is brilliantly written in the very best Hecht style, but when you boil it down I am afraid it is too morbid of a movie." The problem was Davis. It was not good enough for her. Maybe "if [she] never played *Of Human Bondage* and we were badly in need of a story for her, this could have worked out." Even then, "the girl [character] is such an out and out slut, and she seems too horrible to bring sympathy."[116] The script was not suitable for their star property; therefore, it was not good for the studio.

PERHAPS IT WAS just too complicated to determine where the player's benefit ended and that of the studio began. If Davis was the biggest star at Warner Bros., then the company's profits depended on her, which means that in some ways her career was indeed at least as important to Warner as it was to the actress herself. Studios often made mistakes, and, it should be pointed out, box office success was not necessarily identical to what a professional actor might consider quality or career development. Yet, artistic disagreements aside, the managerial methods devised by Hollywood executives suggest that, despite the draconian contracts and the paternalist attitude, studios had an interest in keeping their stars theirs and also shining. Actors often decried the terms of their employment. Producers, in contrast, often tried to belittle the role of stars or their ability to break out without managerial help. All in all, if, as Davis claimed, "once you're in the profession fame is your tangible reward," it had to have been a symbiotic relationship.[117]

CHAPTER FIVE

Shooting

Cameraman Virgil E. Miller chose to open his 1964 memoir, *Splinters from Hollywood Tripods*, with an observation made by former secretary of labor Maurice J. Tobin:

> Some of the brightest stars in Hollywood are the fellows who never get their names in lights—no glamour magazines carry their pictures—they never appear in previews—BUT, no picture could be made without them. . . . We are so busy applauding the leading lady or the leading man, we fail to notice the beautiful jobs done by the cameramen, electricians, grips, property men, make-up men and women, set-dressers, hairdressers, sound men, costumers and others. I like to think of these people as Hollywood's 400—the men and women from the 40-odd unions, without whom there would be no pictures and no stars.

As a member of the behind-the-camera workforce, Miller wished to dedicate his book to these "forgotten people who have been so sadly neglected by the press and the public—those without whom the other half could not function."[1]

These "forgotten" figures certainly numbered in the hundreds or even thousands. With the resources available to the big studios due to the industry's vertical integration, the production lots in and around Hollywood were tremendous apparatuses, swarming with people and activity. By the mid-1940s, 30,000 men and women were employed in the Los Angeles film industry.[2] These various craftsmen worked in close proximity to one another on the studio lots and were capable of producing almost anything one could imagine. Director George Cukor, for example, remembered that when he was making the movie *Camille* for MGM in the mid-1930s, "it was decided" that the casino set had to include a statue of the goddess of chance. "This was at five o'clock in the afternoon and we were shooting the next morning," he recalled. "I came in the next morning, there it was, larger than life," in marble white, about ten feet tall, and equipped with both rudder and cornucopia. Such ingenuity and efficiency were not out of the ordinary.

"They had tremendous resources," Cukor said, especially "the technical part of it."[3]

Each studio was an ecosystem, one in which the stars were more of a looming presence than the beating heart. The it-takes-a-village nature of the era becomes apparent if we consider the spatial organization of a production center such as the Warner Bros. studio in Burbank. Purchased in 1926, the property was essentially sixty-eight acres of farmland, but by the 1940s the company had expanded it, turning it into more than a hundred acres of offices, sound stages, and back-lot settings, inside which worked about 3,500 employees.[4] The main entrance was on Olive Avenue, "flanked by well-kept lawn, carpeting a grove of tall pine trees." Upon entering the main gate, the first thing one encountered was "the two story Administration Building, where in the foyer, Grant Donnelly ... functioned as a receptionist and guardian," serving, essentially, as the indispensable gatekeeper, separating insiders from what actress Anna Q. Nilsson once termed the "Heartbreak Lane in Hollywood, leading by a circuitous path to the gates of the many studios."[5]

Those allowed to pass Ms. Donnelly were the various contributors without whom there would indeed be no pictures and no stars. Charles F. Greenlaw Jr. was assistant to the Warner Bros. general production manager during the 1940s. In his unpublished autobiography, he described in detail the premises of his extensive workplace. His account reveals not only the vast network of craftsmen operating on the studio lot, but also the space accorded to each group of professionals. The administration building accommodated all the studio's upper echelons: "Cy Wilder's Accounting Department, Max Arnow's Casting Office, the Story Department, the Producers ... and the Executives." Further east on Rowland Avenue (today Warner Boulevard), the street stretching between the main entrance and Riverside Drive, stood the more eclectic Music Building, where "the Music Library files, and offices for composers and arrangers occupied the west wing." However, the rest of this "one-story building" was taken up by production manager "William Keonig ... and the Unit Managers" who "shared most of the space." This arrangement left only a "few small offices" assigned for the use of directors and assistant directors.

It seems that important work was often performed in confined spaces. Close to the main administrative building were "the so-called First National cutting rooms. . . . These were tiny spaces, each barely large enough to accommodate the cutter, his movieola and the necessary film bins and tacks." This was also a noisy area, since the editing rooms had no soundproofing and the "doors were open in hot weather."[6] Editor Margaret Booth recalled the compact, "hopelessly cluttered" room at MGM, where she performed her "artistry," in quite the same manner.[7] Fellow editor Frank Atkinson called it "a small room" where a cutter "runs hundreds of thousands of feet of film under a light and sometimes makes a story where there is none."[8]

Each building housed additional important collaborators. Across from the "cutters' domain" was the Wardrobe Department. Greenlaw remembered it as a "vast enterprise, with a number of designers . . . under long term contract." There were two tailor shops, one for men and, "on the upper floor, a huge ladies work room."[9] To call all the workers in this department designers is a bit too general. One wardrobe employee at MGM stressed the fine differences: "At any big studio there is a huge staff of experts in the art of cutting and tailoring, exclusive fur workers, needle women, and hand embroiderers—each to do his or her specialized bit in creating these costumes for the screen."[10] Similarly, "the Makeup Department, run by Perc Westmore," could appear like a "mob-room," with mirrors, makeup tables, and "separate make up rooms" for the "star make-up artists and hairdressers."[11] Yet here too the craftsmen were more than mere technicians. When makeup expert Jack Dawn wanted to hire new workers for his staff, he had to interview "more than 500 applicants, and each one . . . had graduated from an art institute."[12]

There were many more specialists. The Sound Department "under the supervision of Col. Nathan Levinson . . . was housed in a two-story edifice." There was a Grip Department "with its own headquarters where equipment was stored, repaired and refurbished, and the Electrical Department maintained a similar autonomous area." The electricians had an in-house painting crew that worked on "lamps and ancillary electrical equipment," which should not be confused with the "separate Paint Department whose responsibility was the painting of sets and studio buildings." That same area also housed the Craft Building, "a cavernous structure . . . which contained the shops for most of the set-building crafts—Metal shop, plumbing, special effects, staff and plaster shop, machine shop, paint shop, and all other miscellaneous arts."

Close to the crafts was the Art Department, presided over by Bert Tuttle and "ensconced on the upper stories of a building attached to Stage Five." It consisted of "offices for the Art Directors, a large drafting room, a model makers' area, and rooms for sketch artists."[13] Hans Dreier, who headed this department over at Paramount, explained that this was complex work, which often combined "art with practical knowledge and executive ability," therefore most studios "keep the most valuable [staff] on a permanent basis."[14] In the same building, a few floors down, was the Camera Department, "whose responsibility it was to hire, assign, and lay off the operators and assistants who worked with the head cameramen; to maintain the camera equipment, and to store raw film, load magazines, and transport exposed negative to the lab for processing."[15]

A separate two-story building was "devoted exclusively to the writers." Greenlaw claimed that this was based "on the theory that if they were all kept in one area their output could be more easily measured and monitored." The Warner brothers aspired to monitor work "wherever possible." They also emphasized maximizing efficiency and conserving resources, even wood. In fact, at a far corner of the studio, next to the river, the brothers installed "extensive scene docks [where] used sets not immediately needed were folded wall by wall and stored." Art directors "were required, wherever possible, to reuse them." Sometimes, due to bad weather conditions or lack of space, some of these sets had to be dismantled. On such occasions, the set parts "were transported to an area on the backlot where workmen dismantled them, removed nails, cut off damaged ends [into] two-by-four and other reusable pieces of lumber, and stacked them on the lumber pile." Greenlaw explained that while this practice may seem ridiculous, at the time "labor was less expensive than raw lumber."[16]

The rest of the studio roster validates this last claim. It included the Research Department, Transportation Department, Property Department, and Scenic Department, as well as the Greens Department "with potted shrubs and trees," the Trailer Department, the Stock Film Library, the Location Department, Payroll, Accounting, First Aid, a studio police force, the Messenger Department, and "even a Telegraph Office."[17] At least in terms of geography, the "forgotten" workers who staffed these areas seemed to have had a more lasting presence in the studio than their more famous colleagues. While writers were accorded merely one building, and directors only a few small offices, Greenlaw's recollections suggest that there was no Actors Department. Instead, the Warner stars appear in his memoir like VIP guests, stopping to visit the various well-established professional domains where they were measured, fitted, and made up before heading to the stage or back lot they happened to be working on that day.

Not all the employees in these departments directly contributed to the film production process. Still, as the words of Miller, Booth, Atkinson, and Dreier demonstrate, many saw themselves as an essential part of the creative endeavor, and with good reason. Unlike Plato's luxurious city, which dis-

tinguished between those "occupied with music and colors" and the "manufacturers of all kinds of articles," the Hollywood studio did not draw such
impermeable lines between arts and crafts.[18] Working in a creative industry, many craftspeople involved in filmmaking could assume the mantle of
artistry. Such an assumption, though, was neither natural nor elementary.

If the creative pursuits of writers, actors, and directors had to be transformed to fit a modern workplace via standardization and commodification,
the journey of traditional crafts went in the opposite direction. For their
work to be thought of as a creative pursuit, tailors, designers, and some of
the technicians who performed services for the motion picture production
companies had to provoke a cultural transformation through which their
technical skills would be socially and professionally recognized as artistic
talents. It was a change in perception more than in work practices, one concerned primarily with respect and recognition rather than with control
over labor power and product. Not all studio trades sought this conceptual
transition. Of those that did, each followed a different path, but in many
cases employees of these so-called supporting fields developed a logic that
framed their work in creative terms while at the same time distancing their
job from its more utilitarian elements. The most emblematic case was that
of cinematographers, who perhaps more than any other "technical" group
managed to bridge the gap between arts and crafts. The cameramen's quest
for artistic validation represents the condition of "Hollywood's 400," demonstrating that for many of them, the goal was more than just to "not be
forgotten"; it was to be remembered as artists.

Arts and Crafts

In aesthetic terms, the line separating art from craftsmanship is quite blurry.
Members of creative industries such as filmmaking are often divided into
two classes: artists perform "the work that gives the product its unique ex-
pressive character," while craftsmen are those "whose skills contribute in a
supporting way."[19] Most employees of such industries might agree with this
terminology; however, the crux of the matter is what counts as a "supportive" task. Here, as may be expected, consensus is hard to find. In the studio
era, many editors, for example, saw themselves as central, claiming that "it
is not extravagant to assert that many pictures were 'made' in the cutting
room."[20] Director Alfred Hitchcock suggested that actors were somewhat
supportive. He often compared the actors' role to that of children or cattle,
and once he even professed that "Disney had the ideal relationship with his

stars," since "he can erase them if they get out of line."[21] In contrast, many writers felt that it was actually directors who received too much credit for their work.[22] Perhaps one has to look beyond the aesthetic jargon.

Historically, craft stands for skill or the ability to "make something skillfully." In labor history, the term is closely tied to professional organizations, from the manufacturing craft guilds of the medieval period to the collective bargaining of skilled craft workers in the nineteenth century.[23] In these terms, beginning in the industrial era, "crafts" were distinguished from "common labors." Craftsmen were skilled workers whose labor required technical knowledge that was acquired in formal apprenticeship or by assisting other experienced craftsmen. In iron manufacturing, for example, such skilled professions included puddlers, heaters, rollers, and nailers.[24] But not all work in large factories involved complex skills: someone had to move the raw material from place to place, to transport the finished goods, to clean up, and in general to work "wherever physical strength was required."[25] These were the common or unskilled workers, the people Karl Marx referred to as "the light infantry of capital."[26]

Motion pictures were a product of the industrial era. They were developed in the same labs and by the same engineers who produced the lightbulb, revolutionized the telegraph, and experimented with iron ore separation and cement. From its very beginning, then, the production of cinema involved the work of skilled craftsmen. The invention of moving pictures in the late 1800s also coincided with the growing power of American craft unions. Following a period of labor unrest whose climax was the Pullman railroad strike of 1894, skilled craftsmen under the leadership of Samuel Gompers and the American Federation of Labor (AFL) distanced themselves from "common laborers" and opted for a more elitist and stable, albeit cautious, form of unionization, which emphasized alignment across a specific craft or trade rather than across industry.[27] This strategy proved itself. Between 1897 and 1903 membership in trade unions mushroomed from 447,000 to 1,913,900.[28]

The organization wave in the United States did not skip the growing entertainment industry. Indeed, in 1893, eleven locals of theater workers convened in New York and established the National Alliance of Theatrical Stage Employees (IATSE). In 1894, the alliance received an official charter from the AFL.[29] As would be the case with a trade union, membership was originally limited to locals of stage carpenters, electricians, and property men. The bylaws emphasized a "strict departmentalization of tasks," which meant "no crossing-over between job classifications," the "establishment of a standard eight-hour work day," and "abolishment of the system of employing actors, supers and other incompetent persons as carpenters, property men, gas men, or stagehands."[30] This last clause might explain why actors were almost a priori excluded from IATSE. The various theatrical unions that formed across the country since the 1870s rose in response to grievances that were specific to nonperformers: layoffs following opening night, replacing traveling mechanics with local stage crews, and hiring janitors and children to replace stage workers, as well as discrimination in wages.[31] It seems that, at least according to their colleagues, actors did not share these problems; they belonged to a different type of theater worker.

With the nickelodeon boom beginning in 1905, IATSE sought to extend its mandate to the burgeoning motion picture industry. First in line were film projectionists. Interestingly, even though AFL-style unionism was supposed to be "pure and simple," aligning with projectionists proved to be anything but.[32] Three different unions claimed that their mandate extended to this novel craft. The International Brotherhood of Electrical Workers (IBEW) assumed that projectionists fell under its jurisdiction over all "use of electrical power for commercial purposes." IATSE naturally saw its domain as encompassing all of show business. Most surprisingly, an early players' association, the Actors' National Union (ANU), felt that it was the most suitable to take control over projectionists, so that together the two groups could increase their power versus motion picture producers. IATSE won this dispute in 1907 when it was granted jurisdiction over all motion picture machine operators.[33] But there is a lesson here, which is that classification of professions and alliances between them are neither natural nor intuitive; rather, they are the result of politics and interests.

Ultimately, it was IATSE's interests and "strict departmentalization of tasks" that came to define and dominate the motion picture business. Slowly but surely, this organization tightened its grip over the growing industry and its various professions. To be sure, this takeover was accompanied by many battles with producers and jurisdictional disputes with other unions, but by the end of the studio era in the 1950s, IATSE practically assumed control over all production work save for acting, directing, writing, and music composition. It became the bargaining unit for seventeen locals, which between them included approximately 160 separate jobs, from directors of photography to property "swing gang men."[34] Therefore, the separation between arts and crafts has clear institutional and historical causes in addition to aesthetic ones. Motion picture crafts are those professions which were successfully lobbied for and claimed by long-standing trade unions, ones associated with more traditional forms of craftsman-ship. The "creative professions" or "talent" were the ones whose history and traditions belonged to the more elusive and hard to categorize realm of "the arts." This institutional division seemed to have been officially ac-cepted by the industry by 1927, with the establishment of the Academy of Motion Picture Arts and Sciences, whose stated goal was to "co-ordinate the forces of the five major production branches," which consisted of "producers, writers, directors, actors, and technicians."[35]

Nevertheless, the form of organization embraced by the motion picture crafts and the type of work they were engaged in kept the border with "the arts" quite porous. IATSE was (and still is) an association of trade unions, but it was also an industrial union that promoted the alliance of all theater workers. The practical implication of this duality is that many studio work-ers had two frames of reference: the tradition of their craft and the creative nature of their industry. In this sense, they were markedly different than craftsmen who belonged to unions such as the United Brotherhood of Car-penters and Joiners or the International Union of Painters and Allied Trades.[36] Like many of their fellow filmmakers, Hollywood craftsmen had a liminal identity—between arts and crafts. This might explain why many card-carrying IATSE members viewed their work as creative and themselves as artists.

Craft to art conversion is in itself a long-standing tradition. Colloqui-ally, the idea of craft pertains to "practical utility" and the making of things "according to the dictates of clients or employers." Art, on the other hand, is believed to be guided by ideals of beauty and free expression. One can certainly turn into the other. The designation of any trade as an art form is, of course, a social construction. It requires a community of people, both from within the practice and from without, to affirm its artistic status. Such social consensus could and indeed did form around certain crafts. In fact, in many ways all arts began as crafts: music was made for religious ritual, and painters were commissioned for portraits.[37] In that sense, the condition of motion picture craftsmen is historically unexceptional. However, as was often the case in the industrial era, scale mattered. Producing entertain-ment in large settings such as the Warner Bros. lot in Burbank, the motion picture business invited many traditional craftsmen to engage in what was not socially considered to be high art but was certainly a creative pursuit. It opened the studio gates to carpenters, needle workers, electrical engi-neers, and many others, and by that also allowed them to take a few steps away from utility on the imaginary craft-to-art continuum.

No profession reflects this motion, as well as the ambiguity of the film-making crafts, better than cinematography. Strictly speaking, cameramen are craftsmen; they "possess certain objective and teachable skills," such as knowing how to operate a camera, process film, and make photographic prints. At least during the studio era, they also learned their trade by semi-apprenticeships or assistantships. The historical origin of their trade is scientific and industrial. Not surprisingly, like many of their peers, with the expansion of the business, motion picture photographers, and especially those among them who earned the status "director of photography," have come to view their work in artistic terms. Yet, probably more than any other trade in the "technical" branch of the Academy, cinematographers came closest to creating a consensual understanding that the "mechanical and chemical process" created with the help of the camera is the result not only of "technique or learned skills" but also of a unique ability and artistic sensibilities. To secure this understanding, an elite class of cinematographers had to distance themselves from the technical origins of their profession and embrace a language and practice more akin to that of directors or writers. That is exactly what they did, via division of labor and a process of "dis-identification" with the mechanical aspects of camera work.[38] Their success was partial; cameramen of all classes eventually came under the IATSE craft umbrella, but their story is emblematic and therefore worth telling. Hand in hand with the medium it represented, cinematography was pioneered by engineers, advanced by showmen, and, ultimately, recognized to some degree as the work of artists.

Get Cranking

One morning in early October 1889, having just returned from a trip to the Universal Exposition in Paris, Thomas Edison headed to his laboratory in West Orange, New Jersey. Upon his arrival, so the story goes, he was greeted by William Kennedy Laurie Dickson, a young apprentice who had moved to the United States from England five years earlier to work for Edison and study electrical sciences. That summer, Dickson oversaw experimentation with his boss's recent idea: "reproducing to the eye the effect of motion by means of a swift and graded succession of pictures and of linking these photographic impressions with the phonograph in one combination so as to complete to both senses synchronously the record of a given scene."[39] That morning, the young engineer "led his master to room V of the building." Inside "was a black wooden box, perhaps the height of a modern filing cabinet. Near the top was a peephole."[40] Following his assistant's instructions,

Edison looked in the peephole. There, within the machine, he saw a miniature Mr. Dickson who walked "out on the screen, raised his hat and smiled."[41]

This flickering image of Dickson was, of course, one of the first motion pictures. The machine projecting it was an early version of the kinetoscope, and the image itself was captured by the kinetograph, one of the first motion picture cameras. In the following years, Dickson kept experimenting with these prototypes with the help of other lab workers such as William Heise. They improved the original models, and when Edison decided it was time to commercialize his newly patented moving image inventions, Dickson and his assistants also started producing movies. In 1894, they "kinetographed" more than seventy-five motion pictures, including *Annabelle Butterfly Dance*, *Buffalo Bill*, *The Wrestling Dog*, and *The Boxing Cats*. At first, the films were made for the peephole machine, but almost immediately Dickson was also at work assisting the development of big-screen projection, new camera patents, and 70 mm film frame photography. By 1896, after he left Edison to help found of the American Mutoscope & Biograph Company, Dickson was a full-time filmmaker, scouring the East Coast for scenes to shoot, as he was put in charge of operating the company's sole camera.[42]

Many of the first cinematographers were like Dickson: inventors turned filmmakers. They had the necessary training to build motion picture cameras, which immediately made them the most qualified to operate those cameras. In fact, in the early years of cinema, those making the movies were usually referred to by the very technical term "operators."[43] They did much more than just operate the machinery, though: they chose the subject, picked performers, and determined the scenery and the shooting angles. One could say it was a system of production based almost completely on their labor. Just like traditional craftsmen, the camera operators "knew the entire work process," and through them the product's "conception and execution were unified."[44] The only other job that had comparable control over the moving images belonged to another kind of skilled technician, the film projector operator. Indeed, if they were not directly involved in designing and building equipment, many of the early cameramen started their engagement with film as projectionists.

Oftentimes it was both. Edwin S. Porter became a projectionist in 1896. He remembered working "for a man by the name of J. R. Balsley and [for] R. S. Pine who bought the state rights of the Vitascope [projector] from Raff and Gammon for California and Indiana." After that, Porter "ran the projectoscope for Daniel and Dowe of Hamilton, Ontario." His experience as an electrician and telegraph operator made him qualified to handle this complex machine and troubleshoot the many problems it encountered. Porter did similar work in New York, where in 1898 he started working as a projector operator at the Eden Musée. While there, as he recalled, he also "built projecting machines [and] cameras of [his] own design." In the fall of 1900, he went to work for Edison. It was a new century, a new workplace, and also a new role. Edison hired Porter to make films rather than project them. He placed him as the photographer in charge of the company's new studio on 41 East 21st Street.[45] From that location Porter's career skyrocketed. Three years later, he produced *Life of an American Fireman* and *The Great Train Robbery*, each of which was (and still is) considered to be a cinematic breakthrough. Porter functioned as projectionist, camera operator, writer, and director all rolled into one.

Cameramen Billy Bitzer, who shot hundreds of films and worked with D. W. Griffith on *The Birth of a Nation* and *Intolerance*, had a very similar story. He started by studying electrical engineering at Cooper Union in New York. Through the connections of a friend, he got a job at Bernard Koopman's Magic Introduction Company, which "dealt in all sorts of new inventions—like a new cigar lighter that burned benzoin." One of the novelties picked up by the company in 1894 was none other than Dickson's mutoscope camera. Shortly after, the Magic Introduction Company turned into American Mutoscope, and Bitzer became Dickson's assistant.[46] He remembered photographing as "fairly easy and gratifying." The same could not be said about "the showing of these pictures," a task that was also Bitzer's responsibility:

> Running the projector was like running a trolley car, in that it made
> a terrible racket. The projector was also hand-turned, like the camera.
> I used every resource I had, including my nose, to control the film so
> that it would not buckle on me. I was scared stiff and almost desperate
> when I realized that I would have so many different things to do—
> flashing titles onto the screen with a separate lantern-slide projector;
> watching the heat from the lamp so there would be no danger of fire;
> looking at the screen to keep the action smooth; and so on. I would
> have to use both hands, one foot, my forehead, and my nose; and
> I was afraid that two eyes would not be enough.[47]

He had other technical duties as well, ones "which no cameraman today would consider part of his job," including "house electrician." Bitzer emphasized that he could fulfill this union-protected craftsmanship because his "course at Cooper Union entitled [him] to that license."[48] Finally, he started making movies on his own for Biograph (the name commonly used for American Mutoscope & Biograph). In this capacity, much like Porter, he was "responsible for everything except the immediate hiring and handling of the actor."[49]

Behind the expanded responsibilities of the cameramen was the commercial success of motion pictures. As the business continued to grow, however, its increasing popularity also brought about the contraction of the cinematographer's work role. Part of the reason Bitzer became an omnipotent filmmaker was that, between 1897 and 1898, Biograph increased its production rate from 350 films per year to nearly 500, a move that called for additional production units and more cameramen to lead them.[50] With the nickelodeon boom, which began after 1905, demand increased even further. Albert E. Smith, a cameraman and the founder of the Vitagraph company, remembered that around that time they "had been training men to take over the camera work." Finding qualified people was not easy. Still photographers proved unsatisfactory, mostly because "the camera required the ministrations of a mechanic." Therefore, they were mostly "training men from the machine shop." This system functioned well, since "early story pictures consisted entirely of movement," and, according to Smith, "the plots of that era would not tax a new enroller in today's nursery school."[51] Soon, however, the skills of these machine shop technicians were insufficient. The growing industry, which increasingly relied on longer and more-structured narrative films, needed more people like Porter, who could think up stories as well as shoot them in dramatically effective ways. The profit considerations of industry heads meant that they also needed their Porters to work fast. As one scholar put it, "The cameraman system could supply films but not as predictably, rapidly, and inexpensively as was necessary."[52] Relying on the abilities of one man was simply too disorganized.

In turn-of-the-century America, as craftsmen and common laborers alike realized all too well, there emerged a top-to-bottom growing consensus that speed was increased by efficiency and that efficiency was maximized by a division of labor.[53] This rationale was not lost on the motion picture industry magnates. They all "realized that the production business must be systemized." A first step was to relieve the cameramen of their story-writing duties. Smith recalled that any "one-reel (thousand-foot) silent was filmed in a single day," and, by 1908, Vitagraph was "producing eight films a week."

To guarantee this fast pace, "story ammunition . . . came from a widely advertised five-dollars-an-idea plan."[54] Biograph did the same. In fact, before he started directing, Griffith sold some of his stories to the company. After he started directing, his cameramen lost some more of their responsibilities: "Soon it was Griffith's say whether the lights were bright enough, or if the make-up was right." Directors were taking charge, assuming some of the functions that were previously embedded in the role of the cameraman. Bitzer, for one, did not mind his diminishing control. To the contrary, as he explained, "a cameraman had enough to do watching the rapidity of action and keeping the hand-cranked camera going at a steady pace to prevent the film from buckling."[55]

Whether film photographers were pleased by it or not, for the next several years their work was steadily confined to that hand-cranked camera. Their primary duties now consisted of "setting up lighting, placing the boundary lines to signal the edges of the set area visible in the image, handling the camera, and providing special effects photography."[56] That was by no means just a technical job, but its creative elements relied on technical know-how. As cinematographer Arthur Miller once said, in those early days, a cameraman could become an artist, but "first he had to be a technician."[57] Most professionals affirmed that "in order to cooperate in the fullest sense with his director," a "dramatic instinct" was a virtue for the cameraman. Still, when they spoke about their work they emphasized that "there are other factors . . . that are necessities," such as "a thorough technical knowledge of the medium and its possibilities and limitations" and, "of course, certain fundamental principles of lighting."[58] When asked about the conditions of the job, the *Moving Picture World* informed its readers in August 1912 that "the salary of a cameraman ranges from $25 to $35 or even more," and he "must be able to judge both daylight and the lighting of the studio, in addition to the general knowledge of photographic work and the motion camera."[59] Cinematographer Norbert Brodin went even further, suggesting that in his line of work, one "must not only be a master craftsman" with regard to "his photographic apparatus"; he must also be "a master of lighting."[60]

By the early 1910s, systematization pushed the cinematographer away from the center of the filmmaking process, placing the director in his stead. But at that point in time, the principles of efficiency were just beginning to take hold in the motion picture industry. While, at first, division of labor fastened camera work to its technical elements, at its zenith it would completely release some cinematographers from the cranking handle.

A Society of Cinematographers

Standardization did not reach its peak until the 1930s. Despite the efforts of companies to regulate the employment of actors or the attempts of producers such as Thomas Ince to implement new managerial methods, throughout the 1910s and early 1920s labor practices in motion pictures were not yet uniform. That was certainly the case for cinematographers. To begin with, there were no strict hiring procedures. Some cameramen were under long-term contracts, others employed by the picture or just by the day. Bitzer often claimed that in the period he worked with Griffith, which lasted until the late 1920s, "there was never a written contract, only a handshake and our trust in each other." Documentation shows he did sign a three-year contract with the director from 1913 to 1916, but this discrepancy suggests that such formal agreements were irregular and uncommon enough that one could forget them.[61] Another cameraman who worked with Griffith, Arthur Sintzenich, left a clear record of instability. In his diary, the years between 1919 and 1922 are a "kaleidoscope of jobs, mostly of short duration, involving a cataract of names, known and unknown." Work usually involved "unlimited hours and intermittent pay." Sintzenich describes many situations in which "two or more cameramen are . . . 'cranking' side by side," or "work simultaneously on different scenes" of the same movie. Job description was also quite loose. When working on set, a cameraman like Sintzenich was on occasion asked to "supervise laboratory work, or edit, or even act."[62]

Most camera professionals never even made it to the set of big studio productions. Feature-length dramas, comedies, and serials supplied work opportunity for a relatively small number of camera operators. Instead, until the end of the 1920s, a more lucrative source of revenue for cinematographers was newsreels. Miller observed that at "every moment throughout the world, cameramen are literally standing by their cameras, waiting for telegrams and cables, waiting for orders, that they may record for your pleasure or enlightenment those world-shaking events that are termed news."[63] Many cameramen made their living responding to such telegrams. Elmer Dyer was one of them. He was a freelance photographer, and throughout the late 1910s his career consisted of responding to announcements such as the following one, issued by the Famous Players–Lasky Corporation in 1919: "Please be advised that the Educational Department of the [company] is about to produce a new screen magazine to be known as the 'Paramount Magazine.' We are very anxious to have you contribute subjects for this reel and you can rest assured that our policy of payment for subjects suitable will be very liberal."[64] Dyer responded by offering to shoot such topics as "Branding Cattle," "Farming Lady Bugs," and "How a Mexican Makes His Rope."[65] The company picked the ones they deemed commercially viable and eventually paid him $510 for one such picture, a sum that included compensation for 340 feet of film, fourteen days' salary, machine storage, and other expenses.[66] Dyer and many like him essentially functioned as pieceworkers.

Nevertheless, even if the labor market was still in relative disarray, cinematographers created their own order. Abiding by the long-standing traditions of craftsmen, motion picture cameramen established clear, albeit informal, channels of socialization, including systems of apprenticeship and several professional organizations. On-the-job training was probably the most traditional element embraced by photographers. "There is just one way to get a position as cameraman with a motion picture concern," explained the *Moving Picture World* in 1912. "You 'get next' to some cameraman. For a time, you act as helper and then, by degrees you are broken in to the work."[67] A few years later, due to a large number of inquiries on the matter, the leading trade paper had to once again underscore the fact that this type of work "can only be learned by actual experience," and "unless you can afford to go and apply in person to different film factories until you get some sort of minor position and then work up by study and application, you had better give up the idea of becoming a cameraman."[68]

The career path of several cinematographers confirms this axiom. George Folsey started as an office boy for Jesse L. Lasky's Feature Play Company around 1914. Ever since he first laid eyes on a studio, he was hooked. So he hung around, taking whatever job he could: "I got to learn how to run the switchboard, I got to learn how to run the elevator, I played parts in pictures." At some point, "they sent me to help a cameraman. I didn't know what I was doing, but I helped him." Folsey stressed that it was not an official position; the film crews of those days consisted of "one cameraman, that was it." As he remembered it, the need for assistance was a natural outgrowth of the heavy workload. The shooting schedule was intense, and the company's cameramen had too many responsibilities to handle on their own. Porter, who was with Lasky at the time, "was so busy that he didn't have time to load the magazines, unload them, and can them and put them away. He had too many other big things to do. So he got his secretary to get him an assistant," just as he would have done if he were still working in the electrical shop or as a telegraph operator. Folsey embraced the opportunity. He assisted J. Searle Dawley, James Durkin, and Emmett A. Williams, among others. Then, in 1919, while working on the set of the picture *His Bridal Night*, the cameraman, Jacques Montéran, quit in the middle of production, and, as so many Hollywood legends go, Folsey got his big break. The director, Kenneth S. Webb, asked him if he could step in. "Well, by this time I'm 19 years old," recalled Folsey. "I'd never shot a picture in my life, but I'd been around with good cameramen [and] I was always watching. I understood about lights and all that, so I said 'sure' so he made me the cameraman."[69] Perhaps this break was Folsey's direct shot to the top; perhaps he had to wait and watch a bit longer; either way, apprenticeship was necessary for promotion.

Sometimes the climb started from below the assistant level. James Wong Howe was one of the most respected cinematographers in Hollywood. He had shot well over a hundred pictures and was nominated for eight Academy Awards and won two of them. In the summer of 1917 he was standing outside the gates of Paramount Studios, hoping to see Alvin Wyckoff. Mr. Wykoff, as Howe referred to him even years later, "was the head of the camera department and also Mr. Cecil B. DeMille's chief cameraman." Howe wanted to become his assistant. Unfortunately, that position was already filled, but Wykoff had another idea. "You know that the cameramen throw their waste film and paper away down there in the camera department," he said to Howe, "and I like to have someone to keep it clean. That'll be your job. When the time comes, if I need another assistant, you'll have the first opportunity." After about six or seven months, as Howe recounted, "Mr. DeMille needed an extra assistant to hold the slate. That's how I became an assistant."[70] Harking back to late nineteenth-century workshops, the establishment of apprenticeship for cinematographers seemed to have come about almost intuitively—a reenactment of the relationship master craftsmen such as Edison had with their underlings.

Another craft-like element embraced by cinematographers was the formation of professional societies. Seeking to advance their trade and secure it, American cameramen started banding together by the early 1910s, without the auspices of IATSE or any other formal labor union. In 1913, a few operators from the Edison Kinetoscope Company formed the Cinema Camera Club in New York City. Two years later the organization boasted "a register of over one hundred and twenty members" and "spacious offices" in the Times Building. At the same time, a similar body, the Static Club, was formed in California, and soon the two established an affiliation and even published two short-lived magazines. "We had no thought of a union, or of using the organization to obtain higher pay," explained one founding member of the New York club. "Our original purpose was to get cameramen to exchange ideas and thus encourage manufacturers to make better equipment, especially lighting equipment."[71] Other more politicized organizations were also attempting to unite the profession. Sintzenich mentioned joining the Society of Motion Picture Craftsmen in 1919, the United Society of Cinematographers in 1920, and the Motion Picture Photographers Association. His notes suggest that these were all sites of professional exchange in which members looked for work, shared technical knowledge, and discussed labor conditions.[72]

Perhaps due to the competition, several members of the Cinema Camera Club decided to solidify their ranks. In December 1918, a reorganization committee met in Los Angeles and formed the American Society of Cinematographers (ASC). A month later the association was incorporated under California law and received an official charter. The society's motto was "Loyalty, Progress and Artistry," and its constitution emphasized "a strive for preeminence, excellence, artistic perfection, and scientific knowledge." But if one goal was to bring "into the closest confederation" the leaders of the profession, another avowed goal was to divide and create hierarchy. Membership in the ASC was by invitation only, with the clear intention of making such affiliation "a mark of honor and distinction based on merit." At least according to this society, "to advance the art and science of cinematography" meant splitting it up, separating the wheat from the chaff, and keeping only those "whose achievements in that field entitle them to membership." Choosing elitism as the safest road for progress, the ASC demarcated the boundaries of the cinematographic profession, leaving many on the outskirts. In its official publications the ASC often emphasized that it was not a union; indeed, in many respects it was just the opposite.[73]

Strikingly, as the studio system expanded, the major film companies embraced the informal hierarchies and practices developed by cameramen. The division of labor embedded in the apprenticeship system and professed by the ASC was easily co-opted into the endeavor to achieve efficiency and standardization that engulfed the motion picture industry in the 1920s and 1930s. The big studios were increasing production and streamlining the production process. To that end, all tasks, including camera operation, had to be routinized. Accordingly, during the 1920s, it became standard practice that three people handled camerawork: the first cameraman shot the primary negative and orchestrated the lighting. The second cameraman assisted the first and, often, literally worked as a second cameramen, operating an additional camera. "The reason for that," explained Howe, "was that they needed two negatives, one for [the] domestic and one for the European market. So they set up the second camera." The third crew member was the assistant, who carried around the equipment, loaded the film, and held "the slate with the clapper on top" that identified the scene and take number.[74] In this regulated system, noted Miller, even "the inexperienced son of the big boss of the studio could not possibly become a first cameraman until he had completed several years as a film loader, assistant, and operator."[75]

Following the introduction of talking pictures in the late 1920s, the size of the camera crew increased, and its subdivisions multiplied. Experimentation with sound recording techniques reshuffled production practices several times between 1926 and 1932, as studios and sound experts tested new technologies and filming strategies. "That was the most difficult period," said Howe. "The sound engineers were responsible. They were really the top men. We had to accommodate them."[76] The main change for cinematographers was the temporary shift to multicamera filming from 1929 to 1931. Spearheaded by Warner Bros., major studios employed the Vitaphone company's sound-on-disc method, by which action and sound were recorded simultaneously but captured separately—the first on film, the second on disc. Due to that fact, it was very complicated to cut the action and change filming positions without disrupting the sound sequence. To counter this problem, companies decided to set up multiple cameras around the set, each from a different angle, enabling the editor to combine takes from all of them while maintaining a synchronized soundtrack.[77]

Orchestrating multiple cameras was a complex endeavor. The machines had to be placed so that they complemented rather than obscured one another, microphones had to be concealed from all, and lighting had to be fixed to fit all angles. Each camera required at least one operator and one assistant, and someone had to coordinate the entire staff. That someone was the first cameramen, whose job now consisted of managing the army of cameras, determining their positions, and deciding on lighting. The men assigned to this new role were no longer operating the machinery. Instead, as *Variety* declared in 1930, they turned into "cameraless cameramen." The formal job description changed as well: "First cameramen on pictures are cameramen no longer. New title lists them as supervising cinematographers."[78] By the mid-1930s, the sound-on-disc method was discarded and replaced by systems that recorded audio optically onto the film. Companies reverted to the single-camera set up, but the new division of labor persisted. Supervising cinematographers soon came to be known as directors of photography, a title that fitted their increasing load of managerial duties and growing distance from the camera crank.

Even without multiple cameras, technological innovations, which improved the quality of pictures and introduced new technical features, also turned the filming task into a complex undertaking and the film crew into a robust labor unit. In 1948, a reporter who followed Howe around the set offered the following description:

> Howe's camera crew consists of an operative cameraman who pans the camera (swings it) and keeps his eyes glued to the finder as he follows the actors. A first assistant cameraman loads the film, handles the focus and changes the stops of the lens under Howe's direction. A second assistant holds the recording slate of the scene numbers used to identify each sequence and keeps daily notes of scenes and footage that have been shot. . . . Working with the camera crew is an electrical crew, headed by the chief electrician, called the "gaffer," his first assistant or "best boy," and another assistant or two. The usual movie set had five or six electricians on the floor and 15 or 20 on overhead. Then there is a unit of three to six grips, who are among the most important laborers on the set. They move the dolly or camera truck on wheels, the camera crane and the "wild" [or] movable walls of a set, and act as jacks-of-all-trades.

The director of photography, or D.P., as he is often referred to, managed all of these people, leading the author of this piece to conclude that "today's cameraman is as much an executive as artist."[79]

As mentioned, this division of labor was formalized by the studios. In late 1933, the ASC assumed the role of a bargaining unit and entered negotiations with a committee representing the major film companies.[80] By January 1934, they reached an agreement stating that the ASC would furnish the studios with "lists of eligible cameramen approved by the Society," from which "the Producers may select Cameramen for employment." The four classifications specified included first cameraman, second cameraman, still cameraman, and assistant cameraman, each of which was matched with a minimum wage scale. The contract signed also acknowledged the managerial duty of the first cameraman or director of photography, indicating that "by virtue of [his] experience and association, he is well-fitted to give aid and assistance to the Producer in the selection of the Camera Staff, and shall hold himself ready and shall help and advise the Producer."[81]

Ten years later, the list of job titles had inflated considerably, comprising director of photography, cameraman, still cameraman, portrait photographer, color technician, technician, assistant, and film loader. At this point, the size of the crew was so large that titles were not enough. Specialization and unionization dictated the specific duties and responsibilities of each role. The 1944 wage scale stated, for example, that the second cameramen are "those who operate cameras and shoot scenes," that a color technician is the one who "has complete charge of the mechanical operation of the camera during the course of a shooting day," that the assistant cameraman "handles the slate and clapsticks," and that the term "film loader" "refers to one who is engaged in the loading and unloading, as well as the handling of equipment."[82] Over a span of thirty years, informal practices and pecking orders turned into official roles and contractual obligations. Directors of photography returned to a managerial role akin to, though far less powerful than, the position they held in the early days of the profession. Commanding a large crew, and free from operating the equipment, those first among cameramen were now also free to explore their artistic potential.

Cameraless Cameramen

The separation of man from machine in the early 1930s inspired many cameramen to embrace an artistic jargon to describe their work. Lee Garmes, who shot *Scarface* (1932) and *Duel in the Sun* (1946), among many other films, preferred the title "photographer," not because of "any snobbish desire," but simply since "the art of photography rather than the physical operation of the camera is the concern of the photographic director."[83] Garmes started his career in 1916 as a "prop-boy," but he immediately manifested a "hankering for fussing around a camera, and no opportunities were overlooked for getting his hands on the instrument." In 1930, IATSE showcased this hankering as a staple of Garmes's career path and used it in an op-ed as an example of "what may be achieved by a combination of ambitious perseverance and applied ability."[84] By the end of the decade, however, Garmes chose to emphasize different capabilities. He now denoted the picture camera as "a simple instrument," and explained that "the quality of a picture photographically and to a great extent dramatically comes, not from elaborate equipment, but from the mind of the man in control of the equipment." Perseverance was beside the point. Garmes no longer tried to get his hands on anything. Instead he "liked to get the 'feel' of the scene before [he] decided how [he] wanted to photograph it." He explained that "unless the photographer is able to do this [abstract exercise], his work, no matter how brilliant technically, will be unsatisfactory and detrimental to the picture."[85]

Such sentiments were echoed by John Arnold, who served as the president of the ASC between 1931 and 1936. He became involved with motion pictures in the early 1910s, working in the engineering department of the Edison Company before he moved to the "motion picture department." He went on to shoot dozens of films and to head MGM's camera department for over two decades. In line with this trajectory, by the late 1930s, Arnold was far removed from his engineering days both temporally and mentally. "A cameraman is in reality an artist," he testified in 1937, therefore, he "cannot be placed in one class, as his individual standing as such has been attained through his artistic temperament and development." In fact, "personality plays an important part in his career." A good cinematographer, according to Arnold, "brings into play all the lore and photographic and dramatic knowledge at his command," which is "the result of years of study and application to the fine arts and works of the world." Arnold's description of his work routine was teeming with technical details, including mentions of tubular globes, lenticular glass strips, silver bromide, and silver chloride. Yet he chose to sum it up by saying, "To any man, who can paint with light and shade, as a painter does with oil and pigment on canvas should rightfully go the title artist."[86] Garmes used the same metaphor, writing that "the photographer must use his lights as another artist would his brushes and colors to paint a scene before him."[87]

The language chosen by these cinematographers demonstrates the kind of work they wanted to be associated with. "Photography to me has as its function and no other, the responsibility of expressing the story in its own dramatic terms," explained Howe. "This is more than mood," he elaborated. "It is photographic drama . . . suited to the emotional quality of the story. Shot by shot, it is suiting the camera to the action," adding, with a hint of self-reflection, "if that doesn't sound too pompous."[88] Whatever it sounds like, his words certainly reflect a sea change from the tangible way pioneer cameramen like Bitzer or Dickson described their engagement with the mechanics of filmmaking.

Self-evaluations notwithstanding, embedding cinematography within the realm of the arts was not an easy enterprise. First, just like all their colleagues and unlike the Renaissance painters they often compared themselves to, directors of photography did not have complete creative control over their work. Despite their artistic manifestos, even the Garmes-Arnold-Howe triumvirate acknowledged their own limitations. "Sometimes I received the script several days before production was due to begin, and took part in conferences with the art director, director, and producers," explained Garmes. "Many times, however, the photographer has much less notice of a new assignment and may even go on the floor without having read the script at all."[89] Arnold, once again, confirmed: "Sometimes [the director of photography] may be tied up on another production until almost the last minute." When that happens, "much of his preliminary work must necessarily be performed by the Studio's Executive Director of Photography or by such of the studio's contract Cinematographers as may be available."[90] Their responsibility in any given picture was limited and often also divided. On top of that, while they managed large crews, directors of photography also had a boss. "The cameraman gets a story," clarified Howe, then "he is assigned a director.... Sometimes the cameraman and the director don't agree. The smart cameraman adapts himself to the director."[91] Or in the words of George Folsey, "It was my understanding that the director was always the boss ... it was his decision, it was his picture and he got what he wanted."[92] As was the case for all filmmakers, the studio routine confined the creativity of cameramen as well as their managerial abilities to well-defined and carefully monitored segments of the production process.

In addition, while many directors of photography saw their work as inherently distinct from the craft of camera operation, other forces in the business felt differently. Chief among those forces was IATSE, which, in 1939, once again (as in 1905) attempted to "take jurisdiction over the entire film industry," this time by demanding that the studios abrogate their contract with ASC and allow IATSE to assume responsibility for all classes of cameramen under its existing affiliate, International Photography Local 659. Thus, IATSE sought to abolish the "dual union in the photographic field," which separated directors of photography represented by ASC and all other members of the camera crew, who typically joined Local 659. The main motivation behind this move was to increase power. As stated by *Variety*, "Takeover of the chief lensers would give the IATSE the two most powerful groups in the industry, cameramen and projectionists," and would enable it "to force the producers to accept any reasonable demands." The catalyst for the move was the separatist nature of the ASC. The attempt to solidify control within Local 659 was a response to a clause from the ASC's agreement with the studios, "which stated directors of photography would be required to perform their services for the producer regardless of any strike that might be ordered by other film crafts or guilds."[93] IATSE sought to enforce an industry-wide craft alliance, and cinematographers of all classes were a necessary part of its vision.

Unsurprisingly, this image of an industrial union clashed with how ASC members imagined their professional field. In 1941, the organization comprised "one hundred per cent of all First Cameramen and Directors of Photography employees of the West Coast," and they were "unanimous in their intention of not affiliating in a union with the balance of the photographic craft."[94] In fact, they found Local 659's attempt to "supervise the affairs of six different classifications . . . an impossible undertaking from any standpoint of good business." According to the ASC, one class clearly did not fit in with the other five: "First Cameramen, by the very fact of their responsibility for the motion picture photography in a production, are the bosses of the balance of their crew," a condition that "precludes the possibility of proper harmony and freedom of action in the operation of a single labor union." In addition, "the salary situation" also "makes universal bargaining a practical impossibility," as the "salaries of Loaders, Assistants and Operative men are at scale," while "the salaries of First Cameramen and Directors of Photography vary through a range of up to two, three, four, and five times the minimum scale," or any amount that reflects their "varying degree of artistry, creative and executive abilities."[95] Representing the likes of Garmes and Arnold, the ASC sought, once again, to distinguish between the creative professionals at the top and the technical craftsmen who worked under them.

Unfortunately for ASC members, their vision was not shared by those occupying the other five classifications. There was a clear conflict of interest between the privileged and the rank and file. Local 659, most of whose members were not first cameramen, sided with IATSE. On December 28, 1941, the union adopted a resolution that called on producers "to recognize the jurisdictional award of first cameramen and/or directors of photography that has been regularly made to this local by the IATSE." An added threat promised that all IATSE employees "shall refuse service where any first cameraman or director of photography is not a member of this local." Assistants and operatives, with some pressure from the alliance, decided that the strength of their craft depended on the unity of the cinematographic ranks. The ASC saw this as a clear sign that "the lower brackets of the camera craft desire to be in a position to dictate to the First Cameramen," a pursuit that would inevitably result in "a continuation of the misunderstanding, division of opinion and lack of harmony which has existed up to the present time in the ranks of the camera craft."[96]

Indeed, the lack of harmony was persistent and ubiquitous. Local 659 stepped up its campaign to recruit ASC members, on occasion resorting to aggressive tactics. In response, the ASC attempted to leverage its position by aligning with the IBEW.[97] All of this was happening amid one of the most tumultuous periods in Hollywood labor history. The year 1941 also saw the start of the nine-month-long cartoonists' strike, which was part of a longer power struggle between the studios, IATSE, and its newly formed contender, the Conference of Studio Unions, led by Herbert K. Sorrell.[98] In July, with encouragement from Sorrell's opponents, the California Fact Finding Committee on Un-American Activities, chaired by State Senator Jack B. Tenney, began its investigation into the film industry's ties to communism, in a prelude to the House Un-American Activities Committee (HUAC) hearings of the early 1950s.[99] To top it all off, in November, the president of IATSE, George Browne, resigned after having been convicted of extortion, throwing the organization into disarray.[100] In December, the United States entered World War II.

Unlike the engulfing conflicts, the dispute among the cameramen was resolved relatively quickly. By the end of 1942, the IBEW withdrew its support of the ASC, and the latter voted to merge with Local 659.[101] This resolution left directors of photography within the organizational envelope of the motion picture crafts, aligning them, at least institutionally, with the balance of the cinematographic craft. Yet, even if as a group they were tied down, as individuals many of them had plenty of reasons to feel artistically elevated. First, as argued by the ASC, the salaries of first cameramen often went above and beyond the minimum specified in basic agreements. For example, Charles G. Clarke's 1933 contract with MGM guaranteed him $300 a week, while the basic agreement signed by the ASC a year later set the minimum for first cameramen at $225.[102] This elevated pay scale was given to Clarke even though, by his own account, he "never felt at home at [Metro]," which "had their top cinematographers," and where he "found [himself] becoming a second unit man."[103] At the same time, Howe, who was one of those top cinematographers, was not required to pay his agent unless the latter could guarantee a weekly paycheck exceeding $450.[104]

Second, beyond the raw numbers, contracts signed by directors of photography accorded them the same unique abilities conferred upon actors, directors, writers, and composers. Just as in the agreements of the "talent class," those signed with first cameramen stated that their services were "of a special, unique, unusual, extraordinary and intellectual character, and of great and peculiar value to the producer." Of course, all these adjectives served primarily as a justification for the contract's more stringent elements and the legal assertion that a loss of said unique services "cannot be reasonably or adequately compensated in damages in an action at law," and would therefore cause "irreparable injury and damage."[105] But in Hollywood the mere entitlement to such a contract, with its dialectics of art and commerce, signified a creative status. Even if, organizationally, cameramen of all classes still belonged to the "technical" or craft section of the industry, contractually, each director of photography was granted a singular artistic talent.

Finally, the contract featured one last conjunction of art, craft, and greed. Cameramen, like all other creative employees, signed over the rights to "all results and proceeds" of their work "without reservation, condition or limitation."[106] Such results consisted of "literary, dramatic, musical, motion picture, mechanical, or any other form of works, themes, ideas, compositions, creations or products." On occasion, the language was even more specific, indicating the assignment of "all invention, developments, improvement and/or discoveries, conceived, made or discovered by [the employee]."[107] In other words, whether they developed stories or mechanical patents, whether they were artists, craftsmen, directors of photography, or mere technicians, they were first and foremost employees, and whatever they produced belonged to the studio and the system.

REFLECTING ON A CAREER that lasted for more than half a century, in 1986 George Folsey was still uncertain about the status of his profession. "I guess it's a craft," he told his interviewer. "I think of it as a craft. Though I think you have to be somewhat artistic, I think you have to have some feeling for painting in your life. You have to have an understanding of light and shade." On further consideration, this veteran cinematographer admitted, "I don't know the difference between an art and a craft, so I don't know which cinematography is. I really don't." Perhaps it was the fact that Folsey started working in the 1910s, the era of camera operators, long before they became directors of photography, that made him reiterate, "I don't think of cinematography as an art." More than anything else, he said, "when I'm doing it, I think of it as a job . . . I feel that my primary job is to make everything to be projected."[108]

Whether one agrees with Folsey's conclusion, the main takeaway is his ambivalence. As a cinematographer, it was difficult for him to ignore the scientific and technical origins of his work. At the same time, it was clear to him that filming motion pictures required a creative sensibility on top of the mechanical abilities. In the end, he was not sure what it all added up to. All he could say for certain was that he had a job. His status as an employee was the only fixed identity. This ambivalence captures the condition of the other "Hollywood 400." Many studio employees held jobs that corresponded with traditional crafts or with professions that had an organizational history outside the realm of show business and the arts. As such, their status within the art world was precarious and in constant need of affirmation. Throughout the studio era, their success was partial. Despite convincing arguments about each profession's indispensable contribution to the creative process, cinematographers, editors, costume designers, and others remained in the "technical" branch of the Academy and within the organizational hold of IATSE. Nevertheless, the ability of people like Folsey to be certain of their "employee" status should not be taken for granted. As we shall see, for those studio workers more fully entrenched in the creative realm, this legal category was far from guaranteed.

CHAPTER SIX

Bargaining

MGM executive producer Irving Thalberg believed that he worked in a "creative business." He thought one could not "say definitely whether picture making is really a business or an art." In fact, he found the issue so complex that, in 1933, he suggested, "It is hard, as a matter of fact, to explain the whole motion picture business situation to a banker—or to anybody else."[1] An outsider simply could not understand.

Indeed, reducing Hollywood companies to either business or art often appeared very difficult, not to say limiting. It was especially so for production managers such as Thalberg. The work of screenwriters was a case in point. In 1935, while conducting negotiations for the Code of Fair Competition for the Motion Picture Industry sponsored by the National Recovery Administration (NRA), studio management, represented by head producers, felt that it was essential to stress the conventional industrial position of writers. The latter were trying to incorporate into the document regulations concerning the fairness of their employment. A committee of studio producers, which included Thalberg, responded to these demands by stating that writers "are to be classified as employees and not as employers." Consequently, writers "are not in competition with the producers [and] as a general proposition, conditions among the writers or conditions in the writers' relations with the producers, are not within the scope of the code." According to the producers, therefore, any demands from the writers "could be adopted into the Code only upon application of the group which originally applied for and agreed to the Code itself, namely, the employers." And they, as employers, did not wish to adopt the writers' demands.[2] The lines were clearly drawn; Hollywood was an industry, producers were its management, and writers were part of the workforce.

That was back in 1935. A year later, the situation had changed. It was April 1936, and the writers, now operating within a professional union, were fighting for their right to collective bargaining. They demanded that the studios recognize their newly formed Screen Writers Guild (SWG). Management once again rejected their demands, this time for a different reason. It was not that the producers had a problem with labor unions. As they claimed in a public statement, signed by representatives of all companies, "for years they have cooperated with the unions and fully sympathized with their proper functions and legitimate objectives." However, per the producers, there was "a wide distinction between labor unions properly organized as such, and organizations of creative employees." Writers may have been employees, but of a special kind, since "not by a widest stretch of the imagination can a writer, whose ability and value cannot be even remotely standardized, place his interest and problems on a place with the man who joins a union" in order "to establish standard wages, working conditions and hours of labor."[3]

Thalberg even took it a step further. A few days after the above statement was released, on May 2, 1936, he held a meeting with all the screenwriters under his employment. As one of them, Charles Brackett, testified, "Mr. Thalberg addressed the writers present more in sorrow than in anger." The vice president in charge of production stated that "writers had no business to belong to anything like a union; that they were artists and should not be members of any organization." Comparing this idea with the comment Thalberg made in 1933, it seems that he found the status of picture-making so "hard to explain" because the way he perceived it was so context-dependent. When he was dealing with the NRA, Hollywood was more of an industry, and screenwriters were part of its workforce. Faced with the demands of organized labor, he preferred to think of Movietown as an artists' colony.[4]

Then again, perhaps it was not complicated at all. Perhaps Thalberg was invoking notions of "exceptionalism" simply to mask what was in essence a very conventional position. When studio bosses suggested that their screenwriters were "not regular employees," all they really meant was that they were not the kind of employees who could lawfully unionize. This, of course, was a managerial tactic typical of the era. When faced with organized labor, many American employers charged that their workers were not in fact "employees" under the law.[5] For Hollywood moguls, the "artistic" argument was simply the most obvious legal recourse. All in all, they attempted to silence their writers the same way any other industrial executive would have.

Due to such managerial orthodoxy, these incidents of producer-writer enmity are telling. On a day-to-day basis, the American motion picture industry relied on its ability to balance a modern, rationalized production operation with a more unstructured creative process. For the most part, maintaining that balance was in the economic interest of all parties involved. However, as the above producer-writer episode illustrates, in times of crisis, when the harmony was interrupted, the creative element was often surrendered. The fact that Thalberg, whose position was to broker between studio management and the creative personnel, sided so unequivocally with the former, serves as a marker here. When the Hollywood system of creative labor encountered labor problems, more often than not it tackled them just the way more "conventional" American industries did.

The word "American" should be emphasized. Throughout its existence, the motion picture business was framed by the larger sociopolitical reality it was operating in, whether it was New York censorship laws or California's open shop policy. Yet, particularly during the 1930s, the policies and legal changes brought about by the New Deal had a significant influence on Hollywood and the reshaping of its labor relations. The rise of creative guilds such as the Screen Writers Guild, the Screen Directors Guild (SDG), and the Screen Actors Guild (SAG), their struggles, the way they chose to pursue them, and the attitude embraced toward them by producers were all molded by the political consensus forged during the Roosevelt era. Thus, Hollywood politics followed the course set by this particular historical intersection of a liberal federal government and a rising labor movement. The ways in which Hollywood overcame its moment of social rupture and the labor practices it adopted in its aftermath were geographically and temporally dependent.

Still, within the political context of the 1930s, and despite the film industry's overall conformity to national trends, the Hollywood labor force maintained some elements of uniqueness. While taking advantage of such programs as those of the National Recovery Administration and the courts of the National Labor Relations Board (NLRB), the members of the creative class also kept their distance. As it turned out, Thalberg was not the only one invoking the ambiguous character of the industry. At several crucial points, many actors, writers, and directors were equally of two minds. Taking advantage of the indecisive nature of their creative business, these creative employees behaved just like their bosses, aligning with traditional industrial labor causes only as long as it served their immediate goals. Just as management flip-flopped on its position toward writers, above-the-line filmmakers went back and forth on their intention to collaborate with and participate in the struggles of back-lot studio workers. Actors and directors especially exhibited only perfunctory support for the New Deal model of state-monitored labor-management relationships. When it came to politics, the ambivalent working class was extra hesitant. Perhaps due to this hesitancy, motion picture people managed to solidify a strong and enduring, albeit conservative, labor movement—a movement that ultimately outlasted many of the 1930s policies and institutions that were responsible for its formation.

The Field and the State

No industry can be studied in isolation. In his theory of cultural production, French sociologist Pierre Bourdieu emphasized that any taste-guided industry is continually affected by the laws governing the fields that encompass it, those of economic and political profit. Any field of cultural production is embedded within a larger "field of power," which is itself rooted in the overarching "field of class relations." As a result, Bourdieu explained, there are "homologies" between the fields. That is, the struggles taking place in inner fields are always overdetermined by and echo the encompassing fields. Specifically, cultural producers, or those who control the cultural industry economically, often express solidarity with their counterparts in the economically dominated positions within the field of politics and class relations.[6] There is always an alignment between the classes within a culture industry and those of society as a whole. Accordingly, ideological struggles at the encircling fields—those of political power and class—are often reproduced at the industry level. In such cases, the owners of production companies tend to be closer to the sources of power outside of their specific industry, assuming those are the wealthy classes that traditionally govern industrial societies.

Such a homology was at work in Hollywood, except that during the 1930s the balance of power in the overarching fields was shifting. Since the appearance of organized labor in the late nineteenth century, the prevailing attitude of American government and business toward the movement was to subvert its legitimacy. Guilds and unions were often accused of inciting conflict and instability, and were faced with charges of corruption, outside agitation, and harboring alien ideological influences. However, following the Great Depression, a new dominant ideological and institutional dynamic formed, one that saw an "amelioration of the labor question." Unions now became "inexorably bound up with a structural solution to the crisis of American capitalism itself." In other words, organized labor became patriotic. Between 1933 and 1937, unions in the United States recruited close to five million new members.[7] The sectors and institutions dominating the power and class relations fields were fluctuating and were no longer confined to big-business owners.

The empowerment of organized labor during the New Deal took a particular form. Unions gained their newfound strength and membership under the auspices of the federal government. In line with its hands-on approach, the Roosevelt administration reformulated the country's industrial relations while reserving an important role for the "new liberal bureaucratic-administrative state" it was fostering. During FDR's tenure, the workers' right to organize was tied to the state: labor organizers could gain power only within the regulatory frameworks of state institutions, for instance, the NRA and the National Labor Relations Board; and unions were not "entities with rights," but instruments chosen by employees via government-supervised elections.[8] The state became an instrumental part of labor relations and, with the aid of lawyers and federal officials, magnified its power to regulate the economy.[9]

Motion pictures were an indispensable part of American life. As such, they too were swept up in the all-encompassing political wave of the New Deal.[10] Some scholars go so far as to argue that what occurred after 1933 in the studio system was no different than the struggles in Detroit's automobile industry or Pittsburgh's steelmaking plants.[11] This claim, however, tells only half the story. Whether or not the film industry behaved just like any other industry, the more important story was *how* the business of filmmaking readjusted according to the emergent economic model of the 1930s. Following the announcement of the Bank Holiday in March 1933, the motion picture business opened its doors to the federal government. Between their participation in the Blue Eagle campaign and their multiple appearances at the NLRB courts, American film companies, management and workforce alike, took part in President Roosevelt's new liberal administrative state. That state, as well as the sociopolitical vision it promoted, shaped the nature of Hollywood's labor strife, supplying the ideologies and institutions with which the industry tackled and resolved it. In addition, at least in terms of labor, the New Deal also marked a break from the industrial order Hollywood was accustomed to. It is to that old order we shall now turn.

Clear Skies, Open Shop

Filmmaking started on the East Coast. Since the invention of cinema at the turn of the twentieth century and throughout most of the 1910s, New York and its suburbs were the center of production. Chicago was second in command. By 1910, however, the climate of these northern cities had become a severe limitation. Nickelodeons were booming across the country, and the demand for films was constantly increasing. To stay in business, companies had to keep up with the growing market, a task that was proving difficult during the long winter months. East Coast studios were not equipped for year-round activity. Some were outdoors—many of them on rooftops—and very few featured artificial lighting, conditions that made shooting problematic or even impossible. As a result, the industry began looking for more-lucrative filming locations in other parts of the United States and beyond. It was not a direct route; there were "detours on the way to Hollywood," and producers were dispatching their crews practically everywhere. Colonel Selig sent out touring companies to New Orleans and Mexico. Vitagraph went as far as Jamaica. The Columbia Film Company was shooting in Oklahoma, and IMP sent Thomas H. Ince to direct in Cuba. Then, during the winter of 1908–9, Kalem led an expedition to Jacksonville, Florida, that was so successful that for a time the city pronounced itself the "World's Winter Film Capitol."[12]

Despite these detours, as early as 1911, Los Angeles and its surroundings were recognized as an important and permanent film center. At the time, all major companies, including Selig, Essanay, Lubin, Kalem, Éclair, and Lasky, had already established some presence in the area. During the 1911–12 winter, Nestor, the western extension of the Centaur Film Company from New Jersey, joined them and launched the first motion picture studio in the adjacent town of Hollywood.[13] Another significant event occurred in 1915, when Carl Laemmle opened Universal City in the San Fernando valley, marking the first permanent setup built to completely replace an eastern studio. Eventually, wartime coal rationing measures, passed in the winter of 1918–19, forced even more companies to consolidate operations in the Los Angeles area, until by 1922 the area's share of American production stood at 84 percent.[14] Significantly, only the production facilities were relocated to the West. The executive headquarters of all companies remained close to the stock market and financial centers in New York. Even so, by the early 1920s, "Hollywood" was already beginning to serve as a synecdoche for the motion picture industry.

Why did they all end up gravitating toward Los Angeles? First and foremost, it was because of its convenient weather. The warm climate of Southern California "provides 320 days for good photography, out of the 365," proclaimed a reporter for the *Moving Picture World* in 1911.[15] A second motive was the varied landscape accessible from the city. Only a short ride away, one could find city streets, sunny beaches, mountains, a desert, and even some snow and forest trees, scenery against which to film any possible story. Another reason was that land was abundant and inexpensive. Companies could easily purchase vast lots on which to build big production facilities like Laemmle's Universal City. Last, but certainly not least, was LA's reputation as the nation's principal nonunion city.

Keeping unions out was more than a reputation; it was a stated mission. General Harrison Gray Otis, publisher and owner of the *Los Angeles Times* and an avowed proponent of "open shop," wrote as early as 1910 that the city was "steadily approaching that magnificent goal for which brave and few men should everywhere contend." That goal was industrial freedom or "the right firmly established for every citizen to freely pursue, under the law, any honest avocation or employment of his choice, and to be protected in that right from disturbance, menace and maltreatment by the whole power of the law."[16] Otis and his allies, the most powerful of which was an organization called the Merchants' and Manufacturers' Association (M and M), pursued this mission vigorously. Under the banner of industrial freedom, they lured people like Henry Ford and Harvey Firestone to bring their factories to Los Angeles in hopes of turning the city into an industrial center. Their boosterism was successful. Forming a coalition of bankers, employers, and Otis's powerful newspaper, they turned the city into what historian Mike Davis referred to as "a paradise of the open shop," with "militant anti-unionism" combined with "scientific factory planning, low taxes, abundant electric power, warm weather, mass-produced bungalows, and a racially selected labor force."[17] Or, as the United States Commission on Industrial Relations reported in 1914, a place where labor "freedom does not exist either politically, industrially, or socially."[18]

Owners of motion picture companies undoubtedly found this atmosphere appealing. As movies were getting longer, more elaborate, and more expensive, the production process required many skilled craft workers such as carpenters, electricians, tailors, painters, and other specialists. The ability to hire these hands at lower costs became an increasingly important factor. Weak unions and a steady supply of new residents in search of work kept wages around Los Angeles very low. How low? Some scholars estimate that they were as much as "a fifth to a third below the prevailing rates in San Francisco, and in some cases half the wage levels of New York."[19] There are several indications that film producers sought to benefit from these profitable conditions, the most important of which was their establishment, in 1917, of the Motion Picture Producers Association (MPPA). Seventeen of the studios on the West Coast, including Fox and Universal, joined this organization, which set uniform labor policies for its members, combated unionization, and kept wages low. A written warning sent out by the association's secretary in the spring of 1920 essentially spelled out the MPPA's class allegiance, alerting affiliates about "the possible infiltration of studio labor by members of the Industrial Workers of the World."[20]

Nevertheless, while wages remained low, some unions did manage to infiltrate the studio lots. The East Coast origin of most producers, as well as their as of yet loose ties with the interests of the more traditional downtown Los Angeles businesses, made labor organizers hopeful about their chances. First among them was the International Alliance of Theatrical Stage Employees (IATSE). Established in New York in 1893, this union extended into a "horizontal combination of locals of crafts closely related to the building trades," as well as the motion picture machine operators, property men, and grips.[21] By 1908, IATSE had opened a local in Los Angeles, but due to the overlap between the film-stage setup and other forms of construction, soon it was competing over jurisdiction. Two of the city's long-standing trade unions, namely, the United Brotherhood of Carpenters and Joiners and the International Brotherhood of Electrical Workers, saw an opportunity to strengthen their position versus the Otis alliance and started sending their own men to work at the studios, thus challenging IATSE's entitlement in the budding film centers. Naturally, such grievances served the interests of studio managements. While producers managed to unite as a class, studio employees were "deeply divided by craft, rival union affiliations, and gender."[22]

This division was clearly felt during the three strikes organized by IATSE, in 1918, 1919, and 1921. In each one of these, studio heads managed to defeat the picketers by locking them out and hiring rival-union or nonunion men. Of course, the film companies also received support from the *Los Angeles Times* and the M and M. Incidentally, these picture business conflicts corresponded with nationwide labor unrest that escalated during World War I, peaking with the 1919 strike wave following the Armistice. IATSE and other AFL-affiliated locals, including musicians, managed to form a united front in 1926. Setting aside their differences, they forced companies into signing the first Studio Basic Agreement, which recognized most unions, granted the eight-hour workday, standardized overtime payments, and formed a committee to settle labor disputes. This agreement did not guarantee a closed shop, however, and was not immune to bickering among the organizations that signed it. In general, the 1920s struggles of what one may collectively call the back-lot craft unions failed to gain meaningful concessions from film companies. Still, these associations of studio craftsmen were the pioneers of Hollywood's labor movement. The creative talent, including actors, writers, and directors, in many ways followed in the footsteps of their less glamorous colleagues.[23]

Indeed, the struggles of the back lot soon found an echo among other studio employees. The year 1919 saw the rise of the Actors' Equity Association. Though officially established a few years prior, it was only after World War I that this organization achieved its first big victory on Broadway and was accorded the jurisdiction of film acting and Hollywood by the AFL. This official affiliation did not necessarily engender enthusiasm on the part of film actors. Actually, Equity had several factors working against it. First, many Hollywood actors started their careers on the screen rather than on the stage, therefore they did not consider a vertical players' union a natural alliance. Second, a "process of fragmentation" created and sustained a "differentiated labor in the sphere of production" between stars and lesser players.[24] Third, until 1922, when the MPPA turned into the Motion Picture Producers and Distributors Association (MPPDA), under the leadership of former postmaster general Will Hays, the studios had no official bargaining unit with which a union could negotiate. Nevertheless, despite these setbacks, following Hays's nomination Equity made several attempts to negotiate a standard contract for Hollywood players.[25] In 1920, determined to strengthen its claim, this actors' union also encouraged the formation of the Screen Writers Guild, which managed to draw some, albeit meager, membership.[26]

Producers were not enthusiastic about the newly formed creative guilds. Therefore, as a protective measure, early in 1927, a few months following the signing of the first Basic Agreement, a group of industry people led by MGM's Louis B. Mayer incorporated the Academy of Motion Picture Arts and Sciences. The stated purpose of this organization was "to aid and encourage the development of the production branches of the motion picture industry, by co-ordinating the forces of the five major production branches of the industry in constructive and cooperative action."[27] These five branches included producers, writers, director, actors, and technicians. The latter was an umbrella term for all trades that could bargain under the jurisdiction and auspices of powerful unions such as IATSE.

During its first years, the Academy engaged in a mixed bag of activities. On the one hand, its membership was far from democratic and was reserved only for a select few who were invited to join by the chartered members. In addition, it was actively working to keep independent labor unions out of the industry. On the other hand, the organization successfully negotiated a basic agreement for extras and bit players and also provided a form of protection for creative employees via the Academy Conciliation Committee, which included members from all participating branches. Furthermore, when, in June 1927, sixteen of the largest studios announced a 10 percent pay cut for all workers earning over fifty dollars a week, the Academy passed a resolution that protested the "blanket reduction" and encouraged the adoption of other reforms.[28] Subsequently, the cut was postponed and then abandoned altogether. Considering these achievements, despite a prevalent trend among scholars to view the Academy as a model company union, one could also think of it as a successful industry-wide "employee representation plan," which gave its members "their first taste of the fruits of collective bargaining."[29]

Still, the Academy proved to be a problematic tool of representation. Its conflicted interests were illustrated most clearly by one of its organizers. Frank Woods was among the founders of the Screen Writers Guild in 1920. Seven years later, he joined Mayer's initiative and served as the Academy's secretary during its first four years. Woods insisted that the project, which "started out in May 1927, with rosy dreams for an idealistic future," was "in no sense a concerted plot of the producers to put one over the talent classes." He claimed that there was a sincere hope that "friendly contact would accomplish more good in the long run than would militant conflict." Unfortunately, he bemoaned, there quickly came a "sad awakening." Woods claimed that already during the negotiations to eliminate the 1927 cut, producers bargained in "bad faith" and used the Academy as a "smoke screen." In 1935, this founding member of the organization had sobered up. He conceded that "conciliation only within the Academy is inadequate for craft settlements."[30] By 1937, Woods did a 180 and was willing to testify that by setting up the Academy, Mayer's real plot was to prevent an "organization that was antagonistic to the producers" by building an alternative, which settled "all differences between the industry itself, without washing the dirty linen."[31]

Woods's reevaluation of the Academy symbolizes the transformation undergone by the Hollywood labor movement from the 1920s to the 1930s. Pleased and proud of their industry's good fortune, studio employees, particularly those associated with the tasks traditionally thought of as creative, did not wish to stir up trouble. Even if they had suspicions about studio bosses and their intentions, creative employees, including actors, writers, and directors, preferred to play along. They were by no means unique. The general prosperity of the Roaring Twenties, division among union ranks, a hostility of most employers to unionization, as well as an industrial embrace of "welfare capitalism" in the form of company unions, thinned the ranks of organized labor across the United States. All that was about to change after 1929. As historian David M. Kennedy remarked, "When the Crash came, the transient generosity of employers was starkly revealed as a shabby substitute for the genuine power of collective bargaining that only an independent union could wield."[32] This revelation did not go unnoticed in the film industry.

Mr. Cantor Goes to Warm Springs

"The dangerous year for Hollywood, as it turned out, was not 1929 but 1933," observed industry historian Lewis Jacobs back in 1939. He explained that, at first, box office revenues had been unaffected by the stock market crash, but two years later demand was falling, theaters were closing, and profits were diminishing rapidly.[33] RKO, Paramount, and Fox went into receivership, and Warner Bros. suffered heavy losses. Only MGM managed to stay afloat, though its earnings shrank considerably. Companies had to find ways to cut spending, and so, on March 9, 1933, when President Roosevelt signed the Emergency Banking Act, a great opportunity presented itself. "Motion picture producers announced tonight that '97 per cent' of the contract film players had agreed to accept a reduction of half their pay checks for an eight week period," reported the *New York Times*.[34] "The order for the salary cuts came from the home offices . . . of the different studios and was described as being the only means of keeping open at all," the *Los Angeles Times* informed its readers, explaining that the measure was "to aid in tiding over the [majors] during the financial stress caused by the Presidential banking holidays." The paper declared, "Stars, directors, writers and other contract people as well as stenographers and smaller paid workers [heeded] the decree without an objection."[35]

The industry's workforce remembered this occasion far less triumphantly. In its review of the Bank Holiday measure, the *Screen Guilds' Magazine* posited the following chain of events:

> When the banks closed in 1933 the producers proclaimed loudly that money could not be moved from state to state and that therefore they would not receive their accustomed receipts during the bank moratorium. Without waiting for any proof that this would be true, they bluntly told the talent members of the board of directors of the

Academy that if they did not order their brothers in the industry to accept a fifty percent cut, they would be held responsible by everyone for closing down the entire industry and throwing thousands out of work. . . . There is no proof to this day that the producers needed the money.[36]

Several writers remembered the studio meetings in which they were asked to take the cut as acts of emotional blackmail. At MGM, "L. B. Mayer played the role of a man in torment, looking sleepless and unshaven. He asked his employees to help him save the studio," recounted Frances Goodrich. "Everyone got very pious and scared about the possibility that the studio might shut down."[37] Actor Kenneth Thomson stated, "A little pressure was used in some cases . . . so that was the situation under which the cut was accepted voluntarily."[38]

Since it was negotiated by the Academy, the measure was undeniably voluntary, though its implementation was made possible only after "a week of bickering, charges of stampeding, and accusations of bad faith." The details of the eight-week program specified that union labor and employees earning $50 a week or less would be unaffected, those receiving between $50 and $75 would take a reduction of 25 percent, and only the salary of those earning over $100 would be cut in half. The members of the Academy's Executive Committee were the ones who suggested that "the high-salaried employees, executives, directors, stars and writers assume the loss," in order to pacify the IATSE leaders, who were adamant in their objection to any wage reductions.[39] Under the circumstances, it was probably the noble thing to do; still, it left many in the creative ranks discontented and feeling discarded by their supposed representatives. At the culmination of eight weeks most companies resumed their regular pay rates. Warner Bros. was the only studio to extend the cut for one more week, a step that triggered the resignation of its executive producer, Darryl Zanuck.[40] Despite the reinstatement of their salaries, writers and actors remained with an acute feeling that "the Academy was the medium through which wholesale theft was committed under the guise of necessity and parliamentary processes."[41] In contrast, they saw how IATSE protected the back-lot workers from such thievery.

During the month following the announcement of the pay cut, the organization of creative labor received two shots in the arm. In April, the old Screen Writers Guild was reorganized under a new constitution and bylaws. It immediately signed up 173 charter members and elected John Howard

Lawson as its president.[42] Brian Marlow, who was one of the reorganizing members, confirmed that the "revitalization of the existing organization grew out of the 50 per cent cut." He explained, "A group of about 15 or 20 [writers] got together . . . at the Knickerbocker Hotel, because they felt that the Academy was not competent to handle their interest [and] they decided to form another organization."[43] During a speech he gave three years later, the next president of SWG, Ernest Pascal, also reminded his fellows that "the Guild was born of the 50% cut."[44] Then, in July 1933, the newly founded Screen Actors Guild joined SWG. The conditions were similar. When asked, "What did the screen actors in Hollywood do after [the cut]?," Thomson, the executive secretary of SAG, answered, "Actors attended Academy meetings during the cut, for the purpose of seeing if there was any way the necessity for the cut could be investigated," and "they protested at those meetings against the cut." Finally, "[they] held a series of meetings, out of which the Screen Actors' Guild was formed."[45]

The 50 percent cut was perhaps the immediate catalyst for the formation of the talent guilds, but it was accompanied by an overarching political change. On May 17, 1933, President Roosevelt introduced legislation that led to the passage of the National Industrial Recovery Act (NIRA) in June of that year. The measure included the famous section 7(a), which accorded industrial workers the right "to organize and bargain collectively through representatives of their own choosing."[46] A few months later, Eddie Cantor, president of SAG, confirmed that it was measures such as this that "gave the actors of Hollywood the concrete encouragement and the proper political setup." He emphasized that both SAG and the Screen Writers Guild "were born of this appreciation" for the president's "warm sympathy for all employees of the nation and his definite determination to improve working conditions."[47]

If there was still a doubt, he stated, "the New Deal is responsible for the organization of the Screen Actors Guild."[48] To be sure, Cantor's sympathies were not unbiased. This actor was a personal friend of Roosevelt's. Still, his language here reminds one of John L. Lewis and other labor organizers who tried to link their effort with that of the administration by saying, "The President wants you to join a union." Even without the explicit language, launching their guilds in the spring and summer of 1933, actors and writers joined other American workers without any previous record of labor activism who tried to unionize. Their inspiration to act corresponded with that of the thousands who joined the United Mine Workers of America, the Amalgamated Clothing Workers' Union, or the AFL ranks.[49]

Even if, initially, the NIRA was only implicitly responsible for the formation of the talent guilds, soon enough it had a direct impact on them. One of the professed goals of the act was to achieve recovery through cooperation between the federal government and industry. The NRA was the agency assigned the mission of setting up "government-sanctioned industrial compacts" in which "production in whole industries would be controlled, and prices and wages would be raised."[50] Starting around July, NRA chief Hugh S. Johnson was working with leading business owners to devise formal "codes of fair practice" for their respective industries. Hollywood moguls, who were accustomed to aligning their interests with those of the national power elite, were quick to jump on the bandwagon. By early September, they had already prepared a draft for their own code with the aid of Sol A. Rosenblatt, the agent in charge of the NRA's Amusement Division.[51] In the film industry, as in most cases, the New Deal code authorities amounted to what is often described as a "cartelization of huge sectors of American industry under the government's auspices." In general, powerful industrial producers used their sway and devised these codes according to their needs, while enforcing production quotas and price policies on their affiliates, essentially ignoring existing antitrust laws.[52] It was a successful cooperation between the homologous dominants.

True to form, the proposed Motion Picture Code guaranteed the oligopoly of major producers. Focusing primarily on the relationship among production, distribution, and exhibition, the owners of Paramount, Loew's, and the other vertically integrated companies assured their continued dominance over the market by warranting such practices as the block booking of pictures and a price discrimination that put independent theaters at a disadvantage. With regard to their creative employees, company managers attempted to introduce some price control. They incorporated three provisions aimed directly at actors, writers, and directors. The first stated that in order "to avoid the payment of sums unreasonably in excess of the fair value of personal services," which "results in unfair and destructive competition," the code authority could "investigate whether [a producer] agreed to pay an unreasonably excessive inducement to any person." In case they found such transaction did take place, that producer would pay a fine of up to $10,000. A second clause specified the formation of an "agency committee," which would, in essence, license talent agents. And a third provision, referred to as the "anti-raiding" clause, prohibited the practice of luring away talent from their existing contract by offering them higher salaries.[53]

With these measures, producers attempted to put an end to what they considered to be the "most serious unfair trade practice" in Hollywood. Growing in tandem with the star system, the "enticement of talent by competitors" and the intervention of agents deeply troubled the pockets of company managers. For example, a studio would have a "long-term contract with an actor at a salary of $1,000 a week," explained RKO president Benjamin B. Kahane in a public hearing on the NRA code. Then, he said, "as much as three years prior to the expiration of [said] contract another producer approached the actor through an agent and made an offer of $3,000 a week." He noted that on some occasions offers would go up to "ten times the existing salary." To avoid accusations, the enticing company refrained from making a direct call for resignation and simply added, "If [the actor] can get out of [the] present contract sooner, we shall be glad to have you." With regard to agents, Kahane portrayed their role as "unrestrained trouble-makers engaged in stirring dissatisfaction among their clients" and playing "upon the fears of employing producers by misrepresenting the offers of others."[54]

Moguls such as Kahane accompanied their NRA campaign with publicity. Not that they were eager to expose the inner workings of their business. On the contrary, studios continued to work tirelessly to suppress representations of Hollywood as a conventional industry and, instead, promoted its image as a glamorous world of entertainment. But with the 1933 labor disputes threatening to eclipse this image, the studios' management reframed the labor discourse in terms that emphasized its own patriotism and moral leadership, while painting their workers' actions, and particularly those of talent and stars, as unpatriotic. They were equating their own adversaries with those of the state. Capitalizing on the popular perception that Hollywood stars earned exorbitant salaries, publicity departments filled the industry's trade papers and fan magazines with articles and advertisements that argued that the stars' "refusal to reduce their salaries indicated a greed and impropriety that was out of step with the national recovery program."[55] One noteworthy piece was published in the November issue of *Screen Book* and featured an anonymous fan letter to an anonymous actor. "I don't begrudge you your fine salary," wrote the fan, "but don't you think all big salaries might be lowered—maybe to $1,000 a week? If what the paper says is true, you earn in one week five times what most of us earn in a year."[56] Considering the influence studio heads carried in such publications, the cloud of anonymity surrounding this exchange makes its authenticity all the more suspect.

Though they did not possess an equal sway over the press, the new working-class affinities of the current administration entailed that by identifying themselves as employees, actors and writers could find some sympathizers of their own within the federal government. Since the Academy and the talent representatives operating within it "participated in the framing of the first draft of the proposed code," this institution now appeared, as Cantor proclaimed, even more "inimical to the interest of actors."[57] A more accurate way of phrasing it would have probably been "more inimical to the interest of stars," as all the contested clauses pertained to those in the higher pay brackets. Still, such stars held the necessary power to turn the actors' union into a meaningful threat. Indeed, in early October, immediately following the appearance of the code's first draft, actors of all classes made a "mass exodus" from the Academy and boosted the ranks of SAG. Numbered among them were prominent names such as Paul Muni, Robert Montgomery, and the Marx Brothers. Then, working together with SWG, the two guilds began "waging unremitting war on [the] provisions" mentioned above. This war consisted mostly of mass gatherings, with some aid from the press. Cantor mentioned, perhaps sarcastically, that they all "owe a debt of thanks to the Hearst newspapers for the publicity given to us in that fight."[58] However, the pinnacle of the effort was a direct appeal to the government.

In mid-October, the guilds sent FDR a wire. Drafted with the help of Laurence Beilenson, the attorney for both SAG and SWG, this wire was steeped in New Deal–inspired language. "The professional people of the stage and screen are patriotic Americans," it began. "They have never failed to respond to any appeal in war or peace." Pointing to the intent, specified in the NRA code, to limit "unreasonable" salaries, the guilds explained that it would not only hurt them but "every employee from the electrician to the star." They charged that "the purpose of this plainly illegal usurpation of power is to do exactly what the NRA forbids: to fix maximum rates of pay." SAG and SWG called the measure "un-American" and emphasized that "the direct result of this attack on the creative element will be to lower compensation of actors and writers in the middle and lower salary classes." With regard to the "so-called anti-raiding clause," the wire affirmed, it "tried to accomplish the same thing in another way. It is not to prevent raiding, but to lower salaries."

The guilds shifted the responsibility for the industry's financial troubles to the producers. Managers wanted to limit what artists could receive. But, asked the two guilds, "if the artist draws a large sum at the box office and receives a small compensation ... who gets the excess? Not the public, but the producer." They asserted "without fear of successful contradiction that motion picture companies have not been bankrupt by salaries." Rather, it was "the purchase and leasing of theatres at exorbitant prices, caused by the race for power of a few individuals desiring to get a stranglehold on the outlet of the industry." SAG and SWG warned the president that "the same individuals who bankrupt the major companies by these policies still control them[,] ... are writing the motion picture code and will directly or indirectly be the Code Authority." Once again, the warring parties were clearly identified: it was the patriotic professionals, the employees, and the lower classes of the industry against the power-seeking moguls.[59]

The wire hit the right nerve, and shortly after, Cantor, the president's friend, was invited to spend Thanksgiving with the Roosevelts in Warm Springs, Georgia. Perhaps unsurprisingly, the SAG representative found "the President warmly sympathetic to our problems, a delightful gentleman, and a real friend of every man who works for his living."[60] Consequently, when the Motion Picture Code was published on November 27, 1934, it featured a presidential executive order suspending the salary limitation and anti-raiding clauses, "pending further report from the Administrator, after investigation, as to whether such provisions should be indefinitely suspended, or modified, altered or changed, or become effective."[61]

Strictly speaking, it was a pure victory neither for the producers, whose code was incomplete, nor for the talent guilds, which were still officially unrecognized by the studios. If there was a clear winner in this round, it was the administration, which managed to implement its political vision of an "administrative state" and position itself as part and parcel of the industry's labor relations. Actors and writers were so convinced about the government's commitment to help workers that they agreed "to proceed to attempt to negotiate a fair minimum basic agreement with producers," not through their own organizations but in the newly formed "Five-Five Committee of the Motion Picture Code [Authority]."[62] In addition, both guilds set aside any notion of a strike, believing that "the slower method of negotiation will be far better for everyone concerned."[63] Industrial peace was maintained.

It did not add up to much. The producers, who did not really want to engage in collective bargaining, and who understood that negotiating with the Five-Five Committees would inevitably lead to a formal recognition of SAG and SWG, stalled the appointment of their committee members.[64]

That delay lasted months, "during which [the guilds] bombarded Washington with letters, telegrams and telephone calls urging the appointment." Finally, the producers yielded, appointing as their representatives executive producers such as Thalberg, Zanuck, and Hal Wallis as well as company owners Samuel Goldwyn and Harry Cohn. These men listened to the demands of the talent representatives, which by that point were no longer confined to upper salary caps and also included written contacts for short-term engagements, clear arbitration procedures, and a special clause prohibiting the practice of hiring from general booking agencies.[65] The producers responded plainly that "they were opposed to any attempt to regulate such matters under the code."[66] By late November 1934, the actors were prepared to declare a "deadlock" and, by February 1935, the writers claimed that they had "exhausted the possibility of negotiation."[67] The sides continued shadowboxing until May, when the Supreme Court struck down the NIRA by declaring it unconstitutional, thus rendering the whole discussion a moot point.

It was an interesting moment, one in which a shift in the ideological and practical preferences of the overarching field, that is, the federal political field, scrambled the traditional power structure. In many ways, the stagnation of the Five-Five Committees reflects what historian Daniel Rodgers referred to as the New Deal's "monumental confusion."[68] Even if in hindsight it appears that during those years Washington was working toward expanding its administrative power, many scholars convincingly argue that, in the words of Alan Brinkley, "the New Deal was, in fact, awash in ideologies" and lacked "any single principle to bind its many diverse initiatives together."[69] It was a hodgepodge of policies, with the government adopting on a trial-and-error basis anything that could bring about economic recovery. Such ideological uncertainty helps explain what, at first glance, might appear as a peculiar standoff in Hollywood, in which two opposing patrons representing different sets of interests both assumed that their claims would be legitimized by the federal government. Facing off in the Five-Five Committees, both studio management and the talent guilds believed that their interests aligned with those of the administration. Both believed that the administration would eventually rule on their behalf. It was a moment when a creative industry encountered a creative government. Alas, when the state was prepared to interfere in favor of labor, it was the exceptional and eternally ambivalent nature of the Hollywood creative workforce that prevented the materialization of a broader and stronger alliance.

An Organization unto Himself

During the 1930s, when a door closed for organized labor another one usually opened. The insistence of the guilds only strengthened their reputation among their jurisdictions. As they grew in numbers, they never stopped looking for ways to achieve exclusive bargaining agreements. This was also when their roads diverged. As the creative labor disputes moved to the next phase, the character of each trade, that is, of acting, directing, and writing, as well as the relative power it held within the system, weighed in and manifested itself in the different trajectories followed by SAG, SDG, and SWG.

Once again, the federal government stepped in. In July 1935, Congress passed and the president signed the National Labor Relations Act. Commonly referred to as the Wagner Act, this "Magna Carta" for the labor movement "guaranteed workers the right to select their own union by majority vote, and to strike, boycott, and picket." It also formulated a list of unfair labor practices by employers, including "the maintenance of company dominated unions, the blacklisting of union activists, intimidation and firing of workers who sought to join an independent organization, and the employment of spies."[70] Back in Hollywood, in an article titled "The Wagner Bill—Reality or Prophecy?," guilds' attorney Beilenson quickly affirmed that it was the former. The meaning of this act is that "collective bargaining is the policy of the United States," claimed Beilenson. He assured his clientele that "if the constitutionality of the Act is upheld the Guilds will gain greatly," and "producers will have to bargain."[71] With that, it appeared that the three parties—talent, management, and government—were ready for another round.

Yet, in keeping with Thalberg's notion of a creative business, the next steps taken by the guilds were not very easy to classify, at least not in terms of class loyalty. As a standard response to complaints filed against them following passage of the Wagner Act, studio managers were consistent. They always claimed that the plaintiffs, be they directors, editors, or script clerks, were not employees under the definition of the law. To be sure, this line of defense was tricky, and on occasion it prompted otherwise very competent attorneys to blurt out such awkward lines as "Writers don't get wages, so far as I know; they get salaries . . . they don't get salaries. They get paid for their work, and it is divided into weekly payments."[72] Still, regardless of its veracity, the studio position was in line with the conventional managerial stand, which questioned the government's right to determine "when it was appropriate for a group of distinctive craftsmen, or specialized workers, to be considered as a separate unit." Executives of motion picture companies joined other corporate groups who resented the Wagner Act for meddling in labor-management relationships.[73] But while brokers like Thalberg and Zanuck chose a clear side, it was the talent guilds that now assumed a somewhat intermediate position.

In the next couple of years, the creative employees of Hollywood participated in the struggle of industrial organized labor and appealed to its new federal resources in a utilitarian, rather than ideological, fashion. The actors, for example, played it both ways. Even before the NIRA's demise, SAG acted as a professional craft union. It became a member of the AFL, the California State Federation of Labor, and the Los Angeles Central Labor Council. In 1936, and again in 1937, the guild made an official request to be included in the Studio Basic Agreement, receiving support neither from the producers nor from the other craft unions. In April 1937, following the upholding of the National Labor Relations Act by the Supreme Court, the actors appealed to the MPPDA to accept its standard contract, once again to no avail. As its attempts to affiliate with the craft unions seemed futile, SAG decided to try a different course of action.

The upholding of the Wagner Act strengthened the ranks of another Hollywood back-lot union, the Federation of Motion Picture Crafts (FMPC). Despite its name, this organization was more akin to an industrial union, as it clumped such varied workers as painters, plumbers, cooks, and set designers under the same roof. On April 30, 1937, to the dismay of both executives and IATSE, the 6,000 FMPC employees staged a walkout from studio lots, demanding recognition of their union.[74] SAG leadership chose this exact moment to amplify its own confrontation with studio management. "Stars and meteorites of the motion picture colony, 4000 strong, voted last night to wait until next Sunday to decide whether they will paralyze a $255,000,000 industry by joining members of [FMPC] in their strike," reported the Los Angeles Times on May 3.[75] On May 5, the same day that the Congress of Industrial Organizations (CIO) announced its support for the protesting studio workers, the guild contributed $500 to the FMPC strike fund.[76] A couple of days later, on May 7, Aubrey Blair, SAG's business agent, released a statement saying, "The actors have voted nearly 100 per cent in favor of the strike." They intended to join FMPC without delay unless the MPPDA "accedes to their various demands," the most important of which was a "Guild Shop" for actors.[77] The headline for the following morning read "Actors' Guild Demands Met." Producers agreed to recognize and negotiate with SAG, a development that, as the *Los Angeles Times* accurately stated, threw a "stumbling block in the path of striking studio craftsmen."[78]

Signing a separate agreement and abandoning the FMPC was a symbolic act. SAG essentially took advantage of a back-lot dispute. It all started with IATSE. As one historian suggested, "If the events of that year were ever made into a movie, [IATSE] would certainly be the villain."[79] By 1937, this mammoth union was markedly different than its 1926 version. For one thing, it had become an enormous power that could shut down the industry. In addition, it had been taken over by Al Capone, who in 1934 placed two of his men, George Browne and William Bioff, at the head of the organization. Bioff, an ex-pimp, quickly orchestrated a working relationship with studio bosses whereby he was "accepting suitcases full of cash" in exchange for a guaranteed "steady supply of docile workers." For these reasons, in its struggle for recognition, the FMPC directly challenged the IATSE's authority over the back lot, an initiative that "immediately attracted the sympathies of all the leftists in Los Angeles." That being said, the FMPC was a weak union, one whose struggle with the studios dated back to 1932. This latest escalation was its hopeful attempt to capitalize on the passage of the Wagner Act, an attempt whose chances seemed even greater with the support of the actors. As it happened, most actors were not really in the mood to strike for the rights of painters and makeup artists.[80]

Shifting loyalty from IATSE to the FMPC and back was a dirty trick. SAG knowingly exploited a dispute among the workers' ranks. The guild was fully aware of the heavy weight its alliance with the FMPC carried and correctly assumed that such a move would help further its own goals. In 1939, the organization did it again as it announced its intent to sympathize with the CIO-affiliated United Studio Technicians Guild, only to back out when IATSE agreed to quit its attempts to unionize Hollywood extras. Time and time again, Hollywood actors demonstrated that they were willing to "use the Left as a stalking-horse in any fight for power."[81] By using other unions in such a way, actors also distanced themselves from a true alliance with any of the voices speaking for the industry's working classes.

Directors played a similar game, though perhaps due to their status in the industry they did not have to resort to such manipulative tactics. Fewer in number than writers and actors, and on the whole better compensated than everyone but the biggest stars, Hollywood directors were slow to organize. It was only on January 22, 1936, that the industry's leading directors, including Henry King, King Vidor, and John Ford, left the Academy and established the Screen Directors Guild. In a public statement, they claimed, "Organization is necessary as a protective measure against [the] growing tendency of studios to attempt reduction of directors' importance and earning power." Their membership amounted to 125 by the end of the month. This was not a conventional union; its members were more concerned with respect than with work conditions. As a testament, in a move *Variety* described as "conservative in a big way," the SDG voted "no affiliation, working agreement or connection with any other talent or craft organization."[82] In this sense, the directors' guild was like the American Society of Cinematographers, which attempted to keep directors of photography apart from the lower ranks of the craft and to form an elitist representative body more akin to a professional organization than a union.[83]

Despite these lofty attempts, the studios maintained their regular stand and refused to recognize the SDG. It should be pointed out that the directors were not 100 percent exclusionary. They did join forces with assistant directors and unit managers, who had already formed their own union in 1931. Company executives excused their snubbing of the guild by claiming that this association did not constitute an appropriate bargaining unit. Luckily for SDG, it was no longer the studio's call to make. By the summer of 1937, the Wagner Act had empowered the newly reformed NLRB to decide whether a group of workers could be considered a unit for bargaining purposes and to supervise the elections by which this unit chose its representatives. As more peaceable measures, such as boycotting the 1936 Academy Awards ceremony, had no effect, SDG turned to the government for help, and in August 1938, the NLRB began hearings on the directors' case.

Simultaneously, the newly appointed president of SDG, Frank Capra, who was also the Academy's president, made another attempt to negotiate directly with the producers. Annoyed by the runaround treatment he received from the head of MPPDA, Joseph Schenck, Capra decided that the guild must move "quickly, gamely, and lethally." On February 15, 1939, he resigned from the Academy and announced that the entire SDG membership would once again boycott the Oscars ceremony, which, incidentally, Capra himself was set to host. In addition, the guild called a strike commencing the following day. Probably due to the looming threat of the latter more than the boycott, an agreement was reached during that same night that recognized the guild, specified conditions for assistant directors, and granted the senior directors' requests to participate in script preparation, cast selection, and editing. Interestingly, the unit managers were left out of the bargain and forced to form their own union. All this occurred before the NLRB made its ruling.[84] For directors, the institutions of organized labor were just a safety net. At the moment of truth, they preferred a peaceful, narrow agreement, catering mostly to the artistic aspirations of a select few, to one negotiated by the government that might have improved actual work conditions for a larger sector of employees.

The relatively quick battles of SAG and SDG correlated to the positions these groups of employees held within the Hollywood system. As shown, when it came to directors and star actors, the big companies developed a complex system of control and nurture. In both cases, while binding the talent to draconian contracts and limiting their creative freedom, the studios also fostered a sense of belonging and solidarity. With directors, it was through the spheres of autonomy they were accorded during the shooting stage. With actors, it was via the network of experts who nourished and maintained the star persona. The big film companies invested in these practitioners because each of them possessed a unique capability, that is, a complex skill or commodity status, that was deemed necessary for efficiency and profits. Therefore, it is not surprising that with these two groups, studio management avoided any real confrontation. Furthermore, the nurturing relationship developed by the companies might also explain why SAG and SDG were so eager to settle their claims and return to the safe spot under the studios' wing. Such a convivial resolution was not readily available for those whose creative contribution was perceived to be slightly less specialized.

The talent group that came closest to a traditional proletariat was that of writers. Unlike the two other creative guilds, SWG was unable to force the producers' hand on its own, and it was only after two separate appeals to the NLRB that the studios finally recognized the union. By the same token, the struggle with SWG exposed the producers at their most employer stereotypical behavior. This was undoubtedly due to the screenwriters' status in the system, which was devoid of the personal power possessed by skillful directors and box office stars. They simply were not as threatening. After all, as an economic analysis of collective bargaining in the industry explained, "a strike of actors immediately halts all photography; a strike of writers does so only after the backlog of previously prepared screen plays has been exhausted." In addition, the report also indicated, "producers probably [had] greater reason to desire free access to the market for story material than for acting talent."[85] With these reasons holding back producers and with writers growing more and more frustrated, compromise was harder to reach.

The long showdown began with the screenwriters' attempt to vertically integrate their union. Discouraged by their failed attempts to gain recognition since 1933, SWG leaders had come to the realization that "the only difference between this labor organization and any other labor union is that we are, under present conditions, unable to cut off the supply of man-power and material." Convinced that without guild shop status they remained "a purely defensive machine, with the danger of disintegrating through sheer inertia," the guild devised a new plan of action. In April 1936, they announced their intention to amalgamate with the Authors' League of America in order to "consolidate all writers in all fields into one strong and unified organization, strong and able to protect [the writer] against the invasion of his rights and to fight for and win what is rightly his." Amalgamation on its own could not guarantee recognition, therefore the SWG board also proposed a new article for its constitution, Article 12, which ordered members "to refrain from contracting for their services or material" beyond May 1938. These two propositions were to be voted on by the members on May 2.[86]

That got the producers' attention. After ignoring the guild for three years, suddenly, in the days leading up to the vote, SWG was all studio bosses could talk about. The dispensability of writers stemmed from the relative ease with which studios could replace them, an advantage they stood to lose if the amalgamation plan went through. In almost every company, writers were called to meetings in which they were addressed by management with regard to the proposed amalgamation and Article 12. "I called them together to tell them we are faced with a demand by the [guild] to represent them, and I wanted to know how they felt about it," recounted Jack Warner. "I wanted to have a little talk with them, as I felt that there would be a slowing down. It was a sort of general pep talk . . . because, as in any industry, where there is friction there is a slow-down of the progress of the work." Warner wanted his writers to remember that "we had all been working here under very favorable conditions, very high salaries." In light of that fact, with regard to Article 12, he explained, "we signed people to seven years," and "it is impossible to sign people for two years because you may work on a story as high as eight, nine or ten months." If writers refused to offer their services beyond 1938, they might "write one or two stories and [the] contract is over." Warner acknowledged, "We like to retain our writers," but only "at the right wages, agreeable to them." Stressing the first person plural, for this studio boss, it was all about solidarity.[87]

Kahane held a similar meeting at RKO. His intention, as he stated, was "to meet with [studio] writers who worked for us and talk this thing over in a sensible and sane fashion." He emphasized, "[Writers] had the same interest as we had; they were interested in earning a livelihood out of the motion picture industry," and "certainly they were not disposed to wreck the industry to make it impossible for [the] studio to carry on." Contrary to past record, he claimed, "there was certainly no objection to a guild," and "if their purpose was to straighten out any grievances they might have, [executives] were glad to listen to them and try to straighten them out." Kahane called SWG leaders "misguided." He clarified that since it was his duty to "protect the stockholders and their huge investment in theaters, studio and facilities," he had to "resist with every legitimate recourse . . . any attempt on the part of writers to control man power and bottle up supply of material," which, he believed, would certainly be the result of the proposed amendments.[88]

Speaking over at Twentieth Century–Fox, Zanuck too paid close attention to the amalgamation and said that he was "personally opposed to dealing with a group of writers who were under the control of another group of writers who hated [the] moving picture business." He thought, "They were foolish. If they wanted an organization, they could have an organization, but let it be an organization that they could themselves control." Harking back to his days as a writer, he explained that he "looked at it from the writers' viewpoint," and that he "certainly wasn't going to have [his] future as a writer jeopardized by a group of people who had obviously shown their hatred of Hollywood." Zanuck stated that authors and playwrights were simply "endeavoring to get a lot of writers under their control," since they "hate the salaries that were made by screen writers because screen writers received 10 times as much money for a picture as they received for a hit play." His was both a unifying and a divisive message. Per Zanuck, producers and writers were united like an industrial family; they had the same interests. Authors and playwrights were like estranged siblings. They were not part of this family and, consequently, did not have its best interest at heart.[89]

Once again, memory of these events differed according to position. The screenwriters remembered the speeches given by their bosses as carrying a far less familial and far more intimidating and threatening tone. Several writers remembered Kahane as being "very belligerent," saying things such as "If you want to fight, we will fight, and the fight will start Monday morning at 9:00 o'clock."[90] James Gow testified that in the studio meeting held the Saturday before the SWG gathering, "Mr. Kahane said that there would be a blacklist" and that the "Guild was being led by a bunch of radicals with

Russian ideas." Gow remembered his boss shouting, "Some of these people should go back where they came from."[91] Anthony Veiller swore that the exact phrasing was "You fellows talk a lot about a blacklist. If this thing goes through, I will show you a blacklist that will blast you out of the business."[92] With regard to Warner, Dalton Trumbo recalled his boss saying that SWG "leaders were Communists, radical bastards, and soap box sons of bitches," and that "there are a lot of writers in the business who are active in the Guild now who will find themselves out of the business and it wouldn't be a blacklist because it would all be done over the telephone."[93] Luci Ward claimed that Warner also added that he "happened to know that the Department of Justice are investigating certain Guild members and there are going to be a lot of cooked geese in Hollywood who will never work in pictures again."[94]

Despite these admonitions, SWG members voted in favor of both amendments. As a result, two things happened, neither of which involved studio recognition. First, on the very next day, May 3, 1936, a group of dissenting screenwriters including James K. McGuinness, Grover Jones, and John Lee Mahin resigned from SWG, and quickly after established a rival organization called the Screen Playwrights. This more conservative union received the support of producers, headed by Thalberg, who told McGuinness, "When you are ready to sit down at a table to talk, let me know and representatives of the producers and myself will sit down with you."[95] By April 1937, the Playwrights even managed to sign a deal with the major studios. As Jones proudly stated, "I think what shocked them was that we asked for so very little."[96] That said, the Playwrights' agreement was a sweetheart deal only in the sense that it helped factionalize SWG and eradicate any plan for amalgamation or constraining of talent contracts. With regard to the betterment of work conditions, the conservative screenwriters were sincere in their intents and achievements. Their contract with the studios included "minimum wage, standardized contracts . . . notice, on request, on whether other writers were working on the same material, no speculative writing without payment, and participation in the credit allocation procedure," all conditions that spoke directly to the writers' main concerns.[97]

The second development was the disintegration of SWG. The producers did not lay down their arms. Encouraged by the formation of the Playwrights, following the May 2 vote, they increased their in-studio pressure on writers. On several occasions managers "disapproved formally of the action taken at the screen writers meeting," and offered resignation slips from the guild, suggesting that "those writers who are willing to withdraw sign those slips."[98] The scare tactics worked, and by June 1, 1936, membership had shrunk from 422 active members and 521 associate members to 211 active members and 169 associates.[99] Remarkably, this decline did not correspond with an increase in the Playwrights' membership. Nevertheless, SWG was inactive for a while until, in a similar fashion to SDG, after the validation of the NLRB in April 1937, it appealed to the board to supervise an election for screenwriters in the motion picture industry.

The studios, now backed by the Playwrights, objected to such elections. In the hearings held by the NLRB, they claimed that filmmaking did not engage in interstate commerce, and therefore that the "National Labor Relations Board has no jurisdiction of this matter; That there is nothing affecting commerce that has been shown by the evidence. . . . That the people referred to as screen writers are not employees," and that therefore they "do not come within the contemplation of the Act, nor does their relationship to the producers of motion pictures come within the contemplation of the Act." Finally, the studios also asserted that the Authors' League was not a proper bargaining unit.[100] Since the witnesses were all members of the creative industry, the dry legal speech was accompanied by more colorful arguments, such as the one delivered by Playwrights member Howard Emmett Rogers:

> Writing is not a standardized form of work. When a bricklayer falls
> off a scaffold the foreman calls a local and asks for another bricklayer.
> I can understand why that man should have an organization taking
> care of his economic problems, because $4 a week difference . . . may
> mean the difference between having a car or sending a boy to college.
> If Mr. John Lee Mahin or Mr. Charles Bricker, or several other
> topflight writers in the picture business, were to start a story tomor-
> row and take ill and die, the producer could not call any organization
> for a writer and say, "We have lost a writer. Send us another one."
> He would have to match John Lee Mahin or Charles Bricker or the
> writer that died. That, to me, is very important in this case. Writing
> is not a standardized form of work. It is creative and the writer
> himself is an organization unto himself.[101]

This description conveniently ignores the practices of writing on committee, reassignment of scripts, and the constant replacement of writers, all concocted by the studios exactly in order to standardize the profession. Nevertheless, echoing Thalberg's remark from May 1936, people such as Rogers saw screenwriters as artists who do not belong in the ranks of organized labor.

On the other front stood people like Brian Marlow, Frank Woods, and Charles Brackett, who insisted that they were employees, thus legally deserving of the right to bargain collectively. On June 7, 1938, the NLRB sided with them. Perhaps it was unsurprising. Though theoretically this institution was staffed with "expert—theoretically non-partisan—administrators," at least in the first few years, many radicals and Communists staffed the NLRB, "belying the neutral patina of expertise."[102] In the screenwriters' case, trial examiner William R. Ringer ruled in favor of SWG, and an election was set for June 28. Regardless of persuasions, the ruling seems to have been in place. Despite the irony of hearing writers earning $1,000 per week testify that they were regular employees, as demonstrated, most writers did not fit in that pay bracket. Moreover, SWG's overwhelming four-to-one victory over the Playwrights in the ensuing elections suggests that most Hollywood writers were indeed united behind this organization.[103]

These results were not enough for producers to admit defeat. They continued stalling and refused to end their agreements with the Playwrights. Finally, in 1939, SWG filed a complaint with the NLRB, charging studios with unfair labor practices. Only after that were producers willing to recognize the guild and start serious negotiations. The first SWG-studio contract was signed on May 1940 and included 80 percent guild shop. By 1945, a second agreement specified 85 percent guild shop, minimum pay of $125 per week, labor arbitration committees, and guild control over the assignment of credits.[104]

Of course, even with the heated hearings at the NLRB, the writers' struggles still diverged from more conventional labor disputes. First, although it took them over six years to get studio recognition, screenwriters never really threatened to go on strike. Perhaps it was because a strike might not have been effective. As mentioned, studios often had a surfeit of prepared screenplays. Then again, perhaps, as the Playwrights' attorney suggested, "strikes are not going to be indulged in by the writers who are getting $3,000 to $5,000 a week."[105] Even though such wealthy scribers were a select few, their support was a crucial element in whatever bargaining power a theoretical strike by SWG held. More significantly, throughout this extended conflict, studio productivity was completely unaffected. Hollywood labor strife seems to have been unrelated to the actual labor. Writer Philip Dunne remembered, "There was a lot of intimidation," and even the bargaining sessions were "really a shouting match, because Zanuck was the chairman of the producers' negotiation committee." The head producer of Twentieth Century–Fox was Dunne's boss, and as the screenwriter understood all too well, "he only knows one way to fight: to go in with boots, teeth, elbows, everything else, and that's the way he did it." In the same breath, he added, "There's no big deal there. [Zanuck] was no worse than anybody else." In fact, "at the very same time that he was fighting the Guild, we made *How Green Was My Valley*, which, after all, was a very powerful statement in behalf of labor organizations." Dunne recalled, "We talked about it very frankly." They talked and shouted, but never stopped writing. Making movies about the troubles of the working class, in Hollywood it was business as usual.[106]

OF COURSE, one should not belittle the achievements of the talent guilds. By the early 1940s, all three of them had signed long-lasting contracts with the big studios that featured major concessions, including increased wages, minimum wages, arbitration of disputes, and, most importantly, an extensive guild shop which covered between 90 and 100 percent of studio employment. These achievements become even more impressive from a distance. In his book about the deterioration of the American working class, Jefferson Cowie writes that by the late 1970s, "the rate of successful organizing efforts had fallen from about 80 percent in the first ten years of the Wagner Act to 61 percent in the 1950s to only 46 percent by 1977." In addition, Cowie explains, "the Wagner Act had lost its teeth, transformed from a mechanism for 'encouraging' unionization and collective bargaining to a legal cul-de-sac from which workers never emerged, falling victim to delay tactics, intimidation, and aggressive employers."[107] In contrast, in Hollywood the triumphs of the New Deal era lasted through the 1970s and beyond. SAG, SDG, SWG, and IATSE remain powerful organizations well into the twenty-first century, orchestrating and even strengthening their hold over a labor force that now extends to other industries such as radio, television, and digital media.[108] Nevertheless, it is important to point out that none of these organizations has been at the forefront of struggles for gender and racial equality.[109]

This suggests that, ultimately, creative talent was a special kind of workforce, one more akin to a traditional craft organization, for which "collective bargaining remained a fundamentally private activity" rather than a political endeavor intertwined with a coalition of labor power led by the federal government.[110] It was also a workforce that included many members who were able to secure better terms of employment through the services of talent agents and individual bargaining than those guaranteed in the standard guild contracts.[111] (The practice of extending talent contracts following suspensions, for example, was discarded only following the personal struggle of actress Olivia de Havilland.)[112] Therefore, it was a labor force that did not fit neatly into the conventional definitions of the industrial jargon.

Still, for a time creative workers were at least fellow travelers. As unique as they may have been, even writers, directors, and actors made use of the federal assistance that became available to organized labor during the 1930s. Moreover, it was only during the New Deal that creative employees managed to erect the powerful unions that still serve them so well. Before 1933, the prevalent opinion within the Hollywood studios held that "the beneficiaries of the industry generally should not allow greedy and selfish cliques to kill the prolific geese which have laid such marvelous golden eggs for all." Asserting its commitment to the working people of America, the Roosevelt administration challenged this maxim and enabled the creative talent of the studios to "stand up," deny this "foul slander," and proclaim with vigor, "This golden goose is a myth, a ghost, to haunt the timid." It was the changing national attitude toward business that empowered the creative workers of the American motion picture industry to "cook the goose," assuring them it was possible to both fight for their rights and keep the golden eggs.[113]

Disintegrating
An Epilogue

The first time Gino Corrado appeared on screen was in 1916. He portrayed a random runner in D. W. Griffith's *Intolerance*. Following that uncredited appearance, Italian-born Corrado was cast as an extra in more than 350 pictures. For the next two decades, probably due to his heavy build, he mostly played the role of "heavies" or gangsters. Then, in 1933, "he became a movie headwaiter," serving Al Jolson in *Hallelujah, I'm a Bum*. "Since then," he remembered, "I have played hundreds of headwaiters, waiters and maître d's, more than anyone in the movies." He served Clark Gable and Vivian Leigh in *Gone with the Wind*, asked Kane's second wife if she wanted another double in *Citizen Kane*, and took an order for Champagne in *Casablanca*'s famous Rick's Café. Corrado treated his job seriously. "I played those roles to perfection," he said. "I have observed the maître de's [sic] at work in Hollywood and elsewhere. I go to restaurants and talk to headwaiters and watch their mannerisms, how to bow, lead to the table, seat a party and so on." He believed that for the camera "everything had to be just so."

Corrado's studious commitment to accurate portrayal turned out to be doubly valuable, for in 1949 he found himself working as a real maître d'hôtel at the Italia restaurant in Beverly Hills. "Things are very quiet around the studios now," he explained. Therefore, when his neighbor offered him a job at the restaurant, he agreed "with the understanding that if anything came along in the way of a movie role, I'd have the privilege of taking it." But this famous extra was not anticipating any such roles. "They have stopped building big restaurant and night club sets in pictures in order to economize," he explained, "and if there are no restaurants and night clubs, how can there be headwaiters?"[1]

Corrado probably never had a real studio contract, even though he was at some point a member of the Screen Actors Guild. Nevertheless, his personal journey "from reel life to real life headwaiter" illustrates the transition of the industry as a whole. Toward the late 1940s, the studios were downsizing. The industry that institutionalized creative labor and integrated popular culture into modern American capitalism was about to turn the corner. Even though 1946 was the most profitable year up to that time in the history of the film business, with cumulative box office revenues of close to $1.7 billion and studio profits totaling close to $120 million, the following years saw a steady, worsening decline. By 1960, average weekly attendance dropped from 90 million to 40 million, the number of films produced per year decreased from 467 to 184, and the number of theaters in the United States fell from 19,019 to 16, 991.[2] Indeed, already in 1949, the screenwriter Herbert Clyde Lewis commented, "swimming pools are drying up all over Hollywood. I do not think I shall see them filled in my generation."[3]

There were multiple reasons behind this collapse. For one thing, alternative spectator amusement industries, particularly professional sports and, beginning in the early 1950s, broadcast television, became powerful competitors. In fact, scholars tend to agree that television alone was the primary reason for the decline in movie audiences between 1948 and 1956.[4] In addition, the postwar rise of the suburbs severely weakened the inner-city first-run theaters, which were now left wanting for patrons, and shifted overall expenditure from amusement to material consumer goods. At the same time, European postbellum recovery introduced protectionist measures in important markets such as Britain and France, making it harder for American companies to sell their pictures overseas. These were combined with rising production costs and attacks by private as well as government groups who challenged the industry's morality and patriotism.[5] Last but not least was vertical disintegration.

In May 1948, the Supreme Court handed down its decision in *United States v. Paramount Pictures, Inc.* Though name checking only one company, this long-standing suit by the Justice Department charged all five majors as well as Columbia, Universal, and United Artists as being in violation of the Sherman Antitrust Act.[6] The Supreme Court concurred, ruling that "price-fixing conspiracies existed between all defendants and between each distributor-defendant and its licensees," and that "there was a conspiracy to restrain trade."[7] As a result, the court ordered Loew's, Paramount, RKO, Warner Bros., and Twentieth Century–Fox to divest themselves of their theater holdings and for all eight companies on trial to enjoin from using monopolistic distribution practices such as "block booking" and renting films on a circuit-wide basis. Enduring as production- and distribution-only firms, the big five and the little three would now be forced to rent their films "picture-by-picture" and "theater-by-theater."[8]

Though this disintegration did not have a direct impact on theater attendance, it did carry tremendous implications for revenues. Sans its theater chain, RKO, for example, found itself in debt for $8.5 million. The company's production-distribution end had been losing money for quite some time and was kept above water by the exhibition branch. On its own, the studio was in the red. The Warner Bros. studio had been in a similar predicament since 1941; its theater chain was responsible for 62 percent of the joint company's profits.[9] Without direct access to box office receipts and the safety net provided by the oligopolistic distribution techniques, film production became a much riskier business. Exhibition was not faring much better. By 1955, theater owners too were complaining about "product shortage" and a "rise in rental terms." As one economist put it that year, "The most important experiment in vertical disintegration under the Sherman Act" could be aptly characterized as "disappointing."[10]

The economic downturn resulting from these combined factors forced all studios into a cost-cutting mode. "Producers grind out films faster in [a] drive to cut production costs," declared the *Wall Street Journal* in August 1949. The paper reported that shooting time had been cut by 25 percent on average since 1946, a trimming that dramatically reduced production budgets. Twentieth Century–Fox cut its overall production expenditure by $500,000 between 1947 and 1949, and Paramount was making its pictures for an average cost of $1,498,000 compared to $1,947,000. Still, as the slump continued, executives felt that "more economies must be made."[11] Some of the other strategies they pursued included, as Corrado bemoaned, a shift toward location shooting outside California, as opposed to constructing expensive in-studio sets, or a shift away from purchasing high-priced story properties. But as it turned out, the key for reducing operation costs was simply to cut down the labor force. Between 1946 and 1956, the number of production workers employed by motion picture companies in Southern California fell from 21,775 to 12,593. The plunge was even more striking in the creative ranks. During the same time frame, the number of actors under contract dropped from 804 to 229, the number of directors fell from 160 to 92, and the ranks of screenwriters collapsed from 490 to 67.[12]

In terms of output, studio downsizing was supported by a parallel and complementary shift in the mode of production that facilitated filmmaking outside the traditional big-company structure. In a process that began in the mid-1940s, Hollywood started leaning more and more heavily on independent production. In the American motion picture industry, being independent meant having "no corporate relationship to a distribution firm," and therefore having to negotiate distribution deals on a temporal or film-by-film basis. David O. Selznick and Samuel Goldwyn, who distributed their pictures via United Artists, were the big independent producers of the industry throughout the 1930s and 1940s. Importantly, despite their smaller structure, most of these production operations were "within the mainstream of the American film industry," employing the same financing sources, film production methods, and labor practices, as well as the same understanding of cinematic quality.[13] Due to this fact, following disintegration, the idea of outsourcing some percentage of the yearly productions to independent operations while concentrating on distribution deals appealed to the big companies. Relieving themselves of the costly burden of producing movies, the former studios could theoretically retain a much smaller permanent staff made up of workers in management, accounting, sales, and publicity, plus a minimal crew to maintain the physical facilities.[14] As *Variety* reported in 1951, "[The] volume of independent films channeled through the majors in participation deals is hitting a new high."[15]

Hollywood was not alone. Large corporate structures with internal labor markets declined in the second half of the twentieth century and were replaced by a looser, more fractured, and "supple" system of production. It is exactly this transition that the theorist David Harvey identified as an essential element of what he termed the "condition of post modernity." Though Harvey located the turning point of this transition later, toward the late 1970s, he still recognized a large-scale transformation in American, as well as global, political economy from a Fordist-Keynesian system of mass production and mass consumption to one based on "flexible accumulation." The latter is characterized by, among other things, flexible patterns of work. Instead of big, vertically integrated companies, in the new flexible pattern, any industry revolves around a small core of employees with permanent status and a larger periphery of easily exchangeable part-time workers.[16] By the late 1950s, such a division of labor was at least ten years in the making for post-disintegration Hollywood. In filmmaking, flexible accumulation was also accompanied by a matching corporate structure of "flexible specialization," in which each picture was produced by many specialized firms coming together ad hoc.[17] In this sense, it seems that the motion picture industry foreshadowed the emerging postmodern economic trends.

Instead of the studio, at the center of the new system now stood the deal. In what some scholars refer to as a "spot-production" or "package-unit" system, the entire industry became one large pool of resources that formed transitory combinations for short-term arrangements, film by film. Every picture was put together from scratch. The producer was still the focal point, organizing the film project by securing financing; negotiating contracts with lead actors, a director, and writers; and leasing "means of production" such as costumes, cameras, lighting, and other technological equipment from a growing list of specialized support companies. The role of the former majors was gradually limited to that of financiers and distributors. The self-contained studio that emerged in the 1920s was all but disappearing by the early 1950s.[18]

THE TRANSITION TO a film-by-film production system naturally entailed the end of the long-term employment contract. As indicated, the number of studio employees decreased dramatically already by 1950. Companies were particularly eager to dispose of their contracts with the creative talent, which placed the largest burden on the budget sheets. Warner Bros. was the quickest to do so. Starting in 1950, the studio terminated the contracts of most of its top stars, including James Cagney, Humphrey Bogart, Bette Davis, Edward G. Robinson, Errol Flynn, Ann Sheridan, and Sydney Greenstreet. The company got rid of its top producers as well; it sold off Jerry Wald's contract to RKO and gradually reduced the role and salary of its executive producer, Henry Blanke. In April 1951, Jack Warner also eliminated the entire story department.[19] Though the rate of downsizing was uneven, and MGM, for example, took several more years to reduce its human assets, during the 1950s the Hollywood labor force, headwaiters and Clark Gables alike, had been forced to adjust to a new normal.

For some, these changes came as a blessing. As much as the big companies wanted to shed their producing duties, by the early 1950s many of the big names in the industry were happy to assume them. Independent production offered several perks to those who were willing and financially able to take the risk. For one, it accorded producers a share of the profits, a benefit that long-term studio contracts hardly ever offered. What's more, operating from within the auspices of independent companies, producers could enjoy the advantages of paying a corporate tax on their proceeds. Changes in the tax code following World War II placed the maximum tax on capital gains at 25 percent and on corporate tax at 52 percent. At the same time, personal income tax climbed to as high as 75 or even 92 percent on yearly paychecks exceeding $100,000, not an uncommon sum among Hollywood high rollers.[20] Finally, as one historian stated, some creative people were simply "tired of studio bureaucracies and wanted to guide their own careers."[21]

As a result, many new production firms appeared across town, and quite a few familiar names added a hyphen followed by the word "producer" to their title. The age of the all-powerful Thalberg-like head producer was over. The position itself continued to appear on studio rosters, and some towering figures like Zanuck remained in place for a few more years. But with the growing reliance on independent production, power was diffused. As one producer put it, "By 1960 it was hard to find a creative producer willing to run a major studio."[22] Selznick's unit-production model, which he realized in his successful independent company, was now the standard practice. Hollywood veterans who entered the production fray included actors Douglas Fairbanks Jr., Ida Lupino, Burt Lancaster, Danny Kaye, and Bogart; directors John Huston, Stanley Kramer, Ken Annakin, Anatole Litvak, George Stevens, Frank Capra, and William Wyler; writer Ben Hecht; and former studio producer Wald.[23] These indie entrepreneurs were unable to avoid studio bureaucracies altogether. As *Variety* explained, most of the independent deals were in "alignment with the large studios," which "suppl[y] second money and guarantees for production." Only with "this accomplishment, indies have little trouble at all obtaining initial coin from the banks."[24] Still, going into business with a studio was a far cry from being employed by one.

This new "semi-independent" status affected producers' work. If previously they vacillated between creative tasks and executive ones, when working outside the studio machine their pendulum often stuck on the managerial side rather than the artistic one. Hal Wallis was particularly troubled by this change. Producing was nothing new to him. Far from it—Wallis was one of the greats, a Thalberg-like executive producer who set the tone for Warner Bros. pictures following Zanuck's departure in 1933. At the helm, he helped bring to light such classics as *The Life of Emile Zola* (1937), *Jezebel* (1938), *Juarez* (1939), and *The Maltese Falcon* (1941), while building the careers of Litvak, Huston, William Dieterle, Bette Davis, and many others. In line with the times, by the early 1940s he "had had enough of this business of being responsible for a program of 20 or 30 pictures a year," and decided to set up his own unit within the studio. "That was the period I made *Casablanca* [1942] and *Air Force* [1943] and *Saratoga Trunk* [1945]," he remembered, "because I could work closely on a limited number of pictures, and I preferred that." In 1944, tensions with Jack Warner inspired Wallis to partner with Joseph Hazen, who served as the Warners' lawyer, and to set up his own independent company in alignment with Paramount.[25]

Independence came at a price. Instead of working closely on his pictures, Wallis found that he spent "more and more time on collateral matters . . . towards the development of deals, arrangements, negotiations, meetings, etc." More often than not, he wasted much of his days speaking with agents and lawyers "mostly on contractual involvement and matters not directly relating to the production of our current picture or the preparation of any future picture." These negotiations, Wallis felt, "[took] me away from what I should be doing, namely, working on my pictures." On any average day, he complained, there was "practically no time to work on my scripts or to read synopses or other material for the future, or to edit."[26] Making deals became his major task, if not his primary one. For Wallis, this was an unwelcome change. "Making pictures was much more fun in the thirties," he said. By the late 1950s, he recalled, "the fun [had] pretty much gone out of it. There are too many difficult elements and provoking elements that enter into the situation."[27]

Typically for Hollywood, not everyone felt the same. The collateral matters that sucked the "fun element" out of the executive producer's work experience certainly improved the work conditions of some creative talent. Wallis's grumbles are telling. As an independent, he found that it was "becoming increasingly difficult to put together attractive packages," particularly "in view of the astronomically high cost of stories and stars."[28] Every little thing had to be agreed upon. Since important stars were "unattached," he explained, they "will not make a commitment for more than one picture at a time, and that in most cases only after [they] read the original material and often the shooting script." That was not all; "the bigger the star, the more the demands." Many stars insisted on the rights "for approval of co-star, of supporting cast, of writer, of director. All sorts of things come into it, which weren't in the pictures some years ago."[29] One producer's loss was another actor's gain. Released from their draconian studio contracts, those actors in high demand could suddenly exercise some control over their careers, as well as creative control over their craft. Now, if a producer felt that the success of a picture required Gable, Gable was no longer required to be in the picture, and if he chose to appear, it would be on his own terms.

This shifting balance of power was not reserved for the acting talent alone. When, in 1953, Wallis tried to hire the directing services of Dieterle, he was shocked to receive a wire "proposing we pay $25,000 with a call on his services for an additional $60,000." In a letter to M. C. Levee, Dieterle's agent, he and Hazen employed any conceivable tactic to try to reduce the amount:

I am sure I do not have to remind you of my own personal relationship with Mr. Dieterle, which commenced at the time he first came to this country for Warner Bros. when I, personally, settled his contractual problems with a German producing firm which threatened to enjoin the rendition of his services in this country. I was in Berlin at the time and handled the matter personally for which I received no remuneration from [sic] Mr. Dieterle—nor did I seek any. I am sure that I do not have to recount Hal's relationship with Dieterle nor our employment of Dieterle when he had fallen into a fallow period, as a result of which Paramount and Columbia contracts followed.[30]

Mutual history was one thing, business in the 1950s quite another. Levee was not moved by this polemic, replying, "It always amuses me to find that you and Hal Wallis are 'shocked' at other people trying to work out what is obvious, a fair and equitable deal."[31] This was a newfound validity, one it is doubtful Dieterle had when he was working under Wallis at the Warner lot in the 1930s.

Well-paid screenwriters also fared well. Employed for short periods, usually on a specific engagement, they too could extract higher sums and exercise more control over their contracts. Already in 1949, Samson Raphaelson's agent advised him that, per his request, his contract with MGM had been reduced to two "employment periods, either of which can be for 40 weeks or for a single assignment," based on his own preference. The writer also had "the primary right to designate the starting date of each of the two [engagements]." In other words, Raphaelson could decide when, and on what, he was going to work.[32] Retained on a film-by-film basis, like their fellow actors and directors, screenwriters could negotiate salaries, schedules, and sometimes even percentage deals. Ben Hecht once joked that in the studio era, "if you could alter your status from that of a writer to that of a card-player or drinking companion, it was a tremendous step up."[33] It seems that by the 1950s, even without resorting to gambling and heavy drinking, a few screenwriters were simply swept up by the organizational rising tide.

For the most part, though, this was not the case. In post–studio era Hollywood, the less popular creative employees were not lifted by a rising tide but caught up in a low one filled with uncertainty and frequent periods of unemployment. By the end of the 1940s, as one talent agent reported, "out of some 1200 members of the Screen Writers Guild, only about 120 are currently employed at all studios." Gone were the days that "Metro alone used to carry that many writers on the payroll."[34] One can imagine that, with the production wheels slowing down, work was hard to come by for the remaining 1,080 SWG affiliates. Many Screen Actors Guild and Screen Directors Guild members shared this fate. Director John Brahm wrote to a friend in 1948, "I am absolutely stunned and stymied by the professional inactivity." His RKO contract had ended the previous October, and by May he had counted "six and a half months now without pay, nine months without work! And nothing in sight." Naturally, "besides the enervating mental situation re the lack of work," Brahm now found the "financial one getting out of control" too.[35] Without the studio back lots and the security offered by long-term contracts, post–studio era workers were relegated to the lower ranks of the industry's hierarchy.

Polarization ensued. The growing echelons of unaffiliated talent opened new opportunities at the very top of the film business hierarchy. As the new center of the system was the ad hoc picture deal, and since the studios had begun outsourcing the means of production, it followed that one important resource, namely, the administration of labor power, was up for grabs. Or in other words, no longer under the studios' auspices, the management of the industry's creative force was on offer, open to new methods of organization and control. During the heyday of the studio system, Selznick confirmed, "there [were] two, and only two, important types of manpower in motion pictures and they [were] equally rare: the great top executive and the great individual picture-maker."[36] By the 1950s, this duo turned into a threesome as the executive producer and the individual director made room for the great talent agent. Creative talent began using the services of intermediaries such as lawyers and agents to organize their employment in the late 1920s. As noted earlier, objection to agent regulation was one of the main battle cries in SWG's and SAG's fight against the 1933 Code of Fair Practice.[37] But as long as the seven-year contract was the standard practice, the interaction among client, agent, and studio was interspersed between long periods of prenegotiated studio employment.

Not that these agents were insignificant. Powerful brokers such as Myron Selznick and Charles K. Feldman spent the 1930s and 1940s introducing services for the studio-bound as well as the freelance or nonexclusive talent. With clients such as Irene Dunne, Claudette Colbert, and George Stevens, Feldman, for example, could renegotiate salaries during the option review periods and determine terms about maximum daily work hours, dressing rooms, and breaks. Most troubling to studios was the practice of "raiding," by which an agent would negotiate a new and more lucrative deal for a client already affiliated with a studio, using the counter-offer to reopen the existing contract. Indeed, the involvement of agents was meaningful enough that producers tried to limit their influence on several occasions during the 1930s. Though many producers and agents often socialized after hours, during the workday they were adversaries, and the former often found the latter to be "craven Hollywood hucksters, fleecing producers of millions" and "contaminat[ing] the rational business methods that supposedly governed the burgeoning studio system."[38] As one such producer at MGM sarcastically wrote to his agent friend Leland Heyward, "Only a mad man would spend months sweating his guts out in a creative effort when life could be so much pleasanter—at least ten per cent pleasanter—when lived on what one can scavenge from the efforts of others without ever putting one's talents to the test."[39]

Still, after the disintegration of the studio system, the so-called scavengers came to the fore. Lew Wasserman was the epitome of the new agent-king. Taking Jules Stein's MCA (Music Corporation of America) into the picture business, Wasserman bought Hayward's agency in 1944. A year later, MCA helped one of its new clients, Olivia de Havilland, triumph over Warner Bros., winning a court battle that set a precedent and prevented studios from extending their talent contracts following suspensions. These moves marked the agency as a major player in the industry.[40] Wasserman firmly established his reputation by negotiating profit participation deals for his clients and offering producers package deals on the agency's stars. This latter practice basically blurred the line between the agent and the producer. After all, wasn't stringing together talent to work on a specific production, and essentially casting the movie, one of the major tasks of a producer? In fact, when in 1952 the new president of United Artists, Arthur Krim, set out to attract star power to his studio, he contacted Wasserman directly.[41] Packaging truly upended the old system; now a project often started in an agency and only then was pitched to studios or independent producers. As one industry scholar pointed out, with Wasserman "the modern studio system was born."[42]

Perhaps surprisingly, despite the ascendance of personal representation, Hollywood unions survived the upheavals intact and were even invigorated. SAG, SDG, and SWG continued to represent their respective creative crafts through the collapse of the studio system, the proliferation of new technologies such as television and cable, and the formation, toward the late 1960s, of new corporate conglomerates. Despite its difficult beginnings, SWG developed into a particularly impressive organization, achieving the long-dreamed-of amalgamation and, ultimately, becoming Writers Guild of America, representing authors of film, broadcasting, and theater. In 1985, the guild further expanded its reach, signing an overarching agreement with sister guilds from Great Britain, Canada, and Australia to form a genuine and exceptional international union.[43] In 2012, SAG formed a similar intra-industry alliance with the American Federation of Television and Radio Artists. And yet, while the guilds proved to be effective representative tools, unlike agencies, they did not become the cornerstone of the new industry. Unions did become the principal organizing mechanism for below-the-line or craft jobs. As in many other industries, the roster system, embraced by most IATSE-affiliated unions, added to the unions' collective bargaining duties and turned them into de facto hiring halls.[44]

That was not the case for the talent guilds. The tentative nature of the talent workers once again sidestepped the more common trajectory of working-class organization and, instead, necessitated an in-between institutional structure, combining collective bargaining with personal representation. Theoretically, the two worked side by side, the guilds protecting the basic minimum standards of employment and the agents testing the maximum, aiming high for the stars. But with the agents veering closer and closer to the center of power, it became unclear to what extent their concerns were aligned with those of the less-than-famous rank and file. Star writers, directors, and actors continued to view themselves as above the line, identifying strongly with their own brand and the product of their labor and only loosely with their position in the industry's labor *structure*. This was especially the case now that a significant number of them were crossing the lines to the hyphenated producing echelons. Aligning both with the employees and the chieftains, the ambivalent working class had someone looking out for them on both ends.

This polarization between fame-holders and fame-seekers was mimicked by the industry's product. Just as the industry discarded the large studio and long-term contract method for a leaner staff roster and spot deals, studios replaced the steady flow of A pictures and occasional prestige epics with a shorter list of well-calculated, big-budget blockbusters as their main source of income. These trends only intensified through the 1950s and 1960s. In addition, with the growing fragmentation of the entertainment market and the corresponding segmentation of the moviegoing audience, production companies, which by the 1970s were reimplanted in new multi-industry companies and on occasion also international conglomerates, also began to diversify. Studios were no longer just in the motion picture business. They were packaging TV movies and TV shows, music videos, soundtrack albums, video games, videocassettes, and even theme park rides. As media scholar Thomas Schatz declared, "Diversification and conglomeration" became the key features of the industry. This was "the New Hollywood."[45]

IS WORKING IN the new Hollywood better? Much of the current discourse suggests that it is. Surveying the transition from the studio era to the film-by-film era, a prevalent and popular position holds that it was a welcome shift from "an older corporate-centered system" to a more "people-driven one." Naturally, say the prophets of this new creative class, the emphasis on people immediately connotes more value to "individuality, self-expression, and openness to difference," as opposed to the "homogeneity, conformity, and 'fitting in' that defined the previous age of large scale industry and organization."[46] As the change in the film industry during the 1950s only foreshadowed the global transition to flexible accumulation, this positive change is attributed to a much larger sector of the workforce. As one scholar put it, "We're all going Hollywood." A diverse group of industries, including arts, advertising, high-tech, pharmaceuticals, and many others, have all adapted themselves to "the individual's rise." It is a new era dominated by a creative class of free agents, coming together for a project and dispersing when it ends—no longer working according to a Taylorist-inspired division of labor, but in a new "tailorist" system, in which each individual sets the terms for him- or herself.[47]

Perhaps. Then again, it is also possible to conjure a somewhat less optimistic batch of associations with individualism—for example, fragmentation, discord, and alienation. While the new Hollywood is certainly not corporate-centered, this does not necessarily mean it is "people-driven." As the source of all interactions has become the project or the ad hoc deal, it might be more fitting to describe the new mode of production as product-centered. Though previously the studio was at the center, the studio system still managed to inaugurate the initial cohort of the creative class. Always putting itself first, any vertically integrated film company was nevertheless dependent on this class. Each studio was dedicated to nurturing and maintaining its large and stable creative labor force. The workers forged in this system developed a complex set of loyalties: to their artistic visions, the products they made, the studio they were working for, the industry as a whole, and, albeit ambivalently, their fellow craftsmen. Thus, while far from a benevolent organization, the studio was a stable workplace, fostering wide-ranging and long-lasting solidarities. In contrast, a film project is by nature ephemeral. Therefore, notwithstanding the possible benefits of such a flexible system, the type of loyalty it encourages is mostly to oneself. Anything else melts into air as soon as the work is over.

It is not my intention to romanticize the studio system. Like any industrial structure, the era that turned creativity into a modern form of work certainly generated much employee dissatisfaction. As Hecht, always the first among the disgruntled, reminisced in 1959, it was all a sham: "The writer was a fake, the director was a super-fake, and the producer was a con man. He had no more reason for getting paid than an usher would have for getting all the money in the theater."[48] Still, while working for a big company may have meant trading in one's independence and, on occasion, also one's artistic integrity, there is something to be said for the security and support offered by these institutions. The standardization of screenwriting, directing, and acting involved at least a partial alienation from the product, a division and commodification of the creative labor, and in the case of stars the commodification of their personas. But the system also invested in its workers and compensated them by offering occupational stability, resources, and opportunity for cooperation, conditions that are very favorable to artistic production. Once employees were under contract, the system delivered these advantages as guarantees, without forcing them to constantly engage with and monitor their market value.

Upon reflection, George Cukor reached a very different conclusion than his colleague Hecht. "Now that the studios are not active," he said in the early 1970s, "they would talk about them as factories and this and that." But, in fact, he observed, he "didn't realize how much they helped. This was all taken for granted . . . now when I try to do some of these things myself, it's enormously difficult to do."[49] Never completely free, in the Hollywood studio system the creative worker was also never entirely alone.

Notes

LBMF   Louis B. Mayer Foundation of Oral History, American Film Institute Center for Advanced Film Studies Oral History Collection, Los Angeles.

MHL   Special Collections, Margaret Herrick Library, Beverly Hills.

NLRB.1   Official Report Proceedings before the National Labor Relations Board: Hearing in the Matter of Metro-Goldwyn-Mayer Studios and Motion Pictures Producers and Screen Writers Guild of the Authors' Guild of America et al., Case No. XXI-R-149, et al., Record Group 340, National Archives at College Park, College Park.

NLRB.2   Official Report Proceedings before the National Labor Relations Board: Hearing in the Matter of Universal Pictures Inc. and Screen Writers' Guild Inc. and Screen Playwrights Inc. Party to a Contract et al., Case No. C-1055 to C-1063, Record Group 1460, National Archives at College Park, College Park.

NYPL   Performing Arts Research Collection, New York Public Library for the Performing Arts, Dorothy and Lewis B. Cullman Center, New York.

OHCC   Oral History Collection of Columbia University, New York.

WHS   Wisconsin Historical Society, Madison.

Introduction

1. Darryl Zanuck, "But I Never Had an Ulcer," *Los Angeles Times*, November 21, 1954.

2. Irving Thalberg and Hugh Weir, "Why Motion Pictures Cost So Much," *Saturday Evening Post*, November 4, 1933.

3. Hal Wallis, "Portrait of a Producer Talking to Himself—with Some Answers from Hal Wallis," draft, 1944, file 233.f-2284, Hal Wallis Papers, MHL. The quote is taken from a draft for an "exclusive guest column" Wallis submitted to gossip commentator Walter Winchell.

4. Reminiscences of Adolph Zukor, interviewed by Joan and Robert Franklin, 1958, transcript, Popular Arts Project, OHCC, 36–37.

5. Crawford to Katherine Albert, November 14, 1941, file 3.f-123, Gladys Hall Papers, MHL.

6. Reminiscences of James Cagney, December 1958, transcript, Popular Arts Project, OHCC, 45.

7. Ibid.

8. Surprisingly, there are very few historical works that tackle the Hollywood studio system as a whole. The most prominent of them are still Robert Sklar,

Movie-Made America: A Cultural History of American Movies (New York: Random House, 1975); Lary May, *Screening Out the Past: The Birth of Mass Culture and the Motion Picture Industry* (New York: Oxford University Press, 1980); as well as May's *The Big Tomorrow: Hollywood and the Politics of the American Way* (Chicago: University of Chicago Press, 2000). Several works picked up the question of labor in Hollywood, usually by focusing on one profession. For the work of writers, see Richard Fine, *Hollywood and the Profession of Authorship, 1928–1940* (Ann Arbor: UMI Research Press, 1985); Nancy Lynn Schwartz, *The Hollywood Writers' Wars* (New York: Knopf, 1982); and Larry Ceplair and Steven Englund, *The Inquisition in Hollywood: Politics in the Film Community, 1930–1960* (Garden City, NY: Anchor Press / Doubleday, 1980). For the work of actors, see Richard deCordova, *Picture Personalities: The Emergence of the Star System in America* (Urbana: University of Illinois Press, 1990); Danae Clark, *Negotiating Hollywood: The Cultural Politics of Actors' Labor* (Minneapolis: University of Minnesota Press, 1995). A number of more recent books touch on the issue of work in order to discuss a broader topic such as class formation, the making of a Hollywood political community, and the importance of women to the industry. See Steven J. Ross, *Working-Class Hollywood: Silent Film and the Shaping of Class in America* (Princeton, NJ: Princeton University Press, 1998); Saverio Giovacchini, *Hollywood Modernism: Film and Politics in the Age of the New Deal* (Philadelphia: Temple University Press, 2001); Hilary A. Hallett, *Go West, Young Women! The Rise of Early Hollywood* (Berkeley: University of California Press, 2013).

9. For more on this concept, see Sean P. Holmes, "The Hollywood Star System and the Regulation of Actors' Labour, 1916–1934," *Film History* 12, no. 1 (January 1, 2000): 97–114.

10. My argument is one of scope and scale. I do not mean to suggest that Hollywood was the only film industry to institutionalize creative labor in the West. Rather, I argue that the American film industry did so in the most meaningful, pervasive, and long-lasting ways. Elements of Hollywood's work organization, such as the star system and division of labor, are visible in European industries as well. However, as several scholars have pointed out, by the late 1920s, the dominance of American companies, due to their vertical integration, economies of scale, and standardization, was undeniable. Moreover, throughout that decade, most of the large European companies had effectively surrendered film production. The French companies Pathé and Gaumont focused on distribution, and Éclair went bankrupt. The Danish Nordisk collapsed, as did a large part of the Italian industry. The British market relied on imports from its inception, and by 1924 only a very small number of films were being made in Britain. The German company Ufa did present a model of vertical integration, but it functioned more as an umbrella organization and less as a standardized company. The various production companies operating within Ufa maintained a high degree of independence until, in 1933, the National Socialist government converted Ufa into a state-controlled company. In short, no other film industry matched the volume and durability of the American studio system both in terms of films produced and in terms of labor force. For more on the European industry and its interaction with American film production, see Victoria de Grazia, "Mass Culture and Sovereignty: The American Challenge to European Cinemas, 1920–1960,"

Journal of Modern History 61, no. 1 (1989): 53–87; Gerben Bakker, *Entertainment Industrialised: The Emergence of the International Film Industry, 1890–1940* (Cambridge: Cambridge University Press, 2008); Klaus Kreimeier, *The Ufa Story: A History of Germany's Greatest Film Company, 1918–1945* (New York: Hill and Wang, 1996).

11. For more statistics on theater attendance during the 1920s, see Richard Koszarski, *An Evening's Entertainment: The Age of the Silent Feature Picture, 1915–1928* (New York: Scribner, 1990), 25–26.

12. Here too my emphasis is on scale. I do not mean to suggest that the film industry was the first to standardize culture. My claim is that it was the first to do so for many occupations and for the largest number of people working in each one of these occupations. Earlier attempts to regulate work in American show business could be found in the theater business and in professional sports, particularly baseball. Yet, in theater, at least until the late 1930s, the combination system separated theater control from production, thus limiting the economic power of any specific company, preventing it from becoming a big employer like Paramount or Warner Bros. Similarly, while the National League attempted to enforce regulations, baseball was controlled by local franchises, even the largest of which were small in comparison to motion picture companies. That said, just as in the case of Hollywood, there is very little scholarship on the business and labor conditions of other entertainment industries and much more to learn. The few studies about the theater business include Sean P. Holmes, *Weavers of Dreams, Unite! Actor's Unionism in Early Twentieth-Century America* (Urbana: University of Illinois Press, 2013); Benjamin McArthur, *Actors and American Culture, 1880–1920* (Philadelphia: Temple University Press, 1984); and the old but excellent study by Alfred L. Bernheim, *The Business of the Theatre* (New York: Actors' Equity Association, 1932). A few great articles about the business of sports can be found in Linda J. Borish, David K. Wiggins, and Gerlad R. Gems, eds., *The Routledge History of American Sport* (New York: Routledge, 2017). A good overview is Benjamin G. Rader, *American Sports: From the Age of Folk Games to the Age of Televised Sports* (Upper Saddle River, NJ: Pearson / Prentice Hall, 2009). For a useful study of baseball, see Harold Seymour, *Baseball: The Early Years* (New York: Oxford University Press, 1989).

13. See Thomas Schatz, *The Genius of the System: Hollywood Filmmaking in the Studio Era* (New York: Pantheon Books, 1988), 8–9. Schatz borrows his title from the French film critic André Bazin, who used it in his 1957 essay "La politique des auteurs." Two other influential works that helped establish the field of "industry studies" within media scholarship are Staiger's chapters in David Bordwell, Janet Staiger, and Kristin Thompson, *The Classical Hollywood Cinema: Film Style and Mode of Production to 1960* (New York: Columbia University Press, 1985); and Douglas Gomery, *The Hollywood Studio System* (New York: St. Martin's Press, 1986). While Gomery is primarily concerned with the decision-making hierarchy and how it affected the film product, Staiger focuses on the mode of production and labor structure. Several edited collections on this topic include Tino Balio, ed., *The American Film Industry* (Madison: University of Wisconsin Press, 1985); Janet Staiger, ed., *The Studio System* (New Brunswick, NJ: Rutgers University Press, 1995); and Thomas Schatz, ed., *Hollywood: Critical Concepts in Media and Cultural Studies* (London: Routledge, 2003).

Perhaps the most comprehensive study of the American motion picture industry is the invaluable ten-volume *History of The American Cinema*, written by various authors including Balio and Schatz, each volume of which covers a decade of filmmaking from the late nineteenth century to 1989. See Charles Harpole, gen. ed., *History of the American Cinema*, 10 vols. (New York: Scribner).

14. As Staiger herself points out, despite the immense importance of her work, the labor system and work routines she describes remain "a template to describe work behavior," and lack a "theory of agency" or an explanation as to "why individuals might pursue acting those routines." This work seeks to build on her studies and offer some answers to this very problem of agency. See David A. Gerstner and Janet Staiger, eds., *Authorship and Film* (New York: Routledge, 2003), 40–43.

15. "Pink Slip Man," a draft of an article about Hal Wallis written by Thomas Wood including Wallis's notes, circa 1942, file 229.f-2260, Hal Wallis Papers.

16. On the importance of such "contemporaneous struggles" across cultural industries, see James W. Cook, "The Return of the Cultural Industry," in *The Cultural Turn in U.S. History: Past, Present, and Future*, ed. James W. Cook, Lawrence B. Glickman, and Michael O'Malley (Chicago: University of Chicago Press, 2008), 291–317.

17. For more about this idea and how it relates to the production of culture, see Paul DiMaggio and Paul M. Hirsch, "Production Organizations in the Arts," *American Behavioral Scientist* 19, no. 6 (July 1, 1976): 735–52.

18. For more on the concept of identification and theories of control in creative industries, see Alan McKinlay and Chris Smith, eds., *Creative Labour: Working in the Creative Industries* (Basingstoke, Eng.: Palgrave Macmillan, 2009), 43–46.

19. Donna T. Haverty-Stacke and Daniel J. Walkowitz, eds., *Rethinking U.S. Labor History: Essays on the Working-Class Experience, 1756–2009* (New York: Continuum, 2010), 3.

20. Herbert G. Gutman, "Work, Culture, and Society in Industrializing America, 1815–1919," *American Historical Review* 78, no. 3 (June 1, 1973): 585. For more of Gutman's work, see Gutman, *Work, Culture, and Society in Industrializing America: Essays in American Working-Class and Social History* (New York: Knopf, 1976). Two other important studies in this tradition include David Montgomery, *The Fall of the House of Labor: The Workplace, the State, and American Labor Activism, 1865–1925* (Cambridge: Cambridge University Press, 1987); and Harry Braverman, *Labor and Monopoly Capital: The Degradation of Work in the Twentieth Century* (New York: Monthly Review Press, 1975).

21. For more on how the women of Los Angeles shaped the city, the film industry, and the national discussions about femininity and women's liberation, see Hallett, *Go West, Young Women!*

22. Karen Ward Mahar's study of women filmmakers suggests that the impact of gender norms was manifested in three different stages: The film industry was "born masculine," and during its first decade, which culminated around 1909, the business was centered around technological expertise, which was "understood as indisputably masculine." During the second stage, which lasted throughout most of the 1910s, a "search for middle class approval" welcomed women both as audience members and as creative contributors, since their presence was thought to lend respectability and

wholesomeness. Finally, as the industry expanded into the corporate world during the 1920s, a need for the approval of the business and financial establishment affirmed the "masculine image of the filmmaker/businessmen" and pushed women out of key positions in the studios. See Karen W. Mahar, "True Womanhood in Hollywood: Gendered Business Strategies and the Rise and Fall of the Woman Filmmaker, 1896–1928," *Enterprise and Society* 2, no. 1 (March 1, 2001): 72–110; quotes from 79, 82, 100. For more, see also Karen Ward Mahar, *Women Filmmakers in Early Hollywood* (Baltimore: Johns Hopkins University Press, 2006).

23. T. J. Jackson Lears, *Rebirth of a Nation: The Making of Modern America, 1877–1920* (New York: HarperCollins, 2009), 93.

24. For more on the lives of African Americans who worked in Hollywood, whether in the film industry or around it, see Donald Bogle, *Bright Boulevards, Bold Dreams: The Story of Black Hollywood* (New York: One World Ballantine Books, 2005). For a more specific look at black actors during the 1930s, see Miriam J. Petty, *Stealing the Show: African American Performers and Audiences in 1930s Hollywood* (Oakland: University of California Press, 2016). For a study of the representation of African Americans in the era's cinema, see Ellen C. Scott, *Cinema Civil Rights: Regulation, Repression, and Race in the Classical Hollywood Era* (London: Rutgers University Press, 2015).

25. Ross, *Working-Class Hollywood*, 9.

26. Robert E. Kuenne, "Conflict Management and the Theory of Mature Oligopoly," *Conflict Management and Peace Science* 10, no. 1 (Spring 1988): 37–57.

27. I am referring here to the Motion Picture Patent Company, which was formed by Edison in 1908 and united the patents of all significant production companies of the time, including Edison, Biograph, Vitagraph, Lubin, Essanay, Selig, Kalem, Méliès, Pathé, and George Kleine, as well as raw stock supplier Eastman Kodak. The Patent Company was commonly referred to as "the trust" for its manifest attempt to control all production and exhibition by essentially forcing both producers and exhibitors to use its products exclusively. See Eileen Bowser, *The Transformation of Cinema, 1907–1915* (Berkeley: University of California Press, 1994), 21–36.

28. Gomery, *The Hollywood Studio System*, 12–26. For a full account of all the major business developments of this time and the initial mergers of all majors, see Richard Koszarski, *An Evening's Entertainment: The Age of the Silent Feature Picture, 1915–1928* (New York: Scribner, 1990), 63–94.

29. For more on MGM, see Gomery, *The Hollywood Studio System*, 27–36; Thomas Schatz, *The Genius of the System*, 29–47.

30. On the origins of Fox, see Gomery, *The Hollywood Studio System*, 37–45; Upton Sinclair, *Upton Sinclair Presents William Fox* (Los Angeles: Privately printed, 1933). The Fox Company ran into serious financial problems during the Great Depression and as a result of some unsuccessful business ventures. To save itself from bankruptcy, in 1935 the company merged with newly formed production firm Twentieth Century and was henceforth named Twentieth Century–Fox.

31. See Gomery, *The Hollywood Studio System*, 46–55; Schatz, *The Genius of the System*, 58–66. Unlike most of the other studios, Warner Bros. was the subject of several interesting studies. See Rudy Behlmer, *Inside Warner Bros., 1935–1951* (New York: Viking, 1985); Nick Roddick, *A New Deal in Entertainment: Warner Brothers in the*

1930s (London: British Film Institute, 1983); Cass Warner Sperling and Cork Millner, *Hollywood Be Thy Name: The Warner Brothers Story* (Rocklin, CA: Prima Pub., 1994).

32. Gomery, *The Hollywood Studio System*, 56–57; and Richard B. Jewell and Vernon Harbin, *The RKO Story* (New York: Crown, 1982).

33. For a partial history of Universal, see I. G. Edmonds, *Big U: Universal in the Silent Days* (South Brunswick, NJ: A. S. Barnes, 1977). Background on Columbia can be found in Edward Buscombe, "Notes on Columbia Pictures Corporation, 1926–41," *Screen* 16, no. 3 (1975): 65–82. As it did not have any production facilities, United Artists is not significant to this study, but it was very significant to the economic structure of the system, and it is also the subject of the best history written about any single Hollywood company. See Tino Balio, *United Artists: The Company Built by the Stars* (Madison: University of Wisconsin Press, 1976).

34. Quotes and data from Balio, *The American Film Industry*, 253–55. In terms of theater numbers, in 1945, the majors owned about 3,000, or about one-sixth of the total number of theaters in the United States. Despite this small proportion, these theaters were all "first-run houses," usually located in big cities and exhibiting new pictures. Such theaters could also charge higher ticket prices and, therefore, accounted for 70 percent of the nation's box office receipts. Of course, the majors invented this theater ranking system exactly to elevate the value of their assets and devalue independent theaters.

35. For more on these as well as other trade practices within the distribution and exhibition branches, see Mae D. Huettig, *Economic Control of the Motion Picture Industry: A Study in Industrial Organization* (Philadelphia: University of Pennsylvania Press, 1944), 113–39; Howard Thompson Lewis, *The Motion Picture Industry* (New York: D. Van Nostrand, 1933), 142–80; Lewis Jacobs, *The Rise of the American Film: A Critical History* (New York: Harcourt, Brace, 1939), 287–301.

36. Gomery, *The Hollywood Studio System*, 65.

37. For more on the effect of television on the industry, see Richard E. Caves, *Creative Industries: Contracts between Art and Commerce* (Cambridge, MA: Harvard University Press, 2000), 92–95.

38. Box office grosses dropped from $1.692 billion in 1946 to $1.376 billion in 1950; studio profits during the same years plummeted from $119.9 million to $30.8 million. For more on how broadcasting affected Hollywood, see Christopher Anderson, "Television and Hollywood in the 1940s," in Thomas Schatz, *Boom and Bust: The American Cinema in the 1940s* (New York: Scribner, 1997), 422–44, as well as 291, 462, and 464 for the relevant statistical data.

39. Caves, *Creative Industries*, 92.

40. See Schatz, *Boom and Bust*, 323–28; as well as Michael Conant, *Antitrust in the Motion Picture Industry* (Berkeley: University of California Press, 1960), 323–28.

41. This book is concerned mostly with the operation of the major studios. The minor studios and independent producers, who were also important players in the system, did not operate exactly like the five majors, and naturally the five vertically integrated companies also had their differences. Still, as Staiger explains, commercial independent production "seems to have organized itself in similar fashion" to that employed by the other companies. Independent "work processes were that of a

hierarchy with divided labor," and its "means of production were identical" to those of the big five and little three. Or, in other words, I believe that the commonalities outweigh the differences in this matter. See Bordwell, Staiger, and Thompson, *The Classical Hollywood Cinema*, 317–19.

42. Pandro S. Berman, interviewed by Mike Steen, August 4, 1972, transcript, Oral History Collection, MHL, 57–60.

Chapter One

1. Hedda Hopper, *Washington Post*, February 18, 1940.

2. Nunnally Johnson, typescript regarding the writing of *The Grapes of Wrath*, folder 7.f-41, Rudy Behlmer Papers, MHL.

3. Darryl F. Zanuck, "But I Never Had an Ulcer," *Los Angeles Times*, November 21, 1954.

4. Quoted in Rudy Behlmer, *America's Favorite Movies: Behind the Scenes* (New York: F. Ungar, 1982), 132.

5. Zanuck, "But I Never Had an Ulcer."

6. Leo Calvin Rosten, *Hollywood: The Movie Colony, the Movie Makers* (New York: Harcourt, Brace, 1941), 238.

7. Richard A. Peterson and David G. Berger, "Entrepreneurship in Organizations: Evidence from the Popular Music Industry," *Administrative Science Quarterly* 16, no. 1 (March 1, 1971): 97.

8. Charles Perrow suggests that when the determining factors are "so vague and poorly conceptualized as to make [them] virtually unanalyzable," decision making often "draws upon the residue of unanalyzed experience or intuition, or relies upon chance and guesswork," all techniques that defy standardization. See "A Framework for the Comparative Analysis of Organizations," *American Sociological Review* 32, no. 2 (April 1, 1967): 196.

9. Paul DiMaggio, "Market Structure, the Creative Process, and Popular Culture: Toward an Organizational Reinterpretation of Mass-Culture Theory," *Journal of Popular Culture* 11 (1977): 437–43.

10. For an introduction to recent studies on the sociology of taste and cultural preference, see Amir Goldberg, "Mapping Shared Understandings Using Relational Class Analysis: The Case of the Cultural Omnivore Reexamined," *American Journal of Sociology* 116, no. 5 (March 1, 2011): 1397–1436; Shin-Kap Han, "Unraveling the Brow: What and How of Choice in Musical Preference," *Sociological Perspectives* 46, no. 4 (December 1, 2003): 435–59; and Richard A. Peterson, "Understanding Audience Segmentation: From Elite and Mass to Omnivore and Univore," *Poetics* 21, no. 4 (August 1992): 243–58. For a history of audience research in Hollywood, see Susan Ohmer, *George Gallup in Hollywood* (New York: Columbia University Press, 2006).

11. DiMaggio, "Market Structure, the Creative Process, and Popular Culture," 442.

12. For a discussion of middle management in this form of managerial capitalism, see Alfred D. Chandler, *The Visible Hand: The Managerial Revolution in American Business* (Cambridge, MA: Belknap Press of Harvard University Press, 1977), 377–414.

13. DiMaggio, "Market Structure, the Creative Process, and Popular Culture," 442.

14. Peterson and Berger, "Entrepreneurship in Organizations," 97. Peterson and Berger borrow their definition of "entrepreneurship" from Joseph A. Schumpeter, *The Theory of Economic Development: An Inquiry into Profits, Capital, Credit, Interest, and the Business Cycle* (Cambridge, MA: Harvard University Press, 1934).

15. Tino Balio, *Grand Design—Hollywood as a Modern Business Enterprise, 1930–1939* (New York: Scribner, 1993), 8.

16. Chandler, *The Visible Hand*, 345–76.

17. Balio points out that Warner Bros. was the only company to remain under the management of its original founders throughout the 1930s. For more information about this time period, see ibid., 15; Andrew Bergman, *We're in the Money: Depression America and Its Films* (New York: Harper & Row, 1972); Lary May, *Screening Out the Past: The Birth of Mass Culture and the Motion Picture Industry* (New York: Oxford University Press, 1980). For more on the economic implications of the conversion to sound, see Donald Crafton, *The Talkies: American Cinema's Transition to Sound, 1926–1931* (New York: Scribner, 1997).

18. Richard Maltby, "The Political Economy of Hollywood: The Studio System," in *Cinema, Politics, and Society in America*, ed. Philip John Davies and Brian Neve (New York: St. Martin's Press, 1981), 48.

19. Jesse L. Lasky, "The Producer Makes a Plan," in *We Make the Movies*, ed. Nancy Naumburg (New York: W. W. Norton, 1937), 1.

20. Jesse L. Lasky, "Production Problems," in Joseph P. Kennedy and Harvard University, *The Story of the Films, as Told by Leaders of the Industry to the Students of the Graduate School of Business Administration, George F. Baker Foundation, Harvard University* (Chicago: A. W. Shaw, 1927), 102–3.

21. Philip Dunne, interviewed by Thomas Stempel, 1970–71, transcript, the Darryl F. Zanuck Project, LBMF, 142–44.

22. The average number of films produced by the major Hollywood companies every year between 1920 and 1948 was 641. Some years, such as 1918, 1921, and 1928, yielded over 800 pictures, while in some of the war years the number dropped below 500, hitting a low of 377 in 1945. More data can be found in Gene Brown, *Movie Time: A Chronology of Hollywood and the Movie Industry from Its Beginnings to the Present* (New York: Macmillan, 1995).

23. Lasky, "The Producer Makes a Plan," 1–2.

24. Lewis Jacobs, *The Rise of the American Film: A Critical History* (New York: Harcourt, Brace, 1939), 9.

25. The search was performed in the periodicals available through the Media History Digital Library, which digitizes collections that belong in the public domain. I searched through the available issues of the *New York Clipper* from 1903 to 1909, the *Moving Picture World* from 1907 to 1909, and the *Nickelodeon*, 1909. See http://mediahistoryproject.org. As mentioned, the word "producer" is used very sparsely, if at all, and for the most part only to indicate its literal meaning as a noun. I say that the term "producer" was probably borrowed from the theater because among the pages of the *Clipper* one can find a limited use of the term with regard to the person who puts on theater plays and performances before any such use can be detected with regard to filmmaking (for example, "And how are you going about placing your new

play—have you found a producer?," in "Miss Clipper's," *New York Clipper*, January 6, 1906, 1166). Such examples are not sufficient evidence, but they suggest that the theatrical use of the term predates its incorporation into moviemaking.

26. For more information on 1907, see Eileen Bowser, *The Transformation of Cinema, 1907–1915* (Berkeley: University of California Press, 1994), 1, 22. As Bowser explains, motion pictures around that time were still rather short. A one-reel picture was typically about ten to twelve minutes long. Due to that fact, theaters screened more than one picture every night.

27. Jacobs, *The Rise of the American Film*, 59.

28. "Baldwin on Wire in Storm," *Moving Picture World*, June 27, 1908, 541.

29. "To Picture Yosemite," *Nickelodeon*, July 1909, 31.

30. "St. George and the Dragon," *Moving Picture World*, June 8, 1912, 933.

31. *Motion Picture News*, June 21, 1913, quoted in Bowser, *The Transformation of Cinema*, 222.

32. "Studio Efficiency," *Moving Picture World*, August 9, 1913, 624.

33. David Bordwell, Janet Staiger, and Kristin Thompson, *The Classical Hollywood Cinema: Film Style and Mode of Production to 1960* (New York: Columbia University Press, 1985), 128.

34. For Taylor's theory of scientific management, see Frederick Winslow Taylor, *The Principles of Scientific Management* (New York: Harper, 1911); for a discussion of the dissemination of Taylorist theories in the United States, see T. J. Jackson Lears, *Rebirth of a Nation: The Making of Modern America, 1877–1920* (New York : HarperCollins, 2009), 258–65. A summary of the contribution of the system of middle management in its early years can be found in Chandler, *The Visible Hand*, 411–14.

35. Janet Staiger names this new organizational structure the "central producer system" in Bordwell, Staiger, and Thompson, *The Classical Hollywood Cinema*, 128–37. The uniform style of production discussed by Staiger is what the book's authors term "the classical Hollywood cinema," and it includes conventions with regard to story causality, narration, time and space layout, etc.

36. Selwyn A. Stanhope, "The World's Master Picture Producer," *Photoplay Magazine*, January 1915, 57–62.

37. Bowser, *The Transformation of Cinema*, 222.

38. "Memoirs of Thomas H. Ince," *Exhibitors Herald*, December 13, 1924, 29–30. This title is one in a series published by the *Exhibitors Herald* in late 1924 and early 1925, and is described as "an autobiography of his fourteen years in the motion picture industry, prepared by the noted producer a short time before his death."

39. For more on Ince's career and his contract with Kessel and Baumann, see Brian Taves, *Thomas Ince: Hollywood's Independent Pioneer* (Lexington: University Press of Kentucky, 2012), 30.

40. "Memoirs of Thomas H. Ince," *Exhibitors Herald*, December 13, 1924, 114.

41. "Ince to Move to Culver City," *Moving Picture World*, October 9, 1915, 272.

42. "Memoirs of Thomas H. Ince," *Exhibitors Herald*, December 13, 1924, 29.

43. "Memoirs of Thomas H. Ince," *Exhibitors Herald*, December 27, 1924, 156.

44. "Memoirs of Thomas H. Ince," *Exhibitors Herald*, December 20, 1924, 31.

45. "Memoirs of Thomas H. Ince," *Exhibitors Herald*, December 27, 1924, 42.

46. "Ince to Move to Culver City."

47. For more on the development of the shooting script, see chapter 2.

48. For more on the operations at Inceville, see Taves, *Thomas Ince*, 53–71.

49. Janet Staiger, "Dividing Labor for Production Control: Thomas Ince and the Rise of the Studio System," *Cinema Journal* 18, no. 2 (Spring 1979): 16–25.

50. Taves, *Thomas Ince*, 90.

51. Thomas Schatz, *The Genius of the System: Hollywood Filmmaking in the Studio Era* (New York: Pantheon Books, 1988), 47.

52. Samuel Marx, *Mayer and Thalberg: The Make-Believe Saints* (New York: Random House, 1975), 18–19.

53. "Laemmle Leaves," *Film Daily*, March 17, 1920, 1.

54. For more about Thalberg's biography, see Marx, *Mayer and Thalberg*; Mark A. Vieira, *Irving Thalberg: Boy Wonder to Producer Prince* (Berkeley: University of California Press, 2010).

55. "Great Executive Job Held by a Boy of 22," *Los Angeles Times*, October 15, 1922, sec. 3, p. 37.

56. "Flashes: Busy Universalists," *Los Angeles Times*, September 1, 1921, sec. 3, p. 4.

57. "Great Executive Job Held by a Boy of 22."

58. Richard Koszarski, *An Evening's Entertainment: The Age of the Silent Feature Picture, 1915–1928* (New York: Scribner, 1990), 211.

59. Vieira, *Irving Thalberg*, 12.

60. Marx, *Mayer and Thalberg*, 33.

61. Quoted in Vieira, *Irving Thalberg*, 14.

62. For distribution purposes, the motion picture industry in the United States used to divide its products into categories corresponding to the price for which they were leased to theaters. The expensive pictures, often referred to as A features, were characterized by a larger production budget, big stars, and a big promotional budget, and were often associated with some higher cultural value. For more on this system of differentiation, see Lea Jacobs, "The B Film and the Problem of Cultural Distinction," in *Hollywood: Critical Concepts in Media and Cultural Studies*, ed. Thomas Schatz (London: Routledge, 2003), 147–60.

63. See Douglas Gomery, *The Hollywood Studio System: A History* (London: BFI, 2005), 32.

64. Movie exhibition houses operated according to a zoning system. In general, theaters were divided into two groups: first-run and second-run. First-run theaters were in the centers of big cities and were usually large, fancy structures, with ample seating and often including new technological innovations such as air conditioning. As a result, admission prices for these theaters were higher. Second-run theaters were smaller and simpler. They were typically in smaller neighborhoods or outside the cities. Under the National Recovery Administration code, implemented in 1933, this distinction was set as a developed zoning system divided into multiple categories with clear zoning, screening priority, and pricing limitations that gave preference to the first-run houses. Of course, by that time most first-run theaters were owned by the big picture companies, and independent ownership was prominent among the smaller second-run or lower theaters. See ibid., 21.

65. Data taken from Maltby, "The Political Economy of Hollywood."

66. Data taken from Vieira, *Irving Thalberg*, 30.

67. Irving Thalberg and Hugh Weir, "Why Motion Pictures Cost So Much," *Saturday Evening Post*, November 4, 1933, 10–11, 83–85.

68. Data about MGM operation as well as a transcript of the 1925 report can be found in Schatz, *The Genius of the System*, 44–46.

69. "The Importance of Able Directors to the Industry," *Film Daily*, June 7, 1925, 13.

70. Pandro S. Berman, interviewed by Sam Grossman and Donald E. Knox for "The American Film Institute Seminar with Pandro S. Berman," January 26, 1972, transcript, LBMF.

71. Ed Woehler, interviewed by Donald E. Knox for "An American in Paris: A Documentary Study of the MGM Studio System," May 19, 1971, transcript, LBMF. A unit production manager or "line producer," as this position is sometimes called, is typically in charge of the budget or day-to-day operation of a film and works under the head producer.

72. Thalberg and Weir, "Why Motion Pictures Cost So Much."

73. Data taken from Marx, *Mayer and Thalberg*; Crafton, *The Talkies*; H. Mark Glancy, "MGM—Film Grosses, 1924–1948: The Eddie Mannix Ledger," *Historical Journal of Film, Radio and Television* 12, no. 2 (1992): 127; H. Mark Glancy, "Warner Bros Film Grosses, 1921–51: The William Schaefer Ledger," *Historical Journal of Film, Radio and Television* 15, no. 1 (1995): 55; John Sedgwick, "The Warner Ledgers: A Comment," *Historical Journal of Film, Radio and Television* 15, no. 1 (1995): 75. As is stated in both Crafton's appendix and Glancy's article, the reliability of the data cannot be assured. Statistics from the studio system are hard to come by, and the data available for scholars was compiled by personnel from within the studios who might have had reasons to tilt it one way or the other. In addition, accounting procedures may have differed from one company to another.

74. Reminiscences of Anita Loos, interviewed by James Gaines, June 1959, transcript in the OHCC, 14–15.

75. Ibid., 23–24.

76. Ibid., 29–30.

77. Marx, *Mayer and Thalberg*, viii.

78. Author and screenwriter James M. Cain for one found Thalberg to be "one of the most unpleasant guys." See Pat McGilligan, ed., *Backstory: Interviews with Screenwriters of Hollywood's Golden Age* (Berkeley: University of California Press, 1986), 121.

79. George Cukor, interviewed by Gavin Lambert between August 1970 and April 1971, transcript, LBMF.

80. King Vidor, *A Tree Is a Tree* (New York: Harcourt, Brace, 1953), 153.

81. Ibid., 121.

82. Nancy Lynn Schwartz, *The Hollywood Writers' Wars* (New York: Knopf, 1982), 128. Hollywood writers were not formally unionized until the late 1930s, largely due to the efforts made by the studios, and in particular MGM, to prevent such organization, a topic discussed in chapters 2 and 6.

83. Reminiscences of Ben Hecht, interviewed by Jan and Robert Franklin, June 1959, transcript, Popular Arts Project, LBMF, 722–23.

84. Ibid., 724.

85. Reminiscences of Anita Loos, 12–13.

86. Thalberg and Weir, "Why Motion Pictures Cost So Much," 85.

87. Glancy, "MGM—Film Grosses, 1924–1948," 131.

88. Ibid., 129. See disclaimer at note 73 above. Domestic grosses represent the money earned from rentals, that is, the percentage taken by the studio from the overall box office profit.

89. Data taken from Schatz, *The Genius of the System*, 45.

90. F. Scott Fitzgerald, *The Last Tycoon: An Unfinished Novel* (New York: Scribner, 1969), 38. Fitzgerald was in the process of completing the novel when he died on December 21, 1940.

91. Schatz, *The Genius of the System*, 48.

92. The moniker "Boy Wonder," which was often used to describe Thalberg, became associated with him following its appearance in a short story by the same title written by George Randolph Chester and published by the *Saturday Evening Post* on May 26, 1923. Like Fitzgerald's unfinished novel, *The Last Tycoon*, Chester's story was part of a series that was inspired by Thalberg's career.

93. David O. Selznick, notes on an interview made with Henry Hart, February 28, 1963, folder 22.f-184, Rudy Behlmer Papers.

94. Ibid.

95. For more on Selznick's biography, see Bob Thomas, *Selznick* (Garden City, NY: Doubleday, 1970); David Thomson, *Showman: The Life of David O. Selznick* (New York: Knopf, 1992).

96. David O. Selznick to Harry Rapf, October 5, 1926, quoted in Thomson, *Showman*, 72.

97. David O. Selznick, *Memo from David O. Selznick* (New York: Viking Press, 1972), 47–48.

98. Schatz, *The Genius of the System*, 74; Gomery, *The Hollywood Studio System*, chaps. 1 and 7. See also note 61 above.

99. Glancy, "MGM—Film Grosses, 1924–1948," 130; Thomson, *Showman*, 71.

100. Selznick to B. P. Schulberg, not sent, June 27, 1931, in Selznick, *Memo from David O. Selznick*, 65–67.

101. David Sarnoff, RCA's general manager, consolidated RKO to exploit RCA's Photophone sound system after all other major companies signed agreements in May of that year with Western Electric for its competing sound-on-disc Vitaphone system. See Crafton, *The Talkies*, 160.

102. Selznick, *Memo from David O. Selznick*, 78–82.

103. Gomery, *The Hollywood Studio System*, 145–46.

104. Selznick, unsent letter apparently intended for one of the RKO executives, August 22, 1932, in Selznick, *Memo from David O. Selznick*, 77–78.

105. Thomson, *Showman*, 128.

106. Selznick to Benjamin B. Kahane, January 27, 1933, in Selznick, *Memo from David O. Selznick*, 83–84.

107. Balio, *Grand Design*, 23.

108. "Paramount Pictures," *Fortune*, March 1937.

109. Henry Herzbrun to Adolph Zukor, March 5, 1935, Adolph Zukor Collection, 2.f-15, MHL.

110. Balio, *Grand Design*, 24.

111. "Paramount Pictures," 198.

112. For more about Paramount during the Depression, see Balio, *Grand Design*, chap. 2; Gomery, *The Hollywood Studio System*, chap. 7; "Paramount Pictures."

113. David O. Selznick to George Cukor, February 25, 1938, file 11.f-106, George Cukor Papers, MHL.

114. "Twentieth Century–Fox," *Fortune*, December 1935, 85.

115. For more about the history of the studio as well as on Zanuck's biography, see Upton Sinclair, *Upton Sinclair Presents William Fox* (Los Angeles: Privately printed, 1933); "Twentieth Century–Fox"; Mel Gussow, *Don't Say Yes until I Finish Talking: A Biography of Darryl F. Zanuck* (Garden City, NY: Doubleday, 1971).

116. There were four Warner brothers. Aside from Harry, Abe supervised distribution, and Jack was the head of the studio. The fourth brother, Sam, who was instrumental in the incorporation of sound, died in 1927.

117. Gomery, *The Hollywood Studio System*, 131.

118. For more on the history of this company, see Charles Higham, *Warner Brothers* (New York: Scribner, 1975); Michael Freedland, *The Warner Brothers* (New York: St. Martin's Press, 1983); Nick Roddick, *A New Deal in Entertainment: Warner Brothers in the 1930s* (London: British Film Institute, 1983).

119. Gussow, *Don't Say Yes until I Finish Talking*, 38.

120. Warner Bros. Studio to Zanuck, December 27, 1926, folder 18.f-148, Rudy Behlmer Papers.

121. Quoted in Gomery, *The Hollywood Studio System*, 133.

122. Data taken from Glancy, "Warner Bros Film Grosses, 1921–51."

123. "Twentieth Century–Fox," 132.

124. Ibid., 134.

125. Philip Dunne interview, LBMF, 34.

126. Reminiscences of Ben Hecht, 726.

127. Zanuck to Henry King, n.d., ca. late September 1938, in Darryl Francis Zanuck, *Memo from Darryl F. Zanuck: The Golden Years at Twentieth Century–Fox* (New York: Grove Press, 1993), 17–18.

128. Philip Dunne interview, LBMF, 117–20.

129. Reminiscences of Nunnally Johnson, interviewed by Charles Higham, July 1959, transcript, Hollywood Film Industry Project, OHCC, 578. Zanuck left 20th Century–Fox in 1956 to work in Europe. He returned in 1962.

130. Reminiscences of Anatole Litvak, interviewed by Robert and Joan Franklin, April 1959, transcript, Popular Arts Project, OHCC, 18.

131. Peter Bogdanovich, *Who the Devil Made It: Conversations with Robert Aldrich, George Cukor, Allan Dwan, Howard Hawks, Alfred Hitchcock, Chuck Jones, Fritz Lang, Joseph H. Lewis, Sidney Lumet, Leo McCarey, Otto Preminger, Don Siegel, Josef Von Sternberg, Frank Tashlin, Edgar G. Ulmer, Raoul Walsh* (New York: Knopf, 1997), 193–94.

132. Ibid., 460.

133. "Films to Pay Homage to Thalberg Today," *Los Angeles Times*, September 16, 1936.

134. "Tribute Paid to Thalberg," *Los Angeles Times*, September 17, 1936.

135. "Films to Pay Homage to Thalberg Today."

Chapter Two

1. Charles Brackett, Address for the Samuel Goldwyn Award for Creative Writing, April 22, 1957, folder 20.f-48, Charles Brackett Papers, MHL.

2. "Writers' Guild Spokesman in Wash. Gives Producers Verbal Rubdown," *Variety*, April 1, 1936, 2.

3. Reminiscences of Joe Mankiewicz, interviewed by Joan and Robert Franklin, January 1959, transcript, Popular Arts Project, OHCC, 8–10.

4. Leo Calvin Rosten, *Hollywood: The Movie Colony, the Movie Makers* (New York: Harcourt, Brace, 1941).

5. Dudley Nichols, "Cooking a Goose," *Screen Guilds' Magazine* 3, no. 3 (May 1936): 7.

6. Howard S. Becker, "Art Worlds and Social Types," *American Behavioral Scientist* 19, no. 6 (July 1, 1976): 703; Howard Saul Becker, *Art Worlds* (Berkeley: University of California Press, 1982); Pierre Bourdieu, *The Field of Cultural Production: Essays on Art and Literature* (New York: Columbia University Press, 1993).

7. William H. Sewell, "A Theory of Structure: Duality, Agency, and Transformation," *American Journal of Sociology* 98, no. 1 (July 1, 1992): 27. Sewell relies on Anthony Giddens's dual theory of structure and aims to introduce the concepts of agency and change to the more conventional sociological theory of structures. His notions of "transposable schemas" and "polysemy of resources" as well as "intersection of structures" build upon Bourdieu's concept of habitus.

8. Recent theories of migration embrace what some scholars refer to as a "diasporic perspective," which draws attention to global connections and networks of activities. Within this framework migrants are no longer thought of as substituting one locale for another but rather as forming new ties that bind various geographic locations together. Adam McKeown, "Conceptualizing Chinese Diasporas, 1842 to 1949," *Journal of Asian Studies* 58, no. 2 (May 1, 1999): 307; Dirk Hoerder and Leslie Page Moch, eds., *European Migrants: Global and Local Perspectives* (Boston: Northeastern University Press, 1996).

9. For more on the turn to narrative film, see David Bordwell, Janet Staiger, and Kristin Thompson, *The Classical Hollywood Cinema: Film Style and Mode of Production to 1960* (New York: Columbia University Press, 1985), 162.

10. The decision was made in the case of *Kalem Co. v. Harper Brothers* on November 13, 1911.

11. For more on these diverse backgrounds, see Edward Azlant, "The Theory, History, and Practice of Screenwriting, 1897–1920" (PhD diss., University of Wisconsin, Madison, 1980), 112.

12. NLRB.1, box 516, vol. 5, October 6, 1937, 595–96.

13. Ibid., 608.

14. Azlant, "The Theory, History, and Practice of Screenwriting," 92. In his unpublished dissertation, Azlant presents the valuable stories of several important pioneer screenwriters and includes lists of their previously uncredited screen works.

15. This "continuity" was later produced under the direction of D. W. Griffith.

16. NLRB.1, box 516, vol. 5, October 6, 1937, 595.

17. Ibid., 608.

18. Bordwell, Staiger, and Thompson, *The Classical Hollywood Cinema*, 138.

19. Lloyd Lonergan, "How I Came to Write Continuity," *Moving Picture World*, July 21, 1917, 403.

20. Bordwell, Staiger, and Thompson, *The Classical Hollywood Cinema*, 146.

21. Quoted in Kevin Brownlow, *The Parade's Gone By* (New York: Knopf, 1968), 275.

22. Clifford Howard, "The Cinema in Retrospect, Part II," *Close Up* 3, no. 6 (December 1928): 32.

23. Azlant, "The Theory, History, and Practice of Screenwriting," 192–93.

24. Lonergan, "How I Came to Write Continuity."

25. For more on the problems with "public screenwriting," see Richard Koszarski, *An Evening's Entertainment: The Age of the Silent Feature Picture, 1915–1928* (New York: Scribner, 1990), 108.

26. For more on this, see the introduction.

27. See Karen W. Mahar, "True Womanhood in Hollywood: Gendered Business Strategies and the Rise and Fall of the Woman Filmmaker, 1896–1928," *Enterprise and Society* 2, no. 1 (March 1, 2001): 72–110; Cari Beauchamp, *Without Lying Down: Frances Marion and the Powerful Women of Early Hollywood* (New York: Scribner, 1997); Karen Ward Mahar, *Women Filmmakers in Early Hollywood* (Baltimore: Johns Hopkins University Press, 2006); Hilary A. Hallett, *Go West, Young Women! The Rise of Early Hollywood* (Berkeley: University of California Press, 2013).

28. Hallett, *Go West, Young Women!*, 51.

29. Beauchamp, *Without Lying Down*, 199, 210.

30. Bordwell, Staiger, and Thompson, *The Classical Hollywood Cinema*, 146.

31. NLRB.1, box 516, vol. 5, October 6, 1937, 608.

32. NLRB.1, box 516, vol. unspecified, October 18, 1937, 1701.

33. Ibid., 1721.

34. Ibid., 1735.

35. Clifford Howard, "Writers and Pictures," *Close Up* 3, no. 6 (September 1928): 38.

36. Ibid., 34.

37. Donald Crafton, *The Talkies: American Cinema's Transition to Sound, 1926–1931* (New York: Scribner, 1997), 4, 8, 13–14; Rick Altman, ed., *Sound Theory / Sound Practice* (New York: Routledge, 1992).

38. Rosten, *Hollywood*, 314–15.

39. Richard Fine, *Hollywood and the Profession of Authorship, 1928–1940* (Ann Arbor: University of Michigan Research Press, 1985), 1.

40. Ibid., 74.

41. Ibid., 12; John Schultheiss, "The 'Eastern' Writer in Hollywood," *Cinema Journal* 11, no. 1 (October 1, 1971): 13–47; Rosten, *Hollywood*, 323.

42. Rosten, *Hollywood*, 322. The ten writers were Robert Riskin, Ben Hecht, Preston Sturges, Claude R. Binyon, Talbot Jennings, Sidney Buchman, Vincent Lawrence, John L. Balderston, John Lee Mahin, and Jack Yellen. The latter was a song lyricist. Each one of them earned over $75,000 in 1938.

43. For more information about Nichols and his screenplays, see Richard Corliss, *The Hollywood Screenwriters* (New York: Discus Books, 1972), 107–24.

44. Nichols, "Cooking a Goose," 7.

45. Reminiscences of Samson Raphaelson, interviewed by Joan and Robert Franklin, June 1959, transcript, Popular Arts Project, OHCC, 49–50.

46. Fine, *Hollywood and the Profession of Authorship*, 16, 104.

47. Charles Brackett, excerpts from diary, January 1936, folder 28f-[20], Charles Brackett Papers. I cannot be entirely sure this was indeed a daily diary maintained by Brackett. The title "diary" might indicate a collection of notes, perhaps in preparation for a memoir.

48. Information on Brackett from Ed Sikov, *On Sunset Boulevard: The Life and Times of Billy Wilder* (New York: Hyperion, 1998), 117–19.

49. Brackett, typed diary excerpt, August 17, 1936, folder 28f-[19], Charles Brackett Papers.

50. Sikov, *On Sunset Boulevard*, 117–19.

51. Brackett, excerpts from diary, 1935, folder 28f-[20], Charles Brackett Papers.

52. Biographical information about Raphaelson can be found in Barry Allen Sabath, "Ernst Lubitsch and Samson Raphaelson: A Study in Collaboration" (PhD diss., New York University, 1979), chap. 2.

53. For more on the history of this movie in relation to sound, see Crafton, *The Talkies*, 12.

54. Quoted in Sabath, "Ernst Lubitsch and Samson Raphaelson," 50–51.

55. Raphaelson to Monty Montross, September 21, 1930, box 3, Samson Raphaelson Papers, Special Collections of Columbia University, New York.

56. Raphaelson to Alfred Wallerstein, March 29, 1930, box 3, Samson Raphaelson Papers.

57. For more on the implications of the 1909 Copyright Act as well as the legal status of hired writers, see Catherine L. Fisk, *Writing for Hire: Unions, Hollywood, and Madison Avenue* (Cambridge, MA: Harvard University Press, 2016), 212–25.

58. Rosten, *Hollywood*, 310.

59. A broader discussion of this hearing follows in chapter 5.

60. Philip Dunne, interviewed by Thomas Stempel, 1970–71, transcript, LBMF.

61. NLRB.1, box 515, vol. 1, September 30, 1937, 102–7.

62. NLRB.1, box 516, vol. 9, October 13, 1937, 1129–31.

63. Reminiscences of Ben Hecht, interviewed by Joan and Robert Franklin, June 1959, transcript, Popular Arts Project, OHCC, 770–71.

64. Quoted in Fine, *Hollywood and the Profession of Authorship*, 118.

65. Edwin Justus Mayer, "Writing for Pictures Is a Rational Thing," *Screen Guilds' Magazine* 2, no. 10 (December 1935): 5.

66. Marx's theory of alienation suggests that in capitalist societies man experiences three types of separations: alienation from his work, that is, lack of control over what he does or a "break between the individual and his life activity"; alienation from his own product, or "a break between the individual and the material world"; and alienation from his fellow men, or "a break between man and man." For more on this, see Bertell Ollman, *Alienation: Marx's Conception of Man in Capitalist Society*, 2nd ed. (Cambridge: Cambridge University Press, 1976), 131–36.

67. Maurice Rapf, "Credit Arbitration Isn't Simple," *Screen Writer* 1, no. 2 (July 1945): 31.

68. For more information about Reyher, see Bruce Cook, *Brecht in Exile* (New York: Holt, Rinehart and Winston, 1983), 39–41; James K. Lyon, *Bertolt Brecht in America* (Princeton, NJ: Princeton University Press, 1980).

69. NLRB.2, box 1724, vol. 13, August 29, 1939, 1357.

70. NLRB.1, box 516, vol. unspecified, October 18, 1937, 1582, 1591.

71. Sheridan Gibney, contract with Paramount Pictures Inc., dated March 30, 1939; Donald Ogden Stewart, contract with Paramount Pictures Inc., dated March 30, 1939, NLRB.2, box 1725, Paramount Pictures Exhibits File.

72. NLRB.1, box 515, vol. 1, September 30, 1937, 106.

73. NLRB.1, box 516, vol. 9, October 13, 1937, 1172.

74. Martin Field, "Who Works for Nothing?," *Screen Writer* 2, no. 1 (June 1946): 37–40.

75. Some of these fields were not mutually exclusive. As was the case with Samson Raphaelson, one might write a short story published first in a magazine, develop it further and offer it as a play, and later sell the rights to a motion picture based on either the original story or the play.

76. For more about the New York extensions of the story departments, see Howard Thompson Lewis, *The Motion Picture Industry* (New York: D. Van Nostrand, 1933), 31.

77. Reminiscences of Albert Hackett, interviewed by Joan and Robert Franklin, September 1958, transcript, Popular Arts Project, OHCC, 30–31.

78. Mayer, "Writing for Pictures Is a Rational Thing," 5.

79. Reminiscences of Ben Hecht, 745.

80. Dudley Nichols, "Mr. Goldwyn Bears Down . . . ," *Screen Guilds' Magazine* 2, no. 2 (April 1935): 7.

81. Statistics are from a salary list published by the Treasury Department and quoted in Rosten, *Hollywood*, 322.

82. Ernest Pascal, "The Author of the Piece," *Screen Guilds' Magazine* 2, no. 6 (August 1935): 6.

83. Nancy Lynn Schwartz, *The Hollywood Writers' Wars* (New York: Knopf, 1982), 9.

84. There were organizations for writers in pictures prior to 1933, such as the Writers Club or the Photoplay Authors' League, but they were rather informal and functioned more like social clubs.

85. For more about the various guilds and unions in the motion picture industry, see chapter 6 as well as Douglas Gomery, *The Hollywood Studio System: A History*

(London: BFI, 2005), chap. 14; Larry Ceplair and Steven Englund, *The Inquisition in Hollywood: Politics in the Film Community, 1930–1960* (Garden City, NY: Anchor Press / Doubleday, 1980), chaps. 1 and 2; Schwartz, *The Hollywood Writers' Wars*; Murray Ross, *Stars and Strikes: Unionization of Hollywood* (New York: Columbia University Press, 1941).

86. For more information about the New York guilds, see John William Tebbel, *A History of Book Publishing in the United States* (New York: R. R. Bowker, 1972); Jack Poggi, *Theater in America: The Impact of Economic Forces, 1870–1967* (Ithaca, NY: Cornell University Press, 1968).

87. For more on the theatrical business practices with regard to playwrights in the 1920s, see Alfred L. Bernheim, *The Business of the Theatre* (New York: Actors' Equity Association, 1932), 113–17.

88. Owen Davis, "What Guild Shop Has Meant to the Dramatist," *Screen Guilds' Magazine* 2, no. 10 (December 1935): 4.

89. For more on the negotiations that led to this agreement, see T. J. Walsh, "Playwrights and Power: The Dramatists Guild's Struggle for the 1926 Minimum Basic Agreement," *New England Theatre Journal* 12 (2001): 51–78.

90. George Middleton, *The Dramatists' Guild: What It Is and Does, How It Happened and Why* (New York: Dramatists' Guild of the Authors' League of America, 1959), 11.

91. Davis, "What Guild Shop Has Meant to the Dramatist."

92. Schwartz, *The Hollywood Writers' Wars*, 18.

93. Raphaelson to Alfred Wallerstein. By "Phillipe Boys" and "Mr. Douglas" Raphaelson is probably referencing Broadway producers, as he goes on to compare the conditions in Hollywood to those in New York, saying that in both cases "mass production, the employment of 'talent,' the necessity for decisions, and the unavoidability of haste account for much."

94. Quoted in Schwartz, *The Hollywood Writers' Wars*, 21.

95. "Comparison of Guild Demands and the Academy's Proposed Revised Writer-Producer Agreement," *Screen Guilds' Magazine* 2, no. 8 (October 1935): 8.

96. The difference between a guild shop and a closed shop, according to the SWG proposition and various articles published in its magazine, was that, similar to the prevalent notion of a closed shop, all screenwriters employed by the studio would be required to join a specified union, namely, SWG. However, the guild itself would be open to all new members the studios wished to hire. In other words, the producers would not be limited to the existing pool of writers, but whomever they chose to employ had to join SWG and work according to the union's conditions and basic agreement with the studios.

97. Ernest Pascal, "What the Screen Writers' Guild Really Wants," *Screen Guilds' Magazine* 2, no. 5 (July 1935): 1, 23.

98. Ernest Pascal, "One Organization for All American Writers," *Screen Guilds' Magazine* 3, no. 2 (April 1936): 3, 15.

99. Ibid., 15.

100. E. E. Paramore Jr. and L. W. Beilenson, "The ABC's of the Amalgamation," *Screen Guilds' Magazine* 3, no. 2 (April 1936): 6.

101. For more about the Communist Party and Hollywood, see Schwartz, *The Hollywood Writers' Wars*, chap. 5; Saverio Giovacchini, *Hollywood Modernism: Film and Politics in the Age of the New Deal* (Philadelphia: Temple University Press, 2001); Michael Denning, *The Cultural Front: The Laboring of American Culture in the Twentieth Century* (London: Verso, 1997); Ceplair and Englund, *The Inquisition in Hollywood*.

102. Victor S. Navasky, *Naming Names* (New York: Viking Press, 1980), 367.

103. Larry Ceplair, *The Marxist and the Movies: A Biography of Paul Jarrico* (Lexington: University Press of Kentucky, 2007), 36–37.

104. Schwartz, *The Hollywood Writers' Wars*, 82. Michael Denning suggests that during the 1930s, the forces surrounding the New Deal, including the Democratic Party, labor unions, the Communist Party, and fellow travelers, represented a Gramscian "historical bloc." In that sense, artists who were sympathetic to the ideas and spirit of the New Deal joined the Communist Party to form the superstructure that solidified the hegemony of FDR and his administration. See Denning, *The Cultural Front*.

105. Quoted in Denning, *The Cultural Front*, 45.

106. Pascal, "One Organization for All American Writers," 16.

107. The American Newspaper Guild, for example, chose the term, since, in 1933, its founding members were divided about whether their organization should resemble "a union or a more exclusive professional association with limited aims." See Daniel J. Leab, *A Union of Individuals: The Formation of the American Newspaper Guild, 1933–1936* (New York: Columbia University Press, 1970), 59–60.

108. Nunnally Johnson, interviewed by Thomas Stempel, 1968–69, transcript, LBMF, 122; Reminiscences of Nunnally Johnson, interviewed by Charles Higham, July 1959, transcript, Hollywood Film Industry Project, OHCC, 591–92.

109. Charles Brackett to Leo C. Rosten, October 6, 1948, folder 12f-[11]R, Charles Brackett Papers. He is referring to Alfred Landon, the Republican nominee in the 1936 presidential election.

110. Charles Brackett to membership of SWG, October 25, 1946, folder 20f-[42], Charles Brackett Papers. Some comments along these lines also appear in a note attached to this letter, and all pertain to the guild's leadership and board election of that year.

111. NLRB.2, box 1725, vol. 7, August 18, 1939, 491.

112. Ibid., 500.

113. He further testified that, upon receiving this offer, he replied, "Well, I believe I told him that I would try to clean up a farmer's daughter for that kind of money at that particular time."

114. NLRB.1, box 516, vol. unspecified, October 20, 1937, 2034–35.

115. Ibid., 2055.

116. Ceplair and Englund, *The Inquisition in Hollywood*, 43.

117. Ibid., 46. Catherine L. Fisk claims that, with control over credits, SWG effectively "reclaimed for writers some of the rights and responsibilities of authors" that they lost under the Copyright Act of 1909. See Fisk, *Writing for Hire*, 4, 137–68.

118. Pascal, "The Author of the Piece."

119. James M. Cain, "An American Authors' Authority," *Screen Writer* 2, no. 2 (July 1946): 13.

120. Clifford Howard, "The Cinema in Retrospect, Part I," *Close Up* 3, no. 5 (November 1928): 16–17.

121. Philip Dunne, "An Essay on Dignity," *Screen Writer* 1, no. 7 (December 1945): 1–8.

122. Raymond Chandler, "Writers in Hollywood," *Atlantic Monthly*, November 1945, reprinted in Raymond Chandler, *Later Novels and Other Writings* (New York: Literary Classics, 1995).

123. Dunne, "An Essay on Dignity."

124. This data refers to the classic studio era, before its termination with the *Paramount* decision in 1948. Some of these men assumed additional roles in later years.

125. Mary McCall Jr., "Facts, Figures on Your % Deal," *Screen Writer* 1, no. 1 (June 1945): 32–35.

126. Philip Dunne, "An Essay on Dignity."

127. Casey Robinson to Jack Warner, March 9, 1942, folder 226.f-2240, Hal Wallis Papers, MHL.

128. Casey Robinson, interviewed by Joel Greenberg, July 14, 1974, transcript, LBMF, 50.

129. Ibid., 207.

130. Casey Robinson to Hal Wallis, March 9, 1942, folder 226.f-2240, Hal Wallis Papers.

131. Jack Warner to Hal Wallis, March 10, 1942, folder 226.f-2240, Hal Wallis Papers.

132. Nunnally Johnson, interviewed by Thomas Stempel, transcript, 220–21; Philip Dunne, interviewed by Thomas Stempel, transcript, 252.

133. Brackett, Address for the Samuel Goldwyn Award for Creative Writing.

Chapter Three

1. The content of this chapter has drawn upon material from Ronny Regev, "Hollywood Works: How Creativity Became Labor in the Studio System," *Enterprise and Society* 17, no. 3 (September 2016): 591–617, published by Cambridge University Press with permission.

2. NLRB.1, box 516, vol. unspecified, October 18, 1937, 1741–46.

3. Ibid.

4. Reminiscences of Henry Hathaway, June 18, 1971, transcript, Hollywood Film Industry Project, OHCC, 37–40.

5. Philip Dunne, interviewed by Thomas Stemple, 1970–71, transcript, LBMF, 34.

6. For further discussion of "conventionalization" in the production of culture, see Clinton R. Sanders, "Structural and Interactional Features of Popular Culture Production: An Introduction to the Production of Culture Perspective," *Journal of Popular Culture* 16, no. 2 (September 1, 1982): 69. Sanders lays out the difference between industries with varying levels of conventionalization. He suggests that, as the need for innovation grows, an industry will be less constrained by conventions.

The production of soap operas, for example, requires less innovation than that of fine art photographs, therefore its division of labor and power relations are more firmly established.

7. Frederick Winslow Taylor, *The Principles of Scientific Management* (New York: Harper, 1911), 8–11.

8. David Montgomery, *The Fall of the House of Labor: The Workplace, the State, and American Labor Activism, 1865–1925* (Cambridge: Cambridge University Press, 1987), 29. Montgomery uses the expression "the manager's brain under the workman's cap" to describe complex work roles within the iron mills that relied on training and traditional knowledge. He borrows the term from International Workers of the World and Socialist Party members William D. Haywood and Frank Bohn. For the original context, see Big Bill Haywood's *Industrial Socialism*, 7th ed. (Chicago: C. H. Kerr, 1911), 27.

9. The struggle between workers and management over control and the craft is discussed in Harry Braverman, *Labor and Monopoly Capital: The Degradation of Work in the Twentieth Century* (New York: Monthly Review Press, 1975), 54–58.

10. Montgomery presents the concept of "functional autonomy," but he does not assign it a great deal of attention or importance. See Montgomery, *The Fall of the House of Labor*, 13.

11. "Putting the Move in the Movies," *Saturday Evening Post*, May 13, 1916, 14.

12. Kevin Brownlow, *The Parade's Gone By* (New York: Knopf, 1968), 7.

13. "Putting the Move in the Movies," 14.

14. Brownlow, *The Parade's Gone By*, 67.

15. Quoted in Adela Rogers St. Johns, "Artistic Efficiency—that's Dwan," *Photoplay Magazine* 18, no. 3 (August 1920): 57.

16. Quoted in Peter Bogdanovich, *Who the Devil Made It: Conversations with Robert Aldrich, George Cukor, Allan Dwan, Howard Hawks, Alfred Hitchcock, Chuck Jones, Fritz Lang, Joseph H. Lewis, Sidney Lumet, Leo McCarey, Otto Preminger, Don Siegel, Josef Von Sternberg, Frank Tashlin, Edgar G. Ulmer, Raoul Walsh* (New York: Knopf, 1997), 52–53.

17. Karen W. Mahar, "True Womanhood in Hollywood: Gendered Business Strategies and the Rise and Fall of the Woman Filmmaker, 1896–1928," *Enterprise and Society* 2, no. 1 (March 1, 2001): 72–110.

18. Alice Guy Blaché, "Woman's Place in Photoplay Production," *Moving Picture World*, July 11, 1914, reprinted in Anthony Slide, *The Silent Feminists: America's First Women Directors* (Lanham, MD: Scarecrow Press, 1996), 139.

19. For more about Blaché and her career, see Alice Guy Blaché, *The Memoirs of Alice Guy Blaché*, ed. Anthony Slide (Metuchen, NJ: Scarecrow Press, 1986); Karen Ward Mahar, *Women Filmmakers in Early Hollywood* (Baltimore: Johns Hopkins University Press, 2006), 29–52.

20. David Bordwell, Janet Staiger, and Kristin Thompson, *The Classical Hollywood Cinema: Film Style and Mode of Production to 1960* (New York: Columbia University Press, 1985), 117.

21. Bogdanovich, *Who the Devil Made It*, 56–57.

22. "Putting the Move in the Movies," 14.

23. During those days, a conventional picture was shot on one reel of film, which was approximately 1,000 feet and lasted around twenty minutes. The term "feature" was given to special pictures that had multiple reels and lasted longer. For more on this, see Eileen Bowser, *The Transformation of Cinema, 1907–1915* (Berkeley: University of California Press, 1994), chaps. 11 and 12.

24. Bogdanovich, *Who the Devil Made It*, 152.

25. Bowser, *The Transformation of Cinema*, 224.

26. *Photoplay*, June 1916, quoted in Lewis Jacobs, *The Rise of the American Film: A Critical History* (New York: Harcourt, Brace, 1939), 160.

27. Jacobs, *The Rise of the American Film*, 161. The expansion of the American motion picture industry during the 1910s and 1920s is also discussed in Bowser, *The Transformation of Cinema*; Richard Koszarski, *An Evening's Entertainment: The Age of the Silent Feature Picture, 1915–1928* (New York: Scribner, 1990); Lary May, *Screening Out the Past: The Birth of Mass Culture and the Motion Picture Industry* (New York: Oxford University Press, 1980); Robert Sklar, *Movie-Made America: A Cultural History of American Movies* (New York: Random House, 1975).

28. Not much has been written about Ince. Some information can be found in George Mitchell, "Thomas H. Ince," *Films in Review* 11 (October 1960): 464–68; and Kalton C. Lahue, *Dreams for Sale: The Rise and Fall of the Triangle Film Corporation* (South Brunswick, NJ: A. S. Barnes, 1971).

29. Quoted in Janet Staiger, "Dividing Labor for Production Control: Thomas Ince and the Rise of the Studio System," *Cinema Journal* 18, no. 2 (1979): 20–21.

30. "Putting the Move in the Movies," 15.

31. Ibid., 97, 99.

32. Rogers St. Johns, "Artistic Efficiency—that's Dwan," 109.

33. Casey Robinson, interviewed by Joel Greenberg, July 14, 1974, transcript, LBMF, 15.

34. Bogdanovich, *Who the Devil Made It*, 261–62.

35. Ibid., 73.

36. Quoted in Brownlow, *The Parade's Gone By*, 96.

37. For more information on Griffith and his work, see, for example, Iris Barry, *D. W. Griffith, American Film Master* (New York: Museum of Modern Art, 1940); Cooper C. Graham, *D. W. Griffith and the Biograph Company* (Metuchen, NJ: Scarecrow Press, 1985); David Mayer, *Stagestruck Filmmaker: D. W. Griffith and the American Theatre* (Iowa City: University of Iowa Press, 2009).

38. For the details of Griffith's compensation agreements, see Barry, *D. W. Griffith, American Film Master*, 13.

39. The advertisement was reprinted in Jacobs, *The Rise of the American Film*, 117.

40. Mahar, *Women Filmmakers in Early Hollywood*, 295–322; Mahar, "True Womanhood in Hollywood." For more on the decline of female filmmakers, see also Koszarski, *An Evening's Entertainment*, 223; Slide, *The Silent Feminists*; Anthony Slide, *Early Women Directors* (South Brunswick, NJ: A. S. Barnes, 1977); Sharon Smith, *Women Who Make Movies* (New York: Hopkinson and Blake, 1975).

41. Bordwell, Staiger, and Thompson, *The Classical Hollywood Cinema*, 136–43.

42. Koszarski, *An Evening's Entertainment*, 211. The small group of directors Koszarski is writing about included Griffith, Lois Weber, Erich von Stroheim, Ernst Lubitsch, Cecil B. DeMille, and Marshall Neilan.

43. Tino Balio, *Grand Design: Hollywood as a Modern Business Enterprise, 1930–1939* (New York: Scribner, 1993), 79.

44. The story of Thalberg and Stroheim, the rise of MGM, and the consolidation of Hollywood as a vertically integrated industry aligned with big business are discussed in the introduction and chapter 1.

45. "Sanity Reaches the Movies," *Magazine of Wall Street*, November 11, 1933, 98, quoted in Balio, *Grand Design*, 79.

46. NLRB.1, box 515, vol. 2, October 1, 1937, 186–88.

47. Ibid., 188–89.

48. Ibid., 190–92.

49. Ibid., 209–29.

50. Dunne, interviewed by Thomas Stemple, 11, 41–42.

51. Nunnally Johnson, interviewed by Thomas Stemple, 1968–69, transcript, LBMF, 56–60.

52. Pandro Berman, interviewed by Mike Steen, August 4, 1972, transcript, LBMF, 3–6.

53. David O. Selznick, lecture given at Columbia University extension film-study group, November 1, 1937, reprinted in David O. Selznick, *Memo from David O. Selznick* (New York: Viking Press, 1972).

54. Frank Capra, "By Post from Mr. Capra," *New York Times*, April 2, 1939.

55. For more on Capra's unique status and relationship with Columbia, see Edward Buscombe, "Notes on Columbia Pictures Corporation, 1926–41," *Screen* 16, no. 3 (1975): 65–82.

56. Bob Thomas, *King Cohn: The Life and Times of Harry Cohn* (New York: Putnam, 1967), 165.

57. NLRB.1, box 515, vol. 1, September 30, 1937, 101–48.

58. Stephen Watts, ed., *Behind the Screen: How Films Are Made* (London: A. Barker, 1938), 14–17.

59. Nancy Naumburg, ed., *We Make the Movies* (New York: W. W. Norton, 1937), 55–57.

60. Thomas Schatz offered a similar description while writing about Capra. Emphasizing the contribution of studio operation to the career of the director as well as the shaping of his pictures, Schatz claimed that Hollywood directors were worthy of the title "consummate studio auteurs." See "Anatomy of a House Director: Capra, Cohn, and Columbia in the 1930s," in Schatz, *Frank Capra: Authorship and the Studio System* (Philadelphia: Temple University Press, 1998).

61. Johnson, interviewed by Thomas Stemple, 159–61.

62. NLRB.1, box 515, vol. 1, September 30, 1937, 148.

63. Reminiscence of Irving Rapper, January 3, 1971, Hollywood Film Industry Project, OHCC, 1.

64. Reminiscence of George Cukor, June 22, 1971, Hollywood Film Industry Project, OHCC, 40.

65. Ibid., 2–4.

66. Ibid., 40.

67. Watts, *Behind the Screen*, 14.

68. Due to the stock company model, in the studio era most star actors were under a long-term contract to one of the studios and therefore were not paid by the day. Still, there was a small but influential group of freelance character actors engaged on a film-by-film basis. In addition, the studios often loaned out their stars to one another. A delay in production forced the studio to extend its engagement with these short-term employees, thus paying them for the additional time. For more on the employment of actors, see chapter 4. On the significance of freelance character actors, see Sean P. Holmes, *Weavers of Dreams, Unite! Actor's Unionism in Early Twentieth-Century America* (Urbana: University of Illinois Press, 2013), 152–54.

69. Naumburg, *We Make the Movies*, 105.

70. For more on film stock technology, see Barry Salt, *Film Style and Technology: History and Analysis* (London: Starword, 1983).

71. Interoffice communication from Robert Forbes to Edward Ebel, October 15, 1941, folder 69.f-2; production reports, July 3, 1942, through October 31, 1942, folder 73.f-18, in Paramount Picture Production Records, MHL.

72. Quoted in Naumburg, *We Make the Movies*, 95–96.

73. As Sean Holmes points out, the practice of scheduling production around sets (filming all scenes that take place at the same set one after the other), as opposed to shooting according to the narrative structure of the picture (filming scenes following the sequence by which they appear in the script), was also influenced by the use of freelance actors and the studios' effort to keep the length of their employment to a minimum. See Holmes, *Weavers of Dreams, Unite!*, 152–54.

74. Kenneth Macgowan, *Behind the Screen: The History and Techniques of the Motion Picture* (New York: Delacorte Press, 1965), 391.

75. Leo Calvin Rosten, *Hollywood: The Movie Colony, the Movie Makers* (New York: Harcourt, Brace, 1941), 283, 323, 333. Class A actor was a category devised by the Screen Actors Guild, and it excluded extras as well as actors who did not receive screen credit.

76. Gene Brown, *Movie Time: A Chronology of Hollywood and the Movie Industry from Its Beginnings to the Present* (New York: Macmillan, 1995), 139.

77. Jan Herman, *A Talent for Trouble: The Life of Hollywood's Most Acclaimed Director, William Wyler* (New York: G. P. Putnam's Sons, 1995), 141.

78. Ibid., 296; Axel Madsen, *William Wyler: The Authorized Biography* (New York: Crowell, 1973), 288–89. Wyler received Paramount stock and signed a five-picture deal with the company, for which he was to produce each of these pictures on salary.

79. Undated eulogy for Carl Laemmle, file 50.f-658, William Wyler Papers, MHL.

80. Wyler to Laemmle, July 3, 1925, file 50.f-658, William Wyler Papers. For more information on Wyler, see Madsen, *William Wyler*; Herman, *A Talent for Trouble*.

81. Rosten, *Hollywood*, 57.

82. Quoted in Bogdanovich, *Who the Devil Made It*, 82.

83. Rosten, *Hollywood*, 291.

84. Herman, *A Talent for Trouble*, 81.

85. Memorandum from Paul Kohner to Laemmle, November 8, 1926, reprinted in Koszarski, *An Evening's Entertainment*, 212–13.

86. Herman, *A Talent for Trouble*, 99.

87. Wyler to Robert Wyler, April 7, 1934, file 59.f-756, William Wyler Papers.

88. According to data gathered in 1938, Frank Capra was the highest-paid director in Hollywood. His yearly income was $294,166. Among the other thirty-four top earners were King, Cukor, Hathaway, Walsh, and Hawks. The latter was one of the few directors who were not under contract with a big studio. Wyler's name did not appear on the list. Information taken from Rosten, *Hollywood*, 292.

89. Studio report on *The Shakedown*, November 16, 1928, file 29.f-400, William Wyler Papers.

90. Laemmle to Wyler, August 2, 1932, file 50.f-658, William Wyler Papers.

91. Interoffice communication from Henry Henigson to Laemmle, December 12, 1927, file 1.f-15, William Wyler Papers.

92. Reminiscence of George Cukor, 35.

93. Interoffice communication from William Lord Wright to Wyler, April 27, 1928, file 24.f-336, William Wyler Papers.

94. Interoffice communication from Wyler to Robert Walsh, May 15, 1928, file 24.f-336, William Wyler Papers.

95. Interoffice communication from Wright to Wyler, May 15, 1928, file 24.f-336, William Wyler Papers.

96. Reminiscences of William Wyler, January 9, 1972, Hollywood Film Industry Project, OHCC, 1.

97. Ibid., 14.

98. Interoffice communication, Warner Bros. Studio, April 19, 1940, copy, file 18.f-146, Rudy Behlmer Papers, MHL.

99. Interoffice communication from Walter MacEwen to Hall Wallis, June 14, 1939, Hal Wallis Papers, MHL.

100. Interoffice communication from Michael Curtiz to Jack L. Warner, February 25, 1944, Hal Wallis Papers.

101. Interoffice communication from Wyler to Henigson, February 3, 1928, file 57.f-736, William Wyler Papers.

102. Paul Nathan to Hal Wallis, June 24, 1942, file 229.f-2257, Hal Wallis Papers.

103. Interoffice communication from Frank Mattison to T. C. Wright, October 7, 1941, copy, file 17.7-139, Rudy Behlmer Papers.

104. Reminiscences of William Wyler, 11.

105. Interoffice communication from Laemmle to Wyler, December 7, 1927, file 1.f-15, William Wyler Papers.

106. Interoffice communication from Henigson to Wyler, February 3, 1928, file 29.f-400, William Wyler Papers.

107. Interoffice communication from Carl Laemmle Jr. to Wyler, October 21, 1929, file 57.f-737, William Wyler Papers.

108. Interoffice communication from Henigson to Wyler, June 10, 1931, file 57.f-736, William Wyler Papers.

109. Interoffice communication from Jack Warner to Wyler, June 27, 1940, file 19.f-252, William Wyler Papers.

110. Interoffice communication from Warner to Wyler, June 11, 1940, William Wyler Papers.

111. Reminiscences of Mervyn Leroy, July 12, 1971, Hollywood Film Industry Project, OHCC, 13.

112. Reminiscences of George Cukor, 4–5.

113. Interoffice communication from Wyler to Henigson, May 31, 1933, file 14.f-192, William Wyler Papers.

114. Interoffice communication from Wyler to Laemmle Jr., November 13, 1933, file 7.f-86, William Wyler Papers.

115. Wyler's labor practices also illuminate the role of Hollywood directors vis-à-vis the question of film authorship. For a discussion of how the historical developments discussed in this chapter relate to recent studies about authorship, see the last section in Regev, "Hollywood Works."

116. Wyler to Robert Wyler, January 5, 1932, file 59.f-755, William Wyler Papers.

Chapter Four

1. Data from Roland Flamini, *Scarlett, Rhett, and a Cast of Thousands: The Filming of Gone with the Wind* (New York: Macmillan, 1975), 12. The rights to the book were sold in July. The price was unprecedented for a first novel.

2. Margaret Mitchell to Katherine Brown, October 6, 1936, file 11.f-106, George Cukor Papers, MHL.

3. David O. Selznick to Katherine Brown, May 25, 1936, reprinted in David O. Selznick, *Memo from David O. Selznick* (New York: Viking Press, 1972), 178–79.

4. Selznick to John Hay Whitney, May 27, 1938, reprinted in ibid., 199–200. Mayer was the head of studio operations at MGM.

5. The exact details of the deal signed in August specified that "MGM would lend Gable to Selznick . . . and contribute $1,250,000 towards the production costs, in exchange for the distribution rights and a sliding-scale percentage of gross profits starting at fifty percent and going down to twenty-five percent over a number of years." Flamini, *Scarlett, Rhett, and a Cast of Thousands*, 106–7. See also David Thomson, *Showman: The Life of David O. Selznick* (New York: Knopf, 1992).

6. Data and quotes from Warren G. Harris, *Clark Gable: A Biography* (New York: Harmony Books, 2002), 189. A similar version of this story appears in Flamini, *Scarlett, Rhett, and a Cast of Thousands*.

7. David Montgomery, *The Fall of the House of Labor: The Workplace, the State, and American Labor Activism, 1865–1925* (Cambridge: Cambridge University Press, 1987), 58.

8. Barry King, "The Star and the Commodity: Notes towards a Performance Theory of Stardom," *Cultural Studies* 1, no. 2 (May 1987): 152.

9. Barry King, "Stardom as an Occupation," in *The Hollywood Film Industry: A Reader* (London: Routledge and Kegan Paul in association with the British Film Institute, 1986), 168.

10. Ashley Mears, *Pricing Beauty: The Making of a Fashion Model* (Berkeley: University of California Press, 2011), 76. Mears is primarily concerned with freelance and project-based employees, yet her observation is relevant here as well.

11. "We Nail a Lie," *Moving Picture World*, March 12, 1910, 365.

12. Lewis Jacobs, *The Rise of the American Film: A Critical History* (New York: Harcourt, Brace, 1939), 86.

13. Kevin Brownlow, *Hollywood—the Pioneers* (New York: Knopf, 1979), 156. For similar accounts, see David A. Cook, *A History of Narrative Film* (New York: Norton, 1981); and Robert Sklar, *Movie-Made America: A Cultural History of American Movies* (New York: Random House, 1975). The persistence of the Lawrence legend is apparent by its repetition in the 2011 TV series *The Story of Film: An Odyssey*, by Mark Cousins.

14. Anthony Slide, *Aspects of American Film History prior to 1920* (Metuchen, NJ: Scarecrow Press, 1978), 1.

15. These instances and other evidence are documented in Janet Staiger, "Seeing Stars," *Velvet Light Trap*, no. 20 (1983): 10–14.

16. For more, see Eileen Bowser, *The Transformation of Cinema, 1907–1915* (Berkeley: University of California Press, 1994), 106.

17. Richard deCordova, *Picture Personalities: The Emergence of the Star System in America* (Urbana: University of Illinois Press, 1990), 46.

18. The stock company model was essentially a permanent company of actors "attached to a specific theater which it controlled and at which it played for a major part of each season." This system developed in the United States during the nineteenth century. For more, see Alfred L. Bernheim, *The Business of the Theatre* (New York: Actors' Equity Association, 1932), 26–31; Benjamin McArthur, *Actors and American Culture, 1880–1920* (Philadelphia: Temple University Press, 1984), 5–8.

19. DeCordova, *Picture Personalities*, 46.

20. For more on the star system in theater, see McArthur, *Actors and American Culture*, 10–16; Bernheim, *The Business of the Theatre*, 26–31.

21. *Moving Picture World*, November 12, 1910, quoted in Bowser, *The Transformation of Cinema*, 117.

22. DeCordova, *Picture Personalities*, 98. For more about the rise of film fan magazines, see Anthony Slide, *Inside the Hollywood Fan Magazine: A History of Star Makers, Fabricators, and Gossip Mongers* (Jackson: University Press of Mississippi, 2010).

23. Reminiscences of Gloria Swanson, September 25, 1958, transcript, Popular Arts Project, OHCC, 14.

24. Reminiscences of Blanche Sweet, interviewed by Raymond Daum between May and August 1981, transcript, OHCC, 62.

25. Reminiscences of Sidney Blackmer, December 1959, transcripts, Popular Arts Project, OHCC, 3.

26. Reminiscences of Lillian Gish, interviewed by Raymond Daum, December 12, 1978, transcript, OHCC, 8.

27. Alexander Walker, *Stardom: The Hollywood Phenomenon* (New York: Stein and Day, 1970), 23.

28. Reminiscences of Mae Marsh, interviewed by Arthur B. Friedman, date unknown, transcript, Popular Arts Project, OHCC, 9.

29. Reminiscences of Albert Edward Sutherland, February 1959, transcript, Popular Arts Project, OHCC, 9.

30. Walker, *Stardom*, 27.

31. Reminiscences of Lillian Gish, 11.

32. Reminiscences of Blanche Sweet, 62.

33. Ibid., 86.

34. Reminiscences of Sidney Blackmer, 3–4.

35. See Jeanine Basinger, *The Star Machine* (New York: Knopf, 2007), xiii.

36. Reminiscences of Mae Marsh, 4. Story repeated in Eve Golden, *Golden Images: 41 Essays on Silent Film Stars* (Jefferson, NC: McFarland, 2001), 92–93.

37. Mae Marsh, *Screen Acting* (Los Angeles: Photostar Publishing, 1921), 51.

38. Reminiscences of Mae Marsh, 7–8. See similar versions in Reminiscences of Blanche Sweet, 33; Reminiscences of Mary Pickford, interviewed by Arthur B. Friedman, 1959, Popular Arts Project, OHCC.

39. Reminiscences of Gloria Swanson, 38.

40. Quoted in Walker, *Stardom*, 60.

41. Gaylyn Studlar, "Oh, 'Doll Divine': Mary Pickford, Masquerade, and the Pedophilic Gaze," in *A Feminist Reader in Early Cinema*, ed. Jennifer M. Bean and Diane Negra (Durham, NC: Duke University Press, 2002), 350.

42. Golden, *Golden Images*, 62.

43. There is no recent biography about Adolph Zukor. Information about Famous Players and the formation of Paramount can be found in Douglas Gomery, *The Hollywood Studio System: A History* (London: BFI, 2005), chap. 1; Adolph Zukor, *The Public Is Never Wrong: The Autobiography of Adolph Zukor*, with Dale Kramer (New York: Putnam, 1953); Will Irwin, *The House That Shadows Built* (Garden City, NY: Doubleday, Doran, 1928).

44. DeCordova, *Picture Personalities*, 50–51.

45. Eileen Whitfield, *Pickford: The Woman Who Made Hollywood* (Lexington: University Press of Kentucky, 1997), 123. David Belasco was a famous theater owner, producer, and director.

46. Information about Pickford's salary from ibid., 112–46; Tino Balio, *United Artists: The Company Built by the Stars* (Madison: University of Wisconsin Press, 1976), 14–17.

47. Reminiscences of Mae Marsh, 24. By 1916, Sam Goldfish had already changed his name to Goldwyn.

48. Upton Sinclair, *Upton Sinclair Presents William Fox* (Los Angeles: Privately printed, 1933), 56–57.

49. Richard Koszarski, *An Evening's Entertainment: The Age of the Silent Feature Picture, 1915–1928* (New York: Scribner, 1990), 261.

50. Benjamin B. Hampton, *A History of the Movies* (New York: Covici, Friede, 1931), 194.

51. Geraldyn Dismond, "The Negro Actor and the American Movies," *Close Up* 5, no. 2 (August 1929): 91–92.

52. There were a few exceptions to this rule, most notably the films *Hallelujah* and *Hearts in Dixie* from 1929. For more on these, see Ryan Jay Friedman, *Hollywood's African American Films: The Transition to Sound* (Piscataway, NJ: Rutgers University Press, 2011). Other exceptions included films made by independent black production companies such as the Lincoln Motion Picture Company of Oscar Micheaux, the Colored Players Film Corporation, and Liberty Photoplays Inc. For more on the movies made by these companies, see Thomas Cripps, *Slow Fade to Black: The Negro in American Film, 1900–1942* (New York: Oxford University Press, 1977), 146–72.

53. For more on how Hollywood handled black performers both on and off screen, see Daniel J. Leab, *From Sambo to Superspade: The Black Experience in Motion Pictures* (Boston: Houghton Mifflin, 1975); Donald Bogle, *Bright Boulevards, Bold Dreams: The Story of Black Hollywood* (New York: One World Ballantine Books, 2005). The one exception to the common experience of black actors in the Hollywood studio system might have been Lena Horne, who had a long-term contract with MGM, though she too suffered from race-based discrimination. See Charlene B. Regester, *African American Actresses: The Struggle for Visibility, 1900–1960* (Bloomington: Indiana University Press, 2010), 174–214.

54. Quoted in Balio, *United Artists*, 13–14. In 1919, the Metro Studio was an independent production company.

55. Tino Balio, *Grand Design—Hollywood as a Modern Business Enterprise, 1930–1939* (New York: Scribner, 1993), 144–45.

56. Koszarski, *An Evening's Entertainment*, 95.

57. Reminiscences of Janet Gaynor, November 1958, transcript, Popular Arts Project, OHCC, 2–3.

58. Ibid.

59. Gladys Hall and Joan Crawford, "I Could Not Ask for More," manuscript for a Joan Crawford autobiography, n.d., file 3.f-121, Gladys Hall Papers, MHL.

60. The MPPDA was established in 1922 in a concerted effort by the major producers to create a self-regulating body headed by former postmaster general Will Hays that would combat the threat of state and federal censorship.

61. Phil Friedman, "The Players Are Cast," in *We Make the Movies*, ed. Nancy Naumburg (New York: W. W. Norton, 1937), 110–11. The official website of the Central Casting Corporation lists its opening year as 1925. Since Friedman gives a specific date, which is at the very beginning of 1926, I decided to adopt his version. It could be that the organization was already operating in some form a month or two before.

62. Balio, *Grand Design*, 145.

63. In the baseball reserve system, players signed one-year contracts that contained an option clause "to be exercised by the club if it so desired" to renew the contract for the next season. If a club exercised the option, the player now had to sign another one-year contract with the same provision, essentially binding him to the club indefinitely. For more on this system, which stayed in place until 1976, and the fight against it, see Braham Dabscheck, "Commercialized Sports, Entrepreneurs, and Unions in Major League Baseball," in *The Routledge History of American Sport*, ed. Linda J. Borish, David K. Wiggins, and Gerlad R. Gems (New York: Routledge,

Taylor and Francis Group, 2017), 268–79; and Harold Seymour, *Baseball: The Early Years* (New York: Oxford University Press, 1989), chap. 10.

64. See Agreement between Melvyn Douglas and Samuel Goldwyn, February 9, 1931, Melvyn Douglas Papers, WHS; Agreement between Warner Bros. Pictures Inc. and Paul Henreid, May, 25, 1942, and Agreement between Katharine Hepburn and RKO Studios Inc., August 31, 1932, RKO Radio Pictures Inc., Correspondence, NYPL.

65. Crawford to Katherine Albert, November 14, 1941, file 3.f-123, Gladys Hall Papers. Norma Shearer was the wife of Irving Thalberg, MGM's vice president in charge of production.

66. Reminiscences of James Cagney, December 1958, transcript, Popular Arts Project, OHCC, 44.

67. Bette Davis, "The Actress Plays Her Part," in Naumburg, *We Make the Movies*, 118.

68. Quoted in Hall, "Clark Gable Tells 'How'—and How!," article manuscript, November 10, 1940, file 5.f-195, Gladys Hall Papers.

69. Leslie Howard, "The Actor–I," in *Behind the Screen: How Films Are Made*, ed. Stephen Watts (London: A. Barker, 1938), 84–87.

70. Paul Muni, "The Actor Plays His Part," in Naumburg, *We Make the Movies*, 131–32.

71. Pandro Berman to Katharine Hepburn, March 27, 1935, file 1.f-14, Katharine Hepburn Papers, MHL.

72. Agreement between Melvyn Douglas and Samuel Goldwyn; Agreement between Warner Bros. Pictures Inc. and Paul Henreid; Agreement between Katharine Hepburn and RKO Studios Inc.

73. Reminiscences of Ralph Bellamy, November 1958, transcript, Popular Arts Project, OHCC, 27.

74. Reminiscences of Carver Dana Andrews, November 1958, Popular Arts Project, OHCC, 23.

75. Reminiscences of Myrna Loy, interviewed by Mr. and Mrs. Robert C. Franklin, June 1959, transcript, Popular Arts Project, OHCC, 20.

76. Agreement between Melvyn Douglas and Samuel Goldwyn; Agreement between Warner Bros. Pictures Inc. and Paul Henreid; Agreement between Katharine Hepburn and RKO Studios Inc. Once again, these morality clauses seem to have antecedents in theater and baseball, but they were not as standardized. See McArthur, *Actors and American Culture*, 21; Seymour, *Baseball*, chap. 12.

77. Reminiscences of James Cagney, 10.

78. Reminiscences of Janet Gaynor, 21–22.

79. Agreement between Melvyn Douglas and Samuel Goldwyn; Agreement between Warner Bros. Pictures Inc. and Paul Henreid; Agreement between Katharine Hepburn and RKO Studios Inc.

80. See Theodor Adorno and Hanns Eisler, *Composing for the Films* (London: Athlone Press, 1994), 55–56n6. Adorno and Eisler reached these conclusions after analyzing similar contracts signed by motion picture composers. In his study of theater acting, Benjamin McArthur suggests that this practice began in the theater business following an 1891 New York Supreme Court decision specifying that managers can-

not prevent actors from joining other companies after breaking their contract unless such a departure caused "irreparable damage" to the show, since said actor's qualifications were "special, unique, or extraordinary." See McArthur, *Actors and American Culture*, 21–22.

81. Walker, *Stardom*, 240.

82. Agreement between Melvyn Douglas and Samuel Goldwyn; Agreement between Katharine Hepburn and RKO Studios Inc.; Agreement between Tim Holt and RKO Pictures Inc., December 15, 1938, RKO Radio Pictures Inc., Correspondence. Supporting actors and bit players did not receive such high sums, but they also did not have to sign such draconian contracts.

83. U.S. Department of Commerce, *Historical Statistics of the United States, Colonial Times to 1970*, part 1, 164. Available online at https://www.census.gov/library /publications/1975/compendia/hist_stats_colonial-1970.html.

84. Statement of production costs for *Double Indemnity*, August 4, 1943, file 59.f-2, and statement of production costs for *Hold Back the Dawn*, 1941, file 101.f-2, Paramount Pictures Production Records, MHL.

85. Hall, "Clark Gable Tells 'How'—and How!"

86. Leo Calvin Rosten, *Hollywood: The Movie Colony, the Movie Makers* (New York: Harcourt, Brace, 1941), 329.

87. Cathy Kalprat, "The Star as Market Strategy: Bette Davis in Another Light," in *The American Film Industry*, ed. Tino Balio, rev. ed (Madison: University of Wisconsin Press, 1985), 355–60. A similar process is described in Thomas Schatz, *The Genius of the System: Hollywood Filmmaking in the Studio Era* (New York: Pantheon Books, 1988), 39–40.

88. W. Robert LaVine, *In a Glamorous Fashion: The Fabulous Years of Hollywood Costume Design* (New York: Scribner, 1980), 27.

89. Friedman, "The Players Are Cast," 107–8.

90. Selznick to Cukor, May 28, 1937, file 11.f-106, George Cukor Papers.

91. Cukor to Selznick, June 3, 1937, file 11.f-106, George Cukor Papers.

92. Cukor was eventually replaced by Victor Fleming.

93. Cukor to Selznick, February 11, 1938, file 11.f-106, George Cukor Papers. The Mrs. Chaplin in question is probably actress Paulette Goddard, who was married to Charles Chaplin between 1936 and 1942 and was considered for the role of Scarlett.

94. Libby Holman to Cukor, June 21, 1937, file 11.f-106, George Cukor Papers.

95. Selznick to Cukor, April 18, 1938, file 11.f-106, George Cukor Papers.

96. Copy of casting options for the role of Blossom, undated, file 11.f-106, George Cukor Papers.

97. Selznick to Cukor, January 14, 1939, file 11.f-106, George Cukor Papers.

98. Selznick to Daniel T. O'Shea, November 21, 1938, reprinted in Selznick, *Memo from David O. Selznick*, 193.

99. Selznick to Henry Ginsberg and O'Shea, December 19, 1938, reprinted in ibid., 200.

100. Agreement between Melvyn Douglas and Samuel Goldwyn; Agreement between Warner Bros. Pictures Inc. and Paul Henreid; Agreement between Katharine Hepburn and RKO Studios Inc.

101. Agreement between RKO Radio Pictures Inc. and Paramount Pictures, Inc. regarding the loan-out of William Holden, July 15, 1947; Agreement between RKO Radio Pictures, Inc. and Walter Wanger Productions, Incorporated regarding the loan-out of Tim Holt, September 13, 1938; Agreement between Twentieth Century–Fox Film Corporation and RKO Radio Pictures, Inc. regarding the loan-out of Tim Holt, March 30, 1946, in RKO Radio Pictures Inc., Correspondence; Agreement between Universal Picture Company, Inc. and Walter Wanger Productions, Incorporated regarding the loan-out of Susan Hayward, 1946; Agreement between RKO Radio Pictures, Inc. and Walter Wanger Productions, Incorporated regarding the loan-out of Susan Hayward, June 26, 1946, in Walter Wanger Papers, WHS.

102. Friedman, "The Players Are Cast," 108.

103. Bill Grady, "Casting," in Watts, *Behind the Screen*, 65.

104. Daniel T. O'Shea to Hal Wallis, October 6, 1944, file 222.f-2175, Hal Wallis Papers, MHL. Richards did play the part of Dilly in the picture.

105. Wallis to Walter Wanger, October 26, 1948, file 225.f-2232, Hal Wallis Papers. The picture in question was eventually released under the title *The Reckless Moment*.

106. Berman to Hepburn, June 4, 1936, file 21.f-277, Katharine Hepburn Papers.

107. Selznick to Joel McCrea, December 6, 1932, file 21.f-213, George Cukor Papers.

108. Klaprat, "The Star as Market Strategy," 360–61.

109. Reminiscences of Myrna Loy, 5–7.

110. Hall and Crawford, "I Could Not Ask for More."

111. Reminiscences of Carver Dana Andrews, 12.

112. Davis, "The Actress Plays Her Part," 118–19.

113. Reminiscences of Lauren Bacall, interviewed by Mr. Benton and Mr. Greene, June 29, 1971, transcript, Hollywood Film Industry Project, OHCC, 3.

114. Reminiscences of Reginald Owen, interviewed by Charles Higham, July 2, 1971, transcript, Hollywood Film Industry Project, OHCC, 12.

115. George Cukor, interviewed by Henry Ehrlich, circa 1975, transcript, file 64.f-941, George Cukor Papers.

116. Paul Nathan to Wallis, August 24, 1942, file 226.f-2240, Hal Wallis Papers.

117. Gladys Hall, "I'll Tell on Myself, Says Bette Davis—and Does," undated, circa 1938, file 4.f-142, Gladys Hall Papers.

Chapter Five

1. Virgil E. Miller, *Splinters from Hollywood Tripods: Memoirs of a Cameraman* (New York: Exposition Press, 1964). Miller claims that Secretary Tobin made this statement in an article titled "Stars without Oscars." However, he does not mention the date or the name of the publication.

2. John H. M. Laslett, *Sunshine Was Never Enough: Los Angeles Workers, 1880–2010* (Berkeley: University of California Press, 2012), 84.

3. George Cukor, interviewed by Gavin Lambert, August 1970–April 1971, transcript, LBMF, 111.

4. For more on the history of the Warner Bros. studio and back lot and its architecture, see Steven Bingen, *Warner Bros.: Hollywood's Ultimate Backlot* (Lanham, MD: Rowman and Littlefield, 2014), 19–23. Bingen's description of the studio focuses on the way it looked in 1967.

5. Description of the Warner Bros. studio is taken from Charles F. Greenlaw Jr., unpublished autobiography, circa 1984, file 54.f-489, MHL. Nilsson quote is from "Advice to Girls Seeking a Motion Picture Career," in *The Truth about the Movies*, ed. Laurence A. Hughes (Hollywood: Hollywood Publishers, 1924), 67. This publication is available via the Media Digital History Library Project.

6. Greenlaw, unpublished autobiography, 49–52.

7. Margaret Booth, "The Cutter," in *Behind the Screen: How Films Are Made*, ed. Stephen Watts (London: A. Barker, 1938), 147, 152–53.

8. Hughes, *The Truth about the Movies*, 343.

9. Greenlaw, unpublished autobiography, 53.

10. Adrian, "Clothes," in Watts, *Behind the Screen*, 56.

11. Greenlaw, unpublished autobiography, 54.

12. Jack Dawn, "Make-Up," in Watts, *Behind the Screen*, 74. Dawn worked at many studios, including Universal, Twentieth Century–Fox, and MGM.

13. Greenlaw, unpublished autobiography, 55–59.

14. Hans Dreier, "Designing the Sets," in *We Make the Movies*, ed. Nancy Naumburg (New York: W. W. Norton, 1937), 81–82.

15. Greenlaw, unpublished autobiography, 61–63.

16. Ibid., 56.

17. Ibid., 61–69.

18. The discussion of the "luxurious city" and classifications appears in Plato, *The Republic*, trans. Benjamin Jowett (Auckland: Floating Press, 2009), book 2.

19. Howard S. Becker, "Arts and Crafts," *American Journal of Sociology* 83, no. 4 (1978): 863.

20. T. J. Crizer, "The Film Editor," in Hughes, *The Truth about the Movies*, 340.

21. See, for example, "Disney Has His Troubles with New Set of Actors," *New York Herald Tribune*, September 10, 1950; "Looking at People," *Chicago Daily Tribune*, October 23, 1940.

22. See Philip Dunne, interviewed by Thomas Stemple, 1970–71, transcript, 11, 41–42, LBMF; or Nunnally Johnson, interviewed by Thomas Stemple, 1968–69, transcript, LBMF, 56–60. Both men are quoted in chapter 3.

23. See, for example, Antony Black, *Guilds and Civil Society in European Political Thought from the Twelfth Century to the Present* (Ithaca, NY: Cornell University Press, 1984).

24. David Montgomery, *The Fall of the House of Labor: The Workplace, the State, and American Labor Activism, 1865–1925* (Cambridge: Cambridge University Press, 1987), 14–22.

25. Andrea Graziosi, "Common Laborers, Unskilled Workers: 1880–1915," *Labor History* 22, no. 4 (September 1, 1981): 516.

26. See Karl Marx, *Capital: A Critique of Political Economy* (Harmondsworth, Eng.: Penguin Books, in association with New Left Review, 1976), vol. 1, chap. 25, sec. 5.c.

27. For more on the Pullman strike and the rise of the AFL, see Bruce Laurie, *Artisans into Workers: Labor in Nineteenth-Century America* (Urbana: University of Illinois Press, 1997); Richard Schneirov, ed., *The Pullman Strike and the Crisis of the 1890s: Essays on Labor and Politics* (Urbana: University of Illinois Press, 1999).

28. Leo Wolman, *The Growth of American Trade Unions, 1880–1923* (New York: National Bureau of Economic Research, 1924), 33.

29. In 1902, due to the addition of several Canadian locals, the word "National" was replaced with "International," hence the acronym IATSE. See Robert Osborne Baker, "The International Alliance of Theatrical Stage Employees and Moving Picture Machine Operators of the United States and Canada" (PhD diss., University of Kansas, 1933), 1–9. The alliance with the AFL was not intuitive, as IATSE was, in many ways, an industrial organization, and many of its founding members were affiliated with the Knights of Labor. However, the loose federation model of the alliance, lobbying within the organization, as well as the decline of the Knights, pushed for a charter with the AFL.

30. These bylaws were incorporated from the constitution of IATSE Local 1, the New York City stagehand union. Quoted in Michael Charles Nielsen, "Motion Picture Craft Workers and Craft Unions in Hollywood: The Studio Era, 1912–1948" (PhD diss., University of Illinois at Urbana-Champaign, 1985), 28.

31. Baker, "The International Alliance of Theatrical Stage Employees and Moving Picture Machine Operators," 2–3.

32. The term "pure and simple unionism" was developed by Samuel Gompers in the 1880s. It referred mostly to unionization that was free from the influence of political parties.

33. Nielsen, "Motion Picture Craft Workers and Craft Unions in Hollywood," 29–35. The main source used by Nielsen is IATSE's *Combined Convention Proceedings*, vol. 1, 1893–1926.

34. For more on the history of IATSE, see chapter 6 as well as Hugh Lovell and Tasile Carter, *Collective Bargaining in the Motion Picture Industry* (Berkeley: Institute of Industrial Relations, University of California, 1955); Nielsen, "Motion Picture Craft Workers and Craft Unions in Hollywood."

35. Article of Incorporation of Academy of Motion Picture Arts and Sciences, March 4, 1927, in NLRB.1, box 518, Petitioners' Exhibits, 1–24.

36. Both unions fought with IATSE in an attempt to win jurisdiction over various groups of studio workers throughout the 1930s and 1940s.

37. Becker, "Arts and Crafts," particularly 862–63, 887. For a discussion of painting in relation to art and craft, see Michael Baxandall, *Painting and Experience in Fifteenth Century Italy: A Primer in the Social History of Pictorial Style* (Oxford: Clarendon Press, 1972).

38. For a broader discussion about the process by which certain crafts transition to the world of art, see Richard W. Christopherson, "From Folk Art to Fine Art," *Journal of Contemporary Ethnography* 3, no. 2 (1974): 123–57. Christopherson focuses on still photographers, but the language he uses is particularly suitable to the case of film photographers. For a similar discussion on the work of sound engineers in the music

industry, see Edward R. Kealy, "From Craft to Art," *Work and Occupations* 6, no. 1 (February 1, 1979): 3–29.

39. William Kennedy Laurie Dickson, *History of the Kinetograph, Kinetoscope, and Kineto-Phonograph* (New York: Museum of Modern Art, 2000), 6. The first edition was published in 1895.

40. "Screen's Best Thriller Turns Out to Be Its Own Short Story," *Boston Daily Globe*, May 30, 1926.

41. Dickson, *History of the Kinetograph, Kinetoscope, and Kineto-Phonograph*, 19.

42. Charles Musser, *The Emergence of Cinema: The American Screen to 1907* (New York: Scribner, 1990), 64–81, 91–100, 145–57. Dickson began working with his later partners at Biograph while still under employment at the Edison labs. He also aided the development of the Latham projection system.

43. Paul C. Spehr, "Filmmaking at the American Mutoscope and Biograph Company, 1900–1906," *Quarterly Journal of the Library of Congress* 37, no. 3/4 (1980): 413–21. In his analysis of the biograph logbooks, Spehr found that the company recorded each production's "number, date, subject, shooting location, the name of the operator, the date the negative was developed, and occasionally some production or release information."

44. Janet Staiger titles this period, from 1896 to 1907, the "cameraman" system of production. See David Bordwell, Janet Staiger, and Kristin Thompson, *The Classical Hollywood Cinema: Film Style and Mode of Production to 1960* (New York: Columbia University Press, 1985), 116.

45. These statements by Porter were given as part of his testimony in the *Armat Moving Picture Co. v. Edison Manufacturing Co.* case of 1902; quoted in Charles Musser, "The Early Cinema of Edwin Porter," *Cinema Journal* 19, no. 1 (1979): 1–38.

46. G. W. Bitzer, *Billy Bitzer: His Story* (New York: Farrar, Straus and Giroux, 1973), 8–9.

47. Ibid., 14.

48. Ibid., 27.

49. Ibid., 69.

50. Musser, *The Emergence of Cinema*, 226; Spehr, "Filmmaking at the American Mutoscope and Biograph Company," 416.

51. Albert E. Smith, *Two Reels and a Crank* (Garden City, NY: Doubleday, 1952), 135, 141, 186.

52. See Staiger's explanation of the transition to the director system in Bordwell, Staiger, and Thompson, *The Classical Hollywood Cinema*, 116–17.

53. For more on these ideas and their penetration into American industry, see Daniel T. Rodgers, *The Work Ethic in Industrial America, 1850–1920* (Chicago: University of Chicago Press, 1978), 50–57; T. J. Jackson Lears, *Rebirth of a Nation: The Making of Modern America, 1877–1920* (New York: HarperCollins, 2009), 254–72. Regarding how these ideas spread beyond the United States, see Anson Rabinbach, *The Human Motor: Energy, Fatigue, and the Origins of Modernity* (New York: Basic Books, 1990), 206–76.

54. Smith, *Two Reels and a Crank*, 143–44, 204–5.

55. Bitzer, *Billy Bitzer*, 69.

56. Bordwell, Staiger, and Thompson, *The Classical Hollywood Cinema*, 150.

57. Quoted in Leonard Maltin, *The Art of the Cinematographer: A Survey and Interviews with Five Masters* (New York: Dover, 1978), 64.

58. Guy Wilky, "The Cameraman," in Hughes, *The Truth about the Movies*, 325.

59. "Inquiries," *Moving Picture World*, August 10, 1912.

60. Norbert F. Brodin, "Something about the Cameraman," in Hughes, *The Truth about the Movies*, 327.

61. Bitzer, *Billy Bitzer*, 67. See also the footnote on that page.

62. Erik Barnouw, "The Sintzenich Diaries," *Quarterly Journal of the Library of Congress* 37, no. 3/4 (1980): 322.

63. Miller, *Splinters from Hollywood Tripods*, 44.

64. Famous Players–Lasky Corporation to Elmer Dyer, April 22, 1919, file 2.f-64, Elmer Dyer Papers, MHL. The letter appears to be a generic one, which was probably sent to several freelance photographers.

65. Dyer to Famous Players–Lasky Corporation, April 29, 1919, Elmer Dyer Papers.

66. Famous Players–Lasky to Dyer, ca. 1919, Elmer Dyer Papers,

67. "Inquiries," *Moving Picture World*, July 13, 1912.

68. Carl Louis Gregory, "Motion Picture Photography," *Moving Picture World*, October 23, 1915.

69. George Folsey, interviewed by Sylvia Shorris, September 1985, transcript, file 1.f-13, Sylvia Shorris Interview Transcripts Collection, MHL.

70. "An Oral History of James Wong Howe," interviewed by Alain Silver, 1969, transcript, file 18.f-213, James Wong Howe Papers, MHL.

71. H. Lyman Broening, "How It All Happened," *American Cinematographer*, November 1, 1921; "Six Decades of 'Loyalty, Progress, Artistry,'" *American Cinematographer*, June 1979. The name Static Club was apparently a reference to the static electricity surrounding exposed film, which was a regular nuisance to camera operators.

72. Barnouw, "The Sintzenich Diaries," 323.

73. "Six Decades of 'Loyalty, Progress, Artistry.'"

74. Bordwell, Staiger, and Thompson, *The Classical Hollywood Cinema*, 150; "An Oral History of James Wong Howe."

75. Miller, *Splinters from Hollywood Tripods*, 135.

76. "An Oral History of James Wong Howe."

77. For more on the multicamera system, see Bordwell, Staiger, and Thompson, *The Classical Hollywood Cinema*, 304–8. For more on the experimentation with sound technology, see Donald Crafton, *The Talkies: American Cinema's Transition to Sound, 1926–1931* (New York: Scribner, 1997); Emily Thompson, "Remix Redux," *Cabinet* 35 (Fall 2009); Rick Altman, *Silent Film Sound* (New York: Columbia University Press, 2004).

78. "Cameraless Cameramen," *Variety*, February 12, 1930, 10.

79. Ezra Goodman, "Lights! Action! Jimmy Howe," *Pageant* 4, no. 5 (November 1948), file 21.f-259, James Wong Howe Papers.

80. "Lensmen Have Minimum Pact," *Variety*, October 10, 1933. The ASC was not the sole bargaining unit claiming to represent cameramen, and in fact many of them were members of IATSE up to 1933. However, disputes between IATSE and the studios earlier that year inspired many to seek the auspices of the ASC, which, in turn, felt that it was entitled to represent the entire profession. Naturally, the studios were eager to negotiate with the more conservative ASC, thus weakening the bargaining position of the powerful IATSE.

81. "Cameramen's Agreement," January 3, 1934, NLRB.1, box 518, Petitioner's Exhibits 25 to 67. The same classifications were maintained by IATSE when it reestablished its jurisdiction over cameramen two years later; they appear, with adjusted pay rates, in the official Studio Wage Scale of 1936 and 1937. See "Studio Agreement and Wage Scale," May 11, 1936; "Studio Wage Scale," April 26, 1937, in the same box.

82. IATSE Local 659 to Linwood G. Dunn, September 20, 1944, file 65.f-982, Linwood G. Dunn Papers, MHL. This correspondence contains a chart with the heading "Studio Wage Scale."

83. Lee Garmes, "Photography," in Watts, *Behind the Screen*, 104.

84. "One of Local 659's Examples for Success through Application," *International Photographer*, September 1930, 28.

85. Garmes, "Photography," 109–10.

86. NLRB.1, box 515, vol. 1, September 30, 1937, 151–61.

87. Garmes, "Photography," 107.

88. James Wong Howe, "Hollywood Camera," article manuscript, July 14, 1945, file 17.f-208, James Wong Howe Papers.

89. Garmes, "Photography," 109.

90. NLRB.1, box 515, vol. 1, September 30, 1937, 163.

91. James Wong Howe, "Course in Direction," article manuscript, July 9, 1943, file 17.f-208, James Wong Howe Papers.

92. George Folsey, interviewed by Sylvia Shorris, pt. 2, February 1986.

93. "IATSE Seeks Film Studio Control by Takeover of Cinematographers," *Variety*, July 12, 1939. The ASC contract that incensed IATSE was the second one signed between the society and the studios, which came into effect in 1939, when the first agreement from 1934 expired.

94. Fred Jackman and Board of Governors of A.S.C. to Fred Pelton at the Motion Picture Producers Association, October 25, 1941, file 3.f-33, Charles G. Clarke Collection, MHL.

95. Official communication from American Society of Cinematographers to its membership, November 27, 1941, file 3.f-33, Charles G. Clarke Collection.

96. An Open Letter to the General Membership from A.S.C., December 29, 1941, file 3.f-33, Charles G. Clarke Collection.

97. "ASC Group Gets Master Charter from IBEW and 70 Other Lensers Bolt IATSE," *Variety*, June 24, 1942.

98. For more on Herbert Sorrell, the labor disputes of the late 1930s, and the cartoonists' strike of 1941, see Laurie Pintar, "Herbert K. Sorrell as the Grade-B Hero: Militancy and Masculinity in the Studios," *Labor History* 37, no. 3 (June 1, 1996):

392–416; Michael Denning, *The Cultural Front: The Laboring of American Culture in the Twentieth Century* (London: Verso, 1997), 403–22.

99. For more on the Tenney Committee and HUAC in Hollywood, see Steven Joseph Ross, *Hollywood Left and Right: How Movie Stars Shaped American Politics* (New York: Oxford University Press, 2011), 89–129; Michael Freedland, *Hollywood on Trial: McCarthyism in Hollywood* (London: Robson, 2007); John Joseph Gladchuk, *Hollywood and Anticommunism: HUAC and the Evolution of the Red Menace, 1935–1950* (New York: Routledge, 2007); Larry Ceplair and Steven Englund, *The Inquisition in Hollywood: Politics in the Film Community, 1930–1960* (Garden City, NY: Anchor Press / Doubleday, 1980); Edward L. Barrett, *The Tenney Committee: Legislative Investigation of Subversive Activities in California* (Ithaca, NY: Cornell University Press, 1951).

100. For more on Browne, his conviction, and his involvement with studio bosses and organized crime in Chicago, see Thomas Schatz, *Boom and Bust: The American Cinema in the 1940s* (New York: Scribner, 1997), 31–34.

101. Rod Roddy, "Hollywood Unions," *Variety*, January 6, 1943.

102. Agreement between MGM and Charles G. Clarke, May 13, 1933, file 2.f-23, Charles G. Clarke Collection; "Cameramen's Agreement."

103. Charles G. Clarke, interviewed by Thomas Stempel, May 5, 1971, transcript, file 2.f-26, Charles G. Clarke Collection. A second unit of a film is responsible for supplementary footage such as atmospherics and establishing scenes that do not require the principal actors. During the studio system era, such units often featured a complete camera crew including a director of photography / first cameraman and assistants. Clarke, for example, spent seven months in China as the second-unit cameramen for *The Good Earth* (1937), where he worked on many of the picture's exteriors, though he never received official credit for it.

104. Agreement between James Wong Howe and Joyce-Selznick, Ltd., July 16, 1932, file 20.f-242, James Wong Howe Papers.

105. See, for example, Agreement between Paramount Picture Corporation and James Wong Howe, October 21, 1954, file 20.f-242, James Wong Howe Papers; Agreement between MGM and Charles G. Clarke; Agreement between Clarke and Twentieth Century–Fox, February 25, 1944, file 2.f-23, Charles G. Clarke Collection. For a broader discussion of such clauses, see chapter 4.

106. Agreement between MGM and Charles G. Clarke.

107. Agreement between Paramount Picture Corporation and James Wong Howe.

108. George Folsey, interviewed by Sylvia Shorris, pt. 2, February 1986.

Chapter Six

1. Irving Thalberg and Hugh Weir, "Why Motion Pictures Cost So Much," *Saturday Evening Post*, November 4, 1933.

2. Legal Arguments against the Proposed So-Called Rules of Fair Practice Governing the Relations between Producers and Writers, February 5, 1935, NLRB.1, box 517, Board's Exhibits 166–314.

3. Statement by Motion Picture Producers, April 26, 1936, NLRB.2, box 1725, Board's Exhibits.

4. NLRB.2, box 1725, vol. 10, August 23, 1939.

5. For more about the contested meaning of "employee" in American labor politics, see Jean-Christian Vinel, *The Employee: A Political History* (Philadelphia: University of Pennsylvania Press, 2013).

6. Pierre Bourdieu, "The Field of Cultural Production, or: The Economic World Reversed," *Poetics* 12, no. 4–5 (November 1983): 321–25. When Bourdieu discusses relational positions between fields, he stresses that they are "partial." In fact, he says, "Such alliances, based on homologies of position combined with profound differences in condition, are not exempt from misunderstandings and even bad faith." Bourdieu acknowledges a true "rapprochement" only between the "literary avant-garde" and the "political vanguard," two groups that, if nothing else, shared the experience of being the underdog in their respective fields. Hollywood actors, directors, and writers were working in the heart of the cultural consensus, and due to that fact, as this book argues, despite their authentic difficulties within the studio system, their rapport with the American working classes was always somewhat lacking.

7. Nelson Lichtenstein, *State of the Union: A Century of American Labor* (Princeton, NJ: Princeton University Press, 2002), 20, 33–35, 52.

8. Christopher L. Tomlins, *The State and the Unions: Labor Relations, Law, and the Organized Labor Movement in America, 1880–1960* (Cambridge: Cambridge University Press, 1985), 102.

9. For more on the role of lawyers in this process, see Eileen Boris, "Labor's Welfare State: Defining Workers, Constructing Citizens," in *The Cambridge History of Law in America*, ed. Michael Grossberg and Christopher L. Tomlins (Cambridge: Cambridge University Press, 2008), 329; Irving Bernstein, *Turbulent Year: A History of the American Worker, 1933–1941* (Boston: Houghton Mifflin, 1970); Robert H. Zieger, *American Workers, American Unions*, 2nd ed. (Baltimore: Johns Hopkins University Press, 1994).

10. For more on the industry's cultural and social influence during the New Deal, see Giuliana Muscio, *Hollywood's New Deal* (Philadelphia: Temple University Press, 1996).

11. Douglas Gomery, *The Hollywood Studio System: A History* (London: BFI, 2005), 186.

12. Eileen Bowser, *The Transformation of Cinema, 1907–1915* (Berkeley: University of California Press, 1994), 152–58.

13. See Kevin Brownlow, *Hollywood—the Pioneers* (New York: Knopf, 1979), 90–107.

14. Richard Koszarski, *An Evening's Entertainment: The Age of the Silent Feature Picture, 1915–1928* (New York: Scribner, 1990), 102–4.

15. Richard V. Spencer, "Los Angeles as a Producing Center," *Moving Picture World*, April 8, 1911, quoted in Bowser, *The Transformation of Cinema*, 160.

16. Harrison Gray Otis, "Los Angeles—a Sketch," *Sunset* 24 (January 1910), quoted in Louis B. Perry and Richard S. Perry, *A History of the Los Angeles Labor Movement, 1911–1941* (Berkeley: University of California Press, 1963), 5.

17. Mike Davis, "Sunshine and the Open Shop: Ford and Darwin in 1920s Los Angeles," in *Metropolis in the Making: Los Angeles in the 1920s*, ed. Tom Sitton and William Francis Deverell (Berkeley: University of California Press, 2001), 101–2.

18. Commission on Industrial Relations, *Final Report* (Washington, DC, 1915), quoted in Perry and Perry, *A History of the Los Angeles Labor Movement*, 16.

19. Robert Sklar, *Movie-Made America: A Cultural History of American Movies* (New York: Random House, 1975), 68. Some memoirs and older histories of Hollywood often list the attempt of independent producers to escape the spies and legal pursuits of the Motion Picture Patent Company as an important reason for the move to Los Angeles. There is little evidence to support this claim, particularly since Patent Company members such as Biograph were among the first to send their own companies to Los Angeles. If anything, the presence of independent producers in California might have only helped stall some of their legal battles. For more, see Bowser, *The Transformation of Cinema*, 150–52.

20. For more on class struggles in the early days of the industry, as well as the story of the MPPDA, see Laurie Pintar, "Behind the Scenes: Bronco Billy and the Realities of Work in Open Shop Hollywood," in Sitton and Deverell, *Metropolis in the Making*, 324.

21. Perry and Perry, *A History of the Los Angeles Labor Movement*, 321. For more on the origins of IATSE, see chapter 5 and Michael Charles Nielsen, *Hollywood's Other Blacklist: Union Struggles in the Studio System* (London: British Film Institute, 1995).

22. Pintar, "Behind the Scenes," 330.

23. For more about these strikes, see Murray Ross, *Stars and Strikes: Unionization of Hollywood* (New York: Columbia University Press, 1941).

24. Danae Clark, *Negotiating Hollywood: The Cultural Politics of Actors' Labor* (Minneapolis: University of Minnesota Press, 1995), 20.

25. For more on Equity and early organization efforts by actors, see Ross, *Stars and Strikes*, 23–47; Perry and Perry, *A History of the Los Angeles Labor Movement*, 337–44; Clark, *Negotiating Hollywood*, 29–36.

26. For early organization efforts by screenwriters, see Ross, *Stars and Strikes*, 48–58.

27. Article of Incorporation of Academy of Motion Pictures Arts and Sciences, March 4, 1927, NLRB.1, box 518, Petitioners' Exhibits 1–24.

28. Sean P. Holmes, "The Hollywood Star System and the Regulation of Actors' Labor, 1916–1934," *Film History* 12, no. 1 (2000): 109–11.

29. For a further discussion on the merits of the Academy of Motion Pictures, see Ross, *Stars and Strikes*, 215.

30. Frank Woods, "History of Producer-Talent Relations in the Academy," *Screen Guilds' Magazine* 2, no. 9 (November 1935): 4, 26–27.

31. NLRB.1, box 516, vol. 5, October 6, 1937, 673.

32. David M. Kennedy, *Freedom from Fear: The American People in Depression and War, 1929–1945* (New York: Oxford University Press, 1999), 25–27.

33. Lewis Jacobs, *The Rise of the American Film: A Critical History* (New York: Harcourt, Brace, 1939), 422–23.

34. "Majority of Players Accept Film Pay Cut," *New York Times*, March 10, 1933.

35. "Film Workers Accept Pay Cut," *Los Angeles Times*, March 9, 1933.

36. "The Academy Writer-Producer Agreement . . . Another Attempt to Destroy the Guild," *Screen Guilds' Magazine* 2, no. 8 (October 1935): 8.

37. Nancy Lynn Schwartz, *The Hollywood Writers' Wars* (New York: Knopf, 1982), 9–10.

38. NLRB.1, box 516, vol. 11, October 15, 1937, 1418.

39. "Majority of Players Accept Film Pay Cut."

40. "Zanuck Resigns from Warners," *Los Angeles Times*, April 15, 1933, 1.

41. "The Academy Writer-Producer Agreement," 8.

42. Schwartz, *The Hollywood Writers' Wars*, 21.

43. NLRB.1, box 516, vol. 8, October 12, 1937, 924–25.

44. Ernest Pascal, "Mr. Pascal Asks a Question," *Screen Guilds' Magazine* 3, no. 3 (May 1936): 4.

45. NLRB.1, box 516, vol. 10, October 14, 1937, 1312.

46. Kennedy, *Freedom from Fear*, 151.

47. Eddie Cantor, "What the Guild Stands for . . . ," *Screen Player* 1, no. 1 (March 15, 1934): 2.

48. Ibid.

49. For more on this wave, see Zieger, *American Workers, American Unions*, 29–31.

50. Kennedy, *Freedom from Fear*, 151.

51. In her book, Schwartz makes the interesting claim that Rosenblatt was in fact the brother-in-law of Lester Cowan, who in 1933 served as deputy in the Academy committee responsible for representing the talent groups in the NRA negotiations. See Schwartz, *The Hollywood Writers' Wars*, 28.

52. For more on the "cartelization" element of the codes, see Kennedy, *Freedom from Fear*, 184.

53. National Recovery Administration, Code of Fair Competition for the Motion Picture Industry, November 27, 1933, in NLRB.1, box 518, Petitioners' Exhibits 1–24, 236–40.

54. Ross, *Stars and Strikes*, 91–93.

55. For more on the studios' reframing of the labor dispute via fan magazines, see Clark, *Negotiating Hollywood*, 70–71.

56. Jay B. Chapman, "Figuring the Stars' Salaries," *Screen Book* (November 1933): 11, quoted in Clark, *Negotiating Hollywood*, 73.

57. ". . . The Menace of the Academy . . . ," *Screen Player* 1, no. 2 (April 15, 1934): 1.

58. "Text of Eddie Cantor's Speech at Annual Meeting," *Screen Player* 1, no. 3 (May 15, 1934): 9.

59. "The Wire to President Roosevelt and the Executive Order," *Screen Player* 1, no. 3 (May 15, 1934): 4, 16.

60. "Text of Eddie Cantor's Speech at Annual Meeting," 9.

61. National Recovery Administration, Code of Fair Competition for the Motion Picture Industry, 216.

62. "Text of Eddie Cantor's Speech at Annual Meeting," 12.

63. ". . . Abuses Must Be Rectified . . . ," *Screen Player* 1, no. 3 (May 15, 1934): 1.

64. Perry and Perry, *A History of the Los Angeles Labor Movement*, 349–51.

65. "Writer-Producer Code Committee Disagrees . . . ," *Screen Guilds' Magazine* 1, no. 11 (February 1935): 3; Legal Arguments against the Proposed So-Called Rules of Fair Practice Governing the Relations between Producers and Writers, February 5,

1935, NLRB.1, box 517, Board's Exhibits 166–314. General booking agencies were akin to human resources services, and they ultimately worked in favor of their owners and studio management, as opposed to personal agents and managers, who negotiated better deals for their clients.

66. "Deadlock . . . ," *Screen Guilds' Magazine* 1, no. 8 (November 1934): 10. See also Legal Arguments against the Proposed So-Called Rules of Fair Practice Governing the Relations between Producers and Writers.

67. Deadlock . . . ," 10; "Writer-Producer Code Committee Disagrees . . ."

68. Daniel T. Rodgers, *Atlantic Crossings: Social Politics in a Progressive Age* (Cambridge, MA: Belknap Press of Harvard University Press, 1998), 412.

69. Alan Brinkley, "The New Deal and the Idea of the State," in *The Rise and Fall of the New Deal Order, 1930–1980,* ed. Steven Fraser and Gary Gerstle (Princeton, NJ: Princeton University Press, 1989), 86.

70. Lichtenstein, *State of the Union,* 36.

71. Laurence W. Beilenson, "The Wagner Bill—Reality or Prophecy?," *Screen Guilds' Magazine* 2, no. 6 (August 1935): 1, 15.

72. NLRB.1, box 516, vol. 11, October 15, 1937, 1430.

73. Zieger, *American Workers, American Unions,* 39–41.

74. For more on this strike, see Ross, *Stars and Strikes,* 191–212; Perry and Perry, *A History of the Los Angeles Labor Movement,* 320–37.

75. "Stars Meet in Secret on Studio Tie-Up," *Los Angeles Times,* May 3, 1937.

76. David F. Prindle, *The Politics of Glamour: Ideology and Democracy in the Screen Actors Guild* (Madison: University of Wisconsin Press, 1988), 30.

77. "Actors' Guild Backs Film Craft Strike," *Los Angeles Times,* May 9, 1937.

78. "Actors' Guild Demands Met," *Los Angeles Times,* May 10, 1937.

79. Prindle, *The Politics of Glamour,* 27–28.

80. Ibid. Bioff and Browne were convicted on charges of extortion in 1941 following the testimony of one studio executive, Joseph Schenck, who implicated them in order to lighten the prison sentence he received for tax fraud. For more on this story, see Gomery, *The Hollywood Studio System,* 186–89; Nielsen, *Hollywood's Other Blacklist,* 25–50.

81. Prindle, *The Politics of Glamour,* 31–36.

82. "New Directors Guild Votes against Any Ties with Other Screen Bodies," *Variety,* January 29, 1936.

83. See chapter 5. In the second agreement signed by the ASC with producers, which came into effect in 1939, directors of photography voted not to affiliate with a strike of any other craft or guild.

84. For a lively description of the struggles of SDG, see Frank Capra, *The Name above the Title: An Autobiography* (New York: Macmillan, 1971), 267–73. For other accounts of the guild, see Perry and Perry, *A History of the Los Angeles Labor Movement,* 356–58; Ross, *Stars and Strikes,* 208–10; Gomery, *The Hollywood Studio System,* 191–93.

85. Hugh Lovell and Tasile Carter, *Collective Bargaining in the Motion Picture Industry* (Berkeley: Institute of Industrial Relations, University of California, 1955), 37–38.

86. Ernest Pascal, "One Organization for ALL American Writers," *Screen Guilds' Magazine* 3, no. 2 (April 1936): 15–17. As argued in chapter 2, amalgamation also appealed to writers for reasons other than the fortification of their guild.

87. NLRB.2, box 1725, vol. 6, August 7, 1939, 240–46.

88. NLRB.2, box 1725, vol. 7, August 18, 1939, 333–87.

89. NLRB.2, box 1725, vol. 9, August 22, 1939, 629–55.

90. NLRB.2, box 1724, vol. 11, August 24, 1939, 1139–40.

91. Ibid., 1014–16.

92. Ibid., 1185.

93. NLRB.2, box 1725, vol. 9, August 22, 1939, 684–85.

94. NLRB.2, box 1725, vol. 10, August 23, 1939, 757–61.

95. NLRB.2, box 1725, vol. 7, August 18, 1939, 490–500.

96. NLRB.2, box 1725, vol. 9, August 22, 1939, 550.

97. Larry Ceplair and Steven Englund, *The Inquisition in Hollywood: Politics in the Film Community, 1930–1960* (Garden City, NY: Anchor Press / Doubleday, 1980), 43.

98. NLRB.2, vol. 11, August 24, 1939, 1008–9.

99. These numbers are quoted in Ross, *Stars and Strikes*, 181.

100. NLRB.1, box 516, vol. 11, October 15, 1937, 1689–91.

101. NLRB.2, box 1725, vol. 9, August 22, 1939, 662–64.

102. Eileen Boris, "Labor's Welfare State," 330.

103. For a detailed account of the elections, see Schwartz, *The Hollywood Writers' Wars*, 123–30.

104. Ibid., 173; Perry and Perry, *A History of the Los Angeles Labor Movement*, 356.

105. NLRB.1, box 515, vol. 2, October 1, 1937, 302.

106. Philip Dunne, interviewed by Thomas Stemple, 1970, transcript, the Darryl F. Zanuck Project, LBMF, 100–112.

107. Jefferson Cowie, *Stayin' Alive: The 1970s and the Last Days of the Working Class* (New York: New Press, 2010), 289.

108. Following amalgamation in 1954, SWG was reorganized and divided into two sister guilds: Writers Guild of America East and Writers Guild of America West. In 1959, SDG united with the New York–based Radio and Television Directors Guild to form the Directors Guild of America (DGA). A similar amalgamation occurred between SAG and the American Federation of Television and Radio Artists (AFTRA) in 2012.

109. In general, Hollywood craft unions did not officially bar women or minorities. However, they tended to reflect the representation, or more accurately the underrepresentation, of women and people of color within their respective branches of the industry, without vocally pushing for change. SDG admitted its first black member, Wendell Franklin, only in 1960 and had only one female member, Dorothy Arzner, between 1936 and 1943. Arzner was followed by the second SDG female member, Ida Lupino, only in 1949. Similarly, the American Society of Cinematographers admitted its first female member, Brianne Murphy, only in 1980. SAG and SWG had a more diverse membership, though the latter admitted its first African American woman member, Mary Elizabeth Vroman, only in 1953.

110. Tomlins, *The State and the Unions*, 101.

111. For more on this comparison, see Lovell and Carter, *Collective Bargaining in the Motion Picture Industry*, 1–3. The role of talent agents is discussed in the epilogue.

112. De Havilland sued Warner Bros. for unreasonable suspension policies. Her case reached the California Supreme Court, which ruled in her favor, undercutting the studio practice of suspending stars for refusing to play a part and then adding the suspension time to the length of the contract. See Charles Higham, *Sisters: The Story of Olivia de Havilland and Joan Fontaine* (New York: Coward-McCann, 1984). Other cases of individual bargaining include the struggle of James Cagney with Warner Bros., for which see Robert Sklar, *City Boys: Cagney, Bogart, Garfield* (Princeton, NJ: Princeton University Press, 1992); and the struggles of Bette Davis with Warner Bros., for which see Thomas Schatz, "A Triumph of Bitchery: Warner Bros., Bette Davis and Jezebel," *Wide Angle* 10, no. 1 (1988).

113. Dudley Nichols, "Cooking a Goose," *Screen Guilds' Magazine* 3, no. 3 (May 1936): 6, 20.

Disintegrating: An Epilogue

1. "From Reel Life to Real Life Headwaiter," *New York Times*, August 7, 1949. Additional information about Corrado can be found in Anthony Slide, *Hollywood Unknowns: A History of Extras, Bit Players, and Stand-Ins* (Jackson: University Press of Mississippi, 2012), 147.

2. Statistics from Thomas Schatz, *Boom and Bust: The American Cinema in the 1940s* (New York: Scribner, 1997), 461–65; Peter Lev, *Transforming the Screen, 1950–1959* (New York: Scribner, 2003), 303–4.

3. Quoted in Garth Jowett, "The Decline of an Institution," in *Hollywood: Critical Concepts in Media and Cultural Studies*, ed. Thomas Schatz (London: Routledge, 2003), 206.

4. Fredric Stuart, "The Effect of Television on the Motion Picture and Radio Industries" (PhD diss., Columbia University, 1960).

5. For more on the moral and political attacks, see Brian Neve, "HUAC, the Blacklist, and the Decline of Social Cinema," in Lev, *Transforming the Screen*, 65–86, and Jowett, "The Decline of an Institution." For more on the HUAC investigation in Hollywood, see Larry Ceplair and Steven Englund, *The Inquisition in Hollywood: Politics in the Film Community, 1930–1960* (Garden City, NY: Anchor Press/Doubleday, 1980); and Andrew Paul, "Making the Blacklist White: The Hollywood Red Scare in Popular Memory," *Journal of Popular Film and Television* 41, no. 4 (October 1, 2013): 208–18.

6. On the same day that it handed down its decision in the *Paramount* case, the Supreme Court also ruled in two additional cases relating to the motion picture industry, *U.S. v. Griffith* and *Schine Chain Theaters v. U.S.*, determining that these two large but unaffiliated theater chains used their buying power to gain unfair advantages over smaller independent theaters. Thus, in essence, the Court cited them for the same violation as the big studios.

7. *United States v. Paramount Pictures, Inc.*, 334 U.S. 131 (1948).

8. For more on this long legal battle and its economic implications, see Simon N. Whitney, "Vertical Disintegration in the Motion Picture Industry," *American Eco-*

nomic Review 45, no. 2 (May 1, 1955): 491–98; and Ernest Borneman, "The United States versus Hollywood: The Case Study of an Antitrust Suit," in *The American Film Industry*, ed. Tino Balio, rev. ed (Madison: University of Wisconsin Press, 1985), 449–62.

9. Borneman, "The United States versus Hollywood," 460.

10. Whitney, "Vertical Disintegration in the Motion Picture Industry," 492, 498.

11. Joseph W. Taylor, "Producers Grind Out Films Faster in Drive to Cut Production Costs," *Wall Street Journal*, August 23, 1949.

12. Irving Bernstein, *Hollywood at the Crossroads: An Economic Study of the Motion Picture Industry* (Hollywood, CA: Hollywood A.F.L. Film Council, 1957). Additional statistics can be found in Schatz, *Boom and Bust*, 333; Lev, *Transforming the Screen*, 26; and Kenneth Macgowan, *Behind the Screen: The History and Techniques of the Motion Picture* (New York: Delacorte Press, 1965).

13. Janet Staiger, "The Hollywood Mode of Production, 1930–1960," in David Bordwell, Janet Staiger, and Kristin Thompson, *The Classical Hollywood Cinema: Film Style and Mode of Production to 1960* (New York: Columbia University Press, 1985), 317–19. Aside from Selznick and Goldwyn, Staiger also lists Charles Chaplin, Monogram, Maya Deren, and Pare Lorentz as important independent producers between 1930 and 1950. The list should probably also include Walt Disney and Walter Wanger. In addition, she cites Sidney Kent, president of Twentieth Century–Fox, who in the mid-1930s estimated that there were between twenty-five and thirty independent firms working in Hollywood around those decades, each producing between three and ten films every year. For more on independent production before the 1940s, see Matthew Bernstein, "Hollywood's Semi-Independent Production," *Cinema Journal* 32, no. 3 (April 1, 1993): 41–54.

14. Lev, *Transforming the Screen*, 26.

15. "New High on Indie Major-Deals," *Variety*, February 14, 1951.

16. David Harvey, *The Condition of Postmodernity: An Enquiry into the Origins of Cultural Change* (Cambridge, MA: Blackwell, 1990), 121–97.

17. Susan Christopherson and Michael Storper, "The Effects of Flexible Specialization on Industrial Politics and the Labor Market: The Motion Picture Industry," *Industrial and Labor Relations Review* 42, no. 3 (April 1, 1989): 331–47.

18. The best description of the disintegrated mode of production remains that of Janet Staiger in "The Hollywood Mode of Production," 330–37.

19. Thomas Schatz, *The Genius of the System: Hollywood Filmmaking in the Studio Era* (New York: Pantheon Books, 1988), 437–38. Wald did not last long at RKO, and he quickly left that studio and set up his own independent production company. Blanke's weekly salary was cut from $5,500 to $3,500 before his "producer" title was replaced by the description "advisory capacity."

20. Macgowan, *Behind the Screen*, 322.

21. Lev, *Transforming the Screen*, 25.

22. Macgowan, *Behind the Screen*, 316.

23. "See '51 as Banner Indie Year," *Variety*, February 28, 1951; "Indie Talent's Top Position," *Variety*, February 13, 1952. Some of these names, particularly Capra,

Stevens, Wyler, and Wallis, had already ventured into independent production in the mid-1940s.

24. "New High on Indie Major-Deals."

25. Reminiscences of Hal Wallis, interviewed by Joan and Robert Franklin, September 1958, transcript, Popular Arts Project, OHCC, 19–20.

26. Interoffice communication from Wallis to Joseph Hazen, October 10, 1958, file 194.f-1923, Hal Wallis Papers, MHL.

27. Reminiscences of Hal Wallis, 23.

28. Interoffice communication from Wallis to Hazen, October 10, 1958.

29. Reminiscences of Hal Wallis, 23.

30. Joseph Hazen to M. C. Levee, November 30, 1953, file 1866, Hal Wallis Papers.

31. M. C. Levee to Hazen, December 4, 1953, Hal Wallis Papers.

32. MCA Artist Management Agency to Raphaelson, date unknown, box 2, Samson Raphaelson Papers, Special Collections, Columbia University.

33. Reminiscences of Ben Hecht, interviewed by Joan and Robert Franklin, June 1959, transcript, Popular Arts Project, OHCC, 753–54.

34. MCA Artist Management Agency to Raphaelson.

35. John Brahm to Samson Raphaelson, May 1, 1948, box 2, Samson Raphaelson Papers.

36. Quoted in Schatz, *The Genius of the System*, 458.

37. See chapter 6.

38. Tom Kemper, *Hidden Talent: The Emergence of Hollywood Agents* (Berkeley: University of California Press, 2010), 2. As Kemper explains, the attempts to limit agents included the 1927 formation of the Academy of Motion Picture Arts and Sciences, which was meant to counter personal representation as a company union, as well as the Academy-inspired 1931 proposed agreement and the 1933 Code of Fair Practice.

39. Eddie Mannix to Leland Heyward, December 10, 1943, box 194, Leland Hayward Papers, NYPL. Ten percent of income was the customary fee of a talent agent.

40. Douglas Gomery, *The Hollywood Studio System: A History* (London: BFI, 2005), 306; de Havilland walked off a set when on loan to Columbia, following which Jack Warner wanted to add time to her existing contract at Warner Bros. to compensate for the time lost due to this incident. With MCA's assistance, the actress found a clause in California labor law that convinced the courts that the studio's demands were unlawful. Kemper claims that the de Havilland episode was more symbolic than revolutionary and merely drew attention to the "weakening of the long-term contract," which was brought about to a great extent by Feldman and other 1930s agents. See Kemper, *Hidden Talent*, 235.

41. "UA, MCA Deal Would Give Top Hypo to Indies," *Variety*, December 26, 1951. See also Lev, *Transforming the Screen*, 28.

42. Gomery, *The Hollywood Studio System*, 307.

43. Ibid., 300–304. As Gomery points out, IATSE maintained its power, serving as the governing umbrella for virtually all industry unions except the talent guilds. It successfully negotiates periodical basic agreements that increase wages and determine strict work hours, resting periods, and minimum wages. Interestingly, as Wasserman left MCA and took over the management of Universal Studios, he also took charge

of all industry labor negotiations. Thus, his immense influence reshaped this aspect of modern Hollywood as well. It is important to point out, though, that despite the strong position of IATSE, studies indicate that since the 1950s, employment patterns display a trend toward increased part-time work for a greater number of employees as opposed to long, steady, full-time employment for a smaller number of workers, which was the dominant trend during the studio system era. See Christopherson and Storper, "The Effects of Flexible Specialization," 336.

44. In a roster system, unions arrange their workers on lists according to seniority. Production companies then sign long-term contracts with the unions and are assigned workers based on the seniority lists. See Christopherson and Storper, "The Effects of Flexible Specialization," 335. The possible conflict of interest between guilds and agents is further emphasized by the fact that these two forces negotiated periodical agreements with one another similar to the ones the guilds signed with the studios.

45. Thomas Schatz, "The New Hollywood," in *Film Theory Goes to the Movies*, ed. Jim Collins, Hilary Radner, and Ava Collins (New York: Routledge, 1993), 8–36. The new conglomerates were not only in the film business; they engaged in the entertainment business writ large. The whole economic idea was to diversify the product beyond one medium. MCA was again emblematic. In 1966, it bought Universal Studios, adding it to its growing empire of music records, television, and talent representation. That same year, Paramount was purchased by Gulf & Western Industries, and in 1969, Warner Bros. was taken over by the Kinney Corporation. Many of these former studios have changed hands many times since then.

46. Richard L. Florida, *The Rise of the Creative Class: And How It's Transforming Work, Leisure, Community and Everyday Life* (New York: Basic Books, 2002), 7–10.

47. Daniel H. Pink, *Free Agent Nation: How America's New Independent Workers Are Transforming the Way We Live* (New York: Warner Books, 2001), 16–20.

48. Reminiscences of Ben Hecht, 710.

49. George Cukor, interviewed by Gavin Lambert, 1970–71, transcript, LBMF, 111.

Index

Abdullah, Achmed, 77

Academy of Motion Picture Arts and Sciences: formation of, 10, 145, 173–74, 254n38; guild membership vs., 180, 185–86; pay cuts (1933) and, 175–77; stated purpose of, 173

actors, 2–3, 6, 9, 11, 16, 21, 108–38; casting process, 92, 93–94, 108, 131, 132–36, 204; commodification of, 110–14, 119, 129–32; contract players, 5, 24, 109–11, 118–19, 122–25, 127–28, 133–34, 173, 179; costs and, 96, 97, 128–29, 197; credits and, 113, 114, 120; extras and bit players, 3, 110, 116–17, 119, 122, 123–24, 174, 195; feature players, 124, 131; film history and, 112–21; freelance, 232n68; gender and, 8, 111, 115–18, 122–23, 132–33; market value of, 119; number of (1938), 97; racial and ethnic stereotypes, 8, 120; stars (*see* star system); stock players, 122–23, 124, 235n18; supporting players, 110, 124; theater workers vs., 114, 145; unions and, 66, 145, 173, 185. *See also* Screen Actors Guild

Actors' Equity Association, 67, 173

Actors' National Union, 145

African Americans, 8, 120, 251n109

agents. *See* talent agents

Air Force (film), 200

Aitken, Harry, 119

Aldrich, Winthrop, 13, 14

Alice Adams (film), 126, 135

alienation theory, 225n66

Allen, Joe, 116

Amalgamated Clothing Workers' Union, 177

American Federation of Labor (AFL), 144, 145, 172, 173, 177, 184

American Federation of Television and Radio Artists, 205

American Mutoscope & Biograph Company. *See* Biograph

American Society of Cinematographers, 155, 157, 159–62, 186; first female member, 251n109; Local 659, 160–61, 162

Anderson, Gilbert M., 81

Andrews, Dana, 126–27, 136–37

Annakin, Ken, 200

antitrust laws, 11, 178, 196–97, 252n6

Arbuckle, Roscoe ("Fatty"), 127

Arnold, John, 159, 160

Arnow, Max, 140

art department, 28, 141–42

artists. *See* creative personnel

Arzner, Dorothy, 251n109

ASC. *See* American Society of Cinematographers

Asian actors, 8

Astaire, Fred, 37

Atkinson, Frank, 141, 142

audience, 28, 32–33, 83, 130; casting and, 108

Authors' League, 66, 68, 71, 72, 188, 191

Aylesworth, Merlin, 37

Ayres, Lew, 103

Bacall, Lauren, 137

Bailey, Malcolm Stewart, 76

Balaban, Barney, 38

Balaban & Katz, 9

creative personnel, 1–8, 11, 17, 28, 120, 146, 165, 166–94, 210–11n10; agents and, 178, 193, 203–4; cinematographers as, 151, 159–64; commodification of, 207; contracts and, 193–94; costs and, 31, 41, 197, 199; crafts separated from, 145–47; executive producer and, 41, 42–43, 201; independent productions and, 199–207; institutionalization of, 7, 28, 195–96; management of, 203–4; option clauses and, 123–25; organization of, 166–67, 173–78, 184, 187, 191, 192, 193; studio system and, 206; subfields of, 48–49; uniform vision and, 89. *See also* actors; directors; screenwriters

credits: actors and, 113, 114, 120; screenwriters and, 61–62, 67, 71, 77, 190, 192

Cromwell, John, 93–94

Cruze, James, 81

Cukor, George, 31, 37, 39, 43, 93–95, 137, 139–40; casting and, 132, 133; directorial positions of, 95, 101, 105; on studio system, 207; top salary of, 233n88

cultural production: Bourdieu theory of, 168, 247n6; Hollywood standardization of, 4, 211n12; organizational model of, 15

Culver City studio, 23, 43, 121

Cunard, Grace, 82

Curtiz, Michael, 103, 104

Davis, Bette, 102–3, 125, 129, 130, 137–38, 199, 200

Davis, Mike, 171

Davis, Owen, 67

Dawley, J. Searle, 154

Dawn, Jack, 141

DeCordova, Richard, 113–14, 118

Dee, Frances, 132, 133

De Havilland, Olivia, 129, 194, 204, 252n112, 254n40

DeMille, Cecil B., 154

Depression (1930s). *See* Great Depression

Deren, Maya, 253n13

Dickson, William Kennedy Laurie, 147–48, 149, 159

Dieterle, William, 200, 201–2

directors, 3, 9, 19, 25, 42, 76–107; artistic sense of, 14, 31, 94; autonomy and, 5, 77–90, 94, 95, 101–7; backgrounds of, 81–82, 84; casting and, 93–94, 117, 132; chain of command and, 102–3; cinematographers and, 151, 160; contracts and, 99–102, 123; costs and, 101, 104, 105, 197; creative control and, 29, 30, 39, 87, 89, 94, 102–5; efficiency and, 95; employee status of, 59; foreign-born, 99; freelance projects and, 103; gender and, 8, 53, 82, 87, 112; golden age and, 82, 94, 97; high pay of, 64, 65, 99, 100, 185, 233n88; independent productions and, 11, 201–2, 203; job description, 88–94; loaning out of, 98; movie industry early years and, 81–86; number in Hollywood (1938), 97; organization of, 184–87 (*see also* Screen Directors Guild); producer differentiated from, 20, 21, 23, 42; production phases and, 102–3, 106; screenwriters and, 51, 73, 76, 89, 90, 91; script and, 39, 91, 92, 93; skills of, 78, 97–98; standardization of, 207; star's choice of, 126; status of, 5–6, 8, 21–22, 76, 144, 167; studio system and, 79–80, 93, 94, 97, 99–100, 106–7; unionization and, 145, 185–86 (*see also* Screen Directors Guild); Wyler's career as, 98–107

discrimination, 8. *See also* gender; race

Dismond, Geraldyn, 120

Disney, Walt, 143–44, 253n13

distribution, 9–10, 16–17, 23, 83, 110, 121–22; antitrust ruling and, 11, 196; block booking and, 10, 17, 178, 196; differential pricing and, 122; foreign, 35, 52; independent productions and,

197–98; Motion Picture Code and, 178; United Artists and, 10, 109, 121, 198; vertical integration and, 9, 122, 196. *See also* exhibitors

division of labor, 78, 87–88, 131–32, 210n10; actors and, 119–20; cinematographers and, 147, 150–51, 155–57; early film industry and, 18–19, 21; employee autonomy and, 79; new "tailorist" system superseding, 206; scenario preparation and, 51, 54; studio system and, 3–8, 77, 110

Dix, Beulah Marie, 51–52, 53, 54
Dodsworth (film), 102
Domino productions, 23–24
Don Juan (sound film), 40
Donnelly, Grant, 140
Double Indemnity (film), 128–29
Douglas, Melvyn, 128, 133
Dramatists Guild, 66, 67–68, 70
Dreier, Hans, 141–42
Duel in the Sun (film), 158
Dunne, Irene, 203
Dunne, Philip, 17, 42, 43, 60, 73, 93, 192–93
Durkin, James, 154
Dwan, Allan, 81–82, 85–86, 99, 100
Dyer, Elmer, 152–53

Eastman Kodak, 96
Éclair (film company), 170
Edendale (Calif.) studio, 21–22, 84
Edison, Thomas, 9, 19, 147–48, 149, 154; Kinetoscope Company, 154–55, 159
editing. *See* film editing
efficiency, 18–20, 22, 25, 29, 38, 77–79, 86–88, 152; cost of inefficient set, 42, 96–97; division of labor and, 155; Selznick and, 35; Thalberg and, 26, 33–34
Electrical Research Products Inc., 38
Emergency Banking Act (1933), 66, 175
Empire productions, 23–24
Enoch Arden (film), 51, 83
equity. *See* Actors Equity Association

Essanay studio, 81, 113, 117, 170
ethnic minorities, 8
European companies, 210–11n10
Everybody's Magazine, 58
executive producer, 1, 14, 15, 17–18, 84, 182, 199, 203; birth of, 23–26; creativity and, 41, 42–43, 201; directors and, 77, 90, 93, 94, 103, 106; independent production and, 203; Selznick origination of, 34, 90; Zanuck as, 39–43, 44, 90, 94
exhibitors, 11, 16, 18, 38, 40, 83, 181; block booking and, 10, 17, 178, 196; decline in, 196; demand for films and, 80–81; economics of star system and, 119; financial problems of, 197; first-run theaters, 27–28, 35, 196; Motion Picture Code and, 178; New York theater chains, 9, 24, 27–28, 121–22; Paramount profitability and, 35, 52; second-run markets, 35; vertical integration and, 24, 122, 197. *See also* box office revenue

Fairbanks, Douglas, 50, 119, 120, 122
Fairbanks, Douglas, Jr., 200
fair practice codes, 66, 165, 178–79, 183, 192, 203
Fallen Angel (film), 126–27, 252n6
Famous Players–Lasky Company, 9, 51, 121
Feature Play Company, 9, 121, 153
Federation of Motion Picture Crafts, 184, 185
Feldman, Charles K., 203
Field, Martin, 63
film, cost of, 80, 96, 97, 105
film editing, 89–90, 143; final cut, 91, 106; rooms for, 140–41
film industry. *See* motion picture industry
finances. *See* box office revenues; budgets; profits
financial institutions, 13, 14, 16, 19, 38
Fine, Richard, 56

Firestone, Harvey, 171
First National (theater chain), 10, 40, 121
first-run movie theaters, 27–28, 35, 196
Fitzgerald, F. Scott, *The Last Tycoon,* 33
Five-Five Committee (Motion Picture Code), 181–82
Fleming, Victor, 105
flexible accumulation/specialization, 198
Flynn, Errol, 199
Folsey, George, 153–54, 160, 163
Foolish Wives (film), 26
Fool There Was, A (film), 119
Ford, Henry, 171; Fordism, 6, 198
Ford, John, 17, 185–86
foreign distribution, 35, 52
foreign film industry, 80, 210n10
Fortune (magazine), 38, 39
For Whom the Bell Tolls (film), 56, 96–97
Fox, William, 9–10, 119, 121
Fox Company, 83, 213n30. *See also* Twentieth Century-Fox
Franklin, Wendell, 251n109
free agents, 206
Freeman, Y. Frank, 38
Friedman, Phil, 123–24, 131, 133

Gable, Clark, 2, 6, 125, 197, 201; *Gone with the Wind* casting of, 108, 109, 195; star status of, 110, 129
gag writers, 52, 54–55, 61, 77, 95
gangster films, 41
Garbo, Greta, 125
Garmes, Lee, 133, 158–59, 160
Gates, Harvey, 76
Gaynor, Janet, 122–23, 124, 131
gender, 212–13n21, 22, 251n109; business codes and, 7–8, 53, 87; equality struggle and, 193; film acting and, 115–18, 133; "New Woman" and, 82; traditional conceptions of, 7–8, 112. *See also* women
Germany, 96, 98, 99, 210n10
Gibbons, Cedric, 28

Gibney, Sheridan, 61
Gillis, Ann, 132
Gish, Dorothy, 117, 119
Gish, Lillian, 115–16, 117, 119
Goddard, Paulette, 129, 239n93
God Is My Co-Pilot (film), 103
golden age (1920–50), 2–3, 22, 33. *See also* studio system
Goldwyn, Samuel, 27, 43, 86, 98, 136, 137, 182; independent production-distribution, 196–97; Wyler and, 102, 103. *See also* MGM
Goldwyn Pictures Corporation, 9, 27
Gomery, Douglas, 4, 211n13
Gompers, Samuel, 144
Gone with the Wind (film), 2, 34, 39; casting of, 108–9, 125, 132–33, 195; distribution of, 109; seventeen writers and, 61
Gone with the Wind (novel), 108–9
Goodman, Theodosia. *See* Bara, Theda
Goodrich, Frances, 64, 67, 176
Gow, James, 189–90
Grady, Bill, 134
Grapes of Wrath, The (film), 13–14
Great Depression (1930s), 11, 41, 56, 59, 65, 168; effects on Hollywood of, 16, 65, 66, 67, 88, 175–79, 230n13. *See also* New Deal
Great Train Robbery, The (film), 149
Greenlaw, Charles F., Jr., 140, 141, 142
Greenstreet, Sydney, 199
Griffith, D. W., 20–21, 23, 25, 151; actors and, 11, 118, 120; *Birth of a Nation,* 8, 21, 149; cinematographers and, 149, 152; *Enoch Arden,* 51, 83; idiosyncratic career of, 86; *Intolerance,* 149, 195; theatrical experience of, 81; Triangle Films and, 84, 86
guilds: continuing power of, 193; exclusive shop, 71, 192, 193, 226n96; formation of, 65–70; international, 205; New Deal and, 177, 178; opposition to, 168, 183; rise of, 167, 180–86, 187, 192, 193; Wagner Act

Lonergan, Lloyd, 52

Loos, Anita, 6, 30, 32, 47, 53–54, 56, 70

Lorentz, Pare, 253n13

Los Angeles area, 22–23, 24, 58, 170–72, 248n19

Los Angeles Central Labor Council, 184

Los Angeles Times, 25, 43, 171, 172, 175, 184, 185

Lost Weekend, The (film), 58

Love Letters (film), 134

Loy, Myrna, 127, 136

Lubin studio, 19, 170

Lubitsch, Ernst, 59, 99, 105

Lupino, Ida, 200, 251n109

MacMurray, Fred, 128–29

MacPherson, Jeanie, 53

Madison, Cleo, 82

Magic Introduction Company, 149

Mahar, Karen Ward, 212–13n22

Mahin, John Lee, 140

majors. *See* "big five" majors

Maltese Falcon, The (film), 200

Maltz, Albret, 69

management theory. *See* scientific management theory

managerial capitalism, 15

Mankiewicz, Joe, 46, 47, 63

Mannix, Eddie, 28

Man's Genesis (film), 117

Marion, Frances, 47, 53, 56, 70

Marlow, Brian, 177, 192

Marsh, Mae, 115, 116–17, 119

Marsh, Marguerite, 116

Marx, Karl, 110, 111, 144, 225n66

Marx, Samuel, 24–25, 31

Marx Brothers, 180

Mary of Scotland (film), 135

Mathis, June, 53

Mayer, Edwin Justus, 61, 64, 67

Mayer, Louis B.: Academy of Motion Pictures Arts and Sciences founding, 10, 173, 174; concentration of power and, 88, 90; *Gone with the Wind* and, 108, 109; mergers and, 9; Selznick

and, 36, 38; Thalberg and, 27–29, 32–33. *See also* MGM

MCA (Music Corporation of America), 204, 254n40, 255n45

McArthur, Charles, 73

McCall, Mary, Jr., 73

McCoy, Tim, 35

McCrea, Joel, 135–36

McGowan, J. P., 116

McGuinness, James K., 70, 190

McKinney, Nina Mae, 120

McNutt, Patterson, 70–71

McNutt, William Slavens, 76–77

Melville, Wilbert, 19–20, 23

men. *See* gender

Merchants' and Manufacturers' Association, 171

Meredyth, Bess, 53, 70

merger movement (1910–30s), 9–10, 16

Merry-Go-Round (film), 26, 88

Merry Widow, The (film), 32–33, 59

Metro Pictures Corporation, 27

MGM (Metro-Goldwyn-Mayer), 6, 16, 86; actors and, 108–9, 121, 123, 125, 127, 137; antitrust ruling and, 11, 196; business model, 28, 34; casting department, 134; cinematographers, 162; consolidation of, 52; cost-cutting downsizing and, 199; Culver City studio, 23, 43, 121; directors, 90, 98, 99; first-run market, 35; formation (1924) of, 9, 27, 88; Great Depression effects on, 175, 176; Loew's distribution and, 9, 27, 33, 121–22; middle management, 28; number of releases per year, 35; photography department, 159; production costs, 30–31; profitability of, 32–33, 41, 73, 109; publicity department, 136; screenwriters, 53, 70, 202–3; Selznick and, 35–37, 39; spending by, 30; Thalberg and, 1, 24, 27–29, 32, 34, 37, 39, 40, 43, 44, 86, 165; Triangle facilities of, 86; vastness of operation, 28–29; Warner Bros. compared with, 41; writers, 70. *See also* Mayer, Louis B.

Miller, Arthur (cinematographer), 151, 156

Miller, Virgil E., *Splinters from Hollywood Tripods,* 139, 142

minimum wage, 71, 190, 192, 193

Mitchell, Margaret, *Gone with the Wind,* 108–9

monogram, 253n13

monopoly, 9

Montéran, Jacques, 154

Montgomery, David, 7

Montgomery, Robert, 180

Moran, Betty, 132

Morning Glory (film), 135

Morrison, Ernest, 120

Motion Picture Code, 178, 181–82

Motion Picture Corporation, 21, 22

motion picture industry: allure of, 1; birth (1890s) of, 8, 147–51, 169; as both business and art, 9, 16, 28; Broadway theater decline and, 56; coherent vision of, 105; comparative salaries and, 64; competitors of, 11, 196; components of, 1–7; copyright laws and, 50, 62, 72; critical reviews of, 50; cultural standardization and, 4, 211n12; disintegration of, 195–207; early years of, 9, 18–24, 53, 81–87; evolution of, 3, 49–55; "forgotten figures" of, 139; golden age of, 2–3, 22, 33; Hollywood as synecdoche for, 170; New Deal impact on, 11, 66, 167–69, 175, 177–82, 193, 194, 227n104; new studios and, 22–24, 121, 170; racial/ ethnic discrimination by, 8, 120; theater chain ownership and (*see* distribution); transition (late 1940s) of, 195–96, 206; unpredictability of, 1; women and, 7–8, 53, 82, 87, 112. *See also* silent era; star system; studio system; talking pictures; vertical integration

Motion Picture Patent Company, 213n27, 248n19

Motion Picture Photographers Association, 155

Motion Picture Producers and Distributors Association, 10, 123, 173, 184, 186

Motion Picture Producers Association, 171–72, 173

Motion Pictures Producers and Distributors of America, 52

movies. *See* motion picture industry

movie stars. *See* star system

movie theaters. *See* distribution; exhibitors

Moving Picture World, 19, 20, 112–13, 114, 151, 153, 170–71

MPPDA. *See* Motion Picture Producers and Distributors Association

Muni, Paul, 126, 180

Murphy, Brianne, 251n109

Music Corporation of America. *See* MCA

mutoscope camera, 149

Nagel, Conrad, 133

narrative, 47–50, 51, 54, 82, 91, 113, 130, 150

National Board of Review, 41

National Industrial Recovery Act (1933), 66, 177–78; unconstitutionality of, 182

National Labor Relations Act (1935). *See* Wagner Act

National Labor Relations Board, 91, 92, 167, 169; directors and, 186–87; screenwriters and, 60, 71, 88, 191, 192

National Recovery Administration, 65, 66, 165, 166, 167, 169; Amusement Division Code, 178–80

Nestor (film company), 170

New Deal, 11, 66, 167–69, 175, 177–82, 193, 194, 227n104

New Playwrights Theater, 67

newsreels, 152

New York: as financing source, 16, 22, 88; labor unions, 172; literary circles,

Stonehouse, Ruth, 82
strikes, 172, 184, 192
Stroheim, Erich von, 25–26, 29, 32–33, 88
Stromberg, Hunt, 28
Student Prince, The (film), 30
Studio Basic Agreement, 184; components of, 172, 173
studio system, 1–12; benefits of, 207; chain of command and,102; demise of, 11–12, 197–207; division of labor and, 3–8, 77, 110; financial problems of, 65, 88, 96; gender and, 7–8, 87; golden age of, 2–3, 22, 33, 76, 94, 97; independent production and, 11, 98, 132, 197–207, 214–15n41; inventors of, 1–2; labor relations and, 162, 173, 193; location shooting, 42, 96, 170–71, 197; merger movement (1910–30s) and, 9–10, 16; modernization of, 34; option contracts and, 123–25; paternalism and, 109, 136, 137; as stable workplace, 206–7; standardization and, 121–29; structure of, 23; time frame of, 9; transition from, 206–7; Wagner Act and, 183–84. *See also* star system; vertical integration
Sunrise (film), 123
Sunset Boulevard (film), 58
Supreme Court, U.S.: antitrust ruling, 11, 196, 197, 252n6; copyright ruling, 50; NIRA ruling, 182; Wagner Act ruling, 184
Sutherland, Edward, 116
Swanson, Gloria, 115, 117
Sweet, Blanche, 115, 116, 117
SWG. *See* Screen Writers Guild

talent. *See* creative personnel
talent agents, 178, 193, 203–4, 254n38
talent guilds. *See* guilds; *specific guilds*
talking pictures (talkies): art world overlap with, 48–49; cinematographers and, 156–64; dialogue and, 40, 46–49, 55–65, 96; directors and, 95;

effect on studio power structure, 88; first, 40; sound technology and, 10, 16, 40, 42, 55, 57, 141, 156; transition to, 55–56
Talmadge, Norma, 116
Tamiroff, Akim, 77
Tarnished Lady (film), 95
tax code, 11, 199
Taylor, Frederick Winslow, 6, 20, 22, 79, 206
television, 11, 196, 204, 206, 214n38
Temptress, The (film), 30
Tenney, Jack B., 162
Tennyson, Alfred Lord, *Enoch Arden,* 51
Thalberg, Irving, 12, 77, 86, 94, 165, 182, 184, 200; achievements of, 1, 24, 44; assertion of authority, 87–88; background and career of, 24–28; casting of stars, 134–35; death of, 43–44; filmmaking philosophy of, 28; Fitzgerald's fictional portrayal of, 33; large writing staff and, 54; MGM production system and, 1, 24–34, 36, 37, 39, 40, 43, 44, 86, 165; screenwriters' status and, 165–67, 190, 191; Selznick and, 35, 36, 37; standardization and, 59
Thanhouser, Edwin, 51
theater (stage), 49, 57, 67, 118, 144–46; actors and, 114, 118, 145; as competition to movies, 56; directors and, 78, 80, 81, 82; production companies and, 66; unions and, 144–46, 173
theaters (movie). *See* distribution; exhibitor
Thomson, Kenneth, 176
Thorpe, Dick, 105
Tobin, Maurice J., 139
trade unions. *See* unionization
Triangle Film Corporation, 23, 84, 86–87, 119
Trumbo, Dalton, 190
Turnbull, Hector and Margaret, 53
Turner, Florence, 116
Turpin, Ben, 113

204, 252n112, 254n40; director's
function and, 90–91, 98, 102–3;
financial problems of, 197, 199; First
National distribution and, 10, 40, 121;
first talkies and, 40; formation of, 10;
Kinney Corporation takeover of,
255n45; production costs (1927–28)
and, 30; screenwriter contract and,
73–74; Screen Writers Guild and,
190; sound technology and, 40; stars
and, 137–38; Wallis and, 1, 44,
103–4, 200, 202; Zanuck and, 40–41,
176
Wasserman, Lew, 204
Waters, Ethel, 120, 254–55n43
Webb, Kenneth S., 154
Weber, Lois, 8, 53, 82, 87
Wellman, William, 37
Western Electric, 40
westerns, 35, 76, 84
Westmore, Perc, 141
What Price Hollywood? (film), 37
White Shadows in the South Seas (film),
30
Wilder, Billy, 58, 62, 73, 99
Wilder, Cy, 140
Williams, Emmett A., 154
Williams, Myrna, 136
Wilson, Carey, 70
Wilson, Elsie Jane, 82
Wilson, Margery, 82
Winwood, Estelle, 132
Wizard of Oz, The (film), 105
Woehler, Ed, 29
Woman Rebels, A (film), 135
women: casting of, 132–33; craft union
members, 251n109; film industry jobs
and, 7, 8, 53, 56, 112, 212–13n21, 22.
See also gender
Wood, Sam, 81, 96, 97

Woods, Frank E., 50–51, 53, 54, 71, 174,
192
World Moves On (film), 103
World War I, 172, 173
World War II, 11, 162
Wrestling Dog, The (kinetograph), 147
Wright, William Lord, 102
writers: authorial authority of, 45,
63–64, 71–72, 74; authorship rights
and, 63–64, 189; Authors' League, 66,
68, 70, 71, 72, 188, 191; contract
protection and, 72; creativity of, 191;
East Coast-West Coast dynamic and,
66–71, 188; freelance, 63; legitimate,
71–72; pay of, 64; theatrical playwrights, 66–67, 68, 70; transition to
screenwriting, 46, 56–57, 67, 70,
71–72, 75; unionization of, 188, 205
Writers Guild of America, 205, 251n108
Wyckoff, Alvin, 154
Wyler, William, 6, 7, 98–107, 126, 200

Yeats-Brown, Francis, 76, 77
Young, Waldemar, 70, 77

Zanuck, Darryl, 12, 17, 77, 182, 184;
background and career of, 39–41;
casting of stars and, 134–35; creative
staff praise for, 42–43; executive
production and, 39–43, 44, 90, 94; on
gamble of moviemaking, 1; resignation from Warner Bros., 176; Screen
Writers Guild and, 189, 192–93;
Twentieth Century-Fox and, 1,
13–14, 39–44, 90, 192–93
Zukor, Adolph, 1–2, 10, 12, 34–35, 121;
Famous Players and, 9, 118, 121; star
system and, 120; theater chain
purchases and, 52. *See also* Paramount
Pictures